The Center for South and Southeast Asia Studies of the University of California is the unifying organization for faculty members and students interested in South and Southeast Asia Studies, bringing together scholars from numerous disciplines. The Center's major aims are the development and support of research and language study. As part of this program the Center sponsors a publication series of books concerned with South and Southeast Asia. Manuscripts are considered from all campuses of the University of California as well as from any other individuals and institutions doing research in these areas.

PUBLICATIONS OF THE CENTER FOR SOUTH AND SOUTHEAST ASIA STUDIES:

Angela S. Burger

Opposition in a Dominant-Party System: A Study of the Jan Sangh, the Praja Socialist Party, and the Socialist Party in Uttar Pradesh, India (1969)

Robert L. Hardgrave, Jr.

Nadars of Tamilnad: The Political Culture of a Community in Change (1969)

Eugene F. Irschick

Politics and Social Conflict in South India: The Non-Brahman Movement and Tamil Separatism, 1916–1929 (1969)

Briton Martin, Jr.

New India, 1885: British Official Policy and the Emergence of the Indian National Congress (1969)

James T. Siegel

The Rope of God (1969)

Jyotirindra Das Gupta

Language Conflict and National Development: Group Politics and National Language Policy in India (1970)

Richard G. Fox

Kin, Clan, Raja and Rule: State-Hinterland Relations in Preindustrial India (1971)

Robert N. Kearney

Trade Unions and Politics in Ceylon (1971)

David N. Lorenzen

The Kāpālikas and Kālāmukhas: Two Lost Śaivite Sects (1971)

David G. Marr

Vietnamese Anticolonialism, 1885–1925 (1971)

Elizabeth Whitcombe

Agrarian Conditions in Northern India. Volume One: The United Provinces under British Rule, 1860–1900 (1971)

Nepal
Strategy for Survival

This volume is sponsored by the
Center for South and Southeast Asia Studies,
University of California, Berkeley

Nepal
Strategy for Survival

LEO E. ROSE

University of California Press

Berkeley, Los Angeles, London

1971

UNIVERSITY OF CALIFORNIA PRESS
Berkeley and Los Angeles, California
University of California Press, Ltd. London, England
Copyright © 1971, by The Regents of the University of California
Library of Congress Catalog Card Number: 75-100022
International Standard Book Number 0-520-01643-2
Printed in the United States of America

To My Parents

Preface

THE progenitor of the present ruling dynasty in Nepal, Bada Maharaja Prithvi Narayan Shah, once aptly described his newly conquered kingdom in the central Himalayas as "a root between two stones." Even in his day—the mid-18th century—Nepal's most formidable problem in the formulation and implementation of foreign policy was the preservation of the country's independence in the face of the concurrent but separate threats posed by the newly emerging dominant power in northern India, the British East India Company, and a slowly but steadily expanding Chinese presence in Tibet. Present-day Nepal thus perceives its critical geopolitical situation in terms of a long tradition as a buffer state and with some deeply ingrained attitudes toward the policies and tactics required to maintain its political and cultural integrity.

Because of Nepal's preoccupation with mere survival, its foreign policy inevitably has a psychological orientation different from that of larger states, including India and China, whose physical attributes are in themselves a fairly reliable guarantee of security. To Kathmandu, the current potentialities of external domination and subversion are not very different in kind—though they may be in degree—from those with which Nepali governments have had to contend for at least two centuries. And if the problems are not particularly new, neither is the repertory of responses devised by the Kathmandu authorities. There is a basic similarity between King Prithvi Narayan Shah's analysis of Nepal's role in the Himalayan area and his selection of tactics and that of the Ninth ruler in his dynasty, King Mahendra Bir Bikram Shah Dev. In part, of course, this can be attributed to the paucity of alternative policies for a country in Nepal's position. Nevertheless, there are choices to be made within this strictly limited framework, and the consistency displayed by widely different groups of decision-makers over a long period is one of the more notable aspects of Nepal's history.

Social scientists in both Western and non-Western countries have usually perceived contemporary international relations in terms of the major powers, both real and potential—the United States, the Soviet Union, the larger Western European states, China, Japan and India. Although some attention has occasionally been directed toward the role of the smaller polities in world politics, the analysis has usually been confined to such ambiguous, indeed nonfunctional, collective units as the "third world," the "under-developed" or "emerging" nations, or the "Afro-Asian states." Only rarely has the policy of a single member (such as Nepal) of one or more of these pseudocommunities been thought to merit consideration in depth.

Such an emphasis on big-power policy studies derives in part from the obvious disparity in terms of real power between these few large states and the rest of the world community. Even now, when it is apparent that there are definite limitations to the capacity of the major powers to direct or even influence developments along the lines they consider in their own interest, those limitations are often attributed to ephemeral and transitory factors that will gradually decrease in importance. Such problems are seldom considered insurmountable, and the possibility that these failures and setbacks are in part manifestations of smaller-state *power* at work has usually been ignored.

These assumptions about power and the exaggerated expectations flowing therefrom are now certainly open to challenge. Not infrequently, in our time, the major powers find their smaller associates in the community of nations unreasonably obtuse in defining and maintaining postures and policies which the latter consider to be in line with their national integrity and sociocultural traditions.

Nepal certainly falls neatly into that category of states. For nearly two centuries, this small Himalayan kingdom has been beset by a seemingly irresistible array of "interested" outside parties, eager to assist, advise and manipulate. No doubt these external elements have imposed some barely tolerable restrictions on Nepal's capacity for independent action, but its rulers have themselves displayed a deft hand in defining and, at times, even circumventing these limitations. This has been accomplished by means of a subtle combination of resistive and cooptive policies devised by the various regimes that have monopolized decision-making powers in Nepal, and by a cultural dynamic that seems to permeate all the articulate political, social, ethnic and regional entities in the state. There has been a remarkably broad consensus in Nepal on foreign policy during most of the modern period, not only on broader objectives but also on tactics. Presumably, that consensus reflects the country's long experience in buffer state politics.

Nepal, therefore, provides a useful case study of the processes and styles with which a small state in a difficult geopolitical situation confronts and confounds the intrusionist and directive policies of the major powers. The context in which Nepal burst into the international community from its self-imposed century of isolation in 1950 adds interest to the analysis. Its sudden emergence, for which the country was ill-prepared politically, economically and psychologically, lent a strong sense of urgency, even a single-mindedness, to the task of devising suitable responses to the persistent intrusion of outside influences. But whereas there was a sweet bloom of innocence to the Nepali world-view in the first stages of that traumatic transitional period, it did not long survive, and the lines of continuity between prerevolutionary and post-revolutionary Nepali foreign policy are readily apparent.

In devising this study, therefore, it seemed essential to analyze and interpret the main features of Nepal's foreign policy and relations with neighboring states from an historical perspective. I have eschewed a strictly chronological approach, however, as inappropriate for those purposes at hand—namely, the extrapolation and analysis of those perceived (and sometimes misperceived) historical experiences which the present formulators of foreign policy consider as useful guides. A modified case-study approach has been used instead, under which a number of crisis points in Nepal's relations with India and China since the mid-18th century have been selected for detailed study. The emphasis is placed upon the nature of the problem posed for Nepal both internally and externally and the various responses devised by the Kathmandu authorities to meet the situation. This does not qualify the historical section as "good history," no doubt, as there is a built-in distortion due to the failure to consider some events that were important in their time but which were either only of immediate significance or were yet another repetition of a familiar pattern of development.

Furthermore, I am not particularly concerned in this study with analyzing the processes or agents of decision-making, but rather with the substance of Nepal's foreign policy. This obviates the relevance of a "systems" analysis, which in any case would be handicapped by the fact that the basic data required for such a methodological approach are neither available nor, I would suspect, attainable. There is also, of course, the question of the appropriateness of this kind of approach for a political system in which decision-making on foreign-policy issues is so greatly influenced by forces external to the polity.

Work on this study has proceeded intermittently for nearly a dozen years, and during that period the author has had the advantage of the comments, criticisms and experience of numerous friends and colleagues in Nepal, India and the United States. I will commence with an expression of thanks to colleagues and assistants in the Institute of International Studies and the Himalayan Border Countries Project at the University of California—Margaret W. Fisher (who first directed my interest toward Nepal), Robert A. Scalapino, Joan V. Bondurant, Thomas Blaisdell, Bhuwan Lal Joshi, Frederick Gaige, Jagadish Sharma, Roger Dial, Kunjar Mani Sharma, Cleo Stoker, Jeanne Allingham, and Ila Jungnickel.

Several officials in the Nepal Foreign Office in Kathmandu and in Nepali Embassies in New Delhi and Washington have done their utmost to interpret the Nepali perspective on Himalayan-area political developments, usually very persuasively and always with exemplary patience and persistence. Many more Nepalis in a political or academic capacity have discussed and debated with me at great length and invariably with both considerable enthusiasm and a good sense of humor, adding immeasurably to the pleasure and profit derived from my research. What follows is by no means an exhaustive list, but I do want to pay a special vote of thanks to several Nepalis whom I interviewed on an extensive scale: Rishikesh Shaha, Surya Bikram Jñawali, Keshar Bahadur K.C., Dr. Dilli Raman Regmi, General Mrigendra Shamsher Rana, Surya Prasad Upadhyaya, General Subarna Shamsher Rana, Gokul Chund Shastri, Bishweshwar Prasad Koirala, and Poorna Bahadur M.A.

I also owe a major debt to Mahesh Chandra Regmi and to the staff members of the Regmi Research Project in Kathmandu who facilitated my research program in many ways and who provided a home base during several field trips in Nepal. In addition, I would like to thank Purna Harsha Bajracharya of the Department of Culture and Archaeology of His Majesty's Government, and Dr. Trailokya Nath Upraity, Vice-Chancellor of Tribhuvan University in Kathmandu, for their hospitality and assistance.

My work in the records of the National Archives of India in New Delhi was facilitated by the staff there, and a particular word of appreciation is due Vijaya C. Joshi, S. N. Roy, and Satya Pal. The excellent resources on Nepal at the Indian School of International Studies in New Delhi were made available. I also profited from discussions with Satish Kumar, Ram Rahul, and Sisir Gupta at that institution and with officials in the External Affairs Ministry in New Delhi and in the Indian Embassy in Kathmandu.

My field work in Nepal and India was supported on various occasions by the Ford Foundation (1956–1958), the American Institute of Indian Studies (1963–1964) and the Institute of International Studies, Berkeley (1961–1962, 1965–1966 and 1967–1968), to whom I express my appreciation. I would also like to thank Richard Adloff and Max Knight for the assistance in preparing this manuscript for publication and Mrs. Virginia Herrick for the map.

Needless to say, none of the individuals or organizations mentioned above should be held responsible for any statements made in this book.

L. E. R.

Contents

Part I
Introduction

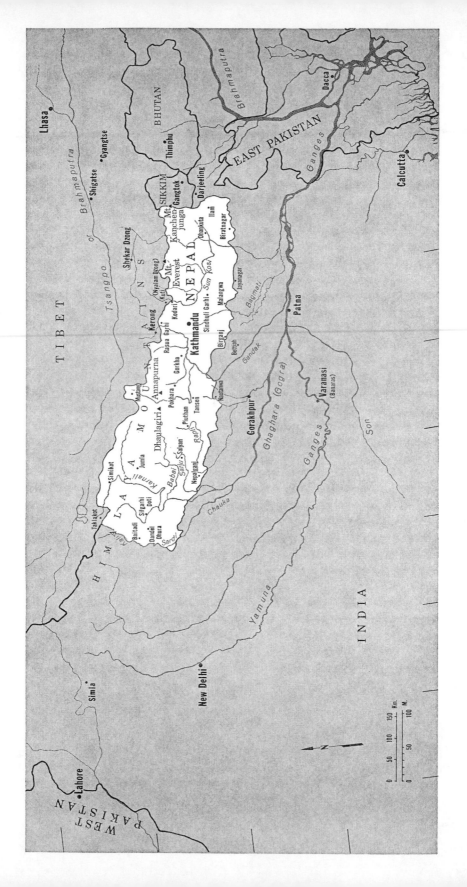

1

The Foundations
of Nepal's
Foreign Relations

NEPAL's foreign policy and the dynamics of its relationship with neighboring states have been conditioned by a complex of factors, of which the political component is only one of the more important. Nepal's cultural relationship with India and Tibet, for instance, or its role in the trade and economic system in the transitional area between south and east Asia could easily be the subject of book-length studies themselves, and indeed several are already in preparation by competent scholars. In this study, therefore, I shall include such factors in my analysis only to the extent that they intrude upon and affect political decision-making or foreign-policy issues. It seems appropriate, however, to begin with a few general remarks on several of these factors in order to place their later treatment in a more comprehensible perspective, and this will be the primary function of the introductory chapter.

THE PHYSICAL SETTING

Nepal's central location on the southern slope of the imposing mountain system that separates the Tibetan plateau from the plains of India has always strongly conditioned the country's history and foreign policy. Modern Nepal controls approximately one-third of the Himalayan bastion upon which south Asia relies for protection —never more so than today. Although that proportion has varied at different periods of Nepal's history, the ruling power in Kathmandu valley usually has controlled access to the principal pass areas in the central Himalayas through which trade has flowed and invading armies have passed in one direction or the other on several occasions. This situation distinguishes Kathmandu valley from similar mountain valleys to the east and west, for it transformed Kathmandu into a major entropôt for trans-Himalayan trade, enriching it, in the process, both materially and culturally.

There are at least eighteen pass areas in the central Himalayan range that can be used as channels of communication between Nepal and Tibet. The two most important, however, are the passes leading to the Tibetan border trading centers of Kerong and Kuti (Kyi-rong and Nyi-lam, respectively, in Tibetan), which have given rise to controversy between the two countries for several centuries. Formed by rivers that have their source in the Bhairab Langur range to the north of the crest of the Great Himalayas, these passes are two of the best in the entire border area because they are low in Himalayan terms (13,000 to 14,000 feet) and are usually not totally impassable in winter. The altitude of the other passes in the central Himalayas, on the other hand, is more than 17,000 feet, and they are invariably snowbound for several months of the year. They are, consequently, of limited utility as trade channels—except for the local inhabitants on either side of the passes—and moreover, they are not as important strategically.

For sound economic and strategic reasons, therefore, it was long a major objective of Nepali foreign policy to establish Nepal's authority over the Kerong and Kuti areas up to the watershed—that is, the Bhairab Langur range. Except for several brief periods, however, Kathmandu was frustrated in that aim by the Tibetans, at times assisted by the Chinese. Indeed, the border in both areas does not even reach up to the summit of the passes in the Himalayan range, but rather lies halfway down the southern slope at about 6,000 feet. As a result, the Tibetans (and now the Chinese) have controlled not only the pass areas but also the approaches to the passes from the south, and thus have had a decided advantage in the several local wars that have been fought in these areas during the past three centuries.

Within Nepal, the dominant topographic features are the complex river drainage system, which cuts through the country in a generally north-south direction, and the three mountain ranges— the Himalaya, Mahabharat, and Siwalik (or Churia as it is known in Nepal)—which lie along an east-west axis. The three principal river systems—the Karnali, Gandaki and Kosi—all have their sources in Tibet, and enter Nepal through spectacular gorges that bisect the Himalayas. South of the crest they are joined by innumerable tributaries, some of them glacial in origin, and eventually make their way down to the plains, where they merge with the Ganges. This river system, with its deep gorges and rugged transverse ridges, vastly complicates east-west communications in Nepal. The natural lines of combat run north-south—a factor that has greatly hampered political and administrative unification in the hill area. Western and eastern Nepal, for instance, are more easily accessible from India than from Kathmandu, with obvious political and economic consequences. Cultural distinctions in the region would doubtless have been even greater than they are if the dominant Hindu culture of northern India had not imposed a broad degree of standardization on the hill communities.

In the approximately 100 air miles between the Gangetic plain and the Tibetan plateau, at least seven distinct zones can be distinguished in Nepal: the Terai, the Siwalik range, the Inner Terai valleys, the Mahabharat range, the mid-montane area, the Himalayan range, and the high mountain valleys of the Inner Himalaya.

The southernmost strip of Nepali territory, known as the Terai, forms the intermediate zone between the Gangetic plain and the Siwalik range. It was once a hot, humid jungle, shunned by both Paharis (hill people) and Madhesis (plains people) during all but the cold season (October-March) because of the prevalence of a virulent form of malaria. The Terai was long considered an important asset in the defense of the hill area, for it made access from the plains extremely dangerous during half the year. Indeed, only in the mid-19th century, when relations with British India had improved, did the Nepal government begin to encourage the clearance of the Terai jungle areas for cultivation purposes.

Even though the Terai, culturally and politically, was peripheral to the hill-dominated polity in Nepal, it was of great economic importance. At the time of Nepal's greatest period of expansion (1770–1814), a favorite Nepali slogan was: "We shall wash the blood from our kukris in the Ganges," signifying the aim of the Gorkha rulers of the country to extend their sway over this valuable lowland region, which was then in a transitional stage as a result of the disintegration of the Moghul Empire in India. The British preempted Nepal in the area, however, and Kathmandu ended up eventually controlling only a narrow strip of territory, averaging 10 miles in width, below the foothills. Nevertheless, this small region yields nearly 75% of the Nepal's total revenue; forests still abound, but several roads now cross the jungle belt and connect the plains with the hills throughout the year.

The Siwalik range, with altitudes of 2,500 to 4,500 feet, is only sparsely settled, for it suffers from a severe shortage of water in the dry season. The inner Terai valleys, lying between the Siwalik and Mahabharat ranges, were also little developed until recently because of the prevalence of malaria. The Mahabharat range, some of whose peaks attain an elevation of nearly 10,000 feet, is Nepal's principal defense wall on the south and, conversely, present-day India's main line of defense against any Chinese thrust from the north in this sector of the frontier. It is too steep to be densely populated, but a few towns—established originally for defensive purposes—are found where trade routes cross the range.

The mid-montane area, located between the Mahabharat and Himalayan ranges, is the most heavily populated region of Nepal and its political heartland. High transverse ridges separate the great river system, and rings of mountains surround the few valleys found in this area. Nevertheless, most of the region lies at 2,000 to 6,000 feet, and intensive cultivation of rice—a *sine qua non* for a Hindu, Indo-Aryan culture—is made possible by an elaborate terracing system.

The Himalayas rise with spectacular abruptness from the mid-montane area, averaging over 20,000 feet in height and reaching 29,000 feet at the highest point—Mt. Everest, or Sagarmatha as it is known in Nepal. Settlements are found up to approximately the 12,000-foot level, above which lies a belt of dense forests, these giving way in turn to alpine pastures and finally the snowline. Some of the highest peaks in the range are on the boundary with Tibet, but others lie well to the south. Beyond the crestline are several wide mountain valleys, known as the Inner Himalaya, which lie at 8,000 to 20,000 feet. Some of these are now part of Nepal, and have been the subject of periodic disputes between Nepal and Tibet. As noted before, however, the two most important of the valleys—Kuti and Kirong—still belong to Tibet.

Nepal's international boundaries with neighboring states are well-defined topographically and have been delimited in a series of treaties and in some places have also been demarcated on the ground. This has not precluded the occasional eruption of minor border disputes, but such disputes have been confined to disagreements over a few square miles of territory. Furthermore, both India and China have formally recognized Nepal's independence in treaties, and no residual claims to sovereignty based upon presumed historical relationships would have any sanction in international law. There is no certainty, of course, that such claims might not be raised notwithstanding in the future by either or both powers if circumstances seemed to make this necessary or expedient.

THE ETHNIC AND CULTURAL MOSAIC

For at least two millenia, the hill areas to the south of the Himalayas have offered shelter to waves of migrants, and the process continues, as the recent wave of Tibetan refugees escaping Chinese rule testifies. The dominant strains in the population of present-day Nepal are Caucasoid (i.e., Indo-Aryan) and Mongoloid, with varying degrees of admixture. Some of these ethnic groups had migrated to Nepal from the east as part of the vast westward movement of tribal peoples from southeast Asia. Others had their origin in Tibet, whereas still others moved northward from the Indian plains or eastward from the hill areas of the western Himalayas.

Systematic ethnological studies in Nepal are as yet in an early stage of development, and the complexities of the ethnic structure are yet to be clarified. We do know, however, that the dominant element socially, politically and economically in most of Nepal is composed of the descendants of high-caste Hindus—mostly of the Brahman or Kshatriya castes—who sought refuge in Nepal at the time of the Muslim invasions of India or even earlier. These families are found scattered throughout the mid-montane area, although rarely above the 6,000-foot level. They form the local elites wherever they reside, and have long dominated political institutions at the central level. In the mid-19th century and thereafter, another wave of Hindu and Muslim migrants from the adjoining areas of India entered the Terai area of Nepal, where today, along with such indigenous communities as the Tharus, they form the bulk of the population.

Another important community of mixed Caucasoid and Mongoloid origins consists of the Newars, centered in Kathmandu valley. They are characteristically an urban group, and the distinctive civilization that developed in the central valley of Nepal is largely their handiwork. There are both Hindu and Buddhist subgroups among the Newars, but Hinduism has held the dominant position in the last two centuries.

The remaining ethnic groups of numerical importance in Nepal are unquestionably Mongoloid in origin. Prominent among them are the Magars and Gurungs, concentrated in the western Nepal mid-montane region, and the Limbus, Rais and Tamangs, who inhabit the hill areas to the east of Kathmandu valley. There are also a number of Mongolid communities of relatively recent Tibetan origin, such as the Sherpas and the Thakalis. It is important to note, however, that Mongoloid origin is no longer synonymous with non-Hindu—usually Buddhist—culture. The Magars, for instance, and to a lesser extent the Gurungs, Rais and Limbus, have been "Sanskritized" (in contemporary anthropological parlance) to a considerable extent.

A syncretic form of Hinduism, encompassing much that is Buddhist or "animist" in derivation, therefore, is the dominant religious and cultural form throughout much of Nepal. The reasons behind the ascendancy of Hinduism are manifold, but probably of greatest importance is the fact that a Brahmanic form of Hinduism has been the religion of most Nepali ruling elites for several centuries. Hindu social and ritual practices carry the highest prestige value, often even among communities of Mongoloid origin. This does not mean, of course, that non-Hindus have always accepted the imposition of Brahmanic Hindu values willingly or that the synthesizing process has been painless. On the contrary, there is still considerable evidence of resentment, even among some communities that have nominally adopted Hinduism, against the enforcement of such Brahmanic principles as the ban on cow-slaughter and on the consumption of alcoholic beverages, and the rigid caste-purification rites. This has tended to obscure Nepal's regional and cultural identity in significant ways, for important sub-cultures derived from the Tibetan Buddhist civilization of central Asia or the highland tribal communities of southeast Asia still exercise a powerful influence in some parts of the country.

Nepali society has been remarkably successful in synthesizing these varied and even contradictory cultural strands into a standard product that is uniquely Nepali in character. But the complex and multidimensional facets of Nepal's cultural heritage play a major part in the Nepalis' comprehension of their role and status in the modern world. They tend to view their homeland as an intermediate zone between south and east Asia, belonging to both regions rather than exclusively to either, and that attitude has been a critical factor in both the modern history of Nepal and its foreign policy.

Nevertheless, the ancient and extremely close cultural and social relationship between Nepal and India is demonstrated in innumerable ways. For several hundred years, for instance, the various ruling dynasties of Nepal have intermarried as a matter of policy with Indian families of equivalent caste status,[1] and this has

_____

[1] Until the latter half of the 19th century, the brides of the Shah rulers of Nepal were often chosen from good—if not always the best—Rajput families in India. When the Rana family gained absolute political power in the mid-19th century and relegated the Shah kings to the status of figureheads, marital policy also underwent a

resulted in a massive exchange of elites that has been of fundamental social, cultural and political importance. There have also been many occasions upon which Nepali rulers have imported prestigious advisors from India, often absorbing them into the existing political system. The first Nepali code of laws, for example, was the product of several reputable Indian Brahmans who were invited to Nepal by King Jayastithi Malla (ca. 14th century), and the 1948 Constitution was in part the work of a team of Indian advisors. Even today, the Brahman priests who administer Pasupatinath temple, the most important Hindu institution in Nepal and the Shah family's personal shrine, are from a village in southern India and were first invited to Kathmandu by a Malla ruler nearly 300 years ago.

The importance of Hinduism as a binding link between these two societies is also readily apparent, if sometimes difficult to analyze in political terms. Several places of pilgrimage in Nepal are visited by thousands of Indians each year, and tours of the major Hindu shrines in India are considered a duty by many devout Nepalis. These pilgrimages are not always motivated solely by a sense of piety and religiosity, however, but at times have had definite political connotations. The first Rana prime minister, for instance, visited several of the holiest shrines in India immediately after his return from England in 1852 in order to prove to his scandalized countrymen that his violation of the caste restrictions against travel across the ocean had not polluted him irreparably in the eyes of the respected Indian priesthood at these shrines. More recently, King Mahendra also made a tour of some of these same shrines at a time when Indian-Nepali relations were at a low ebb, thus emphasizing to the Indian public his status as the only Hindu king in the world, and moreover, one who, under traditional Hindu political philosophy, is considered to be a manifestation of Vishnu.

The common Hindu heritage of the two countries is further reinforced by other forms of cultural and intellectual ties. A large proportion of the Nepali elite has received at least part of its education in India and has absorbed, if only subconsciously at times, the ethos and spirit of that educational system. Similarly, many Nepali political and governmental leaders served their political apprenticeship in India, and the political idioms of Nepal are still largely a reflection of those prevalent in India at any given moment. Educated Indians and Nepalis, therefore, speak the same political language to a far greater extent than would be true with respect to Nepalis and Americans, British, Russians or Chinese. It is impos-

---

gradual change. Thereafter, it became the practice for the Shahs to accept Rana brides, often under some duress. The Ranas, on the other hand, adopted the old Shah practice of seeking brides for their sons from reputable Rajput families in India.

sible to foresee just how important this form of linkage may be in determining Nepal's role in Himalayan-area developments, but it certainly could prove to be a crucial factor in any large scale conflict in this region.

THE HISTORICAL BACKGROUND

The relationship between the hill areas of present-day Nepal and the Gangetic plains to the south has been a close one for nearly three millenia and perhaps much longer. There can be no doubt that the intellectual, religious and social forces that have molded modern Nepali society, whether Hinduism, Buddhism or contemporary political ideology, have stemmed almost exclusively from India. Moreover, Nepali political traditions since at least the time of the Emperor Ashoka (ca. 4th century B.C.) have been closely integrated with those of northern India and cannot be properly comprehended except in conjunction with the basic trends prevalent in the Gangetic plain. In the formation of foreign policy, for instance, Nepal has been influenced as profoundly as any area of India by the dicta on interstate relations that are generally attributed to the Indian "master statesman," Kautilya. The major dynastic lines throughout Nepal since at least the 11th century—and for Kathmandu valley and the far-western hill areas, several centuries earlier —have been of high-caste Indian origin proudly proclaiming their descent from prestigious ruling and warrior (kshatriya) families of India. Although Nepal maintained its political independence throughout this period, its history is so closely intertwined with that of northern India that even a summary analysis of this relationship would be both too lengthy and tediously repetitive.

It was only in the seventh century A.D. that the emergence of a powerful kingdom in Tibet with its capital at Lhasa transformed Kathmandu valley, an isolated sub-Himalayan backwater, into the intellectual and commercial entrepôt between India and central Asia. Presumably, limited trade had been carried on across the Himalayas via Kathmandu prior to that period,[2] but it was not until the seventh century that political relations also assumed a crucial importance. Chinese and Tibetan records assert that the early Tibetan

---

[2] T'ang dynasty records, based largely on the reports of Chinese pilgrims who traveled through Tibet and Nepal en route to India in that period. mention the great wealth of the cities of Kathmandu valley and the important role of the mercantile community there. [See, for instance, Tu Yu, *T'ung-Tien* (Encyclopedia of Source Material on Political and Social History), vol. 46, Chuan 190, pp. 18b–19a.] This suggests that trade between Nepal and Tibet was already flourishing, as Kathmandu's commercial prosperity has traditionally depended upon trade with Tibet.

ruler, Song-tsen Gampo (Srong-bstan Sgam-po) exercised some form of authority over Kathmandu valley, reportedly for having helped King Narendra Deva and his family regain the throne that had been usurped by a powerful minister, Amshuvarma, two decades earlier. "For this service," the Chinese source states, "he had to subordinate Nepal to Tibet."[3]

Nepali *vamshavalis* (chronicles) record the visit of a Tibetan king to Nepal during the same period (i.e., about 640), and also acknowledge that a Nepali princess—perhaps a sister of Narendra Deva—became the wife of Song-tsen Gampo and assisted in the introduction of Buddhism into Tibet. Nepali historians, however, deny that Kathmandu was ever subordinate to Tibet, basing their conclusions on stone inscriptions and historical traditions that are comparatively full for that period.[4]

Whatever the character of Nepali-Tibetan relations, the events of the first half of the 7th century paved the way for the opening of a new channel of communications between China and India across the Himalayan passes, and also led to the first direct contacts between Nepal and China. A Chinese pilgrim, Hsuan-chuang, visited Nepal in 637, but he had journeyed to India via the established route through Kashmir and Turkestan.[5] The first official Chinese mission to Nepal, led by Li I-piao and Wang Hsüan-Ts'ê, used the new route through Tibet. It was warmly welcomed by Narendra Deva in 644,[6] possibly because the latter's relations with Song-tsen Gampo of Tibet were proving irksome.

For the next two decades, the route through Tibet and Nepal was followed by many travellers between India and China. Official contacts between the Nepal Court and the T'ang dynasty were also maintained. In 647, Chinese records indicate, a Nepali envoy visited Changan with presents for the Emperor.[7] Four years later, shortly after the death of King Song-tsen Gampo, Narendra Deva sent another mission to China. It is possible that these direct rela-

---

[3] *Ch'in-T'ang-Shu* (Old History of the T'ang Dynasty), vol. 40, Chuan 198, pp. 1a–1b. The invaluable Tibetan documents found at Tunhuang, consisting of a chronological account of events in Tibet from 650 to 747, record that Tibetan kings resided in Nepali territory on several occasions as if it were part of their domain. (J. Bacot et al., *Documents de Touen-Houang Relatifs à l'Histoire du Tibet*, Paris, 1940, pp. 29–52.)

[4] D. R. Regmi, *Ancient Nepal*, Calcutta, Firma K. L. Mukhapadhayay, 1960, p. 214.

[5] *Ta-T'ang-Hsi-Yu-Chu* (Records of the Western World in the Great T'ang Period) compiled by Hsuan-chuang and edited by Pien-chi, Chuan vii, 648 A.D. (Japanese edition, *Ta-Tsang Chin*, vol. 51, p. 910). There has been some disagreement among scholars as to whether Hsuan-chuang had actually visited Kathmandu valley. A careful analysis of the terminology used by the compiler, however, strongly suggests that he did.

[6] *Fa-Yuan-Chu-Lin* (Forest of the Pearls of the Garden of Buddhist Law), compiled by Tao-shih, Chuan 29, 668 A.D., (Japanese edition, *Ta-Tsang Chin*, vol. 53, p. 504.)

[7] Huang Sheng-chang, "China and Nepal," *People's China*, May 1, 1956, p. 9.

tions between Nepal and China caused uneasiness at the Tibetan Court, for this was the last occasion upon which an official Nepali mission to China was permitted to cross Tibet for nearly 700 years. The alliance between Tibet and China, formalized by the marriage of a Chinese princess to Song-tsen Gampo, disintegrated after the latter's death in 650. When hostilities broke out between Tibet and China a decade later, the trans-Himalayan route between south and east Asia was barred, and it remained closed for several centuries. References to Nepal virtually disappear from T'ang and succeeding dynastic histories.[8] Even during the Yuan (Mongol) dynastic period, when these alien rulers of China exerted a powerful influence in Tibet, direct political contacts with Nepal were never reestablished.

The Ming dynasty (1368–1644), which succeeded the Mongols, failed to maintain a significant influence in Tibet but did manage to establish diplomatic relations with the Rama family of Patan (Kathmandu valley),[9] one of the political factions then contending for control of the valley. During the period from 1384 to 1427, five Chinese missions and seven Nepali missions were exchanged between the two courts.[10] The rival Malla family, however, abruptly terminated all diplomatic contacts with the Ming dynasty once Kathmandu valley had been unified under its authority in 1427,[11] and many years passed before relations between the two countries were renewed.

The 16th and 17th centuries were a crucial period in the relations between Nepal and Tibet. By 1600, Tibet was in a state of

---

[8] A Chinese Buddhist monk, Chi-yeh, visited Nepal during his journey through south Asia (964–76), but he had entered India via the Turkestan route. During the Yuan period, a Nepali artisan and architect, Arniko, was a prominent figure at the court of Kublai Khan. Contemporary Chinese and Nepali publicists attach great significance to Arniko as a symbol of friendship and "ages-old" cultural relations. The Yuan dynastic records, however, are ambivalent about Arniko's origin. All they tell us is that he was an artisan and builder who had earned a great reputation in Tibet before being brought to Peking. While it is probable that he was a member of the thriving Newari artisan community in Tibet, this cannot be ascertained from the Chinese records. Nepali sources do not even mention his name nor his activities in Tibet and China, and this may indicate that Arniko was an isolated phenomenon rather than an example of Nepali-Chinese cultural relations.

[9] *Ming Shih-lu* (Veritable Records of the Ming Dynasty), Nanking edition, 1940, vol, 22, Chuan 159, p. 66. The Chinese difficulty in distinguishing "r" and "l" sounds led the Mings to assume that they were dealing with Buddhist "lamas" rather than Hindu "Rama" family kings.

[10] For accounts of these various missions see *ibid.*, vols. 27, 30, 32, 35, 47, 48, 51 and 63; see also *Ming Shih-kao* (Draft History of the Ming), compiled by Wang Hung-hsu, 1714, vol. 80, Chuan 309; *Ch'in-ting Hsu Wen-Hsien-T'ung-Kao* (Supplement to the T'ung-tien Encyclopedia), 1767, Chuan 148. L. Petech used some of these sources in his *Mediaeval History of Nepal*, Rome, 1958, p. 210.

[11] Radhakrishna Choudhary, "Nepal and the Karnatas of Mithila (1097–1500 A.D.)," *Journal of Indian History*, XXXVI:1 (April 1958), p. 130.

near-chaos as a result of the struggle between competing Buddhist
sects and the more basic regional conflict between the two central
Tibetan provinces, of which Lhasa and Shigatse are the political
centers. The powerful figure of the Fifth Dalai Lama, the head of
the Gelugpa (yellow) sect of Tibetan Buddhism, gradually gained
control, both spiritual and temporal, over Tibet in the first half of
the 17th century, with the valuable assistance of the Khoshote
Mongols.[12]

During this critical period, two ambitious kings of Nepal,
Rama Shah of Gorkha (1606–33) and Pratap Malla of Kathmandu
(1624–74), took advantage of Tibetan weakness to seize control of
the vital border-pass areas through which most of the trans-
Himalayan trade passed. Rama Shah's incursions into Tibet occurred toward the end of his reign, probably from 1625 to 1630,
after he had conquered the intervening territory between Gorkha
and Kirong district in Tibet.[13] The first Gorkhali invading force
was defeated, and the severed heads of the two commanders were
sent to the Panchen Lama at Shigatse. Rama Shah led another army
into the Kerong area, defeated the Tibetans at Khinchog and advanced as far as Kukurghat. He reached an agreement with the
Tibetans under which the boundary line between Gorkha and
Tibet was drawn at Kukurghat, thus giving Rama Shah control
over one of the main channels of communication between Nepal
and Tibet.

This posed a serious problem for the Kathmandu merchant
community, which normally used the route through Kirong in their
trade with Tibet. The Kathmandu Raja, Pratap Malla, decided
against contending directly with the Gorkha ruler for control of
Kerong, but sought instead to bring the second major trade route,
via Kuti, under his authority. An army commanded by his brother,
Bhim Malla, was sent to Kuti in the 1630's and again in the period
between 1645 and 1650. On the second occasion, Bhim Malla over-
ran the border district and advanced some distance toward Shigatse
before he was met by the deputies of the Dalai Lama, with whom he
negotiated a peace settlement.

The terms of this treaty were, in summary:

1) Kathmandu was granted joint authority with Tibet over the border
   towns of Kuti and Kerong.[14]

---

[12] Snellgrove and Richardson, *A Cultural History of Tibet*, New York, Praeger, 1968,
p. 195.

[13] S. V. Jñawali, *Rama Shah ko Jivan Charitra* (Biography of Rama Shah) Darjeeling,
1933.

[14] By 1645, the Tibetans had regained control of the Kerong area from Gorkha. This
probably occurred shortly after the conquest of Tsang province by the fifth Dalai
Lama in 1642.

2) The Newari merchant community of Kathmandu valley was permitted to establish 32 trading houses at Lhasa.

3) The Kathmandu court was given the right to post a representative (Nayo) at Lhasa.

4) Tibet agreed not to impose any charges or customs duties on Newari merchants who were engaged in the trade with Tibet.

5) Tibet promised to make a token payment in gold and silver annually to Kathmandu.

6) It was agreed that Nepal would mint coins for Tibet; Tibet would use these coins internally and would either provide the silver required for their minting or would pay for Nepali coins with gold.

7) Tibet agreed that all trade with India, even though conducted by other than Newari merchants, would be channeled through Kathmandu valley in preference to the routes to the east (i.e., via Sikkim, Bhutan or Towang).[15]

Thanks to the treaty, the merchants of Kathmandu valley gained a virtual monopoly over the lucrative trade between India and Tibet,[16] as well as the right to extend their commercial activities to Lhasa.[17] The Kathmandu Raja also profited substantially from the process under which he minted coins for the Tibetan government, for he deducted a certain percentage of the silver provided by Lhasa as his fee for this service. These Nepali coins, called "Mahendramalla" by the Tibetans, were the sole currency in circulation throughout Tibet for more than a century.[18]

Kathmandu's joint authority with Lhasa over the border towns of Kuti and Kerong apparently lasted only about 25 years. A Jesuit missionary, Father John Grueber, who travelled through the area in 1661, described Kuti as "one of the two chief cities of the Kingdom of Nekbal."[19] However, another Jesuit missionary, Father

---

15 C. R. Nepali, "Nepal ra Tibet ko Sambandha" (Nepal-Tibet Relations) *Pragati*, Year II, Issue IV, no. X.

16 The importance of the trans-Himalayan trade to Nepal is shown by the custom still prevalent among high-caste Newars in which a person dressed as a Tibetan is included in marriage processions. This implies that the groom's family has trading connections with Tibet, and thus is wealthy. Purna Harsha Bajracharya, "Newar Marriage Customs and Festivals" *Southwestern Journal of Anthropology*, vol. 15 (winter 1959), p. 420.

17 Although Newari merchant houses had operated elsewhere in Tibet prior to this time, it was apparently under the provisions of this treaty that they were first allowed to establish agencies in Lhasa.

18 It has been suggested that the system under which Nepal minted coins for Tibet had originated earlier, probably in the reign of King Mahendra Malla of Kathmandu. The Nepali coins circulating in Tibet even in the late 18th century were known as "Mahendramalli" to both the Tibetans and the Nepalis. However, the name had originated in Nepal, as such coins had first been minted during the reign of that ruler, and even coins minted by his successors retained the same name.

19 T. Astley, *A New General Collection of Voyages and Travels*, London, 1745–7, vol. IV, p. 653.

Ippolito Desideri, who resided in the same area for six months in 1721, reported that "not long ago the fortress and the province of Kuthi were subject to the Rajah of Kattmandu; now they are subject to the Kingdom of Lhasa."[20] Neither Nepali nor Tibetan documentary materials specify when or how Kathmandu lost its authority in the border districts, but a Chinese source notes that the Fifth Dalai Lama, who died in 1683, had regained the areas of Tibet that had been seized by Pratap Malla.[21]

The establishment of a presence in Tibet by the Ch'ing (Manchu) dynasty in the early 18th century, in the form of two Manchu Ambans (Residents) at Lhasa, did not lead to an immediate renewal of relations with Nepal on a protracted basis. Kathmandu sent an embassy to the Ambans in 1732,[22] probably on the occasion of Jaya Prakash Malla's succession to the throne. But nothing seems to have emerged from this contact, for neither Chinese nor Nepali records mention any further exchanges between Nepal and the Chinese officials in Tibet during the next half-century. Such exchanges had to await political changes in Nepal, India and Tibet in the late 18th century, as a result of which China became, for the first time, an important factor in Himalayan-area politics.

SOME PSYCHOLOGICAL ASPECTS OF NEPAL'S WORLD VIEW

The Nepali world view in the modern period appears to be primarily a reflection and extension of its perception of the country's two enormous neighbors, India and China. The Nepali comprehension of these two great powers has been strongly conditioned by the history of Kathmandu's relations with them, as recorded in Nepal's chronicles, mythology, and artistic and architectural achievements and as reflected in the syncretistic character of its national culture. For more than two millenia, Kathmandu valley has served as a storehouse for external influences, primarily Indian in origin, as well as a transmitter of cultural influences, either Indian or the syncretic Nepali product, across the Himalayas. Thus, Nepal has played a dynamic role as both preserver and transmitter of cultural and intellectual phenomena in the Himalayan area.

---

[20] Fillipo de Filippi, *An Account of Tibet, the Travels of Ippolito Desideri of Pisotia, S. J., 1712–1727*, London, 1932, pp. 130–31.
[21] *Chin-ting K'uo-er-k'a Chi lueh* (Official Summary Account of the Pacification of the Gorkhas), Peking, 1796, Book 13, Chuan 20, pp. 5b–13b. Cited hereafter as *Chin-ting.*
[22] Klaproth's translation from the Chinese of an "Account of Different Tribes in Tibet," *Asiatic Journal*, Vol. III, (2nd series), September–December, 1830, p. 324.

The contemporary Nepali elite is fully cognizant of this brilliant tradition and is eager to maintain Nepal's status as a bridge between south and east Asia.

There are, however, substantial qualitative and quantitative differences between Nepal's historic relationship with India and that with China. As has been noted, relations with the former have been intimate and continuous on virtually all levels of contact for at least 2,500 years. The major cultural and religious influences in Nepal—whether Hindu or Buddhist—have stemmed from India, as have the dominant political and administrative concepts and institutions. In contrast, Nepal's relations with China have been intermittent at best, and usually have been restricted to the official level (e.g., governmental missions) prior to 1950, and even thereafter. Indeed, there were long periods when Nepal and China were virtually unaware of and uninterested in each other's existence. The fundamental distinction in the intensity of its relations with India and China has had a profound effect upon Nepal's perception, and in fact its capacity to perceive, these two very different societies.

Nepalis seem to apply basically different sets of criteria in evaluating India and China. A Nepali psychologist has described this dichotomy in the following terms:

Nepalis had to reckon with the Indians so long and so often that they are more prone to infer the latters intents quickly than to observe their overt behavior. Due to the high degree of intimacy between the two countries through the ages, whatever the Indians do in actual practice is not considered as important as what the Nepalis think the Indians mean. With the Chinese, however, it is a different story. Historically, the Nepalis had so few occasions to become acquainted with the Chinese mind that they are still in the process of observing Chinese overt behavior vis-à-vis Nepal. In spite of all that has happened between China and India in recent years, Nepali elites are still disinclined to probe into Chinese intents and motives.

He argued that China has reaped a considerable advantage from the fact that its relationship with Kathmandu has avoided the extremes of excessive intimacy and complete indifference, and that it has usually been maintained at a level of diplomatic propriety. Such a relationship has been impossible for India, given the intensely intimate nature of Indo-Nepali relations. As a result, India's statements and actions are interpreted by Kathmandu in the context of Nepali assumptions about New Delhi's motives and intentions rather than its overt behavior.[23]

---

23 Bhuwan Lal Joshi, "The Psychological Basis of Nepali Attitudes to China and India" (unpublished Ms.).

This imbalance in Kathmandu's perception of India and China has influenced the role Nepal has defined for itself in its relations with these two great powers. As we shall note later, under the special interpretation given to nonalignment by King Mahendra, Nepal must treat China and India on the basis of absolute equality, at least superficially. Indeed, a whole new historical mythos, recently formulated in Nepal, aims at proving that cultural and intellectual influences from China and India have been *equally* important in shaping Nepali social values and culture. Factually, this is nonsense, but psychologically it makes very good sense.

Why should this be the case? Part of the answer can be found in the very closeness of the ties between Nepal and India. Differentiation from India in cultural as well as political terms is today considered essential if a viable and distinct Nepali national identity is to evolve and the country is to escape eventual absorption into the Indian mother culture. There is probably nothing that makes Nepali intellectuals more uncomfortable than the still unabated propensity of Indians to harp upon the fact that, as President Hussain of India stated during his visit to Kathmandu in 1968, "relations between Nepal and India were as old and stable as the earth itself and nature has bound the destinies of the two countries together."[24] Precisely because there is a fundamental truth in this assertion, some hypersensitive Nepali intellectuals have been impelled to attempt to concoct an ahistorical but equally lengthy and close relationship with China as a counterbalance. This was unnecessary so long as the patently alien British ruled India, but it became a matter of extreme urgency once the Indians had become masters in their own house and some voices in India were beginning to speak of Mahabharat, or "Greater India." Before long, the need to establish a separate cultural identity for Nepal had been widely accepted in Nepali intellectual, political and even religious circles, and became an important factor in shaping Nepali preferences—if not always policy—on foreign-policy issues.

ECONOMIC LIMITATIONS ON FOREIGN POLICY

As suggested by the preceding analysis, a narrow economic-determinist interpretation of Nepali foreign policy would be deficient in several respects even though economic considerations normally play the major role in decision-making on such issues. Nepal's society is predominantly agricultural with an economic system that is better described as subsistence than as market-oriented. Never-

24 *Gorkhapatra*, Oct. 13, 1968.

theless, it is extremely sensitive to external economic influences, particularly those stemming from India—a fact which imposes severe limitations upon Nepal's capacity to devise what is now usually called an "independent" foreign policy.

For at least several hundred years prior to 1900, the prosperity of Kathmandu valley and the intermediate areas along the main trade routes was largely dependent upon Kathmandu's status as an entrepôt for trans-Himalayan trade. Changes in the trade structure almost invariably were unmitigated disasters for Nepal, undermining the main source of economic dynamism in a society with few easily exploitable alternative resources. It is not surprising, therefore, that Nepali elites placed a high value on the preservation of this trade system, of which they were the principal beneficiaries, or that contemporary Nepali elites emphasize—indeed, overemphasize—the importance of its revival to Nepal's economic development and progress.

Nevertheless, it is a fact that in more recent decades trade with India has become far more crucial to Nepal's economic welfare than the entrepôt trade. This can be attributed to several factors: (1) the opening of alternative trade routes to Tibet by the British; (2) the development of an intensive system of cultivation in the Nepal Terai capable of producing a large food-grain surplus for export to the neighboring districts of India; and (3) capital investment in the Terai by Indian entrepreneurs eager to escape the more restrictive regulations imposed by the Indian government. Today, direct trade with India accounts for approximately 90% of Nepal's total commerce, and this proportion would not be reduced significantly even if an unrestricted entrepôt trade with Chinese—controlled Tibet were reinstituted. Nepal's overdependence upon India for the supply of vital commodities is a constant irritant in relations between the two states. It is nevertheless unavoidable, given existing geopolitical, cultural and political considerations, and there is an aura of wishful thinking in much Nepali speculation about the potentiality of trade diversification.

Although there is also some local trade across the northern border with Tibet, it amounts to only perhaps one-twentieth of the local trade with India and is, therefore, of minor significance to the economy of Nepal as a whole. However, it has long played a vital part in the livelihood of the small Tibetan-origin communities, such as the Sherpas, who inhabit the northern border area and whose integration into the broader Nepali polity has always posed a serious problem for the Kathmandu authorities. Historically, this trade was also of some importance to Nepal because Tibet was the principal source of supply for that vital commodity—salt. Disputes over the salt trade, usually centering around the exchange rate between Tibetan salt and Nepali rice, were chronic until Nepal finally obtained a more reliable and cheaper source of supply in India in the early 20th century.

The pattern of migration into, within and out of Nepal is another important factor in its relations with neighboring states, particularly India, Sikkim, Bhutan and Burma. As noted before, until approximately a century ago the flow of migration was primarily from the surrounding areas into Nepal. The growing pressure on land in Nepal caused by those migrations and the population growth in the mid-montane areas to the west of Kathmandu valley, however, gradually reversed the process. Initially, this took the form of movement from the central hill areas to the less-populated eastern and far-western mid-montane districts, but the supply of land there was quickly exhausted.

There were large unexploited tracts of land in the Nepal Terai suitable for cultivation and which the Nepal government was eager to have settled. The hill people, however, generally avoided the hot, malarial Terai, preferring to migrate to the hill areas of India —Darjeeling, the Assam hills, Dehra Dun—and to Sikkim and Bhutan, where the climate and ecology were familiar and hospitable, or to the newly developing industrial centers in northern India, where jobs were available. The settlement of the Terai, therefore, was largely left to immigrants from India, with the result that there is now a large, still unintegrated minority of Indian origin in Nepal and an equally large and distinctive Nepali minority scattered around India.

With the exception of a few state-owned industries constructed with Chinese and Russian aid, the industrial development of Nepal during the past three decades is also mainly the handiwork of Indian capital and technical investment. At times this has been accomplished through direct agreements between Indian industrial firms and the Nepal government; more often it is the result of covert Indian investment through Nepali front men. Furthermore, what is probably the single most important element of Nepal's economic development, the hydroelectric projects on Nepal's major river systems has been made possible almost entirely by Indian economic aid.

All of these factors have contributed to the present situation under which Nepal is a virtual adjunct of the Indian economy, badly exposed to developments in India that are beyond Nepal's capacity to influence, much less determine. Kathmandu's autonomy in devising economic policies is extremely limited, not only on such obvious matters as international trade but even with respect to ostensibly internal questions such as land reform, currency, industrial policy and taxation. The first question the Nepal government must ask itself in formulating policy on such issues is: how will this affect relations with India? The second question, being asked more and more frequently today, is: how can we change this situation? The responses devised so far, however, have had only limited utility and have not basically altered the relationship between the two states.

Part II
Confrontation Politics in the Himalayan Area, 1770-1845

2

The Old Order Collapses: The Nepali-Tibetan War of 1788-89

A STRONG, unified kingdom in Nepal in the early decades of the 18th century would have been strongly tempted to take advantage of Tibetan disunity and disorder to revive Kathmandu's traditional territorial and commercial objectives in Tibet. Fortunately for Lhasa, the various principalities in central Nepal were in no condition to contemplate adventurism to the north of the Himalayas. The three Malla kingdoms centered in Kathmandu valley were absorbed in their narrow internecine dissensions while the Gorkha Raja, Prithvi Narayan Shah, was slowly but steadily drawing a noose around the valley in his long-range campaign aimed at domination of the entire central-Himalayan area.

The trade system with Tibet played a crucial role in these complex maneuvers in Nepal, for it was the primary source of revenue for the various contenders. By 1757, the Gorkha Raja had seized control of the trade route to Tibet via Nuwakot valley and Kirong, and was thus in a position to cut off commerce with Tibet through this channel at his own discretion. He refrained from such action, probably because of the revenue derived from customs duties, but he did insist that Gorkha's role in the trade structure be formally acknowledged. Under a treaty between Kathmandu and Gorkha signed in 1757, it was agreed that:

1) representatives of both Gorkha and Kathmandu would be stationed in Tibet and all loads of goods would be jointly inspected;

2) Gorkha and Kathmandu would share equally in the minting of coins for Tibet;

3) all gold, silver and currency brought either from Tibet or India would be shared between the two courts; and

4) all inhabitants of Kathmandu or Gorkha going to Tibet would take the route through Nuwakot on the way to Kirong.[1]

This treaty was never implemented. Indeed, it could never have become operative without the concurrence of the Tibetan authorities, who were disinclined to accept innovations in the trade and coinage systems and were already suspicious of Gorkha's long-range objectives. The Kathmandu ruler, Jaya Prakash Malla, managed to open the route through Kuti for his beleaguered merchants for a short time, but Gorkha soon moved to block this channel of communication as well as the main route south from Kathmandu to India. This was accomplished by 1763. A tight economic blockade imposed on the valley by the Gorkha Raja set the stage for the final conquest of the Malla kingdoms six years later. For the first time in centuries, the entire central-Himalayan hill area was controlled by a single ruler, whose ambitious plans for empire-building were by no means exhausted. The next major task he faced was to seek and obtain an accommodation with the ruling powers in Tibet and northern India.

During the long Gorkha-Malla war, trade between India and Tibet had been severely disrupted by the isolation of Kathmandu valley from contacts to the north and south. It was expected that the termination of hostilities would result in the revival of the "traditional" trading system, but the policies adopted by the Gorkha conquerors of Nepal soon indicated that this was unlikely. Nepal's relations with Tibet and the East India Company deteriorated rapidly after 1769 despite the efforts of the three governments to reach a settlement on several occasions. An analysis of the factors behind these failures provides the proper background for the Nepal-China-Tibet imbroglio of the 1788–92 period.

TRANS-HIMALAYAN TRADE STRUCTURE

Under the Mallas, much of the trade between India and Tibet had been conducted by Kashmiri (i.e., Muslim) merchant houses, with headquarters at Banaras or Patna, and by Gosains (Hindu merchant-pilgrim-mendicants). Prithvi Narayan suspected both groups of having encouraged the ill-fated Kinlock expedition which

---

[1] C. R. Nepali, "Nepal ra Tibet ko Sambandha," *op. cit.*

the British had sent to the aid of the Mallas in 1767. The Gosains were summarily expelled from Nepal, and such severe restrictions were imposed on the Kashmiri merchant houses that by 1774 only two were still functioning in Nepal. Two other Kashmiri trading houses opened branches in Bhutan after being expelled from Nepal, but as they were prohibited from trading in broadcloth and several other popular commodities, the volume of trade declined drastically and did not compensate the firms for the losses sustained because of the closure of the route through Nepal.[2]

One of Prithvi Narayan's most cherished objectives was the reestablishment of Kathmandu as the principal entrepôt in the trans-Himalayan trade structure, but on quite different terms than those the Mallas had enjoyed. The Gorkha Raja was determined to gain a virtual monopoly on the trade between India and Tibet by "closing the roads through the east and the west."[3] During the critical 1769–88 period, the Kathmandu Darbar (Court) labored constantly to forestall the opening of alternative trade routes through areas not under its control, and the vigorous military campaigns of the Gorkhalis in the hill areas to the east and west of Kathmandu are best comprehended in relation to this basic economic objective.

The maintenance of the Gorkhali armies in the field had virtually exhausted Nepal's treasury, which had to be replenished if Prithvi Narayan's ambitious expansionist program was to be implemented. The Malla rulers had derived a substantive revenue from direct participation in the trade structure, often in partnership with the Kashmiri and Gosain trading interests. Political considerations having induced Prithvi Narayan to exclude non-Nepali firms from Nepal, he had to devise new techniques to derive revenue from the trade system. This was to be accomplished through the establishment of a trade mart at Parsa Garhi, on the main route from India to Kathmandu, and at several points on the Tibetan border.[4] Under the system proposed, the Indian and Tibetan traders would bring commodities to the trade marts, where they would be purchased and transshipped by Nepali merchants. This policy, however, was not acceptable to Tibet, which in 1770 closed the trade routes to Nepal and suspended all commercial transactions between the two countries.[5]

---

[2] *Home Series, Misc.* (IOL, No. 118, Sept. 21, 1775: The Bogle Journal.

[3] Yoga Naraharinath and Baburam Acharya (ed.), *"Sri Panch Bada Maharaja Prithvi Narayan Shah ko Divya Upadesh"* (Divine Counsel of King Prithvi Narayan Shah the Great) Kathmandu, 1953, p. 10.

[4] S. B. Jñawali, *Nepal Vijeta Shri Panch Prithvi Narayan Shah ko Jivani* (Live of King Prithvi Narayan Shah, the Conqueror of Nepal). Darjeeling, 1935, pp. 79–82.

[5] The Panchen Lama's interest in the revival of commerce with India had induced him to send an envoy to Banaras, the headquarters of several trading companies, in

Tibetan-Nepali relations were also worsened by the old dispute over the circulation of Nepali-minted coins in Tibet. Both Ranjit Malla of Bhaktapur and Jaya Prakash Malla of Kathmandu had exploited that practice as a means of financing the war against Prithvi Narayan. The value of the coins minted under this arrangement was debased by reducing the ratio of silver to other metals, thus bringing the Malla kings large profits, but undermining Tibetan confidence in the debased currency. Lhasa was no longer prepared to continue the system unless Nepal accepted responsibility for the financial losses Tibet had incurred.

On several occasions prior to 1769, Prithvi Narayan had attempted to gain a foothold in the lucrative trade in currency with Tibet, but without any substantial success.[6] One of his first acts after the conquest of Kathmandu valley was to send a deputation to Tibet with a large number of newly minted coins of the proper alloy, struck in his name. The Tibetan government was asked to sanction their circulation. The merchants of Lhasa and Shigatse, however, refused to accept the coins, and the Tibetan authorities agreed to allow their use only if Gorkha was prepared to buy back— at its face value—all the debased Malla currency then in circulation in Tibet. Kathmandu rejected this proposal outright. While Prithvi Narayan was prepared to guarantee that all newly minted coins would contain silver and other metals in the prescribed ratio, he was not willing to absorb the heavy losses that repurchase of the Malla currency at its face value would have entailed for Nepal.

Tibetan and Nepali negotiations on this issue foundered on two points: (1) the exchange rate between silver or gold and the coins minted by the Gorkhas, and (2) the exchange rate between the new "pure" Nepali coins and the older "debased" coins. The Tibetan Government conceded the right of Nepal to derive a profit from the minting of the coins, though it naturally wished to keep

---

June 1771, apparently on the conviction that the trade through Nepal was not likely to improve in the near future. A monk was sent to India, ostensibly on a pilgrimage but actually to establish contacts with Chait Singh, the Raja of Banaras. Chait Singh was also interested in reviving the trade and sent the Gosain, Acharya Sugatigiri, to Shigatse with presents for the Panchen Lama. In 1773, the monk returned and met Chait Singh again at the Panchen Lama's request. Two Gosains accompanied the monk on his return to Tibet, and were still at Tashilhunpo when Bogle arrived there in November 1774. [L. Petech, "The Missions of Bogle and Turner According to the Tibetan Texts," *T'oung Pao*, XXXIX (1949), 335–37].

6 Prithvi Narayan started minting coins in accordance with the traditional terms between Nepal and Tibet in 1749. [Baburam Acharya, "Nepal ko Samkshipta Vrittanta," *op. cit.*, pp. 44–45.] Gorkha concluded a treaty with Lhasa legalizing the circulation of Gorkha coins in Tibet in 1755 and then two years later reached an agreement with Kathmandu on the same subject. [Ramji Tiwari (ed.), *Aitihasik Patra Sangraha: Dosro Bhog* (Collection of Historical Documents, Part II), Kathmandu, 1964.]

the gap between the value of the silver and gold it sent to Nepal and what it received in return at a minimum, while Nepal wished to maximize its profits. However, an agreement on this question probably could have been achieved if the debased-currency question had not entered into the picture, for here the position of the two parties was widely divergent. The Tibetans asserted that the currency sent to Tibet violated the agreement between Tibet and the Malla Kings concerning the proper ratio between silver and baser metals in these coins. As Tibet had paid the nominal rather than the true value of the coins, it insisted that the Gorkha conquerors of Nepal should bear any loss involved in their exchange with new "pure" coins, arguing that a one-for-one principle should be applied. Gorkha, on the other hand, maintained that as the debased coins had been minted by their enemies, the Mallas, they bore no responsibility for their redemption. Nepal argued that the coins should be exchanged on the basis of their relative value, holding generally that the exchange ratio should be one new for two of the older coins.

The Company's Role.—Direct British intervention in the trans-Himalayan trade system was greatly facilitated by a series of events in the eastern Himalaya shortly after the Gorkha conquest of Kathmandu valley. Bhutan, under the vigorous leadership of the temporal authority in that state, Deb Raj Desi Shidariva, emerged as an important element in trans-Himalayan political developments. The degree of Gorkha-Bhutani coordination in these events is still problematical, but it is known that Prithvi Narayan and Desi Shidariva communicated regularly.[7] They apparently perceived a mutual interest on a number of questions, including the need to control access through the Himalayas. In 1768–69, Bhutan suddenly seized the Chumbi valley, then part of Sikkim, and brought the important routes into Tibet through that area under its control. Two years later, the Bhutanese attacked the Indian principality of Kuch Bihar, seizing control of the state and capturing its Raja. This brought part of the access area between Sikkim and the plains under Bhutani control. At the same time, the Gorkhalis launched a campaign against what is now eastern Nepal, which had as one of its primary objectives the trade route from Morang district in the Terai through the Walung Chung pass on the Tibet border.

If these campaigns had been successful, the entire central and eastern Himalayas would have been under Gorkhali-Bhutani control, with the single exception of the exposed trade route through Tawang in what is now Kameng district of the North-East Frontier

---

[7] Jñawali, *op. cit.*, p. 78.

Agency of India.[8] It turned out, however, that Bhutan had over-extended itself in its expansionist program. Sikkim, with Tibetan encouragement, expelled the Bhutani invaders from the Chumbi valley in 1772. Even more disastrous for Bhutan was the British intervention in support of the Raja of Kuch Bihar.

Tibet had assumed an importance in Hastings' eyes that seems rather astonishing when one considers the rather tenuous nature of the British position in India in the 1770's. The diversion of British energies from the plains into the hills was not calculated to improve or strengthen the Company vis-à-vis the other Indian powers, but there were several considerations which seemed to Hastings, and to the directors of the Company in London, to make it incumbent upon Calcutta to further this project. The trade with Tibet, though not significant in the total picture of the Company's commercial relations with India, had been a valuable one and was believed susceptible of considerable expansion. The tales of Tibet as a land of gold and great wealth had permeated down into India and were often believed even by the usually hard-headed Scotsmen who predominated in Company posts. This seemed to be substantiated by the fact that the Tibetan trade resulted in a "flow of specie into British territory . . . at a time when the Company was being criticized for exporting gold and silver to China."[9] The trade with Tibet, in contrast to that with China, gave rise to a favorable balance at a time when the Company was facing serious financial difficulties at Canton. Moreover, it was hoped that trade could develop with western China via Tibet, with Indian subjects of the Company allowed access to these areas still inaccessible to its merchants at Canton.[10]

However, an equally weighty factor, in Hastings' view, was the hope that Tibet could serve as a channel of communication with the Chinese court at Peking. The British had long objected to the trading system in China, under which their commercial activities

---

[8] A trade route from Banaras and Muzapur through the independent principalities of Palpa, Pokhara and Mustang into Tibet was still open, but the difficulties of the terrain made it a relatively inferior route. The trade routes farther to the west were not adjacent to areas then under British control. The Company, therefore, had to look to the eastern Himalayas for an alternative route. This situation changed rapidly with British expansion to the west in the next three decades, as this opened up other possibilities.

[9] Alistair Lamb, "Tibet in Anglo-Chinese Relations: 1767–1842," part I, *Journal of the Royal Asiatic Society*, parts 3 and 4 (1957), p. 162.

[10] A good summary of Hastings' views on this question can be found in the Minute he prepared on the establishment of commercial intercourse with Tibet and other northern states. (Home Department, Public Branch, (IOL) Original Consultation No. 1, Apr. 19, 1779.)

were limited to the port of Canton. It was generally assumed by Company officials that the adverse conditions under which they operated were in part the result of the prejudices and narrowness of the local Chinese officials, and that if they could present their complaints directly to Peking many of their problems would be solved. Despite its naïveté, this attitude was influential in shaping Hastings' policy toward Tibet.

The Governor-General was vaguely aware of the Dalai Lama's status as the spiritual mentor of the Chinese Emperor, and that the Panchen Lama was a highly respected religious figure in China as well as Tibet. He greatly exaggerated the influence these two prelates wielded in the totality of Chinese policy-formation, but he was correct in assuming that they could serve, if they so desired, as a medium of communication between Calcutta and Peking, for they then enjoyed the privilege of direct communication with the Emperor. That both lamas would be averse to assuming such a dangerous and unrewarding role is a fact that the Governor-General could not have been expected to comprehend. One wonders, however, what Hastings' attitude would have been towards relations with Shigatse if he had understood the manner in which the British were being entangled in the complex Tibetan political situation. At that time, and throughout most of the 19th century, it was a basic principle of British policy to avoid any activity on the northern frontier area likely to arouse the Chinese court.

After the failure of the Kinloch expedition in 1767, the Company had decided to utilize other tactics in its efforts to open the trade route through Kathmandu. James Logan was instructed to visit Kathmandu valley and the eastern Terai area in the winter of 1769–70. He was provided with two letters strikingly different from one another, one to Jaya Prakash Malla of Kathmandu and the other to Prithvi Narayan Shah of Gorkha,[11] and was instructed to decide in the light of the circumstances which of these letters should be delivered. By that time, however, Gorkha had completed the conquest of Kathmandu valley and it was obvious to Logan that Prithvi Narayan Shah was the man with whom he would have to deal. The Gorkha Raja's disinclination to consider proposals on this subject, however, forced the abandonment of the entire project.

The failure of the Logan mission made it obvious to the British that trade with Tibet could be developed only by using alternative trade routes. Contacts had been made previously with an exiled

---

11 *Banaras Residency Records*, Uttar Pradesh Central Record Office: both letters are dated Oct. 31, 1769.

Raja from Morang province in the eastern Terai, and it was hoped that the route through the Morang and the hill areas of what is now eastern Nepal or up the Tista River through Sikkim could be developed. The conquest of Morang and the Darjeeling area by the Gorkhas in 1773–74, however, precluded the use of these routes without an agreement with Kathmandu. The British then turned to the route to Tibet through Bhutan, and it was under these circumstances that Hastings welcomed the Kuch Bihar Raja's entreaties for assistance against the Bhutanese.

Prithvi Narayan, well aware of the possible implications of the Bhutanese actions in Kuch Bihar, urged the Deb Raj to avoid open hostilities with the British,[12] but the warning came too late. British intervention in Kuch Bihar, and the defeat of the Bhutani forces in the pass (*duar*) areas on the Indian border, led to a major political upheaval in Bhutan. Desi Shidariva was removed from office by a faction that immediately sued for peace to forestall the threatened British invasion of central Bhutan. They sought the intervention of the Panchen Lama as a mediator in the dispute and agreed to receive a British mission to discuss peace terms. The new Deb Raj signed the 1774 treaty with the head of the British mission, George Bogle, thus making Bhutan the first hill state to reach an agreement with the Company. To the surprise of both the Bhutanis and Tibetans, however, Bogle insisted that his mission should also proceed to Tashilhunpo for discussions with the Panchen Lama.

Nepal's concern with these developments first took the form of an embassy to the Panchen Lama to suggest that he mediate between the Bhutanis and the Company in order to prevent the introduction of British influence in the hills. In his reply, the Panchen Lama acknowledged the wisdom of the suggestion but could not resist the temptation to point out to Gorkha that the situation would not be so serious if Kathmandu had been less obstructive on the trade question and had not encouraged Bhutan to behave along the same lines.[13] Nepal's advice in this instance almost militated against its own broader interests. It was the Panchen Lama's offer to mediate the dispute that resulted in the first official contacts between Tibet and the Company and led directly to the admission of the Bogle mission to Tibet.

The Nepali reaction to the Bogle mission was vigorous in both the military and diplomatic spheres. While the mission was still in Bhutan, the Gorkhalis launched an invasion across the Arun river and into Morang district in the Terai, cutting off the route to Tibet

---

12 D. R. Regmi, "English and Bhutanese Relations," *New Review*, March 1942, p. 240.
13 Petech, *op. cit.*, pp. 339–40.

through the Walung Chung pass.[14] Prithvi Narayan sent another envoy, Lal Giri, to Tashilhunpo with letters for the Regent of the Dalai Lama and the Panchen Lama. According to Bogle, the Raja wrote:

He did not wish to quarrel with this state, but if they had a mind for war, he let them know he was well prepared, and desired them to remember that he was a Rajput; that he wanted to establish factories at Kuti, Kerant, and another place, upon the borders of Tibet and Nepal, where the merchants of Tibet might purchase the commodities of his country and those of Bengal, and desired their concurrence; that he would allow the common articles of commerce to be transported through his kingdom, but no glasses or other curiosities, and desired them to prohibit the importation of them also; that he desired them further to have no connection with the Fringies [English] or Moghuls, and not to admit them into the country, but to follow the ancient custom, which he was resolved likewise to do; that a Fringy had come to him upon some business, and was now in his country, but he intended to send him back as soon as possible, and desired them to do the same with us; that he had also written about circulating his coin, and had sent 2,000 rupees for that purpose.[15]

While carrying on their diplomatic negotiations with the Panchen Lama, the Gorkhalis continued their aggressive military program to the east of the Arun river. That campaign eventually embroiled them in hostilities with Sikkim, which came to the aid of the Limbu community, with which it had strong historical ties.[16] The death of Prithvi Narayan Shah in early 1775 halted the conflict temporarily, because Nepal's attention was diverted to internal developments surrounding the succession of the new Raja, Pratap Singh.

In Tibet, meanwhile, Bogle had failed to obtain the assent of the Panchen Lama to a commercial treaty, and had returned to India. With the death of Prithvi Narayan, the Panchen Lama hoped to achieve a satisfactory settlement of the trade and coinage questions with Kathmandu. This would make it unnecessary to come to terms directly with the British, a much more dangerous move for him in view of the objections raised against relations with the Com-

---

14 However, the Gorkha Raja instructed his officers to avoid hostilities with Tibet at all costs. "Not even four digits of land should be occupied beyond the border of Lhasa," he declared. [Yogi Naraharinath (ed.), *Itihas Prakas ma Sandhi Patra Sangraha* (A collection of Treaties in the Illumination of History), Kathmandu, 1966, pp. 187–8.]
15 C. R. Markham, *Narratives of the Mission of George Bogle to Tibet and of the Journey of Thomas Manning to Lhasa*, London, 1879, p. 158.
16 Prithvi Narayan had earlier assured Tibet that he had no designs on Sikkim and wrote the Tibetan authorities in 1770 that "Sikkim belongs to you and we shall not occupy it." [C. R. Nepali, "Nepal ra Tibet ko Sambhanda" (Nepal-Tibet Relations), *Pragati*, II:4 (n.d.) pp. 103–14.]

pany by both Lhasa and Peking.[17] The Panchen Lama wrote Pratap Singh immediately on hearing of his succession:

You have now succeeded to the throne, and it is proper that you attend to the happiness of your people, and allow all merchants as Hindoos, Musselmen and the four castes, to go and come, and carry on their trade which will tend to your advantage and good name. At present they are afraid of you, and no one will enter your country. Whatever has been the ancient custom let it be observed between you and me. It is improper that there should be more on your part and it is improper that there should be more on mine.[18]

Pratap Singh responded immediately. A new delegation, headed by the recently appointed Vakil to Tibet, Rup Narayan Karki, was sent to the border in the Kuti area, where it met the Tibetan envoys, Shalu Khenpo and Depon Padstal. A *gachha patra* (treaty), concluded in August 1775, stipulated:

1) The rate of exchange between gold and silver would be either fixed jointly between the two governments or determined by the merchants, who would settle their own rates and conduct their own transactions.
2) Coins of the proper (i.e., traditional) alloy would be sent to Tibet by the Nepal government and accepted there.
3) The position of the Newari Mahajans (merchants) and shopkeepers in Lhasa should remain unchanged.
4) The eastern and western "Madesh-parbat" (plains-mountain) routes to Tibet should be closed even for "Sanyasis" (Gosains), Indians and merchants.[19]

This treaty was not completely satisfactory to either government, for it did not settle the critical dispute with regard to the debased Malla currency then circulating in Tibet nor did it provide the type of trading structure preferred by the participants. It did, however, allow for a temporary lull in the troubled relations between Nepal and Tibet, a breathing spell that both powers needed badly because of serious internal complications.

A representative of the Sikkim Darbar was also present at the treaty deliberations, and an agreement was reached between Nepal and Sikkim in the presence of the Tibetan delegation. The boundary between Sikkim and Nepal was fixed; Tibet consented to pay Rs. 4,000 in compensation to Nepal for the death of four Brahmans

17 Markham, *op. cit.*, pp. 148–49; Tsepon Shakabpa, *Tibet, A Political History*, New Haven, 1967, p. 155.
18 Home Series, Misc. No. 219 (IOL): The letter from the Panchen Lama to Pratap Singh is quoted in a report from Bogle to Hastings.
19 Buddhiman Singh Vamsavali, *op. cit.*,; Dhanabajra Bajracharya, *Triratna Saundarya Gatha* (An Account of the Beauty of the Tree Jewels), Kathmandu, 1963, p. 274.

who had been sent as messengers to the Sikkim court; and Kathmandu agreed to refrain from further aggression against Sikkim and to sever all connections with the Bhutanis. Once his authority had been firmly established in Kathmandu, however, Pratap Singh violated the Sikkim treaty almost immediately. Gorkhali forces invaded southwest Sikkim in late 1775, but met with only indifferent success, and a virtual stalemate ensued along the boundary as defined in the 1775 treaty.

NEPALI-BRITISH RELATIONS

The only tangible benefit the British derived from the Bogle mission—other than an improvement in their knowledge of the Himalayan area—was the treaty negotiated with the Deb Raja of Bhutan after Bogle had failed in his efforts to obtain a commercial agreement with the Panchen Lama. Bhutan agreed to allow Hindu and Muslim merchants of the Company to pass freely through its territory between Bengal and Tibet. Combined with the Bhutan-British treaty of 1774, the arrangement seemed to provide the basis for the opening of a new trade route to Tibet. It soon became obvious to the British, however, that Bhutan was not likely to prove an acceptable substitute for the Kathmandu route. The Hindu and Muslim trading firms evinced very little enthusiasm for the difficult and dangerous trip to Tibet through Bhutan and expressed preference for the continuance of efforts to reach an agreement on the trade question with the Gorkha Raja. Furthermore, the Deb Raja of Bhutan faced strong internal opposition to his policy towards the English, which was considered to be contrary to the established customs of the country as well as exceedingly dangerous and likely to lead to an increase in British influence.[20]

Under these circumstances the British renewed their efforts to reach a rapprochement with Nepal. The territory seized by Kinloch in 1767 had already been restored to the Gorkha Raja after he agreed to pay an annual rent of 30 elephants to the Company.[21] In 1776, the British recognized Gorkha's authority in the eastern Terai district of Morang which had been conquered two years earlier by the Gorkhalis. In 1783, a British boundary commissioner decided in favor of the Nepali government in a dispute between Gorkha and an Indian zamindar, Mirza Abdulla, over Rautahat and Pachrauti

---

20 S. Turner, *An Account of an Embassy to the Court of the Teshoo Lama in Tibet*. London, 1800, pp. 107–21.
21 Bengal Public Proceedings. SN 37, Jan. 10–Dec. 16, 1771, pp. 148–53: Board Resolution, Aug. 10, 1771.

districts. Moreover, the British unilaterally initiated a free-trade policy when, after 1786, they stopped collecting duties on goods imported from Nepal. Finally the Calcutta government decided to discontinue its practice of withholding from Kathmandu the revenue for those territories concerning which there was a jurisdictional dispute. These several agreements between Nepal and Calcutta did not solve all the numerous border disputes that grew out of the expansion of both powers into the area at the foot of the hills, but they did allow for a period of relative stability while the attention of both powers was principally directed elsewhere. They also helped prepare the ground for the conclusion of the 1792 commercial treaty between Nepal and the Company.

These conciliatory moves, while welcome in Kathmandu, did not completely allay the suspicious attitude of the Nepali Government. Prithvi Narayan Shah's warnings on the dangers inherent in involvement with the British dominated Nepali councils during the reign of Pratap Singh (1775–77) and the Regency of Rani Rajendra Lakshmi (1780–85). A party favorable to commercial relations with the English did exist, but the leader of this faction, Bahadur Shah, was exiled from Nepal, first by his half-brother, Raja Pratap Singh, and again after the Raja's death, by the Regent.

While seeking a rapprochement with Nepal, Calcutta did not abandon its efforts to open a trade route to Tibet despite the almost total lack of success of its earlier policies. In 1779 the Company had planned to send Bogle to Peking at the same time that the Panchen Lama would be visiting the Chinese capital. It also decided to send Gosain Purangir to Tibet with orders to accompany the Panchen Lama's party to Peking if possible.[22] Hastings hoped that through the direct intercession of the Panchen Lama, Bogle would be able to facilitate the Company's operations in China as well as obtain the approval of the Chinese government to the opening of a commercial exchange between Bengal and Tibet, since it was presumed, erroneously, that Bogle's failure to obtain a trade agreement with Shigatse in 1775 had been due primarily to the opposition of the Chinese.

This attempt had to be abandoned, however, because of Bogle's death in India in 1779 and the Panchen Lama's death in Peking in 1780. It was then decided that a second effort should be made

---

[22] Purangir arrived at Tashilhunpo after the Panchen Lama's departure for Peking. He followed, and was present at the time of the Lama's death in Peking. Purangir's account of these events (Turner, *op. cit.*, pp. 419–33) should be read with some caution as his report was affected by his personal stake in the Bengali-Tibetan trade as well as by his close relations with certain factions at Tashilhunpo.

directly with the Tashilhunpo officials, and Samuel Turner was dispatched to Tibet in 1783 on the pretext of carrying the congratulations of the Calcutta government to the new Panchen Lama. He followed the same route through Bhutan that Bogle had used, noting during his visit in Bhutan the serious internal difficulties faced by the Deb Raj, which made the trade route through this area unreliable. His talks at Tashilhunpo were unproductive so far as any concrete results were concerned, nor did he feel it necessary, or perhaps worthwhile, to reactivate Bogle's agreement with Bhutan.

THE FIRST NEPALI-TIBETAN WAR

Nearly 20 years of multilateral consultation and negotiation had not sufficed to solve or even mitigate the serious differences among the powers involved in the central Himalayan area. The trade situation may have been slightly improved over what it had been in 1770, but the structure of trans-Himalayan commerce was still unsatisfactory to all parties concerned. Moreover, Tibet and Nepal had been unable to reach an agreement on the coinage question, which was a serious blow to Nepal's financial viability.

The period between 1780 and 1788 witnessed a number of important changes in political leadership throughout this region. In Tibet the Panchen Lama died and was succeeded by an infant, and the Dalai Lama at Lhasa finally reached his majority. In Nepal, power had been concentrated in the hands of the Regent, Bahadur Shah, whose approach to foreign policy and commerce varied in certain respects from that which had characterized Nepali councils of state since the time of Prithvi Narayan Shah. In India, the energetic and imaginative Hastings had been replaced as Governor-General by Cornwallis, a man whose interest in events to the north was sporadic and minimal. All these factors contributed to the course of events in the crucial period between 1788 and 1793 in such a way as to encourage the intrusion of Chinese influence while limiting the role of the Company in developments in the Himalayan area during the next quarter-century.

The arrival in Kathmandu of the Ninth Karmapa Lama, the Shamar Trulku, an important Tibetan religious-political leader, in the spring of 1788 was the catalyst that set in motion a whole series of events during the next five years. The Lama's connections with various political and religious elements in Tibet, amply evidenced by the role he played in negotiations between Nepal and

Tibet in 1789,[23] provided Nepal with an unprecedented opportunity to intervene in the internal dissensions then prevalent in Tibet. The Nepali invasions of Tibet in 1788 and 1791 were not merely conflicts between Nepal and Tibet nor were they only raids aimed at the seizure of loot. More fundamentally they constituted an intervention in Tibetan politics and an attempt by the Gorkhalis to support those Tibetan political factions whose interests were, temporarily at least, most closely aligned with those of Nepal. Kathmandu may even have harbored the hope of replacing the Ch'ing dynasty as the nominal suzerain of Tibet, at least for Tsang and the western Tibetan districts.

Other considerations also induced Bahadur Shah to assume the risks inherent in any venture against Tibet. He must have considered it unlikely that China would interfere directly in any dispute between Nepal and Tibet, except possibly as a mediator insisting that Chinese rights and interests be respected. Nearly 40 years had passed since the last vigorous intervention by Peking in Tibet, and the Chinese officials in Lhasa had been comparatively quiescent during the minority of the Eight Dalai Lama—that is, since 1758. Moreover, Bahadur Shah must have felt that the Himalayan barrier between Tibet and Nepal, as well as the great distance any Chinese army would have to travel and over which supplies would have to be brought, made it unlikely that even the Manchus could launch a successful attack against Gorkha's home base.[24] Under these circumstances the Regent was confident that the attack against Tibet could be launched with relative immunity to effective retaliation.

Bahadur Shah may also have hoped to use the war to silence the internal opposition to his regency. Some of his more dangerous

---

[23] Chosdup Gyatse, the Shamar Trulku, was the brother of both the late Panchen Lama and of the Drungpa Trulku, the Regent for the new Panchen Lama. He was also related to the Dalai Lama's family, and his niece was married to Kalon Tenzin Paljar Doring, a scion of the influential Doring family in Lhasa. The Shamar Trulku, therefore, had familial connections in both Shigatse and Lhasa, as well as religious ties with red-sect religious institutions in Tibet, Sikkim and Bhutan. Shamar Trulku fled from Tsang in 1786 through Sikkim. He came to Kathmandu in the spring of 1788, after extensive negotiations with the Nepal Darbar and immediately prior to the launching of the first Gorkhali invasion of Tibet.

[24] According to the well-informed British agent, Abdul Kadir Khan, Shamar Trulku served as an advisor to Bahadur Shah on Chinese affairs. (*Political Proceedings*, Cons. No. 15, Oct. 3, 1792, *op. cit.*). The Lama must have minimized the dangers of Chinese intervention and encouraged Bahadur Shah to assist him in regaining his position in Tibet. According to the Chinese records, Shamar Trulku was conspiring "to seize the office of Panch'en Lama." [Imperial Edict dated 1st month, 58th year of Ch'ien-lung, quoted in W. W. Rockhill, "The Dalai Lamas of Lhasa and Their Relations with the Manchu Emperors of China, 1644–1908," *T'oung Pao*, II, Ser. 2 (1910).] But it is more probable that he had the Regency as his goal.

opponents were shipped off to the battle front under close supervision, thus removing them from Kathmandu. Moreover, a successful war of foreign conquest would greatly enhance the Regent's
prestige and influence in Nepal, a factor he could not ignore now
that King Rana Bahadur was approaching his majority and was
proving increasingly intractable. Bahadur Shah must have realized
that the regency could not be maintained much longer and that a
different basis for his authority had to be established if he was to
avoid being set aside within a few years. The Regent was even suspected of trying to create an opportunity to depose his nephew and
to seize the throne for himself—an ambition he is alleged to have
cherished earlier.

Shamar Trulku had brought part of the Panchen's private
treasury with him to Nepal, but the story that Nepal was instigated
to attack Tibet by the Lama's description of the plunder awaiting
a conqueror is an obvious fabrication. Thousands of Nepali traders
and pilgrims had traveled in Tibet, and the immense wealth of the
monasteries there was no mystery to Kathmandu. It is evident from
the course of events that the Nepal Darbar was interested in more
than loot, for there were better methods of gaining economic benefits from Tibet than the ravishing of a few monasteries. Trade and
the currency question were still the main considerations motivating
Kathmandu in this adventure. Shamar Trulku presented the Darbar with an opportunity for intervention in Tibet, but not a reason.

In the spring of 1788 a Tibetan monk arrived in Kathmandu
on a pilgrimage, and Bahadur Shah took advantage of his visit to
send letters to Tibet demanding a settlement of the currency question and protesting about the quality of salt imported from Tibet.
Nepal threatened to seize the four border districts of Tibet in the
Kuti and Kerong pass areas and, rather curiously, to hold Shamar
Trulku (who had just arrived in Kathmandu) as a hostage if it did
not receive satisfaction on these questions. Shamar Trulku also
sent an appeal directly to the Dalai Lama asking to be ransomed on
the Nepali terms.[25]

The Kashag (cabinet) in Lhasa rejected the Nepali demand for
the devaluation of the debased Malla currency in Tibet and furthermore, according to the Nepali sources, closed the trade routes
between the two countries as a protest against Kathmandu's hospitality to Shamar Trulku. When the Kashag's reply reached Kath-

---

[25] Shakabpa, *op. cit.*, pp. 157–58; and *Chin-ting, op. cit.*, 13/20. pp. 5b–13b. Kirkpatrick reports that Nepal, "considering that it would be improper to commence hostilities against (Tibet), determined to transmit a representation of the whole to the
Chinese Emperor." (*op. cit.*, appendix 1, p. 340). Neither Nepali nor Tibetan sources
mention this letter, however.

mandu, the Darbar implemented the decision made earlier to invade Tibet if its demands were not met. The Gorkhali forces crossed the border in July 1788 and seized the four districts in the Kuti and Kerong pass area between the border and the Bhairab Langur range—Nyanang (Kuti), Rongshar, Kyirong (Kerong) and Dzongka (Jhunga). They met only slight resistance except at Dzongka, which was captured after a brisk engagement. The Kuti detachment pushed on to Tingri, which fell without much of a struggle, and then laid seige to Shekar Dzong, the principal defense position on the route to Shigatse. The Tibetans put up a stout resistance there, however, and the Gorkhalis retreated to Kuti but retained control over the four border districts.[26]

The Gorkhali forces in eastern Nepal launched a simultaneous attack on Sikkim in mid-1788, with a two-pronged attack through Ilam aimed at the Darjeeling area and the winter capital at Rabdentse. The primary objective was the trade route through the Chumbi valley and Sikkim that the Tibetan government had opened in 1784, in violation of the 1775 Nepali-Tibetan treaty and in disregard of strong and repeated protests from Kathmandu. The invasion met with immediate success. Rabdentse was captured and all of Sikkim west of the Tista came under Nepal's control. This gave the Gorkhalis a common border with Bhutan, which then held the Kalimpong area to the east of the Tista. The Bhutan government, however, was still dominated by the political faction that had deposed the pro-Gorkha Deb Raja in 1773, and apparently was disinclined to coordinate policy with Kathmandu. The Sikkim ruler, Tenzing Namgyal, withdrew first to his estate in the Chumbi valley and then to Lhasa to seek Tibetan assistance. By this time the fighting in Tibet had reached a stalemate, and there was also a temporary cessation of hostilities in Sikkim which left Nepal in control of all of the state west of the Tista river.[27]

The invasion of Tibet and Sikkim placed the various contend-

---

[26] Chin-ting, *op. cit.*, 13/21, pp. 11a–14b; Shakabpa, *op. cit.*, pp. 158–59; Som Dhwaj Bisht, *Shahi Sainik Itihas* (History of the Shah Army), Kathmandu, 1963, p. 50). The size of the Nepali invasion force has been disputed. According to the Tibetan commander at Shekar Dzong, the Gorkhali contingent on the front consisted of 5,000 troops supported by 3,000 porters (Shakabpa, *op. cit.*, p. 159), which seems reasonable. There is also some confusion in Nepali published sources on the depth of the Gorkhali penetration into Tibet, some historians asserting that they captured Shigatse on this occasion. The most authoritative Nepali, Tibetan and Chinese sources, however, agree that Shekar Dzong was the farthest point reached by the Gorkhalis and that they were repulsed there.

[27] Tsepon Shakabpa claims that a Tibetan detachment from Shekar Dzong came to Sikkim's assistance and helped drive the Gorkhalis out of the country (*op. cit.*, p. 160). This does not agree with either the Sikkimese or Nepali chronicles, however. If a Tibetan force was sent to Sikkim, the most it accomplished was to prevent the conquest of the area of the state east of the Tista river. According to the Sikkimese chron-

ing political groups in Tibet in a painfully complex position. The officials at Tashilhunpo, led by Regent Drungpa Trulku, were caught in a swirl of contending and contradictory interests. In view of Shamar Trulku's role, they viewed the Gorkhali invasion with considerable apprehension because it constituted a challenge to the political and religious hegemony of the yellow sect in Tsang province. But to turn to Lhasa for assistance was dangerous, particularly in view of the prevailing situation, with a minor Panchen Lama at Tashilhunpo and a Dalai Lama who had reached his majority at Lhasa. Furthermore, an appeal to Lhasa for assistance meant ultimately an appeal to China. This also was likely to result in a diminution of Tsang's limited autonomy in its relations with Lhasa, considering Peking's policy of utilizing the office of the Dalai Lama as the instrument for the extension of its own influence throughout Tibet.

Under these circumstances, Tashilhunpo's instinctive response was to seek terms with the invaders while also appealing elsewhere for military assistance—i.e., to powers who were neither in a position nor disposed to interfere in internal Tibetan politics. A secret deputation was sent to Calcutta in November 1788. In a letter remarkable for its frankness, Drungpa Trulku (writing in the name of the Panchen Lama) reported the Gorkhali invasion of Tibet:

This gave me great displeasure, and when the Chinese Subahs [Ambans] who are in Lassa heard these particulars they wrote to the King of China. Doubtless he will send troops from Koota [China]. God knows what will happen to the ryotts [peasants] when the troops arrive. On seeing this, I was anxious of making peace with the Ghourkally and on that account I was sending an Arzee to the Emperor of China, requesting he will not send troops, but the [Nepal] Rajahs intentions are different, and he does not abide by his Engagements . . . My second request [the first was for an answer to his letter] is that your Lordship will send a large force against the Ghourkally Rajah, and anihiliate (sic) him at any rate. This will be a great mark of kindness and friendship. At this time I will make peace with the Ghourkally, if he agrees, it is well, but if which God forbid, peace does not take place, in that case a large army will come from Koota and go to Napal. Then if the Ghourkally being without resources, shall make a request for aid and assistance, your Lordship will not comply with this demand. This will be a great kindness to me. How can I sufficiently urge this matter. The most perfect kindness is requisite. As from of old a friendship has been firm with the English, I have written your Lordship with very great hopes. My ultimate request is that my former requests he complied with and an army be sent against the Ghourkally, and he be killed. But if your Lordship should not think this advisable,

---

icle, Bhutan sent supplies to the Sikkim Raja while he was fleeing from Sikkim but apparently no military support. (*Sikkim: A Concise Chronicle*, Gangtok, 1963, p. 8.)

in that case show kindness towards me. Consider well my requests and never grant him assistance. Whenever your Lordship's troops shall march towards Napal, I hope that you will act as from yourself and that my name and correspondence be known to no one. Your Lordship will shew such kindness and favor to my request, that no stranger may be acquainted with a word thereof, because we will write to the Emperor of China that a peace has been concluded with the Ghourkally and that he will decline sending troops. God forbid that the King should be informed of my correspondence with your Lordship for this will bring down ruin and destruction on me and in this respect your Lordship will keep my requests a profound secret. How often shall I presume on making this request. Your Lordship is wise and will learn everything from the conversation of the people I have deputed to your presence and treating my people with favor will comply with the above written request, and speedily send them back to this quarter as I am anxiously waiting for them.[28]

Tashilhunpo also attempted to instigate troubles for Kathmandu south of the Himalayas by encouraging the principality of Jumla in western Nepal to renew its intermittent hostilities with the Gorkhalis.[29] Jumla responded immediately, seizing Mustang (a Gorkha protectorate) and some villages to the south of Mustang. It paid heavily for its rashness the following year after the warfare in Tibet had reached a stalemate. Two Nepali armies invaded Jumla and brought it under the domination of Kathmandu for the first time.

By the end of April 1789, Tashilhunpo had learned that no assistance could be expected from the British. In a letter dated February 29, 1789, Cornwallis replied to the Panchen Lama that sending an army to Shigatse would be too expensive; that the Company had suffered no provocation or injury from the Gorkha Raja; and that the Chinese Emperor might be displeased with any British interference in Tibet that had not been directly solicited by Peking. Cornwallis promised not to render any assistance to Nepal, but expressed his reluctance to maintain the secrecy requested with regard to the Tashilhunpo-Calcutta correspondence in view of the Company's extensive commercial stake in the maintenance of friendly relations with China.[30]

The Peking court had been informed of the Nepali intrusion

---

[28] *Secret Proceeding* No. 5, Jan 26, 1789: Panchen Lama to Cornwallis, dated 1 Seffner, 1203 Fassily (Nov. 1, 1788), and received at Calcutta on Jan. 22, 1789. For another translation see *English Translation of Persian Letters Received*, vol. 29, no. 41 (1789).
[29] In his letter to Cornwallis, Drungpa Trulku demonstrated a lack of confidence in Jumla when he wrote: "but in my ideas, the Jumla Wallah will not have the power of making war, and on this account only I have written to your Lordship." (*Ibid.*)
[30] *Home Series Misc.*, vol. 608, Bengal Consultation of Mar. 9, 1789.

into Tibet by the Chinese Amban (Resident) at Lhasa, Shu-lien, but apparently in rather ambiguous terms. The Emperor ordered his aide-de-camp, General Pa-chung, and the Governor of Szechuan, Ao-hiu, to proceed to Tibet to investigate the situation.[31] An advance detachment of 2,000 men under Chêng-têh reached Lhasa in early 1789. At the Chinese commander's request the Kashag deputed one of the Kalons (Ministers), Tenzin Paljor Doring, to accompany the detachment to Tsang. Chêng-têh advanced as far as Shigatse, where he halted to await the arrival of the main Chinese detachment. It was only at the instigation of the Kalon and other Tibetan officials that the Chinese commander finally agreed to advance to the support of the garrison at Shekar Dzong, which was preparing to attack the Gorkhali force in the border districts.[32]

Pa-chung and the other Chinese officials in Tibet hoped to settle the dispute by negotiation. The Tibetan government was divided on the question, most of the civil officials urging continuation of the war. Under Chinese pressure, however, Lhasa sent the father of the young Panchen Lama and the secretary of the Sakya Lama to Shekar Dzong to open negotiations with the Gorkhalis if the situation seemed auspicious. A correspondence was established with Shamar Trulku, who suggested that they come to Kerong along with a representative of the Dalai Lama for talks with him and a Nepali delegation. Kalon Doring was instructed to act on Lhasa's behalf in these talks, and the three men set out for Kerong in May 1789. Discussions began shortly thereafter with Shamar Trulku and the Nepali deputies—Bam Shah, Harihar Upadhyaya and Nara Singh Shahi.

THE 1789 TREATY

In the talks, Nepal first demanded full compensation for expenses involved in the war as well as the "50 dharnis of gold" which, under the 1775 treaty, was to be paid to the other party by the government that violated the agreement.[33] When this was rejected by the Tibetans, the Nepalis then demanded the cession of Kuti district and the payment of an annual tribute from Tibet of 1,000 *dotsed* of silver (valued at more than Rs. 150,000). The Tibetans refused to agree, and the negotiations were on the verge of collapse. Finally, the secretary of the Sakya Lama proposed a for-

---

[31] *Chin-ting, op. cit.,* 23/38, pp. 9a–15b.
[32] Shakabpa, *op. cit.,* pp. 159–60; citing the autobiography of Kalon Tenzin Paldor Doring.
[33] C. R. Nepali, *Shri Panch Rana Bahadur Shah* (King Rana Bahadur Shah), Kathmandu, 1964, p. 89.

mula which both sides accepted,[34] and the treaty was signed on
June 2, 1789.

There is no single authoritative text of the 1789 treaty, and
indeed there are striking discrepancies in the Nepali, Tibetan and
Chinese sources on the agreement. Apparently, the "treaty" actually consisted of a number of letters exchanged between the contract-
ing authorities, each dealing with specific topics and in some cases
signed by different combinations of officials for both sides. As given
by the more reliable sources, the terms finally agreed upon were,
in summary, as follows:

1) Nepal agreed to withdraw from the four border districts of Tibet
   that had been occupied during the hostilities. The boundary in the
   Kuti area was defined so as to conform to the terms of the treaty between Pratap Malla of Kathmandu and Lhasa in the 17th century,
   under which the border market-town of Kuti was jointly administered by both governments.[35] The border of Kerong reverted to
   that prevailing prior to the hostilities.
2) Tibet agreed to pay an annual tribute of 300 *dotsed* of silver, the
   equivalent of 9,600 taels of Chinese silver or Rs. 57,600 at the rate
   prevailing in Tibet—Rs. 6 per tael. (The figure usually cited in
   Nepali and western sources is Rs. 50,001, but this does not agree with
   the exchange value of silver mentioned in these sources.)
3) Tibet agreed to accept and use newly minted Nepali coinage at the
   rate of one new coin for two of the debased Mala coinage. Kathmandu also agreed to mint *suki* (i.e., quarter-rupee) coins for Tibet.[36]
4) Nepal promised never to invade Tibet again.[37]
5) Nepal was granted the right to maintain a Vakil (envoy) at Lhasa
   (thus no longer having to depend upon the head of the Newari trading community at Lhasa as its representative).

---

34 For his assistance, Nepal presented the Sakya Lama with Timal Kot ("Tima
Erhjang" in the Chinese sources), a small estate on the Nepal-Tibet border. [C. R.
Nepali, "Nepal-Chin Yuddha" (Nepal-China War). *Sharada*, 21:1 (April–May 1956),
p. 203.] According to the Chinese documents, however, the Sakya Lama never took
over the administration of the estate, which was restored to Nepal after the 1791–
92 war.

35 This was the only territorial concession made to Nepal in the treaty. Some Nepali
sources maintain that other parts of Kuti and Kerung district were ceded to Nepal.
While a claim was made to the part of Kerung that had been seized by Gorkha during
Ram Shah's rule and later recaptured by the Fifth Dalai Lama, the Kathmandu
Darbar did not insist upon this concession in the agreement.

36 Kalon Doring insisted to the Chinese that the exchange rate had been set at 1½
old coins for 1 new one. (*Chin-ting, op. cit.*, 23/38, pp. 9a–15b.) The difference here
may be due to the method of calculating value in relation to the Chinese tael. Previously the rate had been nine old coins to one tael. In the agreement it was set at
six old coins and twelve new coins to the tael, or a 2–1 ratio, but a 1½–1 ratio if
the previous value of the old coins was used.

37 This stipulation is mentioned only in *Chin-ting* (*op. cit.*, 13/28, pp. 5b–13b) as an
agreement between the Nepali delegation and Pa-chung. It is unclear from this source
whether the Tibetans were also a signatory to this agreement.

6) Trade between Tibet and India was to be channeled solely through Nepal, and the alternative trade routes through Sikkim and Bhutan were to be closed.

7) A Tibetan Lama was to visit Kathmandu[38] each year "to bless the temple" (i.e., Swayambhu Nath).[39]

The official Chinese account of these events maintains that Kalong Doring had grave doubts about Lhasa's willingness to accept the treaty. Three days after the signing of the agreement, the Kalon and Shamar Trulku met and agreed to a modification of the tribute clause. Under this addendum, with which Bam Shah and Harihar Upadhyaya reportedly concurred, Nepal agreed to consider a reduction of the tribute at the time of the second annual payment if a senior Tibetan officer was deputed to Kathmandu to discuss the question.[40]

The roles played by the Chinese officials in Tibet in these events later became a subject of controversy at the Peking court, each of the officials either denying knowledge of the treaty terms or placing responsibility for its approval elsewhere. According to the Nepali sources, the Chinese Amban served as a mediator in the negotiations and was fully aware of the terms of agreement.[41] The most authoritative Tibetan source, however, insists that the Chinese officials were invited to Kerong only *after* the treaty had been signed.[42]

Whether Pa-chung, Ao-hiu and Chêng-têh actually knew the terms of settlement is still unclear. Chinese sources state that the agreement had been reached without the knowledge of the Chinese officials but that Pa-chung, eager to end the business, approved the

---

[38] Clauses 5 to 7 are mentioned only in the official Chinese source. (*Ibid.*) Kalon Doring, in his autobiography, states that it was also agreed that Nepali subjects in Tibet who commit a crime should be tried by the Nepali representative in the area (quoted in Shakabpa, *op. cit.*, p. 161), but this extraterritorial provision is not cited in other sources.

[39] A "text" of the 1789 treaty, based upon records in the Jaisi Kotha (Tibet-China Relations Office) of the Nepal Foreign Ministry has been published in *Itihas Prakas ma Sandhi Patra Sangraha* (*op. cit.*, vol. I, p. 20) and as an appendix in Bishnu Prasad Poudel, *Nepal's Relations with Tibet: 1792–1856* (unpublished Ph.D. dissertation, Indian School of International Studies, New Delhi, 1963). This consists of two documents, one concerning the coinage question and the other, reparations. But it is clear from other Nepali as well as Tibetan and Chinese sources that these were not the only terms agreed to in the negotiations. For these other provisions, see *Chin-ting, op. cit.*, 4/3, pp. 11a–13a; 5/6, pp. 1a–2a; 7/9, pp. 22b–26b; 13/20, 5b–13b, 23/38, 9a–15b; C. R. Nepali, "Nepal-Chin Yuddha," *op. cit.*; and Shakabpa, *op. cit.*, p. 161.

[40] The addendum is cited in Shakabpa (*op. cit.*, p. 161) and, in a slightly different form, in Chin-ting (*op. cit.*, 13/20, pp. 5b–13b). No Nepali source mentions the addendum, but there are indirect references to its contents in some Nepali documents, particularly with reference to the status of Tibetan officials sent to the Kathmandu Darbar.

[41] C. R. Nepali, "Shri Panch Rana Bahadur Shah." *op. cit.*, p. 91.

[42] Shakabpa, *op. cit.*, p. 161.

treaty anyway once Nepal had agreed to send a mission to Peking. Ao-hiu and Chêng-têh followed Pa-chung's lead, but it is uncertain whether any of the three had actually read the document. In the official Chinese account, Kalon Doring is stated to have declared later that he had never shown the text of the treaty to any Chinese official.[43] What is even more surprising is that Nepal must have cooperated with Tibet in keeping the precise terms of agreement from the Chinese, as Pa-chung met the Nepali delegation at Kerong and, apparently at his own request, returned with them to Kathmandu for discussions with the Nepal Darbar.

Why the Chinese officials did not insist upon being informed of the details of the treaty is never made clear. One reason undoubtedly was their unwillingness to become involved in a difficult and costly campaign across the Himalayas, and in the circumstances discretion may have seemed preferable to valor. It seems probable, however, that bribery was resorted to, and that the Tibetan factions which wanted to keep Chinese intervention to the absolute minimum had managed to convince the Chinese officials, through monetary donations, that no further action was warranted.

There are no similar ambiguities with respect to the role of the Chinese Emperor and the Peking court in these events, for it is clear that neither was informed of the terms of the 1789 treaty. Pa-chung merely reported that he had obtained a promise from the Gorkhalis to withdraw from Tibetan territory and never to attack Tibet again, and that the Nepal Darbar desired to send a mission to Peking to "present their submission" to the Emperor. He also mentioned, in passing, that Tibet had assumed an obligation to pay Nepal a certain sum each year, but classified this as "land rent" rather than tribute.[44]

Kathmandu also played its part in keeping the Peking court ignorant of the terms of the agreement. The Nepali mission that visited Peking in 1789–90, at Pao-tai's suggestion, never mentioned the terms of the treaty to the court officials or the Emperor during the four audiences they were granted. Apparently the Nepalis shared the apprehensions of the Tibetans with regard to the reactions of the court were it to learn of the treaty provisions. That these fears were justified is demonstrated by Ch'ien-lung's scornful rejection of the rationalizations offered in defense of the treaty once he had learned of its existence.

At first glance, the Dalai Lama's role in these curious proceedings is somewhat enigmatic. He was determined to resist the Nepali

43 Chin-ting, *op. cit.*, 23/38, pp. 9a–15b.
44 *Ibid.*, 13/20, pp. 5b–13b.

incursions which threatened the stability of the political-religious system in Tibet based on the predominance of the yellow sect. When Pa-chung reached Lhasa in the spring of 1789, the Dalai Lama strongly urged a vigorous military campaign against the Gorkhas:

I am a Buddhist. I do not want at all to kill human beings by military actions, but as the Gorkhas do not believe in Buddhism and want to suppress the yellow sect, and as I am afraid the yellow sect would collapse hereafter, so I suggest that military action be taken and then all the frontier disputes would be settled and only this could protect the yellow sect.[45]

The principal Chinese source on these events informs us, incredibly enough, that the Dalai Lama was not aware that several Tibetan officials, including Kalon Doring, were in the process of negotiating an agreement with Nepal and that he never gave his assent to the treaty despite the fact that, under Tibetan practice, it could have no true validity without his seal.

It was impossible, however, to keep the Dalai Lama completely in the dark about the Kerong proceedings, for the "tribute" payments to Nepal could come only from his treasury. Kalon Doring and his associates attempted to disguise these payments as "land-rents" for the areas (of Tibet) which the Nepalis restored to Tibetan authority after the signing of the treaty and as "tariffs" on Tibetan salt exported to Nepal. The Kalon explained that Tibet had had to recognize the validity of the treaty signed a century and a half earlier with Pratap Malla, and that the Gorkhas had agreed to withdraw from the border districts they had seized only on the payment of yearly land-rents to Nepal for the territories involved.[46] However, this was an obvious subterfuge used by the Kalon to conceal from the Dalai Lama the true nature of the concessions he had been forced to make to Nepal in order to obtain its consent to a peace settlement.

The Nepali delegation to China, headed by Hari Shah and Balbhadra Khawas, left Kathmandu in the fall of 1789 and spent 14 months on its journey to and from the Chinese capital. It was received with full honors by the Chinese court and remained in Peking for 45 days, during which it was granted four interviews with the Chinese Emperor. Gifts from the Nepal Raja were presented to the Chinese Emperor and more valuable gifts were given to the delegation in return, for presentation to the Raja. The Manchu title of *Erdeni Wang* (Brilliant King) was granted to Rana

---

[45] *Ibid.*, 17/28, p. 10a.
[46] *Ibid.*, 13/20, pp. 5b–13b.

Bahadur, and the Regent, Bahadur Shah, received the Chinese title of *Kung* (Duke). The requisite ceremonial robes for the bestowal of these titles were sent to the Nepal Raja and his Regent, along with the usual sanctimonious letter instructing Rana Bahadur to "maintain peaceful relations with the Dalai and Panchen Erdini Lamas, and observe the existing regulations."[47]

POST-TREATY DEVELOPMENTS

The conditions under which the 1789 treaty had been concluded made it inevitable that its terms would be honored more in the breach than in the observance. The concessions made by the Tibetan representatives struck too decisively at basic Tibetan interests and were more than the Tibetan economy could easily support. Disputes concerning the application of the various treaty provisions began almost immediately after the signing of the agreement, and it soon became obvious that the treaty had contributed little to the settlement of these controversies.

The tribute payment for the year 1789 was duly made by Kalon Doring, who collected the 300 *dotseds* of silver from various monasteries and individuals in Tsang province on his promise to repay them out of the Dalai Lama's treasury. The Gorkhali troops were then withdrawn from the Tibetan border districts—which may explain why the tribute payment was made so promptly by the Tibetans. When the Kalon returned to Lhasa he reported to the Dalai Lama on these proceedings. The Lama was dissatisfied with the whole affair but under the circumstances felt obligated to refund the money to Kalon Doring and to give a tentative endorsement to the arrangement, despite his suspicions about its true import. Shortly thereafter, however, he sent a team to the border districts to investigate the situation, and two officials to Kathmandu to request a reduction of the annual tribute payment under the addendum to the treaty.[48]

Bahadur Shah refused to meet with the two envoys on the ground that they were of low rank, and dispatched his own letter to Lhasa demanding full compliance with the treaty provisions. The Dalai Lama decided that discussions should be opened anew with Nepal through a representative directly appointed by himself. The envoy was instructed to tell the Nepal Darbar that the tribute

---

47 Secret E No. 264, July 1911: Patent of Office dated Mar. 5, 1790, from the Chinese Emperor to Rana Bahadur Shah.
48 Shakabpa, *op. cit.*, p. 162.

system was unjust and that the Dalai Lama was not prepared to authorize the payment of the second annual installment.[49] Kathmandu rejected his argument and again demanded the faithful observance of the treaty provisions. The envoy was not authorized to accept this demand, and the discussions ended.

More fuel was thrown on the flames at this point by the refusal of the Tibetan authorities to implement the clause in the treaty setting the exchange rate between new Nepali coins and the debased Malla coinage. The Nepal Darbar had wasted no time in sending a quantity of newly minted coins to Tibet. The merchant community there, however, still opposed a one-for-one exchange rate, and most of them refused to accept the new coins. The old Malla coins continued to serve as the principal medium of exchange in Tibet and no significant number of new coins were put into circulation.

The Nepal government was even frustrated by the Tibetan authorities in its attempt to send a *vakil* (diplomatic representative) to Lhasa. Kathmandu, with some justification, had long been dissatisfied with the system under which the head of the Newari merchant community at Lhasa also served as the channel of communication between the two governments. The Newari merchant houses, for instance, also held large quantities of the old Malla coins and were as opposed to an unfavorable exchange rate as their Tibetan colleagues. Doubting the reliability of the Newari representative, Bahadur Shah decided to send a mission to Lhasa in late 1789 to demand compliance with the treaty and to threaten the renewal of hostilities as the alternative. The mission, headed by Keshar Narsingh, received little satisfaction from the Tibetan government, as the Dalai Lama refused to pay the tribute or to do anything about the circulation of the new coins in Tibet. The Nepali delegation remained in Lhasa until December 1790 and apparently returned to Kathmandu with the Nepali mission then on its way back from Peking.

It was at this point that the Dalai Lama decided to recall his former Regent, Ngawang Tsultrim, from Peking. On his return to Lhasa in February, 1791, the Regent strongly castigated the Kashag for having accepted the 1789 treaty and supported the Dalai Lama's demand for a modification of its terms. In view of the Nepali threat to renew hostilities, however, it was decided to send two high officials to Nepal with one-half of the annual tribute for 1790-91. The envoys were instructed to pay this sum only if Nepal agreed to surrender the copies of the treaty in their possession and accepted the

---

[49] *Chin-ting, op. cit.*, 13/20, pp. 5b–13b.

Tibetan position that this would be tantamount to a cancellation of the treaty. They were also to emphasize the close relationship between Tibet and China and to warn that Chinese assistance would be sought if Nepal should again aggress against Tibet.[50] Kathmandu did not accept these proposals but did modify its position somewhat by agreeing to reconsider the treaty after the full amount of the "tribute" for the first three years had been paid.[51] However, the Darbar was unwilling to negotiate with anyone other than the highest Tibetan officials, and requested that Kalon Doring and the uncle of the Dalai Lama be sent to the frontier to meet a Nepali delegation.

The Kashag was agreeable to the Nepali proposal, but the Regent was strongly opposed and refused to approve the dispatch of yet another mission to Nepal. He died on April 29, 1791, however, and the Kashag was now in a position to reassert its authority. Kalon Doring and Kalon Yuthok were instructed to proceed to Kuti, nominally to repair the monastery there but actually to meet Shamar Trulku and the Nepali delegation—Damodar Pande, Bam Shah, and Subha Bhaginath. The Kalons brought 150 *dotseds* of silver, constituting the balance of the tribute payment for 1790–91.

The sequence of events at the Kerong meeting is still obscure, as the Nepali, Tibetan and Chinese sources give contradictory versions. According to the Nepali accounts, the Tibetan delegation reached Kuti first and were plotting to arrest Shamar Trulku with the assistance of a Tibetan military detachment. While the Nepali delegation was still one day's march from Kuti, the story goes, "Tibetan spies" made an unsuccessful attempt to seize Shamar Tulku, thus alerting the Nepalis to the evil intentions of the Tibetans. Thereupon, Damadar Pande and Bam Shah led a strong military detachment to Kuti, arrested the Tibetan delegates and sent them to Kathmandu under the supervision of Shamar Trulku. Enraged at the treachery of the Tibetans, the Nepali version continues, Damodar Pande immediately launched an attack deep into Kuti district.[52]

This version of the affair suffers from a number of major discrepancies which makes its credibility doubtful. In the first place, the arrest of Shamar Trulku would not have been of any great ad-

---

50 *Loc. cit.*

51 C. R. Nepali, "Nepal-Chin Yuddha," *op. cit.*

52 This version is drawn primarily from *loc. cit.*, but similar accounts are found in most Nepali sources as well as in some western-language works. In a letter to the Chinese Commander in Tibet, dated July 16, 1792, Rana Bahadur gave a similar version of the affair. [*Wei-Tsang T'ung Chi* (Topography of U and Tsang), Shanghai, 1936.]

vantage to the Tibetans even assuming that the Lhasa officials were outraged at his treason, which itself seems unlikely. Tibet's dispute with Nepal was over much more basic issues than the position of the red-hat "refugee" in Kathmandu. In this respect it should be noted that Shamar Trulku had never been a major object of dispute between Nepal and Tibet in the numerous negotiations that had taken place since his flight to Nepal, and that later on it was the Chinese rather than the Tibetans who made the demand for his surrender a condition for peace. Furthermore, the presence of a large Nepali force on the Kuti border, ready to launch a major military campaign in Tibet, was scarcely a fortuitous coincidence. The decision to renew the war with Tibet must have been made before the departure of the Nepali delegation for Kuti, because Damodar Pande and Bam Shah would never have initiated a war on Tibet without first referring the question to Kathmandu—unless they had already received orders to do so.

The Tibetan version is more plausible.[53] While on their way to Kuti, the story goes, Kalon Doring and Kalon Yuthok received a letter from the Tibetan officer at Kuti stating that the Nepali delegation had reached the border and were making warlike preparations. The Kalons forwarded this warning to the Kashag, but were ordered to continue on to Kuti without a military escort in order not to arouse the suspicions of the Gorkhalis. They reached Kuti on the occasion of the Hindu festival of Mahadeva. The local Nepali official there asked and received permission to observe the holiday in the courtyard of the Kuti fort, which was in the Tibetan section of the town. Gorkhali soldiers, disguised as coolies and rice traders, entered the fort and during the course of the celebration suddenly attacked the Tibetan party. The two Kalons were arrested and sent in chains to Kathmandu, while three other Tibetan officials and 35 attendants were killed. Wherever the truth may lie, by late summer of 1791 hostilities were renewed between Nepal and Tibet on a greater scale than before and with far more serious consequences.

---

53 Shakabpa, *op. cit.*, pp. 63–64.

3

China's Trans-Himalayan Adventure: The Nepali-Chinese War, 1791-93

THE failure of the Tibetans to implement the 1789 treaty was a grievous blow to Bahadur Shah. A faction at the Nepal Darbar had been skeptical of the "forward policy" in Tibet from the very beginning. The 1789 settlement, which signified the achievement of political and economic goals that had long eluded the Darbar and also promised to provide the economic support for further military campaigns, temporarily corroborated the Regent's judgment and solidified his prestige and influence at court. When it became apparent that Lhasa was unwilling to implement the terms of the agreement, however, the ephemeral character of Bahadur Shah's "triumph" was starkly exposed. Nepal had gained little except the right to complain incessantly against Lhasa's violation of its treaty obligations as well as a pretext for another thrust into Tibet.

For Bahadur Shah, the consolidation of the victory over Tibet was indispensable if he was to retain a virtual monopoly of power at the Darbar. He faced the unpleasant prospect of having to deal with a king who had come of age and who was known to be antagonistic to the Regent. The clique of advisors around Rana Bahadur included several of Bahadur Shah's most dangerous enemies, and only the success of the Tibet policy might strengthen his position sufficiently to enable the Regent to withstand the challenges that were in the offing. Inasmuch as there was little prospect of achieving these objectives peacefully, given Lhasa's generally negative attitude, Bahadur Shah had to convince the court of the practicality of another expensive campaign across the Himalayas. The comparative success of the 1788 expedition, limited in scope though it was, fanned the enthusiasm of certain groups, particularly among the military classes, but there were many *bharadars* (courtiers) who realized that it was unwise to expect results as favorable to Nepal again.

Opposition to Bahadur Shah's policy centered in the royal family itself, which still exercised a predominant influence at the Nepal court. Two half-brothers of the Regent, Srikrishna and Balbhadra Shah, were particularly active in undermining Bahadur Shah's position. They also shared a strong dislike for Shamar Trulku who, they felt, wielded too great an influence over the Regent and whose interests, they suspected, did not necessarily coincide with those of Nepal—or theirs. Srikishna Shah was particularly antagonistic to the Lama who had been instrumental in the former's dismissal on corruption charges from his post at Kuti during the occupation of that area in 1789. Thus, when consulted by Bahadur Shah, both men strongly opposed a second invasion of Tibet. The Regent, incensed at their opposition, removed Srikrishna from all official posts and had Balbhadra transferred to a comparatively minor post some distance from Kathmandu.[1]

Another important member of the royal family, Hari Shah, who had led the 1789–90 mission to Peking, also came out strongly in opposition to the foreign policy of Bahadur Shah. Hari Shah, like some present-day Nepali leaders, had been captivated by the gracious treatment he had received at the Peking Court, and had become an ardent supporter of a pro-China policy. The Regent and Hari Shah had been close friends, but the latter's opposition to the second invasion of Tibet led to his removal from all posts, and the two men became bitter antagonists. The opposition faction was not yet strong enough to force Bahadur Shah's resignation or even to oppose his policy successfully in view of the Regent's great influence with the army, but they did represent a potential threat and their opinion could not be completely ignored.

From the sources available, it is unclear whether Bahadur Shah

---

[1] The substance of this analysis is based on the remarks made by a captured Gorkha officer, described as a "close servant of Rana Bahadur," to the Chinese commander in Tibet. (*Chin-ting, op. cit.*, 13/21, pp. 11a–14b) This report is substantiated in part by Kirkpatrick who stated: "The predecessor of the present Choutra was his older brother, Bulbhudder Shah, whom the Regent found it expedient to supersede on account of his intractable spirit." (Kirkpatrick, *op. cit.*, p. 199.)

anticipated Peking's response to another Gorkhali invasion of Tibet. Later, in a letter to the Chinese commander, the Regent (writing in the King's name) claimed that he had been deceived on this point by Shamar Trulku.[2] This seems unlikely, however. The Nepali mission to Peking had returned to Kathmandu bearing a letter from the Emperor warning Nepal against a renewal of hostilities with Tibet.[3] Presumably, therefore, Bahadur Shah was prepared to risk war with China, confident that the limited military capacity of the Manchu empire in the area could be effectively counterbalanced if the need arose.

THE SECOND NEPALI-TIBETAN WAR

On August 6, 1791, approximately 4,000 Nepali troops under the command of Damodar Pande, Dev Datta Thapa and Bam Shah crossed the Tibetan border and seized the trade center of Kuti.[4] The army advanced swiftly along the main trade route to Shigatse, captured Tingri in mid-August, and then overwhelmed the small Tibetan detachment at Shekar Dzong. The important monastic and trade center of Sakya fell on September 13 without any opposition. Indeed, the Gorkhalis received a friendly welcome from some of the red-sect monks at this monastery, who presented the commanders with *khatas* (ceremonial scarves).[5] This was another illustration of the confusion in loyalties that marked the red sect—of which Shamar Trulku was a prominent leader—during the war. The Nepali army reached Shigatse on September 17, and immediately prepared to launch an assault on the small Tibetan force there. Drungpa Trulku, the Regent of the young Panchen Lama, fled with his charge and most of the Tashilhunpo treasury on the approach of the Gorkhalis, closely followed by the Tibetan detachment and almost the entire population of this yellow-sect institution.[6]

---

2 *Wei-Tsang T'ung Chi, op. cit.*, pp. 276–77: Letter from Rana Bahadur to Fu K'ang-an, dated July 28, 1792.
3 *Secret E* No. 264, July 1911: Patent of title from the Chinese Emperor to Rana Bahadur Shah, Mar. 5, 1790.
4 Most Nepali and Western-language sources have exaggerated the size of the Nepali invasion force, which is usually placed at around 18,000 men. The official Chinese source (*Chin-ting, op. cit.*, 3/2, pp. 1a–3a), based upon contemporary Chinese and Tibetan reports, places the figure at 3,500 to 4,000 men.
5 *Chin-ting, op. cit.* 2/3, pp. 1a–3a.
6 Later, in a letter to Fu K'ang-an, Bahadur Shah stated that he had been assured by Shamar Trulku that the monks at Tashilhunpo would flee on the approach of the Gorkhalis, who would then be free to plunder the monastery at will. (*Wei-Tsang T'ung Chi, op. cit.*, pp. 276–77).

After the capture of Shigatse, Damodar Pande demanded that Tibet pay 50 *dharnis* of gold as a fine for their violation of the 1789 treaty as well as the 600 *dotseds* of silver due Nepal as tribute for 1790 and 1791. On Tibet's rejection of the demand, the Gorkhalis plundered Tashilhunpo monastery, stripping the walls and altars of the gold, silver and jewels donated in the course of centuries by devotees. The value of the loot, even in a monetary sense, has never been calculated, but the destruction of irreplaceable works of art—many by Newari artisans—was the greater tragedy. The contrast between the behavior of the Gorkhalis at Tashilhunpo and at Sakya, where the equally wealthy red-sect monastery was left untouched, is significant. Obviously, long-term political and economic considerations rather than the urge for plunder were uppermost in the minds of the Nepali leaders.

China's Response. The immediate Tibetan and Chinese response to the Nepali invasion was nearly as confused as in 1788. Once again, many Tibetans were more concerned with the prospects of Chinese intervention than with the depredations of the Gorkhalis. If Nepal had again limited its activities to small-scale warfare in the border area a considerable distance from Shigatse and Lhasa, both Tibetan and Chinese policy might have taken a different direction. But the conquest of Tashilhunpo, the political center of Tsang province, and the possibility of an advance on Lhasa, made it imperative for the Tibetans and Chinese to take vigorous countermeasures. The reactions of the Chinese officials immediately concerned, however, were at best ambivalent. These were the men who had played the same game two years before; who had not informed the Emperor of the exact nature of the 1789 treaty; and who were now greatly embarrassed by the new Nepali invasion because it was likely to lead to a detailed investigation of the 1788–89 events. General Pa-chung committed suicide almost immediately on hearing news of the hostilities—a great convenience for the other officials, who thereafter blamed him for all that had occurred two years earlier.

Despite the reluctance of the Chinese officials in Tibet and Szechuan to take positive steps, Peking soon made complete inactivity impossible. On hearing of the invasion from the Amban, Pao-tai, the Emperor ordered Ao-hiu, the Governor of Szechuan, to go to Tibet once again. He was instructed to warn the Nepali leaders that a Chinese army would be sent to Tibet and that Nepal would be treated much more severely than in 1789.[7] Ao-hiu procrastinated, however, and merely dispatched Chêng-têh to Tibet

---

[7] *Chin-ting, op. cit.,* 3/1, pp. 3b–6b.

with a small force which advanced at a very leisurely pace. The Imperial Court began to suspect that more than normal bureaucratic apathy was being displayed on this occasion, and its suspicions were heightened by the activities of the Amban in Lhasa. Pao-tai had played a prominent role in the Tibetan defense preparations, but had not been able to stem the advance of the Gorkhalis. Lacking confidence in the reliability of the Tibetan army and officials, he recommended that the Dalai and Panchen Lamas withdraw to the China-Tibet border area.[8] The Dalai Lama rejected this advice, however, and was later supported in his decision by the Emperor.

The Amban, still unaware of the Emperor's displeasure with his actions (it required more than a month for communications between Peking and Lhasa), continued to advocate an accommodation with Nepal in his letters to the Chinese court, emphasizing the difficulties and expenses involved in a campaign across the Himalayas. Moreover, Pao-tai reported that the young Nepali Raja, Rana Bahadur Shah, who had not yet assumed power himself, had opposed the invasion of Tibet. The Raja should not be punished, Pao-tai argued, for actions which were the responsibility of his subordinates.[9]

By now the Emperor had lost all confidence in the Chinese officials on the spot, and his most renowned military commander, Fu K'ang-an, was ordered to take command of the army sent to Tibet. The abandonment of Tibet, the Emperor declared, would be a severe blow to the Ch'ing dynasty's interests in view of the Dalai Lama's status as the religious head of the Mongols.[10] It would not be sufficient merely to force the withdrawal of the Gorkhalis from Tibet, the Emperor argued, as they could then prepare for further incursions across the Himalayas secure in the inviolability of their home base. Nepal had to be taught a lesson that would be remembered for all time, and this could only be accomplished through an invasion of Nepal and the punishment of those officials responsible for the recent events.[11]

It should be noted that the Emperor's orders for the invasion of Nepal were issued before word of the plundering of Tashilhunpo monastery had reached Peking. The widely held assumption that the Imperial Court's decision to invade Nepal was due to anger over the wanton ravishing of this revered yellow-sect institution is not correct. News of it may have strengthened the Emperor's resolve

---

[8] *Ibid.*, 4/4, pp. 20a–21b.
[9] *Chin-ting, op. cit.*, 6/7, p. 1a.
[10] *Ibid.*, 3/2, pp. 28b–30b.
[11] *Ibid.*, 4/3, pp. 13a–16b.

to crush Nepal, but his decision was prompted by political and strategic considerations that were more crucial.

In Tibet, meanwhile, the Nepali army at Shigatse began a general withdrawal on October 4, 1791, by way of a more direct but extremely rugged pass in eastern Nepal rather than Kuti.[12] The choice of this route proved disastrous, as the crossing was made too late in the year. Heavy snowfalls impeded the progress of the army, causing many deaths as well as the loss of some of the Tashilhunpo loot.[13] These manpower losses substantially weakened Gorkhali military power when it was about to undergo its greatest test.

The onset of winter did not put a halt to either military operations or diplomatic exchanges and maneuvers. The first countermove by the Tibetans and Chinese was to incite the Sikkimese and Tsongs (Limbus) to attack Gorkhali posts in the Tamur River valley in eastern Nepal. After a fierce 12-day running battle, the Tibetan-led force was defeated at Chainpur and Siddhipur in early 1792. At about the same time, a small Nepali force under Sardar Amar Singh Thapa fought its way through the Kerong area to the Brahmaputra (Tsangpo) River, and then returned to Nepal via Muktishetra.

On the diplomatic side, Pao-tai sent a Chinese officer to Kathmandu in mid-November 1791 with a letter to Bahadur Shah demanding (1) the restoration of the Tashilhunpo loot, (2) the release of Kalon Doring, and (3) the return of Shamar Trulku to Tibet. According to the well informed British agent, Abdul Kadir Khan, the Chinese officer was treated with contumely and was finally sent off with the Regent's rejection of the terms offered.[14] This was only after an intense and lengthy debate within the Darbar, however. In its reply, Nepal merely reiterated its grievances against Tibet and added the allegation that Pao-tai had been bribed by the Tibetans to countenance their refusal to pay tribute to Nepal.[15]

Kathmandu's growing concern with the situation is shown by the elaborate attempts made to obtain intelligence of Chinese intentions from Tibet. At the request of Shamar Trulku, Kalon Doring wrote to his colleagues in Lhasa asking them to intervene in favor of the Nepalis.[16] Shamar Trulku also corresponded with

---

12 Kirkpatrick remarked that his route was chosen in preference to Kuti because the "commanders . . . were aware they should find it impracticable to elude the examination of the officers stationed (at Kuti), in order to take an account of the booty they had acquired" (*op. cit.*, pp. 215–16).
13 B. Acharya, "Nepal ko Samkshipta Vrittanta" *op. cit.*, p. 98.
14 *Political Proceedings*, Oct. 3, 1792, Cons. #15.
15 *Chin-ting, op. cit.*, 11/18, pp. 24a–25b and 14/23, pp. 17b–18a.
16 *Wei-Tsang T'ung Chi. op. cit.*, p. 275.

various Tibetan officials through two Newari merchants with trading interests in Tibet, allegedly in order to obtain information
concerning the plans of the Chinese.[17]

The Chinese, meanwhile, were busily preparing the ground
for an invasion of Nepal the following spring. In October 1791
the combined Tibetan-Chinese military forces began operations to
clear all Nepali troops from the pass areas through which the invasion would be launched. In November, the Gorkhalis were forced
to retreat from Tingri and in February 1792 the fort at Kuti was
captured after a month-long seige. The Chinese were even busier
in the diplomatic sphere. Fu K'ang-an arrived in Tibet in January
1792—having taken the route through Kokonor (Tsinghai) rather
than Chamdo in order to save a month's time on the journey to
Tibet. He immediately initiated efforts to obtain the support of
various powers whose territory bordered on Nepal, and letters were
written to Sikkim, Bhutan, and Jumla and to the British authorities
at Calcutta.

Fu K'ang-an's communication to the Governor-General at Calcutta, received only in July 1792, called upon the "Philings" (i.e.,
"Feringhi" or English) to do all in their power to punish the
Gorkhas. In the grandiose style often affected by Chinese officials
he wrote:

All the Rajahs to the westward directing their attention to the good
government of their own countries, and never deviating from their
loyalty, have, under the protection of the most high Emperor, remained
content with the possession of their ancient dominions. . . . The original
country of the Goorkha Rajah is of very inconsiderable extent, but he
has by force taken possession of the territories of the neighbouring
Princes. He has carried his depredations into Bhote, and committed the
most atrocious actions. As the country of Bhote and its inhabitants are
subject to the Emperor of China, this incursion can be considered in no
other light than a robbery. Nothing better in future is to be expected
from this man. The benefits of his Imperial Majesty's protection and
country are diffused over a thousand Kingdoms. I shall certainly pursue
to destruction all those persons who were concerned in this violent and
unjust undertaking. . . . I, the Chanchoo, have marched with a prodigious
army, exceeding lacks and crores in numbers, with the intention of making war on him for the contempt he has shewn to the Imperial authority. . . . It behoves the Rajahs of all the adjacent countries to obey my
commands. Any clemency towards the Goorkha Rajah, after the crimes
he has committed, would be universally condemned. The Imperial army
is now preparing to attack him, and as your dominions border on his,
you should commence hostilities against him at the same time, and pass-

---

[17] *Chin-ting, op. cit.*, 14/22, pp. 10a–12a.

ing your own frontiers, carry the war into the enemy's country. . . . Let the Princes of all the neighbouring countries cordially uniting on the same enterprize use their utmost endeavours to destroy these robbers. Let them be put to death and let their eyes be plucked out and their hands, feet cut off and sent to me. Whoever has the merit of this action, I the great Chanchoo will reward him liberally, and when the intelligence of his success is reported to his Majesty he will confer on him the most honourable marks of his favor, and present him with a magnificent Khelaut. I desire you after due consideration of what I have written to pursue the proper measures for executing my wishes. I, the great Chanchoo, speak not in vain. Immediately on the receipt of this letter, I desire you to send me a distinct account of the time and place on which you commence your operations, and the route by which you advance.[18]

Letters were also sent to the Governor-General by the Dalai and Panchen Lamas. These had been dictated by Fu K'ang-an, however, and were carried to Calcutta by the same messenger—the gosain Purangir—who carried the Chinese commander's letter.

These overtures from the Chinese and Tibetan authorities placed the Company in a very embarrassing position for, scarcely a month earlier, it had signed a treaty of commerce with Nepal. In November 1791 Abdul Kadir Khan had been sent to Kathmandu with the British terms for an agreement.[19] There was still strong opposition to the treaty within the Darbar, but Bahadur Shah could muster enough support to overcome the opposition.[20] In February 1792 a Nepali deputation, consisting of Sher Bahadur Shah (a half-brother of Rana Bahadur), Bam Shah and Balbhadra Shah, arrived in Patna and discussed the terms of the treaty with Duncan. Finally, on March 1, 1792, the first treaty between Calcutta and Nepal was signed.

In these circumstances, procrastination seemed to be the best response to the Chinese Commander. As Cornwallis explained:

The Commercial treaty that we have concluded with Nepal, and the friendly advances lately made to us by the Rajah should induce us to

---

18 *Political Proceedings*, Apr. 22, 1793, #17.
19 *Banaras Residency Proceedings*, Sept. 12, 1791: First proposed draft of the Nepali-British treaty prepared by Duncan for Cornwallis's approval. Duncan in a letter to Cornwallis, expressed his view that unless a British subject was allowed to remain in Kathmandu to supervise the implementation of the treaty, it would never become effective. (*Ibid.*, Duncan to Cornwallis, Sept. 12, 1791.) This is the first instance in which the British raised the issue of the establishment of a Residency in Nepal, an objective that later became of primary importance to Calcutta. In this instance Duncan's suggestion must have met with strong opposition in Nepal, for the subject is not mentioned in the commercial treaty finally concluded.
20 A. Campbell, "Sketch of Relations Between the British Government and Nepal from their Commencement to 1834 A.D." *Board's Collection* (IOL), vol. 1619, 1836–37; see a note by Brian Hodgson on the original Ms. of this report.

endeavour, as far as it can be done by safe and justifiable means to preserve him and his country from destruction, and it is equally incumbent upon us not only to avoid giving offence to the Chinese, but to neglect no opportunity that affords a prospect of opening a communication with an officer of rank in that State. The union of these objects renders it necessary for us to be extremely delicate and circumspect in our conduct.[21]

Several months passed before an ambiguous reply was sent to the Chinese and Tibetan authorities, and this did not reach them until after Nepal and China had concluded a peace settlement.

The Emperor, hoping to lull the Nepalis into a false sense of security, had been displeased with Fu K'ang-an for having written to these "barbarian tribes," (i.e., Calcutta, Sikkim and Bhutan), as he feared that news of the Chinese intention to attack Nepal would reach Kathmandu through these sources.[22] He sent instructions to Fu K'ang-an to invite Rana Bahadur to come personally to the border, in the hope that this would deceive the Nepalis into concluding that Peking was inclined to settle the affair peaceably and thus deter them from making the necessary preparations to meet the Chinese invasion.[23] Fu K'ang-an complied, and twice sent letters to Rana Bahadur and Bahadur Shah in this vein, but received no answer; he doubted, however, that the letters had the desired effect, for he noted that the Gorkhalis were busily fortifying the pass areas on the frontier.[24]

The Chinese commander also tried to exploit the presence of Newari traders in Tibet. The head of that community told Fu K'ang-an that the Newars and other subject peoples in Nepal were antagonistic to their Gorkhali conquerors and would not aid them against the Chinese army. Seven of the Newari traders were brought into Fu K'ang-an's camp to serve as guides in Nepal and also to penetrate behind the lines to incite the Newars against the Shah dynasty.[25] One of these was sent to Kathmandu in January 1792 to seek out Bahadur Shah's political opponents, Balbhadra Shah and Srikrishna Shah, and encourage them to seize the Regent and Shamar Trulku. The Newari entered Nepal by a seldom-used pass, but even this route was closely guarded by Gorkhali troops, who arrested him and sent him to Kathmandu. Bahadur Shah himself interrogated the trader but was unable to confirm his suspicions. The agent was kept under detention, however, and was unable to

---

[21] *Political Proceedings*, Oct. 3, 1792, Cons. No. 17; Minute by Cornwallis, Oct. 3, 1792.
[22] *Chin-ting, op. cit.*, 14/23, p. 7a.
[23] *Ibid.*, 13/21, pp. 8a–9b.
[24] *Ibid.*, 17/28, pp. 1a–b.
[25] *Ibid.*, 12/20, pp. 18a–19a and 15/25, pp. 75–96.

contact either of the supposedly dissident Nepali leaders. Finally, Bahadur Shah sent the Newari back to Tibet with a message for Fu K'ang-an in which for the first time he stressed the threat posed by what the Chinese records called the "tribe of Tilapacha" of south "Chakar" (i.e., the British)[26] to Tibet, and argued that Nepal served as a screen between India and Tibet. "If you grant more grace to us, we will continue to bar the way when Tilapacha makes trouble. If you do not, then we will let them occupy Tibet."[27]

By May 1792 the Chinese force in Tibet under Fu K'ang-an had increased to 13,000 men—mostly drawn from Szechuan province and from the Khampas of eastern Tibet—plus another 3,000 men in reserve on the Tibet-China border. The Tibetan army had expanded to nearly 10,000 men (7,000 from Gyarong district in Kham and 3,000 from central Tibet) under the command of Kalon Harkhang. The joint commanders decided that this was a strong enough force to accomplish the task at hand, and in June 1792 they launched the campaign against Nepal.[28] The army was divided

---

26 According to the French Sinologist, Imbault-Huart, "Ti-li pa-tch'a est un grand Etat situé au delà des frontières du sud-ouest; les pays qui en dépendent portent les noms de Kô-l-kô-tâ (Calcutta), P'i-leng, A-tra-lâ." ("Un Episode de Relations Diplo matiques de la Chine avec le Népal en 1842," *Revue de l'Extrême-Orient*, vol. 3, 1887, p. 14.)
27 *Wei-Tsang T'ung Chi*, op. cit.; letter from Bahadur Shah to Fu K'ang-an, received in April 1792, pp. 245–46.
28 For the most authoritative Chinese accounts of the war, see *Chin-ting*, op. cit., which contains the texts of the more important communications between Peking and the Chinese officers in Tibet from 1791 to 1793 as well as information on the 1788–89 hostilities, and *Wei Tsang T'ung Chi*, op. cit., in which are found the texts of the letters exchanged between the Nepal Court and the Chinese Commander, Fu K'ang-an, during the campaign in Nepal. For shorter accounts that add some information to the official documents, see Chao-I, "*Ping-ting K'uo-er-k'a Shi lue*" (A Summary Narrative of the Subjugation of the Gorkhas) in Chuan IV of *Huang-Chao-Wu-King-Chi-Sheng Yangchow*, 1792; and Wei Yuan *Ch'ien-lung Cheng K'u-erh-k'a chi* (Narrative of the Conquest of the Gorkhas by Chi'ien-lung) from *Sheng-wu-chi* (Military Exploits of the Ch'ing Imperial Era). The latter work has been translated into French by Camille Imbault-Huart under the title "Histoire de la Conquête du Népal par les Chinois, sous le regne de Tc'ie Long," *Journal Asiatique*, vol. 12 (October-December, 1878), pp. 348–77. An English translation by H. S. Brunnert is included in Perceval Landon, *Nepal*, London, 1928, vol. II, app. XXI, pp. 275–82. Many inaccuracies exist in both translations, which should be used with caution.
The only Tibetan source available to the author that can be considered authoritative is Tsepon Shakabpa, op. cit. Unfortunately, the account of the 1791–92 war is not very detailed and is inaccurate in some places. Its most important contribution is that it stresses the role of the Tibetan army and officers in the Nepal campaign, something which is ignored in the Chinese, Nepali and Western-language sources.
A number of important Nepali accounts of the war have been published in the last two decades, and these add substantially to our knowledge of this affair. One of the first and best is C. R. Nepali's "Nepal-Chin Yuddha" op. cit., pp. 202-16. The most detailed narratives of the war itself are found in S. D. Bisht, *Shahi Sainik Itihas*, op. cit.; D. Bajracharya, *Triratna Saundarya Gotha*, op. cit., appendix C, pp. 265–311; an extract from a Gorkhali "military annals" in *Itihas Prakash*, op. cit., vol. V; B. P. Poudel, "Nepal's relations with Tibet," unpublished Ph.D. dissertation,; and B. R.

into two units: the main force under Fu K'ang-an and the Tibetan general, Kalon Horkhang, invaded Nepal through the Kerong pass (the shortest and most direct route to Kathmandu once the Himalayan range is crossed), and a subordinate force under Cheng-teh used the Kuti pass. The division of the army was to serve two purposes: first, to prevent the Gorkhalis from concentrating their strength for the defense of Kathmandu, and secondly to protect the supply lines of the main force by preventing the Gorkhalis from raiding across the border through the Kuti pass area, which is located between Kerong and Shigatse.

The first battles in the 1792 campaign occurred on the Kuti front in early June. A Tibetan force had recaptured Kuti two months earlier but had been deterred from any advances by a heavy snowfall. Reinforced by Chinese units, the Tibetans attacked the Gorkhali force at Khasa, forcing them to retreat to Listi, where a strong fortified position was prepared. The Tibetan-Chinese force assaulted Listi, but were beaten off with heavy losses. They retreated eight miles to the border area and set up their own fortified camp there. The Nepali detachment remained at Listi and the fighting on this front had reached a stalemate by the beginning of July.

The hostilities on the Kerong front began in mid-June. The main army under Fu K'ang-an and Kalon Horkhang, consisting of approximately 6,000 Chinese and 6,000 Tibetan troops, attacked and defeated the small Nepali detachment at Kukurghat, between Kerong and Dzonka. After a week's siege, Kerong was captured on June 28, and the Chinese-Tibetan force advanced toward the border post on the Trisul Gandaki river, near Rasua.[29] Fu K'ang-an divided his force, outflanked the Gorkhali defenders, and forced

---

Acharya *Nepal ko Samkshipta Vrittanta, op. cit.,* pp. 96–100. Some of the records in the Jaisi Kotha (Tibet-China Office) of the Nepal Foreign Office were also available to the author.

British Indian sources add another facet to the source materials on the war. The account of the origin of the war in Kirkpatrick, *op. cit.,* is particularly useful because the author was in Nepal in 1793 and had excellent, if not always reliable, contacts in the Kathmandu Darbar. The National Archives of India (New Delhi) and the India Office Library (London) contain most of the reports on the 1791–92 war sent to Calcutta by British agents.

29 The Chinese used leather cannons which fired five or six shells before bursting and "worked wonders" in assaults on Nepali fortifications. (Historicus, "Nepal-China Relations" *op. cit.,* p. 42). One of these cannons is still preserved at the National Museum in Kathmandu. A Chinese commentator vividly described the traditions of the Rajput caste as followed by the Gorkhalis: "People of that country conducted the war just as in the ancient manner. They fought only after sending us a written challenge fixing in advance the date for battle. However, our army did not bother with whether it was day or night but always sought the best opportunity to launch an attack, so frequently we caught them unaware. Though they criticized the Chinese army for acting thusly, contrarily to the ancient manner as they thought, they could

them to retreat to Syapni where reinforcements under Sardar Prab-
hal Rana joined them. The Chinese commander again divided his
force and sent one unit through a by-pass to the rear of the Nepali
army. On July 24 and 25, both wings launched an attack which
routed the Gorkhalis again.

The series of defeats inflicted upon the Nepali army caused a
major political crisis for Bahadur Shah and his principal advisor on
Chinese and Tibetan affairs, Shamar Trulku. The death of the
later on July 3, 1792, apparently a suicide, was a blow to the Regent.
According to the official Nepali version, Shamar Trulku had contracted smallpox in March and finally died of this illness—more
than three months later. Fu K'ang-an noted that the date of the
Lama's death coincided exactly with the date the Chinese armies
crossed into Nepal, and concluded that either the Lama had been
murdered by the Gorkhalis or the Kathmandu Darbar was circulating fraudulent stories of his death and hiding him elsewhere. However, the death of the Lama was verified by Kalon Doring and two
captive Chinese officers who were ordered to view the body by a high
Nepali official. The two officers reported to Fu K'ang-an that there
was one pockmark under the Lama's right eye and one on his hand,
but that his body was "blue and purple," which they felt indicated
he had died of poison.[30]

The Chinese armies scarcely had crossed the borders before
Kathmandu sued for peace. In a letter dated July 16, 1792, brought
by the two Chinese officers mentioned above, Bahadur Shah placed
the entire blame for the previous year's misadventure on the late
Shamar Trulku. The Chinese commander was asked to arbitrate
the dispute between Nepal and Tibet, and Kathmandu agreed to
abide by his decision. A second letter, dated July 2, reiterating
these sentiments, was carried to the Chinese camp by Kalon Doring.
In his reply, dated August 2, Fu K'ang-an insisted that Bahadur
Shah and Rana Bahadur were equally responsible, and that one or
both of them should present themselves at the Chinese camp to request forgiveness. He also dismissed the coinage issue and stated
categorically that the 1789 treaty was not valid, as it had been privately concluded by Kalon Doring under compulsion.[31]

---

not resist us and a great number of them were killed so that finally they did not dare
to continue their resistance and offered their submission." (Chao-I, *op. cit.*, Chuan IV).
30 *Ibid.*, 22/37, pp. 22b-23a. Abdul Kadar Khan, who was in Kathmandu at the
time of Shamar Trulku's death, reported that "the lama poisoned himself." (*Political
Proceedings*, Oct. 3, 1792, Cons. No. 15. Bahadur Shah, in a letter to Fu K'ang-an, may
have implied this when he reported that Shamar Trulku, on being told he would
be turned over to the Chinese, "turned pale" and died shortly thereafter. (*Wei-Tsang
T'ung Chi*, *op. cit.*, pp. 276–77).
31 *Wei-Tsang T'ung Chi*, *op. cit.*, pp. 272–79.

The Darbar replied on August 5 to Fu K'ang-an's letter, indicating their interest in a peace settlement. A four-man delegation consisting of Bhutu Pande, Ranjit Pande, Narsingh Gurung and Balbhadur Khawas was sent to discuss terms. In a letter dated August 13, Fu K'ang-an listed the following conditions for a settlement:

1) The remains of Shamar Trulku would be sent to the Chinese camp for investigation.
2) The family, followers and servants of Shamar Trulku would be handed over to the Chinese.
3) Nepal would restore all the Tashilhunpo plunder.
4) The two copies of the 1789 treaty held by Nepal would be surrendered to the Chinese.
5) The Gorkhali army on the front would be withdrawn from their positions opposite the Chinese-Tibetan force, which would be allowed to occupy a more suitable camp site.

If these conditions were accepted, Fu K'ang-an promised that the Gorkhalis would be considered as members of the Chinese family and would not be "disturbed." If Nepal rejected these terms, however, the Chinese-Tibetan army would advance to Kathmandu.[32]

When no answer had been received by August 19, Fu K'ang-an ordered an attack upon the Nepali forces, now under the command of Kazi Damodar Pande, entrenched on the heights above the Chinese camp. After three days of heavy fighting, the Nepalis were again outflanked, and were forced to retreat to Dhaibung on the Betravadi river, the principal defense position for Nuwakot valley and scarcely 20 miles from Kathmandu. The defeat led to near-panic in the Kathmandu Darbar, which ordered the state treasury removed to Makwanpur. The Darbar was badly divided over the policy to pursue in this crisis, the Regent's opponents advocating immediate surrender whereas Bahadur Shah proposed the concentration of all forces against the Chinese invaders.[33] Finally, a compromise was reached under which reinforcements were sent to the front under the command of Srikrishna Shah, an opponent of Bahadur Shah, and the bulk of the Nepali forces in eastern and western Nepal were summoned back to Kathmandu posthaste.[34] At the same time, another letter, dated August 26, was sent to Fu K-ang-an, agreeing to the terms he had proposed, with two excep-

---

[32] *Ibid.*, pp. 279–80.
[33] C. R. Nepali, "Nepal-Chin Yuddha," *op. cit.*
[34] This delay frustrated the Shah dynasty's goal of bringing the entire Himalayan hill area from Bhutan to Kashmir under its control. Ten years later, when the expansion program was renewed, Ranjit Singh had created a powerful Sikh empire in the Panjab and was extending his authority into the hills, barring the way to Nepali expansion to the west.

tions: neither Rana Bahadur nor Bahadur Shah would come to the Chinese camp to offer their submission nor would the Gorkhali forces be withdrawn from the battle positions they then occupied.

In accordance with these terms, the remains of Shamar Trulku and his confidential servant, Chi-lung, were sent to Fu K'ang-an's camp on September 3, along with the Lama's personal possessions and some of the plunder from Tashilhunpo.[35] Ten days later Damar Shah came to the Chinese camp with more of the loot from Tashilhunpo and with a letter from Rana Bahadur which stated that Nepal would send another mission to China.[36] Fu K'ang-an would not accept the terms expressed in Rana Bahadur's letter of August 26, however, as Bahadur Shah had not come personally to conclude the agreement.[37]

Despite an unbroken succession of impressive victories, by September the position of the invading force was critical. Heavy losses had been suffered in battle, and many more men became victims of the virulent form of malaria prevalent in the river-valley area in which the army was encamped. Reinforcements were not readily available, and as supplies could be brought in only with difficulty, there were serious shortages of food and ammunition. Moreover, the army could not be maintained in its present position for more than four to six weeks, since by the end of October snow might impede the transit of supplies and men across the Himalayan passes.

The alternatives open to Fu K'ang-an were to accept the Nepali terms or to attempt an advance on Kathmandu, where adequate supplies could be obtained. The latter course was adopted, and in the second week of September the Chinese-Tibetan armies were once more ordered to the attack, Dhaibung being the immediate objective. A fierce battle was fought near the ford of the Betravadi river. The Gorkhalis successfully defended their positions, however, and forced the invaders to retreat to their previous positions after heavy loss of life, including the "junior Chinese commander."[38]

---

[35] *Wei-Tsang T'ung Chi*, pp. 286–87. Apparently the Nepalis did not surrender all the plunder from Tashilhunpo, despite their promises to the Chinese. Commenting on the return of the 1793 Nepali mission to Peking, the Buddhiman Singh Vamsavali states: "After reaching Nepal they reported to King Rana Bahadur Shah. This King had stored in his treasury much of the property looted from Shigatse so he offered a golden roof to the Bhairabi temple at Nuwakot."
[36] *Ibid.*, p. 287.
[37] *Chin-ting, op. cit.*, 23/39, pp. 21a–24a.
[38] Neither the official Chinese history of the war nor Chao-I's version mentions this last battle, but Wei Yuan's account (*op. cit.*), written six decades after these events, admits that Fu K'ang-an suffered a setback in the final battle. Nepali sources, such as C. R. Nepali ("Nepal-Chin Yuddha," *op. cit.*) and S. D. Bisht ("Shahi Sainik Itihas,"

The Emperor, aware of the influence of climatic factors on a campaign across the Himalayas, had authorized Fu K'ang-an to settle the conflict on the best terms possible, if necessary not even demanding that Rana Bahadur and Bahadur Shah offer their "submission" in person.[39] As the army lacked the strength to push forward to Kathmandu and would shortly have to retreat to Tibet with its mission unaccomplished, Fu K'ang-an decided to agree to a settlement based for the most part upon the terms proposed in the Darbar's letter of August 26. He made one last effort, however, to induce the King and the Regent to come personally to his camp for the signing of the treaty. Bahadur Shah refused the invitation for himself and the King, but sent Dev Datta Thapa, a leading Kaji (minister) at the Nepal Darbar, to the Chinese camp to arrange the settlement and then proceed to the court at Peking.[40]

The Nepali delegation arrived at the Chinese camp on September 23 with the Darbar's latest letter. In the discussions between Fu K'ang-an and Dev Datta Thapa, the latter apparently accepted an additional stipulation—namely, that Nepal would send missions to China every five years with presents for the Emperor.[41] Fu K'ang-an then agreed to "temporarily" withdraw his army from Nepal. A note to that effect was sent to Kathmandu, and its reply, dated September 27, was received the following day.

On the basis of these instructions, Kaji Dev Datta Thapa and Fu K'ang-an concluded an agreement on September 30, 1792,[42] and the withdrawal of the Chinese-Tibetan army began a week later. As in 1789, the terms of settlement were embodied in a series of letters exchanged between the two governments rather than in a single document. Although there are some differences in the available documentary sources as to the contents of the agreement, it is generally agreed that the following terms were included:

---

op. cit.) describe this battle in considerable detail. Shakabpa (*op cit.*, p. 169) mentions that Kalon Horkhang, the Tibetan commander, died during the Nepal campaign, but it is not clear whether he is the "junior commander" who was killed in the Dhaibung battle.

39 *Chin-ting, op. cit.*, 23/39, pp. 1a–b.

40 *Wei-Tsang T'ung Chi, op. cit.*, pp. 298–300.

41 This was in accordance with the Emperor's instructions that Nepal should be obligated to send a "tribute" mission to China every three or five years as did the other "Tributary" countries such as Annam and Korea. (*Chin-ting, op. cit.*, 23/39, pp. 24a–28a.

42 *Wei-Tsang T'ung Chi, op. cit.*, pp. 330–31 and 304–5. None of the sources give an exact date for the signing of the agreement, but September 30 is the date of Fu K'ang-an's letter to the Nepal Darbar stating that he had accepted the terms in their letter of September 27 (*loc. cit.*). The Emperor's ratification of the agreement was promulgated on Oct. 31, 1792 (*Chin-ting, op. cit.*, 25/42, pp. 13a–15a), obviously as soon as Fu K'ang-an's report reached Peking by special courier.

1) Nepal and Tibet would maintain fraternal relations and would not engage in hostilities against each other. Disputes between the two governments would be submitted to the Amban at Lhasa for settlement.
2) Nepal would send a mission to Peking every five years with gifts[43] for the Emperor. The Chinese government would arrange facilities for the mission in China (i.e., bear the cost involved), and would send gifts to the Nepali Raja in return.
3) A Chinese officer would demarcate the boundary between Nepal and Tibet in the Kuti and Kerong area.
4) China would come to Nepal's assistance in the event of an attack by a foreign power.
5) Nepal would return the articles seized at Tashilhunpo monastery and would send back the remains of Shamar Trulko along with his family and followers.
6) Nepal would never again raise claims based on the 1789 treaty or the coinage question.[44]

Thus peace was reestablished on terms that were neither humiliating nor catastrophic for Nepal. Bahadur Shah's adventurism had brought the Shah dynasty to the brink of disaster, but in the final analysis, the war had little permanent impact on the country or on its military capacity. The Darbar reverted to the fundamentals of Prithvi Narayan's foreign policy, under which a tenuous and non-threatening relationship with China was assiduously preserved and contacts with the British were reduced to the minimum necessary to avert a complete severance of relations.

The Peking court, determined to avoid expensive military campaigns in these distant regions, reassessed its traditional "minimum involvement" frontier policy in order to bring under control those factors that had been mainly responsible for the recent hostilities. Ironically, it was Tibet that was most directly affected, for it became a primary objective of Chinese policy to reduce the ex-

---

43 Nepali documents invariably refer to the items sent to the Emperor as "gifts" (i.e., "saugauli") rather than tribute, and uses the same term for the more valuable objects sent in return by the Emperor to the King of Nepal.

44 No copies of the 1792 agreements have been located as yet in the Nepal Government archives. A Nepali publication (Naraharinath, *Itihas Prakash ma Sandhi Patra Sangraha, op. cit.,* vol. II) gives what it calls the "essence of the Nepali-Chinese treaty of 1792, but does not indicate the source. This seems to be based upon the so-called text of the 1792 treaty published in Pudma Jung Bahadur, *Life of Maharaja Sir Jung Bahadur of Nepal* (Allahabad, 1909, pp. 7–8), which also fails to cite any document. A summary of the war is found in Kirkpatrick, (*op. cit.,* App. I). Shakabpa (*op. cit.,* p. 168) gives the terms as summarized by Kalon Doring in his memoires. No Chinese document available to the author gives the terms of the agreement, but they are found scattered through Fu K'ang-an's reports to the Emperor (*Ching-ting, op. cit.*) and letters to the Nepal Darbar (*Wei-Tsang T'ung Chi, op. cit.*)

tensive autonomy that Lhasa and Shigatse had exercised under the previous arrangement. Peking moved to curb those factions in Tibet suspected of activities inimical to China's predominant influence. A series of regulations were enacted by the Li-Fan-Yuan (Colonial Office) in Peking,[45] designed to enhance the powers and status of the Ambans in Lhasa and to reduce the authority and autonomy of the Dalai Lama and other Tibetan officials. These proved to be paper reforms, however, and Hugh Richardson is correct in his conclusion that "whatever the intentions of the 1793 reforms, the substance of Chinese authority was in practice no greater than it had been before."[46]

Neither was the Peking Court much more successful in altering the terms of relationship between Nepal and Tibet. At one point during the hostilities, the Emperor had contemplated the restoration of most of the petty principalities conquered by Gorkha during the preceding two decades. In fact, however, Nepal maintained its borders reasonably intact under the terms of settlement. There was a minor adjustment of the boundary in the Kuti and Kerong areas, but when the Darbar complained to the Ambans in 1793 that two small areas which rightfully belonged to Nepal under the 1792 agreement had been seized by the Tibetans, the latter were ordered to withdraw. Later, the Nepalis contrasted China's generosity on the territorial question with British policy in 1816, further proof to them that largely nominal association with distant Peking was preferable to close ties with British India.

On the trade and currency questions, the Emperor's initial response in 1791 had been to order the expulsion of all Newari trading firms in Tibet and to ban the use of Nepali coins.[47] Both these policies, however, were modified later. In October 1792 the Emperor agreed that the Newari traders should be allowed to remain in Tibet so long as they were registered in the population records—i.e., had become Tibetan subjects. Fu K'ang-an objected on the grounds that the Newaris would leave Tibet under these conditions and that this would be inconvenient because most foreign commodities were imported into the country through Nepal.[48] The Emperor concurred, if rather reluctantly, but did suggest that there should be some delay in the reopening of trade so that Nepal

45 "Li-fan-yuan-tse-li" (Regulations of the Colonial Office), 1816, as translated by W. W. Rockhill in "Tibet, A Geographical, Ethnographical and Historical Sketch Derived from Chinese Sources," an extract from *Journal of the Royal Asiatic Society of Great Britain and Ireland*, 1891, reprinted in Peking, 1939, pp. 7–13.
46 H. Richardson, *A Short History of Tibet*, London, 1262, p. 72.
47 *Chin-ting, op. cit.*, 4/3, pp. 2b–5b and 13a–16b.
48 *Ibid.*, 27/46 p. 21a.

would not look on this concession as indicative of Chinese weakness.[49] By 1796, nevertheless, Newari merchants were trading with Tibet again on essentially the same terms as before the war.

During the war, the Emperor had also decreed that henceforth Tibet should use Chinese currency and Nepali coins should be removed from circulation. Transportation problems made this impractical, however, and Peking finally approved the establishment of a mint at Lhasa instead.[50] Nepali coins continued to circulate in Tibet, but were exchanged at parity with Tibetan coins,[51] and the introduction of new Nepali coinage into Tibet was strictly forbidden.[52]

BRITISH-NEPALI RELATIONS: 1793–95

Calcutta had been acutely embarrassed by the requests for assistance from both sides in the 1791–92 war. The 1792 treaty of commerce with Nepal represented a long-sought goal of Company policy, but it was far overshadowed in importance by the China trade and the necessity to avoid offending Peking. It is uncertain whether any direct or implied promises were made to Kathmandu during the negotiation of the treaty,[53] but Bahadur Shah seems to

---

49 *Ibid.*, 27/46, pp. 5a–6a.
50 *Ibid.*, 8/11, pp. 10a–12b.
51 *Loc. cit.*
52 Approximately a decade later the Kathmandu Darbar, under the leadership of Bhim Sen Thapa, attempted to reintroduce this practice on a limited scale. Bhim Sen requested permission to send some Nepali coins with a mission that was going to Tibet to attend religious ceremonies for the late King Rana Bahadur Shas. The Ambans were opposed to the circulation of newly minted coins but were prepared to allow old Nepali coins to be brought with the mission.
Bhim Sen Thapa saw an opportunity to accomplish his purpose by a bit of mild deception. He ordered that new coins, "with the same content as that of a coin 6 months or 1 year old, should be minted with the old press." C. R. Nepali, *Janaral Bhimsen, op. cit.*, appendix, pp. 294–98.
The Nepali delegation, headed by Dalbhanjun Pande, visited Lhasa in the late fall of 1807, bringing Rs. 14,411 in newly minted but old-style Nepali coins, ostensibly as donations for the religious rites on Rana Bahadur's behalf. The Ambans detected the real purpose of the mission, however. and thwarted this plot in a most sophisticated fashion. They instructed the Tibetan Kalons to "withdraw all the new coins . . . to the treasury of the Dalai Lama and to provide coins, minted at Lhasa, in exchange. The new coins brought this time, will not be circulated in the markets." *Ibid.*, pp. 98–100: Letter from the Chinese Amban to Raja Girban Juddha, Oct. 2, 1807. Thus, the Ambans effectively sabotaged Nepal's attempt to introduce new coinage into the Tibetan commercial system and at the same time avoided antagonizing the Tibetans who expected to benefit from the "donations" received for the religious ceremonies.
53 Neither the archives at London and New Delhi nor the Banaras Residency records contain the documents concerning the actual negotiations of the 1792 commerce treaty in Kathmandu from November 1791 to February 1792. This is particularly curious, since the records on the same subject for the periods immediately before and

have been convinced that an appeal for assistance would not be ignored in Calcutta. In mid-August 1792, when the invading army was pushing deep into Nepal, the Regent, in Rana Bahadur's name, appealed for "ten guns together with ammunition, and ten young Europeans versed in the management of artillery."[54] Approximately two weeks later, another letter was sent to Calcutta, this time requesting that British troops be sent to Nepal's assistance.[55]

Cornwallis, after considerable procrastination, decided that "the commercial advantages that Bengal may obtain by a friendly and open intercourse with both countries" (i.e., Nepal and China) made it "no less political than humane in us to interfere our good offices and endeavour to re-establish peace . . ." The Governor-General informed the Board at Calcutta that he proposed to send a deputation to Nepal

to assure him that it is our earnest wish to extricate him from a ruinous war, but at the same time to state that . . . the amicable correspondence that we have held with the Lamas, and the commercial connexion which has long subsisted between our country and that of the Emperor of China preclude us absolutely from committing hostilities against either of those powers without any provocation on their part.[56]

A letter expressing these sentiments but announcing Cornwallis' intention to "depute a gentleman in my confidence to you" to mediate the dispute was sent to Kathmandu on September 15.[57]

Cornwallis also took the opportunity to reply to the letters received nearly four months earlier from the Dalai and Panchen Lamas and Fu K'ang-an.[58] In his letter to the Dalai Lama he stated that "I shall be happy if my amicable interference can in any shape contribute to reestablish harmony and peace between you and the Rajah of Napal, and I shall be ready to use it in the way of a friend

---

after Abdul Kadir Khan's mission to Kathmandu can be found in full in the Banaras Residency records (U.P. Central Records Office, Allahabad) and in part at London and New Delhi.

[54] *Political Proceedings*, Oct. 3, 1792, Consultation No. 9: Rana Bahadur Shah to Cornwallis, received at Calcutta Aug. 22, 1792.

[55] Ibid., Consultation No. 11: Rana Bahadur to Cornwallis, received at Calcutta Sept. 5, 1792.

[56] *Ibid.*, Consultation No. 17, Minute by Cornwallis dated Oct. 3, 1792.

[57] *Ibid.*, Consultation No. 13.

[58] In explaining this delay, Cornwallis stated that it had been impossible to obtain translations of the several letters in the "thibetan character" and that he had not been sure the "Persian papers which accompanied these letters were proper translations of their content." This was a rather lame excuse at best. These letters were first sent to Banaras for translation and then finally accompanied Kirkpatrick to Nepal where they were translated by a servant of Gujraj Misra. Obviously, therefore, the Governor-General's replies were based upon the "Persian papers."

and mediator between you." The Governor-General announced that he would "depute a gentleman in confidence to that quarter" [i.e., Nepal] for this purpose once the summer monsoon ended.[59]

The envoy chosen by Cornwallis was Captain William Kirkpatrick. Before his deputation even began preparations for departure, however, a peace treaty had been concluded between Nepal and China, thus obviating the need for mediation. Rana Bahadur, who for the first time was beginning to act on his own initiative, wrote Cornwallis in mid-October 1792 that, in these circumstances, "the Gentleman who may have been elected to effect an accommodation, may not be at the trouble of coming."[60]

Mediation had been merely one of the objectives of the British in proposing a mission to Nepal, however, and the relevance of these other considerations was not diminished by the peace settlement. Letters were sent to Kathmandu by Cornwallis, Duncan and Abdul Kadir Khan expressing the "satisfaction" the Company would feel at the reception of the Kirkpatrick mission. Gujraj Misra, meanwhile, explained to the Darbar the dangers involved in declining to permit the entry of the mission at this late date. The political situation in Nepal was still very delicate, and the Bahadur Shah faction continued to exert a strong but no longer decisive influence. His position being weakened by this division of sentiment, Rana Bahadur, reluctantly and with little grace, wrote Cornwallis giving his permission for Kirkpatrick to proceed to Nepal.[61]

Kirkpatrick received detailed instructions from the Governor-General specifying the objectives of his mission,[62] which were (1) to persuade the Kathmandu Darbar to pay the "strictest attention to the commercial treaty," (2) to attempt to settle all boundary disputes between the Company and Nepal, and (3) to make general observations on the government, religion and customs of the Nepalis and to enquire into the trade between Nepal and Tibet and the roads and geography of Nepal and neighboring countries. Not

---

[59] *Political Proceedings*, Oct. 3, 1792, Consultation No. 14: Cornwallis to Dalai Lama, Sept. 25, 1792.
[60] *Ibid.*, Nov. 2, 1792. The Chinese and Tibetans also wrote Calcutta that it would be unnecessary to send a mediator to Nepal, but these letters were not received until June 28, 1793, nearly 4 months after Kirkpatrick had left for Nepal (*ibid.*, July 12, 1793, Consultation No. 14: (Fu K'ang-an to Cornwallis) and No. 15 (Panchen Lama to Cornwallis).
[61] *Ibid.*, Jan. 17, 1793, Consultation No. 15, Rana Bahadur to Cornwallis, received at Calcutta on Jan. 2, 1793. As was often the case in Nepal, the Nepali delegation which came to Patna to escort Kirkpatrick was led by two men—Bam Shah and Dinanath Upadhyapa, the former a supporter and the latter an opponent of the 1792 commerce treaty.
[62] *Ibid.*, Jan. 14, 1793, No. 20b.

mentioned in the orders but repeated orally to Kirkpatrick was Cornwallis' instruction that the envoy should, if the situation seemed favorable, raise the question of a British residency at Kathmandu.

Although the British, with the support of Gujraj Misra and Bahadur Shah, could "induce" Kathmandu to receive Kirkpatrick, the sentiment of the Darbar remained strongly adverse. When Kirkpatrick crossed the Nepal frontier in mid-February 1793, he was amazed to discover that his journey would not take him to Kathmandu but to Nuwakot, where the court had recently moved "to celebrate Holi." Led along a route which circumvented the capital, Kirkpatrick finally reached Nuwakot around the first of March. Rana Bahadur's unfriendly disposition towards the mission was apparent in the Envoy's first presentation to the Darbar, for the usually loquacious Raja "was wholly silent."[63] Rana Bahadur returned to Kathmandu shortly after Kirkpatrick's arrival, but Bahadur Shah remained at Nuwakot to carry on the discussions with the envoy.

By March 10, Kirkpatrick realized that there was little possibility that any concrete results would flow from his mission and that even his continued presence in the country beyond the end of March "was a matter altogether out of the contemplation of this Darbar." Gujraj Misra also impressed upon Kirkpatrick the threat which the Envoy's continued presence in Nepal held for Bahadur Shah. If the Regent should attempt to detain Kirkpatrick in Nepal against the decided opinions of "his coadjutors in the administration," the Rajguru argued, they might use this issue to persuade Rana Bahadur to dismiss Bahadur Shah and assume full powers himself. Under such circumstances, Kirkpatrick decided that it was futile even to bring up the question of the establishment of a residency and that it was best to leave as if under his own volition.

On his return journey the British envoy was permitted to visit Kathmandu, where he dined in the royal palace at the invitation of the Regent. Bahadur Shah expressed his hopes for a renewal

of the personal interviews which had been so agreeable to him and signified his desire to be informed particularly what Powers our Government were in amity with, or otherwise, to the end that, having *now* determined to esteem the friends and enemies of the Company as his own, he might regulate his carriage towards them accordingly.[64]

---

[63] *Political Consultation* No. 11. Mar. 18, 1793: Kirkpatrick to Cornwallis, Mar. 5, 1793.
[64] *Political Consultation* No. 23, Apr. 12, 1793: Kirkpatrick to Cornwallis, Sugauli, April 4, 1793.

Rana Bahadur was not present on this occasion, though he did take a silent part in the ceremony in which Kirkpatrick formally took his leave from the Darbar.

By April 4, 1793, Kirkpatrick was back in India. Despite Cornwallis' statement that he was "entirely satisfied with the whole of your conduct," the results of the mission were negligible from the British point of view. Indeed it may even have been harmful, for the presence of a British envoy solidified the opposition to Bahadur Shah and to the treaty of commerce. It is impossible to determine to what extent the deposition of Bahadur Shah in 1794 was due to Cornwallis' obstinacy in insisting on Nepal's reception of an envoy, but the embarrassment caused the Regent by Kirkpatrick's presence is evident even in the letters of that rather thick-skinned observer. The only solid achievement for the British in this affair was the comparatively comprehensive report prepared with the invaluable assistance of Gujraj Misra and Abdul Kadir Khan, for this gave the Company, and twenty years later the Western world, its first detailed account of Nepal.

POSTWAR POLITICS IN NEPAL

The war with China brought in its wake a serious challenge to Bahadur Shah's previously unrivaled influence at the Kathmandu Darbar. The party opposed to the Regent's rule was not strong enough to bring about his downfall immediately, for he still enjoyed substantial support from various factions in Nepal whose personal interests were closely tied to his own. In the Regent's party were found certain elements of the royal family including Bam Shah and the half-brothers of Rana Bahadur, who had regal ambitions of their own; the *Kala* (black) Pande faction led by Damodar Pande; a Brahman faction led by Gujraj Misra; the Palpa royal family (with whom Bahadur Shah had matrimonial ties) whose position as a semiautonomous vassal of the Gorkha dynasty made the Palpa Raja an important figure in Nepal; and finally, a host of civil and military officials who owed their position to the Regent. In the royal camp was another segment of the royal family including Srikrishna and Balbhadra Shah (half-brothers of Bahadur Shah and uncles of Rana Bahadur); the Thapa family, of whom the best-known member at that time was Amar Singh Thapa; the "Gora" (white) Pande faction; a group of Brahmans led by Dinanath Upadhyaya and later including Raghunath Pandit; and in addition, numerous ambitious Nepalis who had been deprived or denied official posts by the Regent.

The first serious setback for Bahadur Shah occurred at the *Panjani* (i.e., annual reinvestment in office) ceremony in July 1792 during the war with China. Bahadur Shah was not reappointed as *Chountria* (first minister), though he did continue to hold the broad powers accruing to him as Regent. For nearly two years an approximate balance of power was maintained between the two factions, but the Regent's position became increasingly untenable as the antagonism of the Raja intensified. Finally, in the spring of 1794, Rana Bahadur assumed full powers himself, and dismissed the Regent from all offices.

It was on this occasion that a Nepali political faction for the first time attempted to invoke Chinese intervention on its behalf in internal Nepali politics. Several months after his dismissal, Bahadur Shah wrote the Amban in Lhasa requesting that a letter enclosed for the Emperor be forwarded to Peking. The Amban rejected this request and sent letters to both Rana Bahadur and Bahadur Shah enjoining them to live in amity. On the subject of the Regent's dismissal, the Amban merely replied that "this is your domestic affair and we have nothing to say about it."[65] Bahadur Shah replied almost immediately and, undeterred by the Amban's reluctance to become involved, asked to be allowed to go to Peking to meet the Emperor. The Amban again informed Rana Bahadur about his uncle's request, and asked whether Bahadur Shah's proposed visit to China had the Raja's approval.[66]

As might be expected, Rana Bahadur was extremely vexed with this news, and ordered the official in charge of the Tibet Relations Office to go immediately to Lhasa with a long list of allegations against the ex-Regent's behavior while in office, including responsibility for the hostilities with Tibet and China.[67] Bahadur Shah was imprisoned and shortly thereafter murdered. But whether his letters to the Amban played a critical role in the Raja's decision is unclear, as internal political developments centering around the ex-Regent's alleged plot to depose Rana Bahadur and place the Raja's half-brother, Sher Bahadur Shah, on the throne would have provided sufficient motivation.

Chinese policy toward Nepal was clearly indicated in these events. The Ambans were free to "advise" the Kathmandu Darbar at the latter's request, but under no circumstances were they to interfere in Nepal's internal politics or support one faction against another. Thus, Nepal's relationship with China, though defined in

---

[65] C. R. Nepali, "Shri Panch Rana Bahadur Shah," *op. cit.*, appendix II, pp. 108–9.
[66] *Ibid.*, appendix III, p. 110.
[67] *Ibid.*, appendix IV, pp. 111–12.

terms of "vassalage" by Peking, never held much political significance for internal Nepali politics. Very early, however, the Nepalis learned the value of an association with China as a deterrent factor in Kathmandu's periodic confrontations with the British. Dr. Buchanan (Hamilton), who spent 14 months in Nepal during 1802–03, commented:

The Gorkhalis are in the habit of saying, that, should they have any dispute with the English, their only formidable neighbour, they will claim the protection of the Chinese, with whose influence over the Company they seem to be much better acquainted than one would have expected.[68]

This was precisely the policy adopted by Nepal in the first half of the 19th century. Whenever relations with the British reached a critical stage, the Nepalis did their utmost to dramatize their relationship with China to the British, in the process often exaggerating and distorting its true character.

Unfortunately for Nepal's plans to use Peking as a balance to the British, the war had also been a bitter lesson for the Chinese. It became clear to the Manchu court that the costs—financial, military and political—of intervention across the Himalayas were prohibitive and best avoided in the future. Nepal's capabilities both in the sphere of international intrigue and on the battlefield were evident to Peking, and distrust of Nepali démarches characterized the attitude of Chinese officials in Tibet for several decades.[69] Every attempt by Kathmandu thereafter to involve China in Nepal's anti-British moves immediately encountered this prejudice. The cautiousness displayed by the Chinese whenever the Nepalis aproached them with grandiose schemes for an alliance against the British was in part a direct result of China's experiences in the 1788–92 period.

In certain respects, the war with Nepal had been a satisfactory affair for Peking, as evidenced by the stone pillar erected in Lhasa to describe the defeat of the "country of the thieves."[70] Indeed, it

---

68 Dr. Francis Buchanan, *An Account of the Kingdom of Nepal*, Edinburgh. 1819.
69 See, for example, the caustic appraisal of the Nepalis by the Amban Sung-yun (circa 1798) in Husung Pei-ch'iai, *Hsi-Tsang T'u Kao* (Maps and Description of Tibet), 1886, Chuan 7, pp. 33b–44b.
70 However, the Emperor may not have been as exultant over the 1792 war as that pillar indicates. In summarizing his view of the peace settlement, he wrote Fu K'ang-an: "On the whole (the Gorkhali) submission is more humble than that of the usurping King of Annam, and perhaps, hearing of his recent visit to Peking, they (Rana Bahadur and Bahadur Shah) may be induced to come later on. Under these circumstances, I will pardon them and withdraw. . . . As matters stand, the success is not such that I can celebrate a formal triumph in the temple. If, therefore, the plunder taken at Tashilhunpo is returned, you may accept their offers" (*Chin-ting, op. cit.*, 23/39, pp. 24a–28a.

was the last impressive military campaign of the Ch'ing dynasty against a foreign power. The vast expenditures required for the campaign, however, had been a disastrous drain upon the Chinese treasury at a particularly inopportune moment, and furthermore had not been offset by territorial acquisitions of any note. Chinese policy quickly lost the dynamism displayed in the war and thereafter became purely defensive in character. It was aimed primarily at the maintenance of the *status quo* to the north of the Himalayas and avoidance of direct involvement in developments to the south of the range.

Obviously, then, Kathmandu was playing a losing game in its efforts to balance the Chinese against the British, and this would have been true even if there had been an approximate equality of power between its two great neighbors. Nevertheless, it is surprising how long the impact of China's military campaign of 1792 was felt. Indeed, several decades elapsed before the British fully comprehended the true character of China's interests in the area or realistically appraised China's military capacity. These events, therefore, had a strong influence upon British policy toward Nepal and other hill areas to the south of the Himalayas, and was one factor that deterred their absorption into the British Indian Empire.

4

Nepal Challenges
the Lion:
The Anglo-Nepali
War, 1814-16

AFTER having surmounted the crisis in its relations with China and
Tibet with considerable difficulty, Kathmandu found itself moving
slowly but inexorably toward an even more dangerous confrontation with British power in India. Bahadur Shah's dimissal from
office in 1794 was a serious setback to the Company's expectations
in Nepal. The new Governor-General, Sir John Shore, commented
that Bahadur Shah had

some months ago resigned the Regency to the Rajah and with it his
influence on which I had some dependance for promoting my wishes.
The only channel through which I can hope to make a favorable impression on the Rajah of Nipaul, is a Brahmin of the name of Gurjraje
Misser . . . who has always been disposed to promote our wishes, and
whom Captain Kirkpatrick found possessed of great influence with the
Court of Nipaul.[1]

Calcutta's apprehensions were justified. The faction that dominated the Kathmandu Darbar from 1794 to 1799 was opposed to
any expansion of relations with the British, and the first casualty of
the Regent's dismissal from office was the 1792 treaty of commerce.
    The Governor-General decided to test the sentiment of the
Nepal court by the dispatch of a "commercial" mission to Kath-

---

[1] Secret Proceedings, Nov. 3–10, 1794, Consultation No. 29: Minute by Governor-
General Shore dated Nov. 10, 1794.

75

mandu under the leadership of the reliable Maulvi, Abdul Kadir Khan. A letter to this effect to Rana Bahadur elicited a rather brusque reply. The Raja argued that he had done all in his power to encourage traders, but that

owing to the war with the Chinese all the Tibet country that is Bhoot, Lassa, Juggesh, etc. that lay in the way has been devastated by the two armies for which reason the country north of Bhoot is not much frequented by merchants. Formerly whatever merchandise they brought from Hindustan used to be bought by the merchants of Bhoot but now when the Hindustan merchants bring articles for trade there is no one desirous of purchasing them . . . so that I do not conceive it advisable just now to send Molavy Abdul Kauder with the merchandise.[2]

The mission was therefore postponed until mid-1795, when Gujraj Misra was finally able to obtain the consent of the Nepal government.

The Maulvi's deputation was not strictly "commercial" as he was given the authority to negotiate with the Nepal government on political as well as economic matters.[3] The urgency with which the British authorities regarded this venture is indicated by the fact that, with some reluctance and at Duncan's insistence, Abdul Kadir Khan departed for Kathmandu in midsummer, thus forcing him to travel through the Terai at the height of the malarial season. This turned out to be a serious mistake, for the Maulvi contracted a near-fatal case of the disease which prevented him from functioning at full efficiency during his six-month residence in Kathmandu. In any case, the opposition of Rana Bahadur and a powerful faction at the Darbar made the success of his mission unlikely. The Maulvi returned to India in March 1796, after having disposed of most of the merchandise he had brought to Nepal as "gifts" to various Nepali officials. The Governor-General concluded that an extensive and profitable trade with and through Nepal was possible but remote, given the preponderant sentiment at the Nepal Darbar.[4]

THE ANGLO-NEPALI TREATY OF 1801

The murder of Bahadur Shah in 1797 did not notably lessen the strength of the faction at the Darbar opposed to Rana Bahadur, for the army remained largely under the influence of several staunch supporters of the late Regent, including Damodar Pande.

---

2 *Ibid.*, Mar. 20, 1795, Consultation No. 22: Rana Bahadur to Duncan, received in Banaras on Feb. 24, 1795.
3 *Political Proceedings*, Mar. 7–11, 1796, Consultation No. 2, Mar. 7, 1796.
4 *Home Series*, Misc. No. 606, Notes on Nepal. pp. 577–603 (IOL), March 1796.

The opposition to the Raja was greatly strengthened in 1798 when Rana Bahadur excluded his eldest son by a high-caste Chhetri wife from succession to the throne and established as heir apparent his infant son by a Brahmani wife—a marriage which violated basic caste principles and shocked the Hindu elite in Nepal. Fearful that the Bharadars would not honor their reluctantly conceded avowals of loyalty to the heir apparent, Rana Bahadur abdicated on March 23, 1799, and placed his successor, Girban Juddha, on the throne of Nepal. He then retired to a life of "religious meditation" in the vicinity of Kathmandu.

The ex-Raja's renunciation of politics lasted only a few months, and by the autumn of 1799 he was again attempting to re-assert his authority in the Darbar. This led to a direct confrontation with the Council dominated by Kaji Damodar Pande, which was strongly opposed to Rana Bahadur's political reincarnation. A civil war seemed imminent until it became apparent that most of the military leaders sided with the Council. Discretion suggested a temporary withdrawal from the political arena in Nepal for Rana Bahadur and his supporters. In May 1800, the ex-Raja set out for Banaras in India with a retinue including his uncle, Balbhadra Shah, Bhim Sen Thapa, Raghunath Pandit, Dalbhanjan Pande (the leader of the "Gora" or "white" Pandes) and Balnar Singh Kunwar (the father of Jang Bahadur Kunwar, the founder of the Rana family regime).

Rana Bahadur's presence in India, where he could both serve as a focus for dissident Nepali factions and bargain with the British authorities for his restoration to power, was an awesome threat to the security of the regime in Kathmandu. This situation was most attractive to Calcutta, however, which found itself in a position to play off competing Nepali factions against each other for its own purposes—namely, the revival of the 1792 commercial treaty and the establishment of a residency at Kathmandu. Captain W. D. Knox was deputed to Banaras to wait upon Rana Bahadur and to offer his services as a mediator in the latter's dispute with the Nepal Darbar.

The ex-Raja's principal objectives in the complicated intrigues that ensued were to reassert his authority in Nepal and punish the men who had forced his exile. This was to be accomplished moreover, without any ironclad commitment to the British that would restrict the independence of his kingdom. The skill with which this was accomplished was a classic of its kind.

Rana Bahadur realized that his most effective weapon was the Darbar's fear that he might gain British support for his restoration to the throne of Nepal. As his first move in these delicate maneuvers, therefore, the ex-Raja offered Calcutta an outrageous proposition under which, if restored to his throne through the intervention of the Company, he promised to pay the Company 37½ percent of the revenue from the hill areas and 50 percent of that from the Terai areas of Nepal. Furthermore, if a time should come when none of his descendants were living, "the whole of the country of Nepaul shall devolve to the administration and controul of the Company."⁵ Rana Bahadur was certain that the British could not accept this proposition which, in effect, obligated the Company to guarantee the Shah dynasty on a perpetual basis for a price that no Nepal government would be willing to recognize except under compulsion from the British.

However, Rana Bahadur also knew that Kathmandu could not be certain that the British government would reject this proposition, which he carefully leaked to the Darbar. The latter would, therefore, be forced either to come to terms with him or to commit a grave political blunder by concluding an agreement with the British. Damodar Pande recognized clearly the dangers inherent in either of these two alternatives; concessions to the British would minimize temporarily the threat posed by the presence of Rana Bahadur within British territory but at the price of alienating important segments of the Nepali political elite. He finally concluded that, all things considered, the former policy was the less hazardous, and threw his powerful support behind the faction in Nepal favorable to the British alliance.

By the autumn of 1800, Calcutta had already decided to seek an agreement with the Kathmandu Darbar rather than with Rana Bahadur, though of course no announcement to that effect was made. Governor-General Wellesley had concluded that it was preferable to pressure the *de facto* government in Nepal into an agreement than to undertake the task of restoring a banished Raja to an insecure throne over the objections of powerful elements in his own country. The latter course would have required the sending of an expeditionary force to Nepal—an action which Calcutta wished to avoid both because of the internal situation within India and Peking's possible reactions.⁶ While the British had no intention of assisting the ex-Raja, they were nevertheless able to use his presence in India as a potent argument in pressuring Kathmandu into accepting the Company's terms for a settlement.

The question of Nepal's relationship with China assumed some importance to Calcutta very early in these proceedings. Al-

---

5 *Secret Proceedings*, June 30. 1802; Consultation No. 15: Paper of Propositions from Rana Bahadur to Wellesley, Nov. 6, 1801.
6 *Secret Proceedings*, June 30, 1802, No. 1: Minute by Wellesley, June 30, 1802.

though Wellesley was confident that a treaty of alliance with Nepal would not endanger the Company's relations with Peking, concern over Chinese sentiments did affect the terms of agreement. For instance, the British rejected Kathmandu's request for the inclusion of a clause stating that "both Governments should cordially consider the friends and enemies of either State to be the friends and enemies of the other."[7] This, of course, was directed at Rana Bahadur rather than Peking, but Wellesley "deemed it advisable to exclude from the treaty such stipulations as might by any latitude of construction be considered to operate as a defensive engagement against the power of the Chinese."[8] Similar considerations also affected Calcutta's attitude toward enforcement of the treaty, it being decided that "the commercial interests of the Company in China would preclude this Government from authorising the adoption of any hostile measures . . . to enforce the observance of the stipulations of the Treaty.[9]

Undoubtedly the most controversial provision of the 1801 treaty for Nepal was the clause permitting a British Residency at Kathmandu. A heated dispute on this subject erupted almost immediately after the appearance of a new Resident, Captain Knox, in the capital. As the man held responsible for the treaty, Damodar Pande's position was severely undermined and his supporters deserted in large numbers to the Rana Bahadur faction.

The Darbar's opposition to the treaty had become so bitter by March 1803 that Knox decided to return to India. This suspension of diplomatic contacts did not have the salutory effect expected, and Wellesley formally abrogated the 1801 treaty on January 24, 1804. His action set the stage for Rana Bahadur's triumphal return to Nepal the following month. Damodar Pande attempted to organize resistance but without success, and he was executed on the orders of the ex-Raja, who was granted full powers during his son's minority. The history of the next decade is essentially that of preparations for the confrontation with British power in India.

PREPARING FOR CONFLICT

Rana Bahadur Shah was convinced that a showdown with the East India Company had only been postponed by the abrogation of the 1801 treaty and that eventually Nepal would have to contend

[7] Anson Campbell, *Supplementary Narrative on Nepal-British Relations.* Unpublished Ms. in the Brian Hodgson Collection (IOL).
[8] *Secret Proceedings*, June 30, 1802, No. 1, Minute by Governor-General Wellesley dated June 30, 1802.
[9] *Home Series*, Misc. No. 515, IOL.

on the battlefield with the superior military power of the British. After regaining a predominant influence in the Nepal Darbar, therefore, the ex-Raja intensified preparations for the expected confrontation. The greatest obstacle to the expansion of Nepal's military capacity, he realized, was the country's limited financial resources. In the search for new sources of revenue, the system under which rent-free land grants (*kusa birta*) had been given to Brahmans was modified, and these lands were either expropriated by the state or else brought within the ambit of the taxation system.[10] It was also at this time that the procedure under which Terai lands were contracted out for five year periods was introduced. These two measures resulted in a substantial rise in revenue, which was used to finance the organization of new units in the Nepal army.

Despite the elimination of Damodar Pande and his principal supporters in 1804, the situation at the Darbar remained explosive. Factional rivalries were so intense that it was a year before Rana Bahadur could finally maneuver his appointment as Regent, gaining full powers to rule in his son's name. The Regent's efforts to use this authority against his enemies, however, culminated in his assassination in April 1806. In the crisis that followed, Bhim Sen Thapa, one of the late Regent's closest associates, acted quickly and effectively to remove the leaders of the opposition faction. Seventy-seven men were either murdered or executed in the aftermath of the assassination, and the Thapa family emerged as the dominant influence in the Court.

One of Bhim Sen's first actions was to increase the tempo of the military campaign in the area to the west of Kumaun. All of the hill territory up to the Sutlej River was either conquered or brought into an alliance system with the Gorkha dynasty. The Nepalis thus came into conflict with Raja Sansar Chand, who held territory east of the Sutlej but whose capital was at Kangra, on the west bank of that river. By 1809, virtually all of Sansar Chand's kingdom had been conquered, with the exception of Kangra. This was the last major obstacle between the Gorkhas and their ultimate objective, the valley of Kashmir, which at that time was independent, faction-ridden, and ripe for the plucking by any determined aggressor. A unified hill state, subordinate to the Gorkha dynasty, appeared to be an imminent possibility, an achievement that might well have altered the future, not only for Nepal, but of India.

It was at this point that Nepal became involved in a major

---

10 Mahesh C. Regmi, *Land Tenure and Taxation in Nepal—The Land Grant System: Birta Tenure*, vol. II, Institute of International Studies Research Series No. 4, Berkeley, California, 1964, p. 88.

conflict with Ranjit Singh, the shrewd ruler of the powerful Sikh (Khalsa) kingdom in the Panjab, who was no less interested than Kathmandu in control of the Sutlej river basin and Kashmir. At the urgent request of Raja Sansar Chand, a Sikh army attacked the Nepali force besieging Kangra and drove it back across the Sutlej. Ranjit Singh did not want to alienate the Nepalis, however, in view of the British threat to his dominion. He suggested an alliance between Gorkha and Khalsa under which the Sutlej would become their boundary in the hill area. Amar Singh Thapa, the Nepali Commander, recommended acceptance of the proposal, but the Darbar, at Bhim Sen Thapa's behest, rejected the offer.[11] Nepal thus lost what was probably its last real opportunity to forge a mutual-defense alliance with the Sikhs.

The Gorkhali conquests in the west also provoked disputes with the British over certain districts in the plains which had been subject to hill Rajas prior to their submission to Nepal. Amar Singh Thapa assumed that all the territories of these Rajas, including those in the plains, now belonged to Nepal, and he occupied these areas in 1810. That move ran counter to the broad aims of Company policy. Colonel Ochterlony, the British commander in the area, was instructed to inform Amar Singh Thapa that "he cannot be permitted to extend his conquests to the districts below the hills," but that the British would not interfere with Gorkha conquests to the west of the Sutlej (i.e., in Sikh territory) in the hills.[12] The Kathmandu Darbar was anxious to avoid hostilities with the British until their own preparations were further advanced. Orders were sent to Amar Singh to comply with the British demands, and the Nepali detachments were withdrawn from the disputed areas.[13]

A showdown with Calcutta was thus forestalled, but Nepal realized that the problem would become increasingly acute in the future. Kathmandu intensified its diplomatic efforts in preparation for the day when the British ultimatum would be delivered. The 1812 Nepali mission to Peking made yet another strong appeal for Chinese assistance in the event of war with the British,[14] and again received the usual evasive reply which, in real terms, amounted to a rejection. The Nepali envoy to central India sought to conclude alliances with such Indian states as Holkar, Gwalior, Bharatpur,

---

11 S. D. Bisht, *op. cit.*, pp. 83–86.
12 *Secret Consultation* No. 4, May 23, 1810. At this very same time the British informed Ranjit Singh that he was free to attack the Gorkhalis in the hill areas to the east of the Sutlej—i.e. in Gorkhali-held territory. The deterioration of Nepali-Sikh relations was of course to the interest of the British and was encouraged by them.
13 *Records of the Ludhiana Agency*, Punjab Government Press, Lahore, 1911, p. 345.
14 *Home Series*, Misc. No. 516: Memorandum from William Moorecraft.

Rampur, Lucknow and Lahore.[15] The most serious stumbling block was the attitude of Rajit Singh, who had become extremely cautious about associating himself with any anti-British coalition that was not certain of success. Consequently, Nepal's attempt to unify the remaining independent Indian states against the British failed, and did all other endeavors of this sort, because of the mutual distrust and suspicions of the Indian princes and their fear of the Company's capacity for retaliation.

THE OUTBREAK OF THE WAR

During the Napoleonic wars, the Company had studiously avoided any steps likely to lead to armed conflict with Nepal. The "forward policy" pursued by Wellesley during his term as Governor-General (1801–05) would probably have been extended to Nepal if the British had not been so deeply involved in central India in campaigns against the Marathas and by the rise of Ranjit Singh in the Panjab. Even so ardent an expansionist as Wellesley hesitated before extending the sphere of military activity to a new front against a formidable opponent, particularly after the renewal of the hostilities in Europe in 1803 forced the British to concentrate their energies at home. From 1805 to 1814, British policy in India was aimed at holding those territories already in its possession, preventing the emergence of any anti-British alliance comprising the Indian states, and avoiding all but the most necessary military ventures.

By 1814 the situation had changed radically. Napoleon had been exiled and a large, well-trained British army was available for service elsewhere. On October 4, 1813, the Earl of Moira succeeded Lord Minto as Governor-General of India and once again the Company government entered into a new policy phase. The first indication of this was the change in attitude toward Nepal which culminated finally in the invasion of that country in the cold season of 1814–15.

The immediate cause of the outbreak of hostilities was the dispute between Nepal and the Company over certain border districts claimed by both powers. These disputes may have been an irritant to the Company, yet it is unlikely that Calcutta would have undertaken such a difficult and expensive military campaign had there not been questions of broader policy which made that particular

---

[15] C. R. Nepali, *Janaral Bhimsen, op. cit.*, appendix pp. 285–91: letter from Pandit Padmapani to Bhim Sen Thapa, Aug. 3, 1814.

war attractive at that particular time. The outstanding consideration, undoubtedly, was the desire to eliminate one of the few remaining threats to British dominance in northern India. The
strategic situation of Nepal, directly to the north of Bengal, the
heart of British administration in India, had long disquieted Calcutta. The Company feared that the Nepalis, whose anti-British
prejudices had been repeatedly demonstrated, might take advantage of any serious reverses the Company should suffer on the outer
extremities of its empire to launch an attack on Bengal that would
cut Calcutta's communications with northern India and possibly
even threaten the capital itself. Furthermore, Nepal had taken
a lead in recent efforts to unite the Indian states into a strong
anti-British alliance. The Gorkhali conquests in the hills had
given some Indian rulers an exaggerated view of Nepal's military
strength, thus reviving their hopes for the eventual expulsion of
the Company from India. The success with which Nepal had
resisted British pressure since 1769 had contributed greatly to
Gorkha's reputation in the plains, and also partly explained the
hypersensitivity displayed by some Company officials on this
question.

Circumstances in India in 1814 were such that the British
could hope to settle the Company's disputes with Nepal without
the immediate danger of involvement elsewhere in India. A treaty
had been concluded with Ranjit Singh in 1809, and the British felt
relatively certain that the Sikh ruler would not take advantage of
a war in the hills to press his claims to the territory east of the Sutlej in the plains. Without Ranjit Singh's support, no alliance between Nepal and the Maratha states could function effectively, at
least until after the former had been soundly defeated. The British
also wanted to take action before Nepal had consolidated its administration in the western hill area, in order to profit by the widespread dissidence still prevalent there.

The most persuasive argument against the war was concern
over Peking's possible reaction. During his brief tenure as British
Resident in Kathmandu (1802–03), Captain Knox had become
convinced that China would not take exception to British intervention in Nepal and had advised Calcutta accordingly.[16] A decade
later, he was supported in this conclusion by two other British
agents, Buchanan and Hearsay, who had broad experience in the
Himalayan area.[17] The Company's Select Committee of Cargoes at
Canton also urged Calcutta to proceed with the campaign against

---

[16] *Secret Consultation* No. 350, 2 May, 1805.
[17] *Home Series*, Misc., No. 515: Memorandum on Origin and Progress of the Nepal
War, Jan. 30, 1816.

Nepal, arguing that "a knowledge and conviction, that the Honourable Company have principally the means of retaliating any measure of injustice or injury is the best, if not the only security, for the preservation of their [China's] trade with this Company."[18]

With these reassurances, Moira wrote Kathmandu on March 11, 1814, demanding Nepal's recognition of British jurisdiction in Sheoraj and Butwal, two of the disputed border districts. The British Collector at Gorakhpur was ordered to seize those districts by force if the Kathmandu Darbar had not returned an affirmative reply to the ultimatum within 25 days. When no reply was forthcoming by the end of the stipulated period, British troops moved into both districts on April 22, 1814, killing a Nepali official in the process.

On receiving the British ultimatum, the Kathmandu Darbar had summoned a Bharadari (General Council) to consider the question. After a long discussion, it was decided to reject the British demands, though there was a serious division in the Council. The commanding officers in the western hills—Amar Singh Thapa, Bam Shah and Hastidal Shahi—were opposed to war, as were the Kala Pandes and Gujraj Misra. Bhim Sen Thapa, however, favored resistance, arguing that this was only the first of the Company's territorial demands and that it was better to face them at once rather than later. When the British detachments were withdrawn from Sheoraj and Butwal in May 1814 because of imminent onset of the malarial season, a Nepali force returned to reassert Kathmandu's authority there. Several Company officials were killed in the process, and this became the immediate *casus belli*. The British completed preparations for an invasion of Nepal once the rainy season was over and extensive military operations through the Terai became possible.

Finally, in September 1814, 16,000 troops—divided into four columns—set out to invade Nepal. The first two divisions, under General Morley and General Wood, had Kathmandu as their objective. After seizing control of the Terai in their respective areas of command and then having met with a series of minor setbacks when they attempted to extend their activity into the hills, both Morley and Wood brought their operations to a virtual halt. The third column, under General Gillespie, which had Garhwal and Kumaun as its target, suffered a major setback in the assault on the fort at Kulunga, during which Gillespie was killed. General Martindell, who assumed command, then advanced on Jaitak, where he

---

18 *Loc. cit.*

suffered an even more serious defeat which compelled his troops to withdraw from that area.

The only notable success scored by the British in the winter campaign of 1814–15 was achieved by the fourth column, led by General Ochterlony. After a long and difficult campaign against the Nepali force under Amar Singh Thapa, Ochterlony forced Amar Singh Thapa to agree at Malaun to terms under which the Nepali army retired with their arms and the territory between the Kali and Sutlej rivers came under the control of the British. This terminated the first campaign, for the rainy season had set in and military operations were no longer feasible.

NEPAL'S SEARCH FOR ALLIES

When it became obvious in August 1814 that a British invasion was imminent, a letter was sent to the Amban at Lhasa for transmittal to the Emperor in Peking. In this communication Kathmandu claimed that the British were planning to invade Nepal in order to force a passage through to Tibet. Moreover, Bhim Sen charged that the Company had promised to pay Rs. 60,000 to 70,000 as a reward if Nepal did not impede the British advance.[19] The Amban, however, expressed skepticism that the British had any such intention, and rejected Nepal's request for financial assistance. "There is no tradition of giving monetary aid by China," he said, and continued: "We Ambans cannot submit such requests to the Emperor. . . . From now on never make such requests in your letters."[20] In fact, however, the Amban had sent a report to the Peking court summarizing the contents of the Nepali letter, and had been supported in his decision by the Emperor.[21]

The Darbar also solicited the assistance of several Tibetan officials, asking them to use their good offices to persuade the Amban to support Kathmandu's request for assistance. According to the Sikkim Raja (a British ally in the war), the Panchen Lama and some civil officials at Lhasa urged China to assist Nepal,[22] but the Regent of the Dalai Lama advised Kathmandu to settle the dispute with the British on the best terms possible.[23] Thus, here again di-

---

19 C. R. Nepali, *Janaral Bhimsen, op. cit.,* appendix, pp. 301–02: Raja Girban Juddha to the Chinese Emperor.
20 *Itihas Prakash, op. cit.,* vol. I, p. 78.
21 Chusei Suzuki, *op. cit.,* p. 171–72.
22 *Secret Consultation* No. 19, Sept. 7, 1816: Captain Latter (on Sikkim front) to Calcutta, Aug. 19, 1816.
23 C. R. Nepali, *Janaral Bhimsen, op. cit.,* pp. 311–12; Regent of the Dalai Lama to Raja Girban Juddha.

vergent positions were assumed by the officers around the Dalai and Panchen Lama and also by the civil and lay officials in Lhasa.

The Amban's discouraging reply to their first communication did not deter the Nepalis from sending several more letters to Lhasa in the winter of 1814–15, describing the serious plight caused by the British invasion and soliciting financial assistance. The situation in the western hills and the Terai was so critical by the spring of 1815 that the Darbar wrote again to Lhasa, stating that the Amban's refusal to forward any letters from Nepal except in conjunction with the traditional quinquennial mission "had shattered all our hopes."[24] In a letter enclosed for transmittal to the Emperor, the Darbar argued that it would have to submit to the British if aid were not forthcoming from China soon. Nepal might then be obligated to give up its traditional relationship with China and become a vassal of the British.[25]

Other letters repeating similar themes were sent to Lhasa during the next few months. Finally, and with obvious irritation, the Amban wrote to the Darbar:

The Emperor is not concerned with whether or not you are associated with the British, or whether or not you honor the British. . . . *When you fight with the British, this happens outside our borders. The soldiers of the Emperor cannot go there.* We Ambans realize that the King [of Nepal] is only a child and that you do not know how to work; so we have not submitted these embarrassing letters to the Emperor."[26]

The Amban's message was in conformity with the instructions he had received from the Emperor, which had commented: "As a matter of fact they can join the Feringhi rule if they like, so long as they send us tribute, and so long as the Feringhi do not cross the Tangut [Tibetan] frontier."[27]

Nepal's appeals to the various Indian states for assistance were no more successful than those to China and Tibet. Bhim Sen sent envoys to the Mahrattas and Sikhs to urge them to stand with Nepal against the British, and to the Deb Raja asking the Bhutanis to invade Assam and Bengal from the east.[28] The reactions of all these regimes were favorable but cautious, as they preferred to gauge their response in accordance with the course of the war. Ranjit Singh, in particular, played his usual devious role in these events,

24 *Itihas Prakas, op. cit.,* vol. I, p. 79.
25 *Ibid.,* p. 78.
26 *Ibid.,* pp. 91–92 (emphasis supplied).
27 E. H. Parker, "Nepaul and Tibet," *Asiatic Quarterly,* VII (1899), p. 72, and Chusei Suzuki, *op. cit.,* p. 174.
28 *Home Series,* Misc. No. 516: D. Scott (Magistrate at Rungpore) to Bengal Government," Nov. 28, 1814.

turning over to the British several letters that had been sent to him by Nepal[29] but also mobilizing his army and moving it to the Sutlej ready to take advantage of any opportunities that might arise.[30] The Bhutanis assembled what military forces they possessed in the western passes (*duars*) into India, but these were too negligible to constitute a serious threat to the British without Tibetan or Chinese assistance.

Although generally disappointed by the failure of its diplomatic endeavours, Nepal was nevertheless encouraged by several developments both to the north and to the south. By the fall of 1815, the reception of a British letter to the Amban on the war had forced him to forward to Peking both the British letter and the various Nepali letters.[31] Nepal, which did not yet realize that the Ch'ing court had already approved the Amban's rejection of Kathmandu's appeal for support, could now hope that Peking would reconsider this decision.[32] This in itself, Kathmandu concluded, might deter the British from launching another campaign in the hills because of the Company's known disinclination to antagonize China. To the south, meanwhile, the Mahratta states had begun mobilizing their forces in central India, and an outbreak of war there seemed imminent.

Nevertheless, it was clear that Nepal could expect little assistance from any quarter during the cold season of 1815-16 when the British were expected to renew their campaign in the hills. Somehow the British had to be dissuaded from taking any further military action until the next rainy season had set in, thus allowing Kathmandu a few months to assess the results of its diplomatic endeavours. The negotiations between their respective representatives during the 1815 rainy season presented the Nepalis with an opportunity for some subtle political procrastination. Kathmandu sought to convince the British that another expensive campaign in the hills was unnecessary, at the same time postponing the actual signing of a peace settlement. These tactics worked for a while, but finally evasion was no longer possible. On November 28, 1815, the Nepali representative, Gujraj Misra, signed an agreement with the British representative, Major Bradshaw. It turned out that the Rajguru had not been delegated plenipotentiary powers, however, and Kathmandu subsequently refused to ratify the agreement. The

---

29 *Ibid.*, Metcalfe (Delhi Resident) to Bengal Government, Nov. 28, 1814.
30 C. R. Nepali, "Nepal ra British Samrajya," *op. cit.*
31 Chusei Suzuki, *op. cit.*, p. 174–75.
32 *Secret Consultation* No. 3, Jan. 11, 1817: Translation of a narrative concerning a mission sent by China to Nepal to investigate certain Nepali statements concerning the origin of the Nepali-British war, written by a "Kashmieree" who was present at the interview between the Chinese and Nepali envoys.

British then decided that another winter campaign in Nepal was unavoidable and General Ochterlony was ordered to renew hostilities.

THE SECOND CAMPAIGN

The Board of Directors of the Company in London had been strongly critical of the strategy employed in the 1814–15 campaign, arguing that a single punitive expedition would have been sufficient to restore British honor and territory.[33] Calcutta therefore decided to concentrate its entire strength in the force under General Ochterlony, which would have Kathmandu as its objective. The invasion began in February 1816, quite late in the cold season because of the delays caused by the peace negotiations. After some initial setbacks, Ochterlony was able to outflank the main Nepali defensive position at Makwanpur, thus circumventing the chief obstacle on the road to Kathmandu.

With the collapse of the main defense line, the Darbar quickly dispatched Chandra Sekhur Upadhyaya to Ochterlony's camp with a copy of the Sugauli treaty bearing the seal of the Maharaja. At first Ochterlony refused to accept the 1815 text, maintaining that the "insincerity displayed by Nepal warranted the enforcement of more severe terms." However, the General modified his views when it became evident that Nepal would not accept any major changes in the agreement. Calcutta was anxious to end this expensive war in the hills, which was "accepted as an unfortunate distraction from the real work awaiting the Company's armies in India Proper."[34] War with the Mahratta states in central India was threatening and the Pindaries in western India were also becoming troublesome again. Moreover, the British army in Nepal could operate only for another two or three months before the rainy season set in and supply problems became serious. Thus, even if Ochterlony had been able to capture Kathmandu, the victory would have been short-lived unless accompanied by a peace settlement with the Nepal government.

Taking these considerations into account, Ochterlony finally decided on March 4, 1816, to accept Nepal's ratification of the Sugauli treaty. The terms of the agreement, although considerably more liberal than those proposed by the Governor-General at the outset of the war, nevertheless constituted a serious loss to Nepal.

---

[33] *Home Series*, Misc. No. 515, *op. cit.*
[34] Edward Thompson, *The Life of Charles, Lord Metcalfe*, London, 1937, p. 164.

The most important provisions of the treaty (1) authorized the British to establish a Residency at Kathmandu, (2) surrendered all of Nepal's hill territories west of the Kosi River as well as the disputed Terai areas below the hills to the Company or its subordinate Indian states, and (3) turned over the territories between the Singalila range and Tista river to the Company, which then restored them to Sikkim. The loss of territory was a serious blow, not only because these districts had provided a large proportion of the revenue which supported the military establishment, but also because Nepal was thus isolated from potential allies among the Indian states. Nepal lost its common frontier with the Sikh kingdom in the Punjab, and its borders to the east, south and west now adjoined territories either under the direct rule of the British or firmly under their control.[35]

CHINA'S ROLE IN THE PEACE SETTLEMENT

The reception in Peking of both the Nepali and British letters concerning the war in late 1815 caused a considerable stir. The Emperor decided to send a small military force to Tibet to ascertain the exact state of affairs.[36] Its commander, General Sai-ch'ung-a (referred to in the correspondence as "Shee Chanchoon"), was met on the way to Tibet by messenger from Nepal who informed him that peace had been concluded between Nepal and the Company.[37] Nevertheless, he proceeded to Lhasa, which he reached in May 1816. The General wrote to the British Governor-General, noting the Nepali allegations that the Company had demanded "free passage" to Tibet and had ordered Kathmandu to pay the British the tribute formerly paid to China. In this letter he commented:

Such absurd measures (as those alluded to) appear quite inconsistent with the usual wisdom of the English. It is probable that they never made the declaration imputed to them. If they did, it will not be well . . . An answer should be sent as soon as possible to Tingaree (Tingri) stating whether or not the English really made the absurd propositions imputed to them. . . . It is probable that they did not. Let them write a suitable explanation to Shee Chanchoon that he may make a correspond-

---

[35] Moira wrote to the Secret Committee at Calcutta that the possession of Kumaun not only would provide the Company with a large revenue but would give it a position on the flank of Nepal and would be the best security against the renewal of "aggression" by the Gorkhas. Moreover, he continued, passes through Kumaun into Tibet would provide a "practical" and "commodious road into Tartary." (*Home Series*, Misc. No. 519: Moira to Secret Committee, May 11, 1815).

[36] Chusei Suzuki, *op. cit.*, p. 176.

[37] *Itihas Prakas, op. cit.*, vol. 1, p. 79.

ing communication to the Emperor, stating that the whole story is a falsehood of the Rajah of Goorkah.[38]

The Chinese letter, received in Calcutta on June 7, urged an immediate reply, but it was a month and a half before an answer was sent. During that time, Calcutta attempted to obtain a clear indication of Chinese intentions through their new Resident in Kathmandu and their ally, the Sikkim Raja, who not only served as an intermediary between the British and Chinese but also functioned effectively, through his representatives in Tibet, as a defender of the Company's activities. The Governor-General's reply, dated August 3, 1816, stated the British case on the origin of the war with Nepal, and placed the blame on Gorkha for the attack on Butwal in which several Company officials were killed. He added:

It has been agreed that accredited agents shall be received by each Government from the other and all the usual offices of amity between neighbouring and friendly states will be studiously performed. The British Government has no views of aggrandizement and only seeks to remain at peace with other states, and no motives of ambition and interest prompt it to extend its influence and authority beyond those barriers which appear to have been placed by nature between the vast countries of India and China.[39]

On the same date as that of his letter to Calcutta, the Chinese commander had also written Kathmandu, expressing the Emperor's displeasure with the allegations contained in the communications from Nepal. If on investigation, he said, "the English have acted as you have written," he would "smite them to the death." But if it turned out, as he suspected, that Nepal had "fabricated falsehoods . . . you will receive the punishment that would otherwise be inflicted on the English." He advised the Darbar to send a deputation to his camp with a letter asking forgiveness for its actions and pledging to continue the traditional relationship with the Emperor.[40]

The Darbar's reply, dated June 10, 1816, again stressed the importance of Nepal to the defense of Tibet and the need for Chinese assistance if Nepal was not to be absorbed into the rapidly

[38] *Secret Consultation*, No. 17, July 13, 1816: Chinese commander in Tibet to Governor-General, dated 23 Jamada-i-sani, 1231 Hijira (May 21, 1816).

[39] *Secret Consultation*, No. 18: Aug. 3, 1816: Moira to Chinese officers in Tibet, Aug. 3, 1816.

[40] *Secret Consultation*, No. 12, July 27, 1816: Chinese commander to Nepal Darbar, May 18, 1816. The Chinese commander lacked both the military strength and the Court's authorization to carry out these threats.

expanding British Empire in India.[41] The Chinese commander's reply of July 31 was, if anything, critical of Kathmandu's behavior. "Not even one of your requests will be fulfilled," he stated, as "we have not come to protect your country or to help you." The letter ended with a threat to invade Nepal "with a mighty force and annihilate you" if the traditional mission to the Emperor was not sent on schedule.[42] Sai-ch'ung-a had planned to add substance to his threats by moving his small force to Tingri, close to the Nepali-Tibetan border. The Panchen Lama and the Tibetan officials who were with the General at Shigatse, however, persuaded him to wait there for the deputation which Nepal had promised to send.[43]

At this point, Kathmandu embarked on some intricate maneuvers. Concern over Chinese intentions may to some extent have prompted the Darbar's curious behavior, but in the main, its motivation obviously had a different basis. Nepal hoped to exploit Calcutta's apprehensions regarding the presence of the Chinese army in Tibet to effect two basic objectives—the withdrawal of the British Resident at Kathmandu and the restoration of part or all of the territory lost in the Sugauli treaty. Bhim Sen and other high officials of the Darbar visited the British Resident, Edward Gardner, on several occasions to emphasize the danger Nepal faced from China because of its new relationship with the Company.[44] Bhim Sen added a new note to these discussions when he informed Gardner that the Chinese had demanded that the periodic mission be sent to Peking and had even insisted that Bhim Sen come personally to explain the reasons for its discontinuance.[45] The Muktiyar then declared that there might be other motives for the presence of the Chinese army in Tibet, as Peking had assumed its "present hostile attitude" upon hearing about the novel turn in British-Nepali relations.[46]

One week later, Gujraj Misra and Chandra Sekhur Upadhyaya expanded on this theme in another discussion with Gardner, asserting that China

---

[41] *Ibid.*, Nepal Darbar to Chinese officers, June 10, 1816.

[42] C. R. Nepali, *Janaral Bhimsen, op. cit.*, appendix, pp. 312–14: Chinese commander to Nepal Dunbar, July 31, 1816.

[43] *Secret Consultation* No. 9, Aug. 24, 1816, and No. 14, Aug. 1816: Letters from the Kuti and Tingri district officers to the Nepal government in late July 1816.

[44] *Secret Consultation* No. 18: Gardner to Bengal government, Aug. 16, 1816.

[45] This appears to be a total fabrication, for there was nothing in the letters of the Chinese commander to Nepal concerning the periodic missions to Peking, at least in the sense implied by Bhim Sen. Moreover, he was deceiving Gardner in stating that the Nepali mission was overdue, as the last mission had gone to Peking in 1812 and the next was not due until 1817.

[46] *Secret Consultation* No. 39, Sept. 14, 1816: Gardner to Bengal government, Aug. 22, 1816.

was deeply offended, considering Nepaul a tributary of the Emperor, at this Government's having entered into war and concluded peace with the English without his sanction or knowledge; and that the Chinese Army had . . . advanced for the express purpose of resenting this offense and entering Nepaul.[47]

Two days later they told Gardner that the Darbar believed "that it was necessary for them to throw themselves into the arms of one of their powerful neighbours, and gave me clearly to understand that they would prefer adhering to us.[48]

With only slight assistance from the Chinese, intentional or otherwise, the Nepal Darbar might have been successful in this little intrigue, for Calcutta was deeply concerned over the presence of the Chinese force in Tibet. At one point Moira was ready to make major concessions on the Nepal question if necessary, to appease Peking. He wrote Gardner that "the avoidance of any engagement with the Nipaulese which might embroil us or even give umbrage to the Chinese, must be regarded as the basis of our entire proceedings." He was even ready to concede the withdrawal of the Residency from Kathmandu if unavoidable "to remove this source of the jealousy entertained by the Chinese." Moira doubted that the Kathmandu Darbar was a reliable source of information on the sentiments of the Chinese, however, and said this must be ascertained through direct communication with the Chinese or through other alternative channels.[49]

Unfortunately for the Darbar's schemes, the Chinese commander in Tibet answered the August letter of the Governor-General in a most friendly manner. Referring to the peace settlement between Nepal and the Company, he commented that "this is perfectly correct and proper also pleasing to the creator and his creatures. . . . Now it is known from your writing that no blame is to be attached to the English Gentlemen in this respect and my mind is satisfied. . . . The Goorkah's story has proved entirely false."[50] Assured now that the Chinese were not disturbed by the establishment of a British Residency at Kathmandu, the whole question of its withdrawal was quietly dropped, and the concern felt earlier by the Calcutta authorities over Tibetan developments was rapidly dissipated.

Relations between Nepal and China were finally reestablished on their former basis through the agency of a deputation, consisting

[47] *Ibid.*, No. 41: Gardner to Bengal government, Aug. 28, 1816.
[48] *Ibid.*, No. 42; Gardner to Bengal government, Aug. 30, 1816.
[49] *Secret Consultation* No. 43, 14 September, 1816: Moira to Gardner, Sept. 14, 1816.
[50] *Secret Consultation* No. 19: Chinese commander in Tibet to Captain Latter, dated 3 Silikada, H. 1231 (Sept. 25, 1816).

of Dalbhunjun Pande, Ranbir Thapa and Bhakt Bir Thapa, which reached Shigatse towards the end of September. The letter from the Nepal Raja stated that "from the first, the Gorkha Raja has existed by the blessing of the Emperor and now under his auspices, he looks to obtain relief and protection, and, in continuing his faithful tributary, to enjoy his favor to the day of judgment."[51] The discussions between the Nepalis and Chinese were relatively friendly after an initial outburst by the Chinese commander, who berated the Gorkhas for their untrustworthiness and stated: "You and the Feringhi have concluded a *gha* (treaty). Both letters agree. When you already have a settlement why do you ask for more. You must live in peace with others."[52]

The Nepali deputies argued that even if the Chinese could not provide assistance to Nepal, at least they should write Calcutta asking the British to withdraw their Residency from Kathmandu. The Chinese commander, however, remarked that "you have told us that the English entered your country for the sole purpose of establishing there a warehouse and on what plea can I attempt to remove merchants for such people are not molested in any country whatsoever." Dalbhunjun Pande replied: "if they were merely merchants it would be of no import but they are soldiers and commanders and what connexion have troops with merchants." The Chinese commander refused to agree to the Nepali request, and said:

The English have written to us that they sent their Resident with your consent. Therefore, at what have you to complain. And as to what your Rajah wrote about the English having demanded of him the roads through Bhote with the intention of penetrating into Bootun and China, it is false, for if they had those views they were not likely to go by Nipaul when they have less circuitous routes.[53]

The Company's Muslim agent, who was present at the meeting, reported that this concluded the interview.

The Chinese commander, however, did finally write Calcutta that "in consideration of the ties of friendship" between China and India, "it would be better and we should be inexpressibly grateful" if the British withdrew their Resident from Nepal.[54] In his reply, Moira said that he would be prepared to agree to this if China would station an agent in Kathmandu to prevent the re-

---

51 *Secret Consultation* No. 25: Oct. 12, 1816: Urzi from Nepal Raja to Emperor of China, dated Sept. 7, 1816.
52 C. R. Nepali, *Janaral Bhimsen, op. cit.*, appendix, p. 305: Letter from Ranbir Thapa to Bhim Sen dated Kartik Sudi 6, Day 7, V.E. 1873 (Oct. 26, 1816).
53 *Secret Consultation* No. 3: Jan. 11, 1817, *op. cit.*
54 *Secret Consultation* No. 6, Jan. 11, 1817: Letter received in Calcutta Dec. 28, 1816.

currence of disputes like those that had led to the recent hostilities. His government was not interested in seeking "to influence the Council of the Gorkha Government in any respect," the Governor-General asserted, noting that the Resident had been warned against interfering in Nepal's internal or foreign affairs.[55] The Chinese commander responded that there was no need to depute a Chinese agent to Kathmandu and thus tacitly accepted the British Residency there.[56]

The withdrawal of the Chinese force from Tibet in 1817 terminated this particular phase of Sino-British Indian relations, and not until about 50 years later did the Himalayan region once again figure prominently in the relations between the Chinese and the British. The war with Nepal and the establishment of a British Residency at Kathmandu marked the reemergence of the Company as an interested participant in trans-Himalayan developments. There was, however, a fundamental difference between British policy in Nepal in the post-1814 period and that of Warren Hastings three decades earlier. Hastings' interest in Nepal had been primarily a reflection of a desire to open Tibet and western China to British commerce, and this policy carried within itself the seeds of dispute between the Company and Peking. Such considerations, however, played no role in Calcutta's decision to resort to war against Nepal in 1814, nor did the Company even contemplate challenging China's predominant influence in Tibet, even indirectly, or altering the relationship between Nepal and China. Calcutta may have hoped that trans-Himalayan trade would develop, but this was at best a secondary consideration.

China's policy in these events was consistent with its broader goals in the Himalayan region. Tibet was an integral part of the Chinese frontier-security system, and Peking was prepared to react to the limit of its capacity to any challenge to its authority there. Nepal fell within a different category, however, and was "outside our borders," according to the Amban. In Peking's view the Kathmandu Darbar was an independent power unbound by any restrictions on its capacity to act in both domestic and foreign affairs except for its treaty obligation to dispatch periodic missions to China.[57]

---

[55] *Ibid.*, No. 7, Letter dated Jan. 11, 1817.

[56] *Ibid.*, No. 69, May 15, 1818: Letter received in Calcutta Feb. 19, 1818.

[57] Until 1912, Nepal's kings and prime ministers frequently received titles from the Chinese Emperor, but it is obvious that neither Nepal nor China considered these as necessary prerequisite to the assumption of office. Politically they might be of importance to the Nepali officeholder, but from the legal viewpoint they had no more significance than the British titles which these same officials received.

This brief episode in the history of the area demonstrated that the Himalayan region was still only a potential source of conflict between China and British India. Peking was interested in the maintenance of the *status quo* so far as its own rights were concerned, but nothing more. The British were not disposed to challenge China's status in the area, at least until matters within India had been thoroughly and favorably settled. Thus, Nepal's foreign policy in the post-1814 period, based on the principle of balancing British and Chinese power, could have only limited success, and then only because of Calcutta's reluctance to take positive action rather than any real balance of strength between Nepal's southern and northern neighbors.

POSTWAR POLITICS IN NEPAL

In contrast to the 1791–92 conflict, the Anglo-Nepali war did not lead to changes of leadership in Kathmandu. Bhim Sen Thapa's most serious rivals were Amar Singh Thapa and Rajguru Raghunath Pandit. The former died under rather mysterious circumstances in western Nepal in June 1816, reportedly while on his way to Tibet to solicit Chinese assistance. The latter was replaced as Rajguru by a Brahman family closely associated with the Thapas shortly after the ratification of the Sugauli treaty. Even more convenient for Bhim Sen was the death in November 1816 of Raja Girban Juddha (who had just reached his majority) and the succession of his two year-old son, Rajendra Bikram Shah. Queen Tripura Sundari was retained as Regent, thus assuring Bhim Sen of continued support in the royal palace.

Bhim Sen was not reconciled to the Sugauli treaty, and wasted little time before renewing his efforts to find external support against the Company. He even took advantage of the announcement of Raja Girban Juddha's death to the Emperor of China to make yet another appeal for support.[58] The reply from Peking however, merely instructed the infant Rajendra to "remain on good terms with his neighbours and attend to all matters with the utmost diligence."[59] Shortly thereafter, the still persistent Muktiyar instructed the regular quinquennial mission to China to make a personal appeal to the Emperor for assistance, but it met with the same negative result.[60]

---

[58] *Secret Consultation* No. 5, Jan. 11, 1817: Rajendra Bijkram Shah to the Chinese Emperor, Dec. 15, 1816.
[59] *Ibid.*, No. 31, July 5, 1817: Chinese Emperor to Rajendra, n.d.
[60] *Ibid.*, No. 16, Oct. 17, 1818: Gardner to Company, Sept. 21, 1818.

Bhim Sen also attempted to reestablish contacts with several of the Indian states in the context of the British-Mahratta war of 1817–18. The Nepali Darbar considered renewing hostilities with the British themselves, but the reverse suffered by the Mahrattas at Khodki in November 1817 dimmed any enthusiasm at Kathmandu for such a foolish venture. Nevertheless, the reorganization and expansion of Nepal's military capacity proceeded at a rapid pace, and Calcutta's expectation that the loss of the valuable Terai lands and Kumaun would force the Darbar to economize by reducing the military establishment proved wrong. Indeed, Bhim Sen's reforms of the revenue system and the revestment of large tracts of Birta (rent-free) holdings made it possible to establish several new regiments. By 1825 the Nepali Army was greatly strengthened both in size and efficiency over the force that had proved so troublesome to the British in the 1814–16 war.

Domestic political developments in Nepal in the 1830–37 period, however, forced Bhim Sen to modify his anti-British posture. The death of Regent Tripura Sundari in 1832 coincided with King Rajendra's attainment of his majority, thus removing two of the most important underpinnings of the Thapa family regime. Open opposition to the Muktiyar was expressed at the Darbar for the first time in two decades, and it was led by the royal family, the Kala Pandes, and the Brahman faction headed by Raghunath Pandit.

With the rapid deterioration of his internal position, Bhim Sen adopted the normal policy in Nepal in such circumstances—seeking external sources of support. An appeal to China would probably have been preferred, but the Muktiyar's experiences with the Peking court had convinced him that significant support from that direction would not be forthcoming.[61] The Company was the only real alternative, and by 1834 a significant change in Bhim Sen's foreign policy became apparent. The most dramatic demonstration of this was the dispatch of Mathbar Singh—the Minister's adopted son and most reliable supporter—to Calcutta with instructions to proceed to England. Bhim Sen's objectives were, first, to convince the British of the sincerity of his new foreign-policy tact and thus to forestall British support of his opponents, and secondly, to reemphasize to Nepal that it was his policy that had prevented more active British intervention in the country after the establishment of the Residency.

---

61 China's failure to aid Burma in the Anglo-Burmese war of 1824–26 probably convinced Bhim Sen of the futility of appealing to Peking for assistance against the British. In any case, no further letters directly attributable to the Muktiyar were sent to China requesting aid after that date.

Calcutta's initial response to Mathbar Singh's proposal to visit London had been favorable, but eventually it was decided to refuse him a passport and merely forward the letter he carried. Mathbar Singh spent nearly four months in Calcutta trying desperately to persuade the British to allow him to be the first high-caste Hindu official to proceed across the forbidden "Kali Pani" (black waters) during the British period, but to no avail. Mainly responsible for the failure of his project was the strong opposition of Brian Hodgson, the British Resident at Kathmandu, who viewed the overthrow of the Thapa regime as essential to the security of the British position in the frontier region.

Bhim Sen's political authority deteriorated rapidly after the failure of his overture to the British. Mathbar Singh had not been back from Calcutta more than a month before the opposition forces maneuvered his removal on a contrived sex-offense charge, thus depriving the Muktiyar of his right-hand man. Bhim Sen managed to gain reappointment as Muktiyar in the 1836 Panjani, but only after the open opposition at Court had been cowed by his still predominant influence with the army. The following year, King Rajendra, upon the death of his 6-month-old son, falsely accused the Muktiyar of having poisoned the child. Bhim Sen and most other leading members of the Thapa family were thereupon arrested and removed from office.

Bhim Sen having been overthrown, the opposition quickly split into contending factions—the royal family, the Chauntarias, the Raghunath Pandit Brahman group and the Kala Pandes—none of which were able to maintain a firm predominance for more than a short time. In the extremely complicated political intrigues that marked the period from 1837 to 1846, King Rajendra attempted to balance one faction against another, countenancing first one group and then, when they threatened his authority, throwing his support to their opponents. The result was a state of near-chaos at the Darbar, which on occasion threatened the very existence of the country.

Brian Hodgson's assumption that Bhim Sen's removal would allow the British to guide Nepal's foreign policy proved to be a grave miscalculation. As early as 1833, Bhim Sen had relegated the management of foreign affairs to King Rajendra as a concession to the latter's demand for greater participation in the administration.[62] Hodgson concluded that this was a purely nominal transference of authority and attributed responsibility for such diplomatic adventures as the Karbir Khattri mission to Lahore in 1834–35 to the Muktiyar rather than the Raja. The Resident dis-

---

[62] Baburam Acharya, "Bhimsen Thapa ko Patan," *op. cit.*

missed Bhim Sen's protestations of innocence as attempts to discredit the allegedly "pro-British" sentiments of the "royal party."[63] In retrospect, however, it is evident that Bhim Sen's private assurances to Hodgson that he was the Company's best friend in the Darbar were no exaggeration. The opposition played its hand with considerable skill, thanks primarily to Gujraj Misra's and Raghunath Pandit's ability to convince Hodgson that the royal party was "our natural allies." A change at court, Hodgson concluded, will probably be, both in its course and results, capable of being honourably and advantageously biased by us."[64] He would have been shocked to learn that at the same time that he was lauding the opposition in messages to Calcutta, an important leader of that group, Rana Jang Pande, was writing a private letter to the Chinese Emperor stating that "even now we can defeat them [the British] if the Emperor orders this to be done, if aid is given and we are restored to our forefathers' posts."[65]

Although the opposition-party factions headed by Raghunath Pandit and Fateh Jang Shah were more moderate than King Rajendra and the Pandes on foreign policy, they were decidedly in a minority in the new regime. Once the incubus of Bhim Sen's Muktiyarship had been removed, Rajendra renewed his efforts to create an anti-British alliance on a grander scale than ever. On July 14, 1837—before Bhim Sen's imprisonment but after he had lost effective control of the administration—Pushkar Shah set out for Peking on the regular quinquennial mission. He carried a letter to the Emperor in which Rajendra described Bhim Sen as a "pro-Feringhi Bharadar,"[66] and requested either troops or a subsidy of Rs. 20 million to oppose the British. He met with Peking's usual "stern refusal" of all requests "for monied aid, and countenance in furtherance of hostility by Nepal" against the Company.[67]

Once in office, the new regime initiated a vigorous diplomatic campaign. Envoys were sent out in all directions: in November 1837 to Nagpur; in January 1838 to Banaras, Rewa, Burma and Afghanistan; the following month to Allahabad, Bhurtapur and Udaipur (Rajasthan), Hyderabad, and Kuch Bihar (Assam); in March to Rewa, Banaras, Mathura, Lahore and Kotah; in April to Hardwar, Bhutan, Gwalior, Scindia, and Lahore again.[68] The

63 *Board's Collection* (IOL), vol. 1709: 1837–38: Hodgson to Calcutta, June 30, 1837.
64 *Political Consultation* No. 36, Dec. 12, 1836: Hodgson to Calcutta, Nov. 17, 1836.
65 C. R. Nepali, *Janaral Bhimsen, op. cit.*, p. 276: Rana Jang Pande to the Chinese Emperor, Dec. 26, 1835.
66 *Ibid.*, p. 277.
67 *Enclosure to Secret Letters: India*, vol. 49, 1838 (IOL): Hodgson to Calcutta, May 26, 1838.
68 This list was compiled from various British Indian records, the most important of

replies to the letters carried by the envoys were usually formal in tone and indicative of the extreme caution with which all rulers in the plains regarded anti-British conspiracies.

By the end of 1837, Hodgson was completely disillusioned with the party he had helped bring to power and was recommending a stern rebuke by Calcutta. Governor-General Auckland agreed that Nepal was the most dangerous enemy the British faced in India but asserted that this was not the time to seek a showdown. The C-in-C, General Fane, disagreed strongly, arguing that the Company had "allowed a thorn to grow in her side, which must greatly paralyze her efforts elsewhere: and which it behooves her to *pluck out and eradicate* at the earliest favorable moment."[69]

As Kathmandu's diplomatic activity continued unabated despite Hodgson's warnings, Calcutta decided in 1838 to post an "army of observation" on the border. Auckland told Hodgson that the army would not be used against Nepal because the campaign just commencing against Afghanistan "renders it inexpedient that we should seek to force on a crisis, at this time, in our relation with Kathmandoo."[70] But the mere threat of British intervention induced Kathmandu to curb its diplomatic initiatives. Hodgson was furnished with a list of 13 missions recalled to Nepal. This also coincided with the return of Pushkar Shah's mission from Peking with the discouraging news that China was still uninterested in backing Nepal against the Company.

A combination of events in 1839—including the British defeat in Afghanistan, the seizure of the throne of Burma by an avowed enemy of the British (who forced the retirement of the British Resident, much to Kathmandu's delight), and the deterioration of British-Chinese relations at Canton—led the Darbar to dispatch missions again in all directions. Auckland decided to defer any retaliatory action, merely noting that "the quarrel is ours, when we choose to enter on it."[71] On his instructions, however, Hodgson threatened war if the Darbar did not mend its ways. The court being rent by factional dissensions, King Rajendra had to agree to an "engagement" in which Nepal promised to "totally cease all secret intrigues whatever by messengers or letters" and "to have no further intercourse with dependent allies of the Company" without British permission.[72]

which were: *Enclosures to Secret Letters: India*, vol. 51, 1838: Col. Alves (Rajputana Agent) to Calcutta, June 27, 1838; *ibid.*, vol. 49, 1838: Hodgson to Calcutta, May 18, 1838; and *ibid.*, vol. 50, 1838, Hodgson to Calcutta, May 1, 1838.

[69] *Ibid.*, vol. 51, 1838: General Fane to Auckland, June 24. 1838.

[70] *Ibid.*, Auckland to Hodgson, Aug. 30, 1838.

[71] *Ibid.*, vol. 59, 1839: Auckland to Council, July 18, 1839.

[72] *Ibid.*, vol. 63, 1839: Hodgson to Calcutta, Nov. 8, 1839.

The crisis in British-Chinese relations in 1839–40 which led to the "Opium War" once again revived Kathmandu's aspirations for assistance from China. News of the dispute at Canton had an immediate impact at the Darbar as Rana Jang Pande, the most inveterate foe of the English, was appointed Muktiyar on February 8, 1840. Two days later, a letter was sent to the Emperor offering to attack the British in India.[73] The Amban refused to transmit the Nepali letter to Peking, however, and informed Kathmandu that the Chinese were perfectly capable of handling the British force then threatening Canton. In his report to Peking, he repeated the time-honored Chinese dictum that frontier states such as Nepal should "be maintained in the most perfect tranquility." On Peking's instructions, he advised the Nepalis to "rest on the defensive and live in harmony with your neighbors."[74] Obviously the last thing Peking wanted was trouble with the British on this distant section of the frontier when it already faced a major challenge in China proper.

The Chinese reverses in the "Opium War" encouraged the King and his Pande supporters to hope that Peking might have become more receptive to an anti-British alliance. Over the opposition of the Fateh Jang Shah ministry, Rajendra contrived the appointment of Jagat Bam Pande as leader of the 1842 quinquennial mission to China. The envoy left Kathmandu in July 1842 with a letter to the Emperor asking for troops or financial assistance to cope with that favorite Nepali bugaboo—an alleged British threat to invade Nepal if it refused to allow the transit of a British army to Tibet. Rajendra also proposed an exchange of the Tibetan district of Taklakot—with its gold deposits—for the vassal principality of Mustang in Nepal.[75] Still another proposal was made by Jagat Bam Pande, who suggested to the Amban a dual Tibetan-Nepali administration of Kerung and Kuti, under which Lhasa would administer these districts for ten years and Kathmandu for three years. Meng-pao's reply expressed amazement that Nepal would even presume to make such an outrageous proposition.[76] By the time Jagat Bam reached Peking, the "Opium War" had been settled, and China was appalled by the thought of disturbances in the Himalayan area. Meng-pao was instructed to reject Nepal's

---

[73] Meng-pao, *Si-Tsang Tsou-shu* (West Tibet Memorial Reports), Chuan 3. An unreliable translation of this letter is found in C. Imbault-Huart, "Un Episode des Relations Diplomatiques de la Chine avec le Népal en 1842," *op. cit.*, p. 9.

[74] Meng-pao, *op. cit.*

[75] Imbault-Huart, *op. cit.*, pp. 18–19: Rajendra to Chinese Emperor, July 1, 1842; and *Enclosures to Secret Letters: India*, vol. 88, 1842, No. 30: Nepal Political Diary, July 11, 1842.

[76] Meng-pao, *op. cit.*, pp. 43a–45b: Memorial to Emperor, Feb. 29, 1844.

request for assistance on the grounds that it was not China's policy "to send troops to protect the countries of the foreign barbarians," such as Nepal.[77]

NEPAL'S DOMESTIC CRISIS

The period from 1841 to 1846 was marked by disastrous internal instability in Nepal as the various contending factions struggled for power. King Rajendra, a resourceful but somewhat vacillating ruler, desperately attempted to play these factions off against each other to his own advantage. The Pandes had proven incapable of wielding power, and the Chountria-Brahman group was considered too subservient to the British Resident. Rajendra therefore invited Mathbar Singh, the adopted son of the hated Bhim Sen Thapa, to return to Nepal from his exile in India. In 1843, after lengthy negotiations, Mathbar Singh agreed to return on receiving a guarantee of personal safety from the King and a promise of his appointment as Muktiyar. On his demand, five of the leading Pandes were executed and several others, including the members of the quinquennial mission which was then on its way back from Peking, were exiled.

It was not long before a conflict of interest developed between the King and the Muktiyar, who seemed to be maneuvering Rajendra's abdication in favor of his 14-year-old son, Surendra Bikram Shah. The King finally turned to Jang Bahadur Kunwar, Mathbar Singh's nephew and supposedly staunchest supporter, for cooperation in the assassination of the ambitious Muktiyar on May 17, 1845. The political situation, which had shown signs of becoming stabilized under the Muktiyar's strong rule, relapsed immediately into a state of confusion which made another stormy upheaval inevitable.

It was also in 1845 that Calcutta decided to seek a showdown with Lahore, something which it had assiduously avoided during Ranjit Singh's lifetime. The British skillfully encouraged the struggle for power that ensued in the Panjab after Ranjit Singh's death in 1839 by throwing their weight against any faction that seemed on the verge of assuming a position of dominance there. By 1845, Afghanistan had been dealt with—although not entirely to the satisfaction of the British—and there was nothing to divert the Company from settling accounts with Lahore, particularly as Nepal, the only possible ally of the Sikh's, was itself riven with internal dissension.

---

[77] *Loc. cit.*, Peking memo to Meng-pao, n.d.

The news of the outbreak of the Sikh-British war in December 1845 temporarily revived Nepal's bellicose attitude towards Calcutta, but the series of defeats suffered by the Sikhs in the initial stages of the war turned this into deep concern over Nepal's own future. Once again, and for the last time until 1962, Nepal turned to China for assistance. The Amban's reply, which was approved by Peking, followed the pattern established earlier and instructed the Gorkhas to "maintain as much as possible good relations with them (Calcutta) and have no misunderstanding with them," while expressing doubts about the alleged British intentions to extend their conquests into Tibet.[78]

The years from 1816 to 1846 had been marked, then, by complete frustration for Nepal in the sphere of foreign policy. Attempts to weld the Indian states into an effective anti-British alliance had been disastrously unsuccessful, and Nepal found itself, by 1846, the only independent Hindu state in South Asia. It appeared to be only a matter of time before Nepal, too, would be absorbed into the ever-growing British Empire in India. Moreover, Nepal's attempts to arouse Chinese anxieties over possible British trans-Himalayan expansion had met with little response. China was hard-pressed to defend the heartland of its Empire from the encroachment of the Westerners and had little strength to spare to meet a challenge on its outer periphery. Chinese policy, aimed at reducing conflict potentialities in this area, could only view with distaste any proposals that might lead to a Nepali-British war. Moreover, China's reputation had suffered greatly because of its humiliating defeat in the "Opium War." By 1846, Kathmandu realized that all its potential allies in India had come under British dominance and that China was both unable and unwilling to provide the type of assistance required to preserve Nepal against British expansion. Under these circumstances a new foreign policy was an obvious necessity, and the period 1846–58 was to witness the emergence of novel policy concepts that basically altered Nepal's role in Himalayan politics.

---

[78] *Ch'ou-Pan-I-Wu Shih-Mo* (Documents concerning the Management of Foreign Affairs), Peiping, Palace Museum, 1930, vol. 38, chuan 75, pp. 24a–26a: Petition: Rajendra to Chinese Emperor, Feb. 13, 1846; and Letter from Chinese Amban to Rajendra, n.d.

Part III
The Emergence of a New Pattern of Inter-Himalayan Relations, 1846-1945

5

Foreign-Policy Innovations Under Jang Bahadur Rana

THE decimation of the Pande family in 1843 and the assassination of Mathbar Singh Thapa in 1845 eliminated two of the principal factions in Nepal and opened the way for several new contenders for power. The year following Mathbar Singh's death was one of political near-chaos, marked by a bitter struggle for the mantle of authority formerly monopolized by the Thapas and Pandes. There were many familiar faces: the royal family, divided into factions centered around King Rajendra, Crown Prince Surendra and Queen Lakshmi Devi; the Chauntrias, led by Fateh Jang Shah and Pushkar Shah; and the Brahmans, with Raghunath Pandit and his brother exercising a strong influence. In addition, there were some new contenders, including the Kunwar family under Jang Bahadur, and the Basnyet family.

A crisis was reached on September 14, 1846, with the assassination of Gagan Singh, the Queen's principal supporter (and rumored paramour). In a state of fury, the Queen summoned all the important political leaders to the Kot courtyard adjoining the Palace. Charges and counter-charges were hurled back and forth indiscriminately, culminating in the massacre of most of the rivals of Jang Bahadur Kunwar and his brothers. More than thirty officials lost their lives, including Fateh Jang Shah, Khadga Bikram Shah and Narahari Bikram Shah of the Chauntria faction, General Abhiman Singh, Dalbhanjan Pande and Rana Gambhir Pande of the Gora Pande faction, and several Thapas. All of Jang Bahadur's major rivals were either killed or expelled from Nepal shortly thereafter, and Jang Bahadur, on September 16, 1846, was appointed Mukhtiyar by King Rajendra.

The following month it was the turn of the Basnyet family to be eliminated from competition. Several of its members were accused of conspiring with the Queen and were summarily executed by the Minister, and the Queen was exiled to Banaras for her part in this affair. A short time later she was followed by her husband, who found that Jang Bahadur had consolidated power in his own hands and was disinclined to accept orders from his nominal sovereign. The King quickly became the focal point for the opposition to the Minister. Most of the recent exiles joined his camp in India in the hope that Rajendra would duplicate the feat of his grandfather, Rana Bahadur Shah. Jang Bahadur, aware of this precedent, attempted to undermine Rajendra's legal position by deposing the King and raising Crown Prince Surendra Bikram Shah to the throne. Rajendra later led a small army across the Nepal border, but he was defeated and was imprisoned in the old royal palace at Bhaktapur to prevent him from interfering in Nepali politics.

Surendra was incapable of handling the strong-willed and ruthless Jang Bahadur, and soon became nothing more than a pawn of the minister. In 1846 a *sanad* (decree) granted Jang Bahadur what amounted to absolute authority. From that time until 1951, the Kunwar family (later given the heroic appellation "Rana" by Surendra) monopolized all governmental authority in Nepal, and the royal family was reduced to the role of a figurehead.

Jang Bahadur's rise to power resulted in a major redefinition of Nepal's foreign policy toward both China and British India. The minister, an eminently practical politician, was well aware of the rapid decline of Chinese power and recognized that distant Peking was neither willing nor able to challenge the British in the Himalayan area. The stream of appeals that had been directed to Peking since the time of Rana Bahadur terminated abruptly after Jang Bahadur's appointment as Muktiyar. Seldom again did any Nepali official seriously contemplate the utilization of China as a counter balance to British power, although Nepal's "traditional" relationship with Peking was retained. Jang Bahadur realized that the basically anti-British policy followed by Rajendra, and supported to a greater or lesser degree by most of the Darbar, would no longer be tolerated by Calcutta. It was essential to have British good will if Nepal were to avoid the fate that had recently overtaken the last of the major Indian states, the Sikh kingdom in the Panjab. This was a bitter pill, but Jang Bahadur accepted its inevitability and thereafter determined his whole course of conduct accordingly.

By 1850, the reorientation of Nepali foreign policy was given additional emphasis with Jang Bahadur's visit to England—the first Hindu "prince" in modern times to undergo the "forbidden" trip across the "black waters." What he saw in England strengthened his view that British rule in India could not be easily overthrown and that it would be futile and dangerous for Nepal to intrigue or participate in intrigues with this as an object. This perspective helped shape Nepal's important role in subsequent events on the plains of India.

RELATIONS WITH PEKING

One of the side effects of Jang Bahadur's rise to power in 1846 was the decision to cancel the quinquennial mission to Peking scheduled to depart in 1847. The reasons for this are not readily ascertainable. It is possible that Jang Bahadur, aware of Calcutta's concern over the 1837 and 1842 embassies, was anxious to avoid adding fuel to the fire. The presence on Indian soil of many Nepali refugees made it imperative for Jang Bahadur to exercise considerable discretion in order to deter the British from supporting his enemies. In these circumstances the minister may have felt that discretion required an interruption in Nepal's normal relationship with China.

Whatever Jang Bahadur's reasons may have been in 1847, the circumstances five years later were different, and Jang Bahadur decided to renew the customary missions to Peking. A major consideration was the seething unrest then prevalent in China, which burst forth in the Taiping rebellion, a conflagration that was to tear China apart for nearly fifteen years. Nepal's interests required first-hand knowledge of these traumatic developments in China. Moreover, the mission would mollify to some extent those Nepalis who had opposed the minister's trip to England in 1851 and were unhappy with the general direction of his foreign policy. Although Jang Bahadur was not disposed to look to China for assistance against the British, he did realize that Nepal's relationship with Peking had served as an effective deterrent to the British in the past and could still be exploited profitably. Finally, there were important economic considerations: missions to China always had a commercial as well as a political character since they were allowed to carry commodities for trading purposes free of any duties or other restrictions. For instance, opium worth nearly Rs. 300,000 was sent to China with the 1852 mission under its diplomatic privileges despite the legal ban on the entry of this commodity into China.[1]

The mission, headed by Gambir Singh, left Kathmandu in August 1852, reached Peking on schedule, and was received with the usual formalities and friendliness.[2] Gambir Singh and his second in command both died in Peking, and the leadership of the mission passed to a junior officer, Lt. Bhim Sen Rana. By the time the mission left Peking, the Taiping rebellion had reached alarming proportions, and Lt. Rana was forced to follow an indirect route to Tibet. By some Nepali accounts, the mission suffered indignities and maltreatment on the return journey, particularly in the Kham areas of eastern Tibet. Contemporary British Residency records, which reported the arrival of the mission in Kathmandu on May 22, 1854, indicate that this had not been the case.[3] It appears that Jang Bahadur later attempted to use the alleged maltreatment of the mission as one of the rationalizations for the invasion of Tibet in 1854. On one occasion, Jang Bahadur even ascribed the death of the two leaders of the mission to the Khampas until he was politely reminded by the British Resident of the letter from Lt. Rana reporting their demise from natural causes in Peking.[4]

CONFRONTATION WITH TIBET

Between 1792 and 1846, Nepal had followed a noninterventionist policy toward Tibet, usually settling disputes as they arose through the mediation of the Amban or through joint negotiations with the Tibetans.[5] By 1853, however, it was obvious that the time had come to review Nepal's long-dormant but not forgotten claims and goals in Tibet. The Ch'ing dynasty in China was involved in a desperate struggle for survival against the Taiping rebels, and

---

[1] *Secret Consultation* No. 50, May 26, 1854: Ramsay to GOI, May 6, 1854 (report on a conversation with Jang Bahadur).

[2] The British Resident reported the rumor that the Chinese Emperor had indignantly refused the Nepali presents on the grounds that Jang Bahadur had gone to England personally to give presents to Queen Victoria and should also have come to China. The Emperor supposedly threatened war on this issue. The Resident thought this implausible as he was shown a letter from the Envoys describing the kind reception they had received in Peking. (*Secret Consultation* No. 50, May 26, 1854.) It seems highly unlikely that Peking, plagued by massive internal dissension, would have even contemplated a war against Nepal for so inconsequential a reason.

[3] *Secret Consultation* No. 42, June 20, 1854: Ramsay to GOI, May 25, 1854.

[4] *Secret Consultation* No. 27, Dec. 29, 1854: Ramsay to Calcutta, Oct. 24, 1858.

[5] See, for instance, the agreement on import duties signed in 1847. Government of Nepal (GON), [Kaushi Tosha Khana, 1904 V.S. (1847 A.D.) as ctied in B. P. Poudel, *Nepal's Relation with Tibet 1792–1856*), unpublished Ph.D. dissertation.]

British attention was concentrated on the war with Russia in the Crimea. Neither power thus was in position to intervene forcefully in the Himalayan area. The internal situation in Tibet was also encouraging. The Sixth Panchen Lama had died the previous year and the Eleventh Dalai Lama was still a minor. The Regent at Lhasa, Yeshi Gyatso Rating, was not a strong figure, and relations between the Dalai Lama's officials and the Kashag, dominated by Kalon Shatra, were often strained. Moreover, some Tibetan factions hoped to use the Taiping rebellion to eliminate the few remaining vestiges of Chinese authority in Tibet, and were prepared to seek Nepal's assistance in this if necessary. During his stopover in Lhasa in 1854 on his return journey from Peking, for instance, Lt. Rana had been told by the Kalons that if the Manchus were overthrown, Tibet would refuse to establish a similar relationship with the successor government in China.[6]

The domestic political situation in Nepal may also have encouraged Jang Bahadur to seek a confrontation with Tibet. His position was not unlike that which Bahadur Shah had faced in 1791. The only real threat to the Minister's authority was the presence on the throne of an antagonistic if submissive ruler who could become the rallying point of a movement of resistance to the Rana family regime. Like Bahadur Shah, Jang Bahadur may have hoped that a successful war against Tibet would provide the occasion for the removal of the reigning monarch and his own assumption of the throne.[7]

Thus, never before had circumstances seemed so favorable or the dangers so minimal for the pressing of Nepali objectives in an "unprotected" Tibet. The decision must have been made by early 1854, for it was at this time that extensive and expensive preparations for war were begun in Nepal. Jang Bahadur tried to disguise these to the suspicious British authorities in India by claiming that China had requested Kathmandu's assistance in the suppression of the Taiping rebellion.[8] After the return of the Nepali quinquennial mission in May 1854, however, the masquerade was dropped. Calcutta was informed of the decision to invade Tibet if Nepal's "just demands" were not granted.[9]

Jang Bahadur advanced various reasons for the dispute with Tibet, including (1) the alleged abuse of the Nepali mission to Peking by Khampas; (2) the maltreatment of Newari traders at

---

6 *Secret Counsultation* No. 50, Aug. 25, 1854: Ramsay to Calcutta, Aug. 5, 1854.
7 Baburam Acharya, "Rana Shahi ra Shadyantra" (Rana Rule and Conspiracy), *Sharada*, I:5 (February–March, 1957), pp. 1–2.
8 *Secret Consultation* No. 51, May 26, 1854: Ramsay to Calcutta, May 6, 1854.
9 *Ibid.*, No. 42, June 30, 1854: Ramsay to Calcutta, May 25, 1854.

Lhasa; (3) expulsion of the Nepali representative (*Nayak*) from Lhasa on insufficient grounds; (4) a boundary dispute in the Kuti area; and (5) the imposition of higher customs duties on imports from Nepal. This list of grievances scarcely added up to a *casus belli*, and indeed most of the points at issue had been settled to the Nepal government's satisfaction at least several months before the outbreak of hostilities. The 1855–56 war was, therefore, an unprovoked act of aggression on Nepal's part. Kathmandu's objectives were far more fundamental than those implied in the Minister's allegations, and even included the ambition to assume China's traditional role as the "protector" of Tibet.

In early 1855 the Nepal Darbar decided to launch a summer military campaign in Tibet if Lhasa did not agree to Kathmandu's extravagant terms: (1) payment of ten million rupees to Nepal in "damages" for the various iniquities suffered by Nepalis at the hands of Tibetan officials; (2) cession of the Taklakot area in western Tibet;[10] and (3) restoration of those sections of Kuti and Kerong districts that had once belonged to Nepal—i.e., the areas to the south of the Bhairab Langur range, the true watershed between the river systems running north into Tibet and south into Nepal. The Ambans and Tibetans were informed that they had until "Baisakh 15" (April 17, 1855) to accept Kathmandu's term, otherwise the Nepali army would advance into Tibet and the price for a settlement would rise correspondingly.[11]

The Tibetan government immediately sent Palden Dondup, the Treasurer of Ganden Monastery and a cohort of Kalon Shatra, to Kathmandu. In a final effort to avert hostilities, Dondup promised that all Nepali subjects residing in Tibet would thenceforth be treated fairly. In reply, however, Jang Bahadur merely repeated the demands listed in his letters to the Kashag. The Lama was not authorized to make such concessions, and left Kathmandu, stating that if he had not returned within the stipulated time period, Nepal should consider this as a rejection of its terms. Palden Dondup failed to reappear, and Jang Bahadur ordered the Nepali army to start hostilities.

In early April Nepali troops launched attacks across the major passes between the two states—from Walungchung in the east to Jara (Taklakot) in the west—the main assaults being centered in

---

10 The demand for the cession of Taklakot was repeated on several occasions during the course of the war. From the Nepali archival records, however, it is unclear whether this referred only to the area around Taklakot or to the vast province of West Tibet from the Mayum pass to the Ladakh border.

11 GON, *Jaisi Kotha Records*: Letters from Jang Bahadur to the Ambans and to the Tibetan Kashag, Feb. 15, 1855.

Kuti and Kerong districts. The first battle occurred on April 3 at Chusan on the Kuti front, where the Nepalis under Dhir Shamsher (Jang Bahadur's brother) defeated a small Tibetan detachment and captured Kuti. The Nepalis advanced as far as Suna Gompa, nine miles above Kuti, where they halted to await further developments. Meanwhile Kerong had been occupied without opposition by the main Nepali army under another of Jang Bahadur's brothers, Bam Bahadur. A Tibetan force at Kukurghat, two days' march to the north of Kerong, was routed, and the Nepali army pushed on to Dzongka, the principal defense position in that area. After a fierce 9-day battle in the latter part of April, the Tibetans were expelled from the fort and forced to retreat to Tingri.

To all intents and purposes, this ended the campaign for the summer of 1855. The Ambans and Kalon Shatra both wrote to the Nepal Darbar in July suggesting a cease-fire until a peace settlement had been negotiated. Jang Bahadur was only too ready to agree,[12] as the campaign had proven far more expensive and difficult than Kathmandu had calculated. The Minister informed the British Resident that he realized that Nepal's initial terms were unrealistic; he would be satisfied with something less than ten million rupees in compensation, he said, but would continue to demand the cession of the four districts in the Kuti and Kerong area to the south of the Bhairab Langur range.

One of the more disturbing aspects of the war to Jang Bahadur was the reaction of Tibetan civil officialdom. According to Nepali sources, Kalon Shatra had agreed not to resist the seizure of Kuti and Kerong districts, and in turn Nepal had ordered its troops to refrain from any looting or shooting unless attacked.[13] It came as an unpleasant surprise to the Nepalis, therefore, when the Kalon sent reinforcements to Dzongka and ordered the garrison to resist the invaders. What induced the Tibetan authorities to reverse their position—if indeed they had actually agreed to a virtual disengagement—is not clear, but the complexities inherent in the monastic-civil-Chinese interrelationship must have made an easy submission to Nepal's terms impossible.

The posture of the Amban in these confusing developments was presumptuous to the point of absurdity. His influence over the Tibetan lay and secular establishments had declined drastically

---

[12] GON, *Jaisi Kotha Records*: Letters from Kalon Shatra to Jang Bahadur, Ashadh Sudi 5, V.E. 1912 (July 19, 1855); and from Bam Bahadur to Kalon Shatra, Bhadra Badi 5, V.E. 1912 (Sept. 1, 1855).

[13] *Ibid.*, Jagat Shamsher to Jang Bahadur, Baisakh Badi 12, V.E. 1912 (Apr. 14, 1855); and *ibid.*, Jang Bahadur to Khadga Kunwar, Chaitra Sudi 12, V.E. 1911 (Mar. 30, 1855).

since 1793, and his advice was often not sought or was ignored if given gratuitously. The Taiping rebellion eliminated even the threat of Chinese military intervention in the Himalayan area. Nepal and Tibet could now proceed to settle their affairs without excessive concern over Peking's attitude, as the Amban's threats to call in Chinese armies were recognized as an empty gesture. Indeed, the Chinese were hard put to retain any position of influence in Tibet, as there was a substantial body of opinions at both Lhasa and Kathmandu favoring their expulsion from the area. Fortunately for the Amban, there were also strong factions in several monastic institutions and at Shigatse who preferred to retain a nominal Chinese presence in Tibet as a counter to their political rivals in the Lhasa administration. Of equal importance, perhaps, was the Amban's unique position, which allowed him to serve as a mediator—but not arbitrator—in disputes between Nepal and Tibet.

Negotiations between Jang Bahadur's emissary, Subha Siddhiman, and the Chinese and Tibetan officials began in Lhasa in May 1855. Tibet was prepared to pay damages amounting to 233,000 "Kala mohurs" but was not willing to cede any territory to Nepal. Subha Siddhiman had been instructed to insist upon Kathmandu's terms, and therefore withdrew without an agreement having been reached. Palden Dondup and a Chinese officer were thereupon sent to the border, with 15,423 silver coins as a first installment in the payment of damages to Nepal and with a letter from the Amban threatening Nepal with various dire consequences if the Darbar refused to accept his terms.[14]

A series of Bharadari (Council) meetings were held in early July, while the Tibetan delegation was on its way to Kathmandu. Jang Bahadur convinced the Darbar that more advantageous terms would be obtained from Tibet than those proposed in the Amban's letter. The Tibetan and Chinese deputies were informed that there was no need to proceed further unless they were prepared to accept Nepal's demands.[15] The envoys went on to Kathmandu, however, and arrived there in the latter half of July. Discussions were carried on for several days, but neither side was willing to make the concessions demanded by the other. The deputation returned to Tibet in August 1855, accompanied by a Nepali Bharadar, Til Bikram Thapa, who had been instructed to continue the talks with the Tibetan and Chinese authorities at Shekar Dzong.

Opposition to the war was increasing in Nepal and discontent

---

14 *Ibid.*, Amban to King Surendra, June 24, 1855.
15 *Secret Consultation* No. 60, Aug. 31, 1855: Ramsay to Calcutta, July 12, 1855.

was widespread in both the army and the public. The difficulties of the summer campaign had quickly disillusioned the military of any expectation of an easy victory, and there was little enthusiasm for a renewal of hostilities. The vast number of porters required to maintain the supply lines to Tibet— estimated at nearly 400,000— deprived many areas of the country of all casual labor and hampered agricultural production. Prices rose rapidly, and the shortage of salt, normally obtained from Tibet, was particularly irksome. Jang Bahadur told Ramsay that he was aware of the unpopularity of the war and admitted that he had difficulty convincing the army and the officials that it had been necessary or that there had been no opportunity to end it except on disgraceful terms.[16]

Jang Bahadur did not seriously contemplate a second campaign in Tibet for, as he later admitted to Ramsay, the first campaign had cost so much in money and supplies that it would be four years at least before Nepal was capable of mounting a further penetration into Tibet.[17] The Minister hoped that if a threatening posture were maintained in Kuti and Kerung, the Tibetans and Chinese would be induced to concede more favorable terms than those yet offered. He admitted, however, that the occupation of those four Tibetan districts cost far more than was gained in revenue, and that Nepal could not long maintain this position unless the occupation was accepted by the Tibetans.[18]

The failure of the talks between Til Bikram Thata and the Tibetans in September 1855 led to a renewal of hostilities, but this time it was the Tibetans, under the vigorous leadership of Kalon Shatra, who took the initiative.[19] On November 5, attacks were launched simultaneously on the main Nepali camps at Kuti and at Dzongka in Kerung. The Kuti assault caught the Nepali garrison completely by surprise, and over 700 men were killed and the rest were forced to flee to Nepali soil. The attack on Dzongka was not as successful, but the garrison there was closely besieged and all communication with Nepal was cut off. The Tibetans had carefully timed the attacks to coincide with heavy snowfall in the Himalayan passes, but Jang Bahadur wasted no time in dispatching new armies in both directions. In December, Dhir Shamsher moved against the Tibetan force at Kuti and Col. Sanak Singh Khattri (a brother-in-law of Jang Bahadur) led the relief army towards Dzong-

---

16 *Secret Consultation* No. 81, Nov. 30, 1855; Ramsay to Calcutta, Oct. 12, 1855.
17 *Ibid.*, No. 45, Aug. 29, 1856: Ramsay to Calcutta, July 15, 1856.
18 *Ibid.*, No. 64, July 27, 1855: Ramsay to GOI, June 22, 1855.
19 Jang Bahadur complained bitterly about the treachery of the Tibetans in launching these attacks, claiming that they violated the cease-fire agreement. See GON, *Jaisi Kotha Records*, Letters from Jang Bahadur to Kalon Shatra, Magh Dadi 1, V.E. 1912 (Jan. 23, 1856).

ka. Dhir Shamsher recaptured Kuti, burned the town and then retired to Listi, well within the Nepal border. The siege of Dzongka was raised by Sanak Singh, but the Nepalis could not prevent the concentration of a strong Tibetan force in the immediate vicinity of the fortress.

After the virtual military stalemate that ensued, negotiations were renewed. In January 1856, a deputation consisting of Palden Dondup, the Kalon Shatra's son, and several officials of the Dharma Raja of Bhutan came to the border for talks with Jang Bahadur's brother, Jagat Shamsher Kunwar. The failure of their winter offensive to expel the Nepali forces from Tibet, combined with the threat of a revolt against Lhasa in Kham, placed the Tibetans in a precarious situation. Kathmandu was also more disposed to be reasonable, as the winter campaign had placed an almost unbearable strain on Nepal's resources. The claim for Rs. ten million in compensation was reduced to a demand for a nominal annual payment to Nepal, and all territorial demands were dropped. Palden Dondup was prepared to accept an obligation to pay Nepal Rs. 1,200 annually for 100 years—even though the Amban had advised against such a procedure—and agreed to the terms proposed by Kathmandu on other questions, such as trade relations and the position of Nepali subjects in Tibet.[20]

These concessions, though welcome, were considered inadequate by the Darbar. Kalon Shatra thereupon decided to come to Nepal himself for further negotiations, which were carried on through February and most of March before an agreement was reached. Probably the most notable feature of the settlement was the fact that its provisions were, in some respects, considerably less favorable to Nepal than Tibet had been willing to concede some months earlier. The terms of the draft agreement were, in summary:

1) The Tibetan Government committed itself to make an annual payment of Rs. 10,000 to Nepal.
2) Nepal promised to come to the aid of the Tibetans if they were attacked by any other "Rajah."
3) Lhasa agreed not to levy duties on commodities brought into Tibet by Nepali subjects.
4) Tibet consented to return the "Sikh" prisoners who had been captured in the 1841 war between Tibet and the Dogra ruler of Kashmir, and Nepal agreed to return all Tibetan prisoners. Nepal also was to withdraw from the Tibetan territory it had occupied.
5) Nepal would be permitted to install a "Bharadar" (i.e., envoy) in Lhasa.

---

[20] *Ibid.*, Jagat Shamsher to Jang Bahadur, Magh Badi 3, V.E. 1912 (Jan. 25, 1856).

6) Nepal was granted the right to establish a trading establishment at Lhasa for the sale of all kinds of merchandise.
7) The Nepal representative at Lhasa was granted the right to adjudicate disputes between Nepalis, Kashmiris and other non-Tibetans in Lhasa. When subjects of Nepal and Tibet were involved in a dispute, the two authorities would jointly settle the case.
8) The two Governments agreed to the mutual surrender of murderers.
9) Tibet was made responsible for the life and property of Nepali subjects in Lhasa. Similarly, Nepal was made responsible for the protection of Tibetans in Nepal.
10) The persons and property of subjects of Gorkha or Tibet who had collaborated with the enemy during the war were to be respected by both Governments.[21]

The first clause of the treaty was the face-saving provision so far as Nepal was concerned, for it made Tibet into a "tributary" state in Kathmandu's interpretation of the terminology. The annual payment was far less than Jang Bahadur had hoped to wring from Lhasa, and did not even begin to compensate Nepal for the heavy expenses of the war—Rs. 2,683,568, according to one source.[22] The Darbar's insistence upon this arrangement should not be viewed in economic terms, however, but rather from the standpoint of the traditional Nepali comprehension of the intrinsic character of interstate relations.

The principle of the sovereign equality of states in the comity of nations, which is essentially Occidental in origin, had not yet made a significant impact on the Nepali world view. On the contrary, relations between states were typically conceived in terms of a superior/inferior syndrome, and equality was possible only when states were too distant to be in contact. It had not been difficult for Nepal to accept a nominally inferior status vis-à-vis China when that state exercised a substantial influence in Tibet. But by the middle of the 19th century the situation had changed, and there are indications within the treaty that Kathmandu's view of Nepali-Chinese relations had also been modified. In the 1856 treaty, for instance, the same honorific—Shri Panch—was employed in reference to both the Emperor of China and the King of Nepal, placing them on a level of equality.

Tibet, on the other hand, was assigned a status inferior to that of both Nepal and China in the treaty, the honorific used in references to the Dalai Lama's government being the decidedly more modest "Shri Sarkar." The annual-payment provision reinforced Nepal's claim to a superior status, as did the second clause in the

---

[21] *Secret Consultation* No. 27, May 30, 1856: text of proposed treaty.
[22] Buddhiman Singh, *Vamsavali*, Nepali chronological manuscript.

treaty, which in effect made Kathmandu the "protector" of Tibet, presumably supplanting China in this role. Indeed, Jang Bahadur told the British Resident that he had agreed to this clause because he assumed that one of the first acts of Kalon Shatra would be "to play false with the Umbah (Amban) and to call upon the Goorkas to assist the Tibetans in throwing off the Chinese yoke."[23] Nepal would then be in position to subvert the authority of the Amban and replace it with that of the Nepali envoy in Lhasa.

The fourth clause of the treaty was included at the request of the British, acting on behalf of Maharaja Gulab Singh of Kashmir to rescue those "Sikhs" (i.e., presumably Dogras) who had been made prisoner in Tibet in 1841. The third, sixth, seventh and ninth clauses were advantageous to the Nepali merchants residing in Tibet, granting them the right to trade in all types of merchandise, exempting them from the payment of duties, and bestowing extra-territorial rights on Nepali subjects in Tibet. The tenth provision was inserted at Jang Bahadur's insistence to protect the inhabitants of Kuti and Kerung who had assisted Nepal during the war.

Jang Bahadur wrote the Amban on March 24, 1856—immediately after the signing of the draft treaty—requesting his formal sanction of the agreement. A few days later he received what he termed an "overbearing and imperious" reply in which the Amban ordered Nepal to submit the treaty for his approval and reserved a veto right. The Minister was incensed and immediately sent for the Tibetan delegates. An altercation occurred at this meeting which led the deputation to request permission to quit Kathmandu. Jang Bahadur, suspecting collusion between the Tibetans and Chinese to prolong negotiations, threatened an invasion of Tibet the following year if the treaty was not ratified. The Tibetan delegation left Kathmandu, and shortly thereafter Jang Bahadur sent Col. Jodh Bikram Thapa to Shekar Dzong to consult with the Amban. The Colonel was told to reject any substantive amendments the Chinese might suggest but was authorized to add complimentary or friendly expressions toward the Chinese Emperor, if requested by the Amban.[24]

CHINESE ROLE IN THE PEACE NEGOTIATIONS

The Chinese officials at Shekar Dzong—the Amban had already returned to Lhasa—first objected to the "tribute" and the "custom duty" clauses. They held that as both governments were tributary

---

23 *Secret Consultation* No. 26, May 30, 1856: Ramsay to GOI, Apr. 2, 1856.
24 *Ibid.*, No. 26, May 30, 1856: Ramsay to GOI, Apr. 2, 1856.

to China it was improper for Tibet to become also a tributary of Nepal. Furthermore, they argued, Nepal should make the same concessions on duties as Tibet. But when these points were rejected by Jang Bahadur, the Chinese asked Col. Thapa if Nepal had been fighting against China or only Tibet and whether the Darbar still respected the Emperor! The envoy replied that Nepal had suffered no provocation from China and had warred only against Tibet. When Col. Thapa agreed to add a statement to the treaty asserting that Nepal would continue to respect the Emperor, the Chinese Amban's seal was added to the document.

There were, in fact, two significant modifications in the treaty as approved by the Amban. The first was the addition of a preamble referring to the Chinese Emperor, the wording of which has been the subject of considerable controversy ever since. Several translations of the treaty from both the Tibetan and Nepali texts have used the expression that the Emperor "shall continue to be regarded with respect," whereas others have translated the preamble as "the Emperor of China shall be obeyed by both states as before."[25] In the official Nepali text of the treaty, the relevant terminology is: "lāi aghi dekhi māni āyā Bamojim māne rahanu."[26] This is properly translated as "will be respected (or honored) as he has been respected (or honored) in the past," and does not connote "shall be obeyed."

The second article of the treaty was also revised, to read:

Tibet and Gorkha have both respected the Emperor of China up to the present time. As Tibet is a land of monasteries and shrines [devoted to] penance and worship, if any other Raja should invade Tibet, Gorkha will give as much assistance as possible.

This modification was considered important by the Chinese for, in their view, it eliminated the possibility that Nepal would be obligated to come to Lhasa's assistance if on some occasion Chinese troops should invade Tibet. The Tibetans did not accept this interpretation of the treaty and on at least two occasions, in 1910 and 1950, tried to put the clause into operation against an invading Chinese Army. As might be expected, Nepal's interpretation of this clause was flexible, depending upon the circumstances.

---

25 For instance, Landon uses the "regarded with respect" version (*op. cit.*, II, appendix XXII, p. 282), whereas Aitchison translates it as "shall be obeyed" (*op. cit.*, XIV). 26 *Itihas Prakas*, *op. cit.*, vol. II, pp. 118–21: Nepali text of the treaty of Thapathali, 1856. Sir Charles Bell used a Tibetan text for his translation of the 1856 treaty, and translated this phrase as "regarded with respect" (*op. cit.*, appendix IV, p. 278). Another translation of the Tibetan text was made by Major W. F. O'Connor at the time of the Younghusband expedition. In both the preamble and clause 2, he used the phrase "paying respect . . . to the Chinese Emperor." [*Secret Dept., Political and Secret Letters from India*, Apr. 14, 1910 (IOL).]

A copy of the treaty with the Amban's seal was brought back to Kathmandu by Col. Thapa, and another copy, with the seals of the four Kalons of the Kashag and thirteen other Tibetan officials, was enclosed in a letter from Kalon Shatra.[27] The letter from the Amban repeated his objections to the first and third clauses but stated that he had been persuaded to give his assent by the Tibetan officials "who are anxious for peace."[28] The letter recommended that Jang Bahadur address the Emperor of China upon the subject and communicate to him an account of all that had taken place.

AFTERMATH OF THE NEPALI-TIBETAN WAR

Jang Bahadur held a grand Darbar to celebrate the ratification of the treaty. He is reported to have declared:

Soldiers, officers, and brothers. You have, by your late achievements, fully realized my hopes of you, and I do not know how to thank you except by wishing you continued glory and success. Your indomitable valour has caused the snow to melt, and the mountains to bend down their heads before you. The Tibetans who had laughed at us have, by your brave arms, been scattered like a flock of sheep across the Bhairav Sarpoor. They who contemned us have sued us for peace; and peace has been granted on terms most favourable to your country.[29]

Even allowing for oratorical license this statement is somewhat of an exaggeration. It is recorded that the soldiers loudly cheered when the treaty was read to them, but as the terms themselves would scarcely have induced such enthusiasm, it may have been due to a sense of relief that another difficult and wearisome campaign in Tibet was not an immediate prospect.

The political repercussions in Nepal in the wake of the 1855–56 war were in no way comparable to those that followed the 1791–93 war. Most of the potential rivals of Jang Bahadur had been disposed of earlier or, like the Pandes, were in ineffectual exile in India. Surendra Bikram Shah, undoubtedly the weakest and least competent of his dynasty to occupy the throne since the time of Prithvi Narayan, was totally incapable of handling Jang Bahadur in the same manner that his great-grandfather, Rana Bahadur, had dealt with Bahadur Shah in 1794 and Damodar Pande in 1804.

The war did have an indirect influence on Nepali politics, however. If the war and the 1856 treaty had been an indisputable

---

27 GON, *Jaisi Kotha Records*: Kalon Shatra to Jang Bahadur, June 21, 1856.
28 *Secret Consultation* No. 49, Aug. 29, 1856: As quoted by Ramsay in a report to Calcutta dated July 28, 1856.
29 Pudma Jang, *op. cit.*, p. 191.

triumph for Jang Bahadur, it is probable that the minister would have used the occasion to remove the Shahs from the throne and establish his own family as the reigning dynasty. Indeed, this might have occurred anyway had there not been strong opposition from Jang Bahadur's brothers. The minister had promised that succession to the ministerial post would be based on the agnate principle —i.e., each brother would succeed to that office by order of seniority. Succession to the throne in Nepal, however, was traditionally governed by the rule of primogeniture, and thus only Jang Bahadur's sons would have been included in the line of succession. While the brothers and their descendants might have been granted the prime ministership in perpetuity, that office would have lost much of the importance that had accrued to it since the time of Bhim Sen Thapa.

Furthermore, Jang Bahadur could not be certain that the army, which stood by complacently while indignities were heaped on King Rajendra and while King Surendra was deprived of all but nominal sovereign powers, would respond similarly to the deposition of the Shah dynasty. The Minister proceeded cautiously, therefore, taking a step at a time on a path that was patently contrived to lead to his ultimate objective—the throne. On July 31, 1856, in conjunction with the final ratification of the treaty of Thapathali, Jang Bahadur resigned his post as premier and "advised" the King to appoint his brother, Bam Bahadur, as his successor. A week later, on August 6, King Surendra attached his seal to a *lal mohur* (royal order) in which Jang Bahadur was given the rather enigmatic title of Maharaja of Kaski and Lamjung (too small ex-principalities in western Nepal) and the revenue therefrom, amounting to Rs. 100,000.

The terms of the *lal mohur* constituted an expansion in the powers held by Jang Bahadur as Maharaja over those he had enjoyed as prime minister. This document, which thenceforth formed the principal legal basis for the Rana family regime, stated:

As the Maharaja of these lands, you should restrain me if at any time, with the assistance of the *umraos* [officers], the people, the army, I try to injure the friendship with the Queen-Empress of England and the Emperor of China. If in your attempts to do so, I apply force, then my *umraos* and army should support you. Whenever Prime Minister Bam Bahadur commits any mistakes in conducting the civil and military affairs of the State, the *panjani*, and friendly relations with the Emperors of China and England, you should advise him. If he persists and refuses to accept advice, then my *mir umrao* and the army should carry out any orders given by you. All these we have given to you. Keep your kingdom happy. In matters of justice we have given you the authority to inflict capital punishment. Live happily with your title of Sri Maharaja of your Kingdom. If any subjects of my country try to plot against your Kingdom and your life, we have authorized you to kill such persons if necessary. These rights will be inheritable by your children. Along with your brothers, according to the roll of succession, we have established for the office of Mukhtiyar your son, Jagat Jang Bahadur Kunwar Rana, who will be the Mukhtiyar after the completion of the roll with Dhir Shamsher Jang Kunwar Ranaji.[30]

In this document, which we can safely presume was dictated by Jang Bahadur, we can readily perceive the motives of the minister. The unclarified relationship between Kaski-Lamjung and the rest of Nepal gave Jang Bahadur a territorial base for the title of Maharaja (King), an important step on the road to Maharajadiraj (Emperor)—the title of the Shah ruler. The procedure under which the powers, honors and revenue granted to Jang Bahadur were to be inherited *by his sons rather than his brothers* was an attempt to circumvent the roll of succession to the prime ministership based on the agnate principle. The brothers were to succeed to the prime ministership but his elder son, Jagat Jang, was to inherit the maharajaship—and the absolute powers that went with that post.

In the ensuing few months, Jang Bahadur moved gradually to assume sovereign powers in Nepal and to deprive Surendra of even his nominal rights and powers. Ramsay noted:

Everything appears to be now done by Jung Bahadoor—or in his name—in all notices, in all proclamations, it is given out that they have been issued by his orders, not by the Sovereign, nor by the Minister; both of whom, except that they are the nominal Government of the State in so far as communication with the Residency is concerned, appear to be mere cyphers, and compared with Jung Bahadoor, are held in no consideration whatever.[31]

In these maneuvers he was thwarted in part by the Resident, who refused to recognize anyone but the King as the sovereign of Nepal, and in part by his brothers, who were opposed to Jang Bahadur's objectives and worked behind the scenes to frustrate them, with eventual success.[32]

---

[30] For the Nepali text of the Lal Mohur, see Buddhiman Singh, *Vamsavali*: Lal Mohur from King Surendra to Jang Bahadur, Aug. 6, 1856.

[31] Ramsay also reported that "the Maharaja whose dread and whose dislike of Jang Bahadur and his party is about equally balanced has acted throughout merely as he has been bid." (*Secret Consultation* No. 55, Aug. 29, 1856: Ramsay to Calcutta, Aug. 6, 1856.

[32] On Jang Bahadur's demise in 1877, Ranodip Singh, the brother who followed him on the roll of succession, succeeded not only to the ministership but also as Maharaja of Kaski and Lamjung. Jang Bahadur's sons had to be content with a place on the roll of succession. From that time on, no distinction was made between the two posts,

EFFECTS OF THE WAR IN TIBET

Political developments in Tibet after the 1855–56 war were also of considerable significance. Despite the assertion of respect for the Chinese Emperor in the treaty, Tibetan officials understood that China lacked the capacity to support the Amban militarily. At almost any time in the period from 1856 to 1910 the Ambans could have been expelled from Tibet if there had been agreement among Tibetans on the desirability of such a course of action. That Tibet maintained a nominal relationship to the Ch'ing dynasty and allowed the presence of an Amban at Lhasa was due to the presence of important political factions in Tibet to whom this was advantageous. Moreover, nominal subordination to China was a protection in the realm of foreign policy, particularly when a threat from British India emerged in the latter quarter of the 19th century. Finally, the ties with China were economically advantageous to some Tibetans, not only because of the trade between the two countries but also because of the large donations given periodically to monastic organizations in Tibet by the Peking Court.

Political instability had become chronic in Tibet once the war with Nepal and the Taiping rebellion had undermined Chinese influence there. In 1858, a bitter dispute broke out between Regent Yeshe Gyatse Rating and Kalon Shatra. The Regent got the upper hand temporarily, in part because of an indiscreet letter the Kalon had sent to Jang Bahadur, and the Kalon was exiled to his family estate. He returned to Lhasa in early 1862, however, and with the assistance of the powerful Drepung and Ganden monasteries, forced Rating to flee to eastern Tibet. The Regent solicited the support of the Chinese—who asked Lhasa to allow him to return —and of the local ruler of Nyarong principality in eastern Tibet, who rose in revolt against Lhasa.

During the riots in Lhasa that accompanied the overthrow of the Regent a Newari trader had been killed. Jang Bahadur took advantage of this "grievance" to write to the Dalai Lama and Shatra, who had now taken the title of *Desi* (prime minister), demanding punishment of the guilty persons and threatening war if Lhasa procrastinated in its usual fashion.[33] In reply, Desi Shatra sent an emissary to Kathmandu in August 1862 to (1) promise a full inquiry into the death of the Newari, and (2) invite Jang Bahadur to recog-

---

and the person who succeeded to the prime ministership acquired the title and prerogatives of Maharaja of Kaski and Lamjung at the same time.

[33] *Political A* No. 26, July 1862: Ramsay to Calcutta, June 20, 1862.

nize him as the ruler of Tibet and correspond with him as such. Jang Bahadur reportedly told the emissary he would recognize Desi Shatra if he managed to maintain his authority in Tibet for another four months.[34]

The following December, Desi Shatra wrote to Jang Bahadur requesting military assistance against the Nyarong ruler.[35] Jang Bahadur thought he detected an opportunity to extend his influence over Tibetan domestic affairs, and offered a force of 3,000 men to the Desi. Shatra suspected Jang Bahadur's bona fides, however, and reduced his request for assistance to the loan of eight mountain guns, ammunition and artillerymen. Jang Bahadur was disappointed, but sent six mountain guns (without artillerymen to handle the weapons) which presumably were used in the struggle to suppress the Nyarong chieftain's rebellion. Desi Shatra died in 1864, and Nepal's subsequent difficulties in obtaining the return of the mountain guns[36] provided yet another cause for dissension.

The year 1856 thus had marked a turning point in Nepali-Tibetan relations, or more precisely, the restoration of the essential features of their relationship as it existed prior to 1792. The period from 1793 to 1853 had been one of comparatively good relations between the two states. Tibet's foreign relations during that period were conducted largely through the Amban's office, which served both as a buffer between Kathmandu and Lhasa and as a mediator whose "good offices" were utilized by both governments whenever disputes arose. This system had virtually collapsed by 1840, and it disappeared almost entirely after 1856. From that time on, both Tibet and Nepal functioned as independent states, and direct diplomatic relations between the two governments were reestablished on their pre–1793 basis.[37]

Although this was enthusiastically welcomed by Nepalis and Tibetans alike, it also increased the potential for controversy between the two states. Indeed, the period after 1856 was marked by serious differences that on several occasions threatened to erupt into hostilities. In 1869 a dispute, nominally over the barter trade in salt and rice between the two countries, was finally settled peacefully. However, the basic causes of the dispute continued to plague relations between Nepal and Tibet. Jang Bahadur, following the example set by Prithvi Narayan Shah and other Nepali rulers,

---

34 *Ibid.*, No. 36, September 1862: Ramsay to Calcutta, Aug. 9, 1862.
35 *Ibid.*, No. 29, November 1863: Ramsay to Calcutta, Sept. 24, 1863.
36 Secret Internal. No. 374, 1869: Dr. Cayl (Ladakh) to Calcutta, Oct. 30, 1869.
37 The letter sent to the Tibetan Kashag by Jang Bahadur in 1855 announcing the declaration of war seems to have been the first occasion since 1793 that the Nepal Darbar had addressed an official communication directly to the Tibetan government, rather than through the Amban's office.

sought an agreement with Lhasa which would guarantee Kathmandu's virtual monopoly of trans-Himalayan trade. The Tibetans, on the other hand, were disinclined to recognize the privileged position accorded Nepal under the 1856 treaty, and resisted efforts to assure its enforcement. Of more importance, perhaps, were Tibetan fears that contacts between Nepal and China, which had increased considerably in the period after 1860, might lead to a *de facto* alliance under which Nepal would help China reassert its influence in Tibet in exchange for Chinese guarantees that Nepal's economic position in Tibet would be protected.[38]

Chinese influence in Tibet revived somewhat after 1871, partly because of the role played by the Ambans in support of the factions that emerged triumphant in the power struggle of that year and partly because the Ch'ing dynasty had finally reestablished its control over most of China. The influence of the Ambans never approached that exerted by their predecessors prior to 1840, but they did reemerge as a factor in Tibetan politics that could not be safely ignored, particularly since Tibetan factions frequently sought the Ambans' support in their internal disputes.

FURTHER CRISES IN NEPALI-TIBETAN RELATIONS

Nepali-Tibetan relations once again underwent a crisis in 1872 when Kathmandu accused Lhasa of permitting the maltreatment of Nepali merchants resident in Tibet. Jang Bahadur talked of war. A partial mobilization of the Nepali militia was ordered for January 1873, and Nepal threatened to withdraw its Vakil from Lhasa and stop all trade between the two countries. The Tibetans suggested the appointment of a joint commission that would meet on the border to settle the dispute. Jang Bahadur rejected this proposal, and finally did withdraw the Nepali Vakil from Lhasa in the fall of 1873. There is no record of a specific settlement having been reached, but by 1875 the situation had improved sufficiently to permit the Nepali Vakil to return to Lhasa. Relations then returned to normal—that is, to an interminable series of petty disputes.

The most serious dispute over the terms of relationship established in the 1856 treaty occurred in 1883 when armed hostilities between Nepal and Tibet again seemed imminent. On April 8,

---

38 For an analysis of this aspect of Nepali-Tibetan relations, see the report to the British government from the Sikkim Vakil at Darjeeling. *Political A*, No. 471, June 1873.

1883, a dispute between a Newari merchant at Lhasa and two Tibetan women over a piece of coral led, a few hours later, to the destruction and plundering of 84 Nepali-owned shops by a mob led by monks from the three main Lhasa monasteries—Drepung, Sera and Galdan. The Tibetan authorities seem to have done little to forestall the riot and were suspected by Kathmandu of having secretly encouraged the mob.[39]

A close analysis of the events leading up to the riot indicates that this was not a spontaneous affair resulting only from the mutual antagonisms often prevalent between the privileged Nepali merchants at Lhasa and their commercial competitors—the monks of the three large Lhasa monasteries—but rather was planned and carried out at the instigation of the leaders of one or more of the Tibetan factions contending for political influence. Indeed, it may have been connected with the concern felt in some Tibetan circles over the closer relations then being established between China and Nepal, which were viewed as a threat to Tibet's virtually complete autonomy. That this riot coincided with the visit of a high Chinese official, Sanbui Hosai, to Kathmandu with "dresses of honor" for Maharaja Ranodip Singh appertaining to the Chinese title that had been conferred on him in 1878, was probably not inadvertent. Tibetans understood quite well that Nepali-Tibetan disagreements placed the Chinese in a difficult position, and they may have hoped to frustrate a Sino-Nepali rapprochement in this manner.

If this was Lhasa's objective, it succeeded—initially at least. Kathmandu, on hearing of the destruction of the Nepali shops, demanded either full restitution of all property or compensation for losses and threatened war if this was not acceded to by the Tibetan government. The Senior Amban, who seems to have suspected some deep, dark design, placed the blame for the riot squarely on the Tibetans and advised the civil authorities to take the requisite measures for the settlement of the affair in conformity with the terms of the 1856 treaty "and to further neighbourly relations of an amicable nature" with Nepal.[40] He also raised a small subscription fund for the plundered Nepali merchants and urged the Tibetan authorities to restore the plundered property. At the request of the Tibetans, the Amban offered 200,000 to 400,000 rupees to

---

[39] This event occurred on the last day of the festival, nearly 2 months in length, which begins with the New Year according to the Tibetan calendar. At that time it was common for 20,000 to 25,000 monks to congregate in Lhasa, and it was then, as it remained until recently, a period of widespread disorder and rowdyism under cover of which political intrigue often flourished.

[40] *Peking Gazette*, June 29, 1883: Memorial from Se-leng-e to Peking Government, n.d., but probably mid-April 1883, (*A Political E* No. 240, April 1884.)

the Nepali Vakil as full repayment for the merchants' losses—estimated by Kathmandu at Rs. 1,700,000—but the merchants rejected this proposal, with the support of the Nepal authorities.[41] For the most part, relations between China and Nepal remained cordial during the dispute, although Nepali officials did tell the British Resident that China was likely to intervene in support of Tibet if the dispute ended in hostilities.

This crisis was an embarrassment to Kathmandu. Despite its threats to resort to arms, the Darbar was well aware that the cost of a Tibetan campaign would far exceed the indemnification that could be expected.[42] Moreover, the internal political situation in Nepal was critical. The dispute between the sons of Jang Bahadur and the late Maharaja's two brothers, Ranodip Singh and Dhir Shamsher, was fast approaching a showdown. Neither side was anxious for an armed conflict with Tibet at that time, for they were primarily preoccupied with preparations for the power struggle that would ensue after the death of the ailing Ranodip Singh.

Kathmandu realized, however, that if Lhasa successfully avoided all responsibility for the 1883 riot, Nepal's position in Tibet would be gravely impaired. Tibet might next move to terminate the annual payments to Kathmandu or even abrogate the 1856 treaty entirely. If Lhasa refused to make concessions, some form of military reprisal appeared necessary—preferably a lightning thrust into Tibet. The Wallung Chung pass in eastern Nepal was chosen for the invasion route, as the 1788, 1791 and 1855–56 campaigns had shown that Kuti and Kerong were too distant from major political and trade centers in Tibet to have the maximum impact. Khadga Shamsher, a son of Dhir Shamsher, was sent to Calcutta to purchase 4,000 breech-loading rifles; these would have given Nepal such an immense superiority in firepower over the Tibetan army that only a comparatively small force would have been required for the trans-Himalayan campaign.[43]

War was avoided, however, and the Darbar arranged a peaceful settlement of the dispute with Tibet. The Nepali Vakil, eighty Nepali merchants, the Tibetan commissioners and two Chinese

---

41 GON, *Jaisi Kotha Records*: Record of talks between representatives of the Nepali and Tibetan governments at Rasua, March–May 1884.

42 Dhir Shamsher estimated to Girdlestone that a campaign in Tibet would cost Nepal approximately Rs. 6,000,000, far more than it could ever hope to obtain from Lhasa either as compensation or indemnification. Girdlestone noted that "there is a vivid recollection of the cost and misery which a similar war in 1854–56 entailed; the army, so far as I can learn, has no desire to repeat the bitter experience of that time, and in the country at large there is no enthusiasm on the subject."*Secret E*, No. 442, June 1884: Girdlestone to GOI, Jan. 16, 1884.

43 *Secret E*, No. 445, June 1884: Memorandum of the conversation between Khadga Shamsher and Governor-General Ripon: Jan. 23, 1884.

officials set out for Kerong in January 1884 to meet a Nepali delegation headed by Col. Tej Bahadur Rana (formerly a Vakil at Lhasa) and Kaji Laxmi Bhakta Upadhyaya. In the initial discussions between the two delegations Nepal demanded total compensation for the losses incurred by Nepali merchants at Lhasa—Rs. 1,447,807. The Tibetan delegation protested that this sum was excessive, charging that the Nepali merchants had padded their account books considerably in estimating their losses. After several weeks of sporadic negotiations, the two delegations signed a four-point agreement on May 26, 1884. Tibet agreed to Rs. 942,098 as compensation, to be paid in annual installments over a seven-year period. It would also restore as much of the plundered property as could be found, the value of which would be deducted from the compensation figure. The Tibetans promised to punish the looters "according to the Laws of Tibet," and cases involving rioters who were beyond the authority of the Tibetan government—presumably Khampas—would be referred to the Chinese Emperor for punishment. For its part, Nepal gave up a claim for Rs. 600,000 to compensate the Darbar for the expenses involved in its war preparations.[44]

The Chinese were obviously delighted with the settlement of this potentially troublesome dispute. In its eagerness to secure an agreement Peking had even promised to loan Tibet a portion of the sum granted to Nepal as indemnification. The Szechuan treasury was ordered to transmit to Tibet 80,000 taels of silver (approximately Rs. 400,000), which Lhasa was free to draw upon for its annual payments to Nepal. The Tibetans were ordered to repay that sum to Szechuan in three installments, but the obligation was fulfilled only very reluctantly and considerably behind schedule.[45] This contrasts strikingly with Lhasa's payment of the sums due Nepal ahead of schedule, an occurrence without precedent in the long history of Nepali-Tibetan relations.[46]

For Nepal, the immediate results of the 1883 dispute had been about as favorable as Kathmandu could expect: it had avoided an expensive military campaign and had received reasonable compen-

---

44 GON, *Jaisi Kotha Records*: Nepali-Tibetan agreement signed on Monday, Jestha sudi 2, 1941 V.S. (May 26, 1884). For an imaginative Chinese account of these negotiations, see the publication by Chao Hsien-chung (the Chinese official who accompanied the Tibetan delegation), *T'ang-Kuo-Hsiu-Ho-Chi-Lueh* (Summary Narration of the Peace Settlement of the Nepal-Tibet Dispute), 1888. This was published privately by the author and should not be considered an official Chinese version of the affair.
45 *External A*, No. 99, January 1886: Memorial from Chinese Resident to Peking, *Peking Gazette*, Nov. 21, 1885. However, according to Shakabpa (*op. cit.*, p. 194) the payment to Nepal was actually provided by Chayan Hutuktu, a rich Mongol who was visiting the Dalai Lama at the time.
46 *Secret E*, No. 544, September 1886: Girdlestone to GOI, Aug. 28, 1886.

sation for the losses suffered by Nepali merchants in the Lhasa riots. Moreover, its relations with China had emerged considerably strengthened in view of the support Chinese officials had given to Nepal's claims against Tibet. On the negative side, the dispute had been a severe blow to Nepali trading firms in Tibet, who were already facing intense competition from Indian goods imported into Tibet via the recently opened Sikkim-Chumbi valley route. During the dispute, much of the trans-Himalayan trade had been taken over by Kashmiri merchants in Lhasa.[47] The Nepalis were never able to restore completely the virtual monopoly they had held in the trade with Lhasa, even though some Newari commercial houses transferred their center of operations from Kathmandu to Kalimpong to take advantage of cheaper transportation costs via Sikkim.[48] Thereafter, the route through Kathmandu was of decreasing importance in the trade between India and Tibet, though the local trade between Nepal and Tibet in such commodities as rice and salt continued undiminished.

For Tibet, the 1857–85 period had been particularly trying, beset as the country was by potential aggressors from several sides—Nepal and the British to the south and China to the east. Though Tibet had suffered financial loss in the 1883 dispute with Nepal, the settlement had not involved a significant expansion of either Nepali or Chinese influence at Lhasa, a result that would have been much more distasteful to the Tibetan authorities than the payment of damages. In mid–1884, Lhasa moved to improve its own relations with Kathmandu, probably to lessen the attraction of a Nepal-China alliance to the Darbar. The Nepali Vakil, on his return to Lhasa, was received with "unusual" honors and, as already noted, the compensation was paid to Nepal ahead of schedule. Despite these rather hopeful signs, however, the 1857–85 period closed essentially as it had opened, with Tibet striving to protect its autonomy while Nepal and China eagerly sought to exploit any and all opportunities to expand their influence there. In these circumstances, instability was certain to remain a predominant characteristic of the relations between these three powers.

---

[47] *External A*, No. 98, January 1886: Account of a Journey of a Chinese Lama from Tashilhunpo to Chu-ka in Bhutan, submitted by F. S. A. Bourne, British Resident Consular, Ch'ung-Ch'ing, Sept. 25, 1885.

[48] Newari merchants operating from Kalimpong and Darjeeling had a further advantage over Indian merchants because of the provision of the 1856 Nepali-Tibetan treaty that exempted Nepali merchants from most Tibetan taxes and duties.

6

Nepal Adjusts to the British "Forward Policy"

A SERIES of momentous events in India in mid-1857 diverted Nepal's attention from Tibet, for it was then that northern India exploded into an anti-British movement that began with the mutiny of the British Indian regiments at Meerut. For the next two and a half years, Jang Bahadur's prodigious energies and talents were devoted to seeking the utmost advantage for Nepal—and himself—in this crisis.

News of the mutiny, which reached Kathmandu in mid-May, caused an intense, bitter debate in the Darbar. Jang Bahadur, convinced that the revolt had little chance for success, argued that Nepal's interests could best be served by aiding in the restoration and preservation of British rule in India. He faced strong opposition within the Darbar and the army, however, because the sympathies of most Nepali officials—including several of Jang's brothers—were with the rebels.[1] To forestall any conspiracies aimed at his authority, Jang Bahadur seized the opportunity caused by the death of Prime Minister Bam Bahadur to reassert direct control over the administration.[2] On June 28, King Surendra announced that he had appointed Jang Bahadur "contrary to his own desire to be

---

[1] According to the Buddhiman Singh *Vamsavali (op. cit.)*, "The Maharaja . . . assembled all the Bharadars and officers and asked them whether or not Nepal should help the British. Everybody said that Nepal should not help the British."

[2] It had been presumed at the time of Bam Bahadur's death that the next brother on the role of succession, Krishna Bahadur, would succeed to the prime ministership, and he actually acted in this capacity for over a month. However, Jang Bahadur may have decided that this endangered his own "India policy," as Krishna Bahadur's sympathies were reportedly with the rebels.

made Prime Minister and Commander-in-Chief with the title of
Sri Sri Sri Maharajah."[3] Jang Bahadur was given absolute powers
by the *Lal Mohur*, which concluded with the statement that "in
fact he may do . . . whatever he may think proper but I have desired
him at once to put to death all who will not obey him."[4]

Aware of the widespread dissatisfaction in the Darbar, Jang
Bahadur held several Council meetings in which he argued that
the British were certain to win and that Nepal could, by assisting
them, regain the territory lost in the 1814–16 war. He also appealed
to the religious prejudices of the Hindu Nepalis who had borne
a grudge against the Muslim ruler of Oudh ever since his predecessor had "loaned" the British twenty-five million rupees during
the Anglo-Nepali war of 1814–16 and had received as payment
title to certain districts in the Terai. The Darbar's objections to
the use of the Nepali army in India might well have been more
vehement if its operations had not been directed against the predominantly Muslim rebel movement in Oudh.

The negotiations between Ramsay and the Nepal Government, which led to the dispatch of a Nepali force to India, had
their ludicrous moments. On May 31, 1857, the Nepal Government
wrote Ramsay:

There is no probability that this Government will receive any orders
from the British Government on such a trifling occasion, yet in consideration of the friendship which subsists between the two states it
would not be consistent with the rules of friendship to keep silent on
hearing such intelligence. I therefore desire to say that we are ready to
execute any orders that may be given to this Government by the Right
Honourable Governor-General.[5]

To Kathmandu's utter surprise, Ramsay replied only two days
later that "I have no hesitation in accepting, on the part of my
Government, the services of three small bodies of Nepalese troops,
consisting of 1,000 men each."[6] Ramsay recorded that, much to his
consternation, "the disappointment which my acceptance of it has
occasioned is very marked, and I much fear that my suggestions
may not be carried out." The Darbar debated Ramsay's proposal

---

[3] *Secret Consultation* No. 472, Sept. 25, 1857: Yaddasht, Surendra to Ramsay, June 28,
1857. Thereafter, until Rana rule was overthrown, the title of Sri Tin Maharaja
went with the office of prime minister.
[4] *Secret Consultation* No. 473, Sept. 25, 1857: Lal Mohur, Surendra to Jang Bahadur,
June 28, 1857.
[5] *Secret Consultation* No. 4787A, Sept. 25, 1857, *op. cit.* On several earlier occasions,
the Nepal Government had offered Calcutta the services of the State Army, but this
had always been politely refused.
[6] *Secret Consultation* No. 487B, Sept. 25, 1857; Yaddasht, Ramsay to Krishna Bahadur,
June 4, 1857.

for two days and finally informed the Resident that (1) the Nepal Government's offer was conditional on the reception of a direct request for troops from the Governor-General; (2) Nepal, being currently engaged in a border dispute with Tibet, could not send 3,000 troops from Kathmandu; and (3) Nepal would lend the troops if the British agreed to bear all the expenses involved. Ramsay reported that he would have withdrawn his request at this point if the unsatisfactory news from India had not made him feel "that this is not a moment to stand upon punctilio." Moreover, on June 5, the Darbar modified its policy and consented to send six regiments (3,000 men) into the British provinces.[7]

Governor-General Canning's reaction to this exchange of notes was distinctly unenthusiastic. The Resident was told:

His Lordship in Council . . . is strongly of opinion that it is only under the greatest emergency, and in the last extremity, that the British Government could condescend to ask, or consent to receive, armed assistance from the Nipal State.

Ramsay was instructed to thank the Darbar for its offer but, unless the Nepali troops had already passed the boundary, explain that their services were not required.[8] One detachment had already left Kathmandu, and the Resident was obliged to request its immediate recall.

Not long thereafter, however, Calcutta decided that the "greatest emergency" and "last extremity" was at hand. On June 23 new instructions were sent to Ramsay in which he was ordered to "obtain from the Government of Nepal the services of 3,000 men and have them despatched at once to Lucknow to the relief of the British position."[9] The embarrassed Resident now had to inform the Nepal Government that he had been mistaken in asking Kathmandu to countermand its previous order, and requested that the six regiments be sent to Lucknow "with all possible despatch."[10]

The Darbar responded immediately. On June 30 (two days after Jang Bahadur had resumed the Prime Ministership) the first detachment set out towards India, and two other detachments followed shortly thereafter. This force was not strong enough to force its way through rebel-held country to Lucknow, however, and Jang Bahadur therefore offered to lead personally a Nepali force of 8,000 men against the rebels. Ramsay reported that Jang's terms

---

[7] *Secret Consultation* No. 487, Sept. 25, 1857: Ramsay to GOI, June 5, 1857.
[8] *Secret Consultation* No. 488, Sept. 25, 1857: GOI to Ramsay, June 13, 1857.
[9] *Secret Consultation* No. 498, Sept. 25, 1857: GOI to Ramsay, June 23, 1857.
[10] *Secret Consultation* No. 542, Sept. 25, 1857: Yaddasht, Ramsay to Krishna Bahadur, June 26, 1857.

if not exactly qualified by actual *conditions*, were attended by embarrassing hints of expectations from the British Government, provided the proposals are accepted, and good service is performed by the Goorkha troops.

A representative of the Maharaja, Ramsay continued, had expressed the hope that the British would remember that it was Jang Bahadur who exercised "supreme power" in Nepal and who had provided this assistance "and that we would either bestow upon him a tract of country elsewhere as a reward for his services, or recognize him as an Independent Prince in Nipal."[11] The Governor-General postponed the acceptance of Jang Bahadur's offer until Delhi, "the head of the rebellion," had been crushed. Once this was accomplished, Oudh became the center of rebel activity and Canning was eager to obtain a larger Nepali force for service in this area. Ramsay was authorized on November 18, 1857, to accept Jang Bahadur's proposal and to express Canning's "entire confidence" in the Maharaja.[12]

Three weeks later, on December 10, Jang Bahadur led 8,000 Nepali troops into India. The army performed creditably in the fighting which culminated in the capture and looting of Lucknow —an event in which the Gorkhas participated to their considerable advantage. Jang Bahadur then met Canning at Allahabad and requested "that he might be seated on the throne of Nepal."[13] While the British were not prepared to countenance Jang Bahadur's usurpation of the throne, they were under an obligation to reward him—and Nepal—for services rendered in their hour of crisis. Canning therefore informed Jang Bahadur that Calcutta would restore the sections of the Terai taken from Nepal in 1816 and given to Oudh.[14] Thereafter, in conformity with this decision, Canning wrote Kathmandu on May 17, 1858:

I have determined on the part of the British Government to restore to the Nepal State the whole of the former Gurkha possessions below the Hills extending from the river Gogra on the west to the British territory of Goruckpore on the east and bounded on the south by Kreegurh and the districts of Baraitch and on the north by the hills.[15]

The territory as delimited in this letter did not include all the Terai lands ceded to the British in 1816, as Jang Bahadur had ex-

11 *Ibid.*, No. 423, Nov. 27, 1857: Ramsay to GOI, July 17, 1857.

12 *Ibid.*, No. 425, Nov. 27, 1857: GOI to Ramsay, Nov. 18, 1857.

13 Secret despatch from Governor-General Canning to the Secret Committee of the Court of Directors, No. 24, June 10, 1858.

14 Secret despatch to Secretary of State from Canning, No. 23, June 10, 1858.

15 *Secret Consultation* No. 124, Aug. 27, 1858: Canning to King Surendra, May 17, 1858. That Canning addressed this letter to King Surendra rather than to Jang Bahadur no doubt caused the Maharaja considerable irritation.

pected. Canning thought Jang Bahadur would be satisfied with the old Nepal-Oudh boundary and possibly even less, but in this he was wrong. The Maharaja quickly evinced discontent and compared this territorial restitution unfavorably with the recompense accorded some Indian princes who had helped the British much less than he. This factor, combined with the refusal of the British to countenance his efforts to usurp the throne of Nepal, irritated Jang Bahadur and impelled him to take a number of steps intended to express his dissatisfaction. He first requested the recall of Ramsay as Resident, and later, when Calcutta had refused this, moved to restrict the activities of British subjects engaged in commerce in Nepal. He also gave a secret refuge to several important rebel leaders, such as Nana Sahib, who found an expensive but safe haven in Nepal.

The Gurkha Recruitment Question.—Perhaps the most potentially controversial move by Jang Bahadur, however, was the imposition of stricter regulations regarding the recruitment of Nepalis into the British Indian Army. This practice had been introduced in 1815, during the Anglo-Nepali war, when a large proportion of the Nepali force that surrendered after the battle of Malaun, mostly Garhwalis and Kumaunis, were recruited into the British service. Three battalions were formed at that time, consisting primarily of hill men from areas outside of Nepal proper, but later also including recruits from the Khas, Magar and Gurung communities in western Nepal. The magnificent fighting qualities of the three battalions were quickly recognized by the British, particularly after their successful employment in the siege of Bhuratpur in 1826. One of the early residents at Kathmandu, Brian Hodgson, enthusiastically expounded the value of these recruits, stressing their relative freedom from caste prejudices and practices as compared with Indian "military classes."[16]

Hodgson's proposal that the Nepal government be persuaded to allow full recruitment of Gurkhas, however, ran counter to the Darbar's "standing prohibition" against Nepalis serving in the British Indian army. This rule appears to have been a general policy rather than a specific order, as recruitment did occur and on a rather wide scale. The Darbar disliked the practice intensely but was not in a position to prevent a certain amount of recruitment. Whenever the British attempted to increase the pace of recruitment, however, or to revise the system for soliciting enlistments, the Darbar would usually devise countermeasures. In 1843,

---

16 C. R. Nepali, "Nepal ra British Gorkha Rifles" (Nepal and the British Gurkha Rifles), *Ruprekha*, V:4 (August/September 1964), pp. 9–10.

for instance, upon the establishment of an "undisguised and large" recruitment depot across the Nepal border, the Nepali authorities arrested a recruiting agent who had been sent into Nepal and widely publicized the ban on enlistment in the Indian Army.[17] Again during the Crimean War, when the British intensified recruitment activities, Jang Bahadur retaliated by barring members of Gurkha units from visiting their homes in Nepal until after their discharge.[18]

The excellent record of the hill battalions in the 1857–58 rebellion, and in particular their relative immunity to subversive propaganda, enhanced the desirability of these recruits for the British. A vigorous recruitment drive was undertaken in 1858, and a number of "illegal" recruitment teams were sent into the Nepal hills to seek volunteers for the five Gurkha Rifle regiments then being reorganized. Jang Bahadur refused to cooperate, however, and obstructed the recruitment program in several ways. Nepali frontier guards were instructed to arrest recruiting agents who penetrated into the hills, using force if necessary.[19] He also issued an order that "no subject of the four classes and thirty-six castes of our country shall go to India for recruitment without any prior approval." Any Nepali who disobeyed, he declared "shall have his houses and lands confiscated. He shall not be entitled to punish his wife's lover if she has one. He shall be liable to capital punishment if he kills his wife's lover."[20] The British were outraged at this turn of events, but decided to postpone confrontation with the Darbar on the recruitment question. In 1864, the Governor-General barred recruiting teams from entering Nepal, and the Gurkha Rifles were instructed to use the services of individual Gorkhalis already in the army to recruit their fellow countrymen.[21]

All of these gestures of defiance by Jang Bahadur may have given his ego some satisfaction, but they did not constitute a significant change in policy towards British rule in India, for there was no real possibility of a return to the pre–1846 situation. What his acts did signify was the Maharaja's pique with the British as well as his assumption that his standing with Calcutta was secure enough to allow him to carry out, on a limited scale, policies that would appeal to the anti-British bias of the Kathmandu Darbar.

---

[17] *Secret Consultation* No. 52, Apr. 19, 1843: Hodgson to GOI, Apr. 10, 1843.

[18] *Political Consultation* No. 11, Aug. 11, 1854, Ramsay to GOI, June 29, 1854.

[19] *Political Consultation* No. 1216, Dec. 31, 1858, Ramsay to GOI, Oct. 15, 1858.

[20] GON, *Jaisi Kotha Records*: Order dated Tuesday, Bhadra Badi 30, V.E. 1915 (August 1858). The phrase "four classes (*varnas*) and thirty six castes (*jatis*)" was the traditional way the Gorkha dynasty referred to its subjects.

[21] *Foreign Dept., Political A*, No. 89, September 1864: Foreign Department Proceedings, Sept. 17, 1864.

Furthermore, this could be done after 1858 without any serious danger of British retaliation, a consideration that had always restrained Jang Bahadur previously because of his fear that Calcutta might lend support to his many enemies who were in exile in India. He may also have been interested in demonstrating in concrete terms that Nepal was an independent state with the prerogatives attributable to sovereignty, in contrast to the feudatory princely states in India that lost even the fiction of sovereignty after 1860.

REVIVAL OF BRITISH INTEREST
IN TRANS-HIMALAYAN DEVELOPMENTS

Since 1792 the British had maintained a compartively aloof attitude towards the trans-Himalayan region, and no serious efforts had been made to extend their influence into that forbidding terrain. By 1860, however, there was a definite revival of British interest in the area, due both to developments in India and China and to British hopes of creating a land route for trade with western China via Tibet. In 1861 a British expedition was scheduled to travel from China to India through Tibet, and Peking had been persuaded to issue passports to the party. Lhasa refused to recognize the validity of the Chinese passports, however, and the expedition had to be cancelled.

Kathmandu's reaction to these developments was predictable, for they constituted a direct threat to Nepal's virtual trade monopoly in Tibet. Jang Bahadur had warned Calcutta that Lhasa was determined to keep the British expedition out of Tibet and was even prepared to go to war with China rather than permit its admission. Ramsay suspected—with a good deal of justification, as it turned out—that Jang Bahadur had encouraged the Tibetans in this attitude.[22]

Frustrated in their efforts to send a party into Tibet through China, the British once again turned their attentions towards Bhutan and Sikkim as possible avenues to Tibet. In 1861, Calcutta extracted the right to construct and maintain roads through Sikkim from the reluctant Raja of that state. At the same time, endemic border disputes with Bhutan caused a crisis in relations between Punakh and Calcutta. The Ambari Fallakotta area of Bhutan had been seized by the British in 1860 for alleged Bhutani oppression

---

[22] *Political A*, No. 302, April 1862: Ramsay to GOI, Apr. 17, 1862.

of Assamese in the *Duar* (pass) areas on the frontier. In December 1863, a mission headed by Ashley Eden forced its way into Bhutan and proceeded to Punakh, where it received "so gross an insult" that Calcutta "had no option but to declare war in November 1864."[23] The military expedition into Bhutan was not a glorious affair, but the government of Bhutan was finally forced to accept a treaty under which the *duars* and the Kalimpong area to the east of the Tista river were ceded to the British.

While the war was still in progress, Bhutan wrote Kathmandu asking the Darbar to mediate the dispute or to "send assistance to us."[24] Jang Bahadur was not inclined to endanger his relations with the British for so futile an undertaking, however, and replied:

You fought with us in our last war with Tibet. How can we help a former enemy? Pray for mercy to the British Government. You must have committed some aggressions, otherwise the British Government would not have molested you . . . Expect no help from us.[25]

There was little Kathmandu could do to thwart the British in Bhutan, but it may not have been coincidental that it was at this point that Nepal decided to revive the periodic missions to China which had been discontinued after the 1855–56 war with Tibet. Several Chinese officials visited Kathmandu between August and October 1864, probably in connection with developments in Tibet (which had reached a crisis stage) but possibly also for consultations on the Bhutan situation and British policy on India's northern border. Certainly China considered it advantageous to develop closer relations with Nepal as one method of protecting its interests in Tibet both from independence-minded Tibetans and from the British. At all events, it was after the receipt of overtures from the Amban at Lhasa that Jang Bahadur decided in June 1866 to send a mission to Peking.[26]

The mission, led by Kaji Jagat Sher Khattri, left Kathmandu on August 2, 1866, and proceeded as far as Tachien-lu near the China-Tibet border, where it was halted by a Muslim rebellion in western China. After several months, the Chinese authorities there asked the Nepali envoy to turn over the presents for the Emperor

23 Major-General N. G. Woodyatt, *The Regimental History of the 3rd Queen Alexandra's Own Gurkha Rifles*, London, 1929, p. 35. Eden's own account of the mission (*op. cit.*) does not make clear just what this "gross insult" consisted of but does indicate that the mission had been a political failure.
24 *Political A*, No. 245, March 1865: Dev Dharma of Bhutan to Jang Bahadur, Dec. 29, 1864.
25 *Ibid.*, No. 246: Jang Bahadur to Dev Dharma of Bhutan, n.d.
26 *Political A*, No. 163, June, 1866: Ramsay to GOI, June 9, 1866.

and promised to forward them to Peking. Jagat Sher reluctantly agreed to this, but spent nearly 2 years at Tachien-lu waiting for permission to proceed to Peking before finally deciding to return to Kathmandu.

The Chinese government's motive in refusing Jagat Sher permission to proceed to Peking is uncertain. Bishop Chauvean, who headed the French Jesuit mission at Tachien-lu and who became well acquainted with Jagat Sher, speculated that the Chinese were trying to "bring down the storm" of Nepal's wrath on Tibet by sending the mission back to Kathmandu dissatisfied, with the hope that China would be able to take advantage of a Nepali-Tibetan conflict to regain its former influence in Tibet.[27] But it was also at this time that China commenced a determined effort to woo Nepal back into closer relations with Peking. A Chinese "envoy" was sent to Kathmandu in May 1870 to consult with Jang Bahadur. The results of these talks must have been considered encouraging by Peking, for on April 19, 1871, another Chinese mission visited Kathmandu to bestow a title upon Jang Bahadur and, presumably, to continue the discussions that had been initiated the previous spring.[28]

Reactions to British Efforts to "Open" Tibet.—British activity on the northern border was becoming increasingly threatening to all the states with interests in that area. In the winter season of 1873–74, the Sikkim ruler was summoned to Darjeeling and informed that (1) his annual subsidy from the Government of India would be increased from Rs. 9,000 to Rs. 12,000 and (2) a British party would be sent to Sikkim to survey a road to the Tibet border. The Deputy Commissioner at Darjeeling, John Ware Edgar, headed the party, which surveyed all the pass areas in the Chola range on the Sikkim-Tibet border. Both the Tibetans and the Chinese were alarmed at this, and the Amban wrote to the Sikkim ruler warning him:

---

[27] *Ibid.*, No. 208, March 1868: Translation of a French document sent by Bishop Chauvean to British authorities regarding the Nepali mission to China, dated Tachien-lu, July 17, 1686. It should be remembered, however, that Chauvean was interested in arousing both the British and Nepalis against Lhasa, which had barred the entrance of Catholic missionaries into Tibet.

[28] According to Jang Bahadur's announcement of this to the British Resident, the title meant: "The highly honored Commander and Controller of Military and Political Affairs, the Augmenter and Instructor (disciplinarian) of the Army, the Aggrandizer of the Country, the Satisfier of the Low and High by increasing the Prosperity and revenue of the Country, the Great Inheritor of Fidelity and Faithfulness to the Salt." (*Political A*, No. 010, July 1871: R. C. Lawrence to GOI, May 22, 1871.) Two years later, the British followed China's example and made Jang Bahadur a Knight Grand Commander of the Most Exalted Order of the Star of India, an honor that Jang Bahadur had hoped to receive after the 1857 mutiny but which had been denied him at that time. (Pudma Jang, *op. cit.*, p. 314.)

Your State of Sikkim borders on Tibet. You know our wishes and our policy. You are bound to prevent the English from crossing our frontier. Yet it is entirely your fault—thanks to the roads which you have made for them in Sikkim—that they have conceived this project. If you continue to act thus, it will not be good for you. Henceforth you must fulfil your obligations, and obey the commands of the Grand Lama Rimboche and those of the twelfth Emperor of China.[29]

Despite this warning, by 1877 a "road" had been completed through Sikkim up to the Jelep pass leading into the Chumbi valley.

These developments increased the anxiety in Nepal, China and Tibet, particularly since there seemed to be little they could do to forestall the British in Sikkim. The Kathmandu Darbar, which had been irritated by the failure of its 1867 mission to reach Peking, had not sent another deputation to China at the scheduled time in 1872.[30] In the spring of 1876, however, Jang Bahadur informed the Amban of his intention to dispatch a mission to Peking in 1877. But before the mission could be sent, Jang Bahadur had died (in February 1877) and had been succeeded by his brother, Ranodip Singh. The new Prime Minister and his younger brother, Dhir Shamsher (who was the real power at the Darbar), were strongly anti-British. They proposed to reestablish Nepal's relations with China on its old basis if this could be accomplished without precipitating an open break with Calcutta. Furthermore, Ranodip Singh faced strong internal opposition from the sons of Jang Bahadur, who questioned the legality of his accession to the prerogatives and powers of the offices held by their father before his death. Ranodip Singh was anxious to obtain Peking's recognition of his accession and, if possible, a Chinese title equivalent to that bestowed on Jang Bahadur, as one means of silencing his opposition.

The mission to Peking under Colonel Tej Bahadur Rana (a cousin of Ranodip Singh) left Kathmandu in July 1877, bearing a letter to the Chinese Emperor.[31] Once again the mission faced difficulties in its efforts to reach Peking, although the Chinese government had earlier given Colonel Rana permission to proceed to the Chinese capital. In November 1877 Peking told the Chinese officials in Tibet that, "owing to the interruptions of communications" in Shansi and Shensi, the Nepali mission should be intercepted in Tibet and the gifts and letter forwarded to Peking. By the time this decree reached Lhasa, however, the Nepali mission had already pro-

---

29 Quoted in L. A. Waddell, *Among the Himalayas*, 2d ed., 1900, p. 411.
30 The Chinese government, however, had granted Nepal an exception on that occasion. Foreign Dept., *Secret E* No. 130, September 1876: Memorial from Acting Resident in Tibet to Peking, published in the *Peking Gazette*, May 11, 1876.
31 For a translation of this letter see *Secret E*, No. 24, March 1888: Surendra Bikram Shah to Chinese Emperor, July 20, 1877.

ceeded towards China, although it did not arrive in Szechuan province until February 1879.[32] No explanation is at hand to account for the unusual length of time spent by the mission in reaching Szechuan, or, for that matter, for the mission having succeeded in leaving Tibet. In any case, permission to proceed from Szechuan to the capital was soon granted, but it was not until December 1879 that the mission finally reached Peking, where it remained until the following May.[33] The homeward journey took nearly as long as the trip to Peking, for it was only on June 18, 1882, that the mission arrived at Kathmandu after nearly 5 years abroad.[34]

This seems to indicate that China had mixed feelings about the presence of the mission in Chinese territory, but such may well not have been the case. Indeed, Peking was becoming increasingly aware of the importance of Nepal to Chinese interests in the Himalaya. Ting Pao-chen, the governor of Szechuan, expressed a popular view when he wrote Peking:

Now fortunately we still have Bhutan and Nepal which both border on Tibet and could become our buffer states. The whole land of Bhutan is still not subjugated to India. With regard to Nepal, because of the strength of their armed forces, the British, at the time they conquered India, could not occupy this land and are still worried about them. Now, if the British wished to penetrate into Tibet, they must take the route through these two countries which could be troublesome to them. If we endeavoured to establish ties with those two countries and frustrated the British intention of establishing connections with them, then Tibet would not lose its strategic passes and we should be covered by a strong screen. At a former time, when the British had annexed Kashmir from the Sikhs in northern India, they already intended to trade in Tibet, which proves that they have had such an intention for a long time. If now we do not associate with Bhutan and Nepal the British surely would try to establish connections with them, and thus Tibet would be exposed and even Szechuan province would have its door opened.[35]

In furtherance of these objectives a Chinese envoy was sent to Kathmandu in January 1878 to confer upon Ranodip Singh the same Chinese title that Jang Bahadur had been granted previously.[36]

---

[32] *Peking Gazette*, Memorial from Szechuan Governor to Peking, Mar. 24, 1879. (Secret Department (GOI) No. 135 of 1879, June 1879.)

[33] The announced departure date of the mission was deferred on several occasions but it finally left after having had at least one audience with the Emperor. *Political A*, No. 84, January 1881: T. F. Wade to GOI, Nov. 1, 1880.

[34] Buddhiman Singh, *Vamsavali, op. cit.*

[35] *Ch'ing-Chi-Ch'ou-Tsang-Tsou-Tu* (Memorials and correspondence concerning the arrangement of affairs during the latter part of the Ch'ing dynasty), Peiping, National Academy, 1938, vol. I, p. 162: Memorial from Ting Pao-chen to Emperor, Nov. 15, 1877.

[36] *Political A*, Enclosure of letter to Secretary of State for India (IOL), No. 33, Feb. 1, 1878: Henvey to GOI, Jan. 18, 1878.

In 1879 Calcutta renewed its efforts to establish direct contacts with the Tibetan authorities by sending to Lhasa Sarat Chandra Das, the best-known of the Indian agents used by the British. Three years later, Colman Macaulay was selected for what was to be the first of several missions to the Tibet border to ascertain whether a direct route into Tibet through Lachen valley in Sikkim was feasible and also to establish contacts with the Tibetan officials at Tashilhunpo. Neither mission was a resounding success. Sarat Chandra Das reached Lhasa but was forced to act with such circumspection that he was unable to carry out his mission effectively.[37] Macaulay toured the area near the Tibet border, but was prevented from actually crossing the frontier by the Tibetan local authorities; nor were his letters to Tashilhunpo transmitted to their destination. Lhasa was still disinclined toward direct relations with the British, a policy Kathmandu enthusiastically endorsed.

ANGLO-NEPALI RELATIONS

After Jang Bahadur's death in 1877, intrafamilial rivalry had become a chronic feature of the Rana regime, the Shamshers (Dhir Shamsher and his sons) and the Jangs (the sons of Jang Bahadur) being the principal contestants under the precarious prime ministership of Ranodip Singh. Dhir Shamsher's death in October 1884 swung the political balance toward the Jang branch, one of whom succeeded as commander-in-chief and was thus next on the role of succession as Prime Minister. Moreover, Ranodip Singh had tended to favor the Jangs, and even allowed Jagat Jang (who had been expelled in 1881 for conspiring against the Prime Minister and Dhir Shamsher) to return to Nepal.

Drastic action was necessary, and soon, if the Shamshers were to retain a dominant position in the Darbar. Fortunately for them, a number of influential British officials, particularly in the Military Department of the Government of India, were inclined in their favor.[38] The British Resident, C. E. R. Girdlestone, was a staunch supporter of the Jangs, but he went on leave in May 1885.

---

[37] Later, when Lhasa learned of the real nature of his mission, all Tibetans involved, no matter how innocently, were imprisoned, their property was confiscated, and some were even executed for their part in the affair. E. Kawaguchi, *Three Years in Tibet*, Banaras and London, 1909, pp. 402–3, and Shakabpa, *op. cit.*, p. 193.

[38] See, for instance, the note of the Adjutant General dated Apr. 4, 1885 (*Secret E*, K.W. No. 2, January 1886). A memo by H. M. Durand of the Foreign Department dated June 3, 1885 (*General A, K.W. No. 1 of Consultations, No. 260–97*, June 1885), however, expressed greater concern over broader political considerations than the recruitment question.

The Acting Resident, Colonel Berkeley, reflected the views of the Military Department, which was now determined to improve the procedures under which Nepalis were recruited into the British Indian Army. Colonel Berkeley quickly reached the conclusion that more concessions on this issue would be gained from the Shamshers than from the Jangs, and was disposed to support that faction of the Ranas.

The Shamshers' opportunity came in November 1885, when Bir Shamsher was selected to command four regiments of the Nepali army scheduled to depart for India to participate in a military display on the invitation of the Indian government. With this force, Bir was in a position to stage a coup d'état. On the night of November 23, several of the Shamsher brothers gained admittance to Ranodip Singh's palace and assassinated the prime minister while he was at his devotions. A document bearing the King's seal appointed Bir Shamsher as the successor to the uncle he had just murdered. The Shamshers accused the Jangs of the crime and used this as an excuse for exterminating their rivals. Jagat Jang and several other members of his family were killed, and others, including the king's mother, took refuge in the British Residency. They were finally allowed to proceed to India on the plea of the Acting Resident, who was prompted both by humanitarian instincts and political expediency, for the presence of the Jangs in India was to prove of inestimable value to Calcutta in handling the Shamsher-dominated government in Nepal.

Bir Shamsher's position was still very insecure, as the loyalty of the Nepali army—which had been strongly attached to Jagat Jang—was in doubt. Recognition of his official status by Calcutta and Peking was absolutely essential if Bir was to hold power. Fortunately for him, Colonel Berkeley proved helpful. Acting on the latter's advice, Calcutta gave a tentative *de facto* recognition to Bir within a week of his accession to office. Some British officials later regretted that more concessions had not been wrung from Bir Shamsher in exchange for Calcutta's recognition of his status. In November 1885, however, Bir's promises to improve the Gurkha recruitment system had been particularly welcome to the British who were then experiencing another period of crisis in their relations with Russia in central Asia.

The Military Department of the Government of India had for some time been determined to effect an improvement in the procedures under which Nepalis were recruited into the Indian army. After Jang Bahadur's death in 1877, for instance, the Resident had sought to take advantage of the power struggle that ensued in the Darbar. On Calcutta's instructions, he requested Ranodip Singh's aid in the procurement of 1,000 "volunteers" for the Gurkha battalions as a demonstration of "his real friendship."[39] The prime minister was in no position to reject this "request" outright, but did what he could to frustrate the British. He agreed to accept responsibility for the delivery of what he termed the "wild and ignorant people of this country" to the recruiting centers across the border.[40] After much procrastination, however, Ranodip Singh collected only about half the number requested, and an estimated seventy to eighty percent of these were physically disqualified—much to the annoyance of the British.

Another opportunity to pressure Kathmandu on the subject of recruitment arose in 1883, when Nepal urgently required British arms and armaments because of the current crisis in its relations with Tibet. The Military Department of the government of India was eager to obtain the right to establish a regular recruitment system within Nepal, and strongly urged Calcutta to seek a *quid pro quo* with Kathmandu that would facilitate this objective. The Foreign Department had somewhat different sets of priorities, but nevertheless reached the same conclusion. British policy toward Nepal was the subject of a long interdepartment note by the Foreign Secretary, H. M. Durand, who stated:

Hitherto we have not regarded it as our duty or our interest to interfere between Nepal and Thibet for the prevention of hostilities. Nepal is not absolutely independent . . . but practically we have treated her as an independent State, having power to declare war and make treaties. She is nominally tributary to China, but China evidently regards her as outside the limits of the Celestial Empire. She is in regular treaty relations with Thibet. That country again is clearly regarded as a portion of the Chinese empire, but as an outlying portion, rather protected than held; and precedent seems to be in favour of the view that China would not be likely to interfere if Nepal and Thibet fell out. So long at all events as the war did not threaten the actual disruption or a permanent conquest of the latter country.[41]

Durand concluded that Britain would be "incurring an unnecessary and undesirable responsibility by any authoritative interference to prevent war, though if the outbreak of war meant an actual serious conflict with China, I should not consider it beyond our rights to insist upon Nepal keeping the peace and submitting its grievances for our settlement." However, unless war between

---

[39] *Political A*, No. 245, February 1879: Impey to GOI, Nov. 25, 1878.
[40] *Political A*, No. 246, February 1879: Yaddasht from Ranodip Singh to Col. Impey, Nov. 21, 1878.
[41] *Secret E*, K. W. No. 2, Consultations No. 438–59, June 1884. Note by H. M. Durand, May 19, 1884.

Nepal and China appeared likely, Durand felt it unwise to call upon Nepal to refrain from war, because

such an interference would reduce Nepal to the level of an acknowledgated feudatory, and might be very unpalatable to her just when we want to keep on good terms. It would also give us much trouble diplomatically, and might end in our finding ourselves involved in differences with China on behalf of Nepal.

I think that any differences with China should be very scrupulously avoided. It is in all ways to our interest to be on good terms with the Chinese. Putting aside the fact that they might give us a great deal of trouble on various parts of our frontiers, and even cause us serious danger under certain circumstances, they are, with regard to future contingencies in the north-west, a possible ally of much value. I would therefore carefully avoid getting into any unnecessary differences with them, whether in the way noted above or in any other way.

Durand suggested that the British government contact Peking and offer to intervene to assure peace between Nepal and Tibet. However, the British should not restrain Nepal from war, and if the Nepalis did invade Tibet

it would be very desirable to let them take with them . . . a first installment of breach-loading arms; and I would certainly . . . allow them to buy other munitions of war in India. However, as an exchange for the arms the Government of Nepal must allow freer recruitment of Gurkhas for the British Army and a definite arrangement should be provided for before arms are sent.

The peaceful settlement of the Nepali-Tibetan dispute, however, eased the pressure on Kathmandu to make concessions to the British on recruitment and the request for arms was allowed to lapse.

The government of India's decision in 1885 to double the number of Gurkha battalions in the Indian army (from five to ten) again brought the recruitment question to the fore. The Resident, C. E. R. Girdlestone, was instructed to seek the Darbar's consent to the soliciting of volunteers in Nepal by British recruiting agents. Ranodip Singh reluctantly agreed that the Darbar would (1) announce in the hill areas that any Nepali is "at full liberty to (enlist) on condition of previously making the local Nepalese District Office acquainted with his intention"; (2) "exert itself to collect recruits"; and (3) allow pensioners from the Gurkha and Assam Rifles to collect recruits under the Darbar's supervision. However, he firmly rejected proposals that British recruiting agents be allowed to operate inside Nepal and that a permanent recruitment depot be established at Kathmandu.[42]

---

[42] *Secret E*, No. 37, July 1885: Girdlestone to H. M. Durand, May 6, 1885.

Bir Shamsher was in such a weak position politically after his succession to the Prime Ministership in 1885 that he was constrained to meet British demands on the recruitment question on the best terms possible. Recruitment teams were still barred from the hill areas, but servicemen in the Gurkha units were now allowed to visit their homes on leave to solicit volunteers. Moreover, Bir had an order published at all appropriate places in Nepal declaring that "if you wish to enlist in British regiments, we give you full permission to go and take British service. There is no prohibition whatever."[43] Thereafter, the Darbar cooperated fully with the British in the collection of recruits, providing the numbers requested in good physical condition and from the proper castes and tribes. By 1890, therefore, the recruitment problems for the Gurkha units had been largely solved, to the immense satisfaction of British army authorities. "For this continued improvement in recruitment," according to one British report, "we have to thank Maharaja Bir Shamsher, as it is only since his accession to power that we have succeeded in filling our ranks with the best classes of Gurkhas."[44]

The Mission-to-Peking Question:—Despite their gratitude to Bir Shamsher concerning the recruitment matter, the British had been careful to provide a safe refuge to the remnants of the Jang faction. Few if any hindrances were imposed on their activities, and there was always the implied threat of British support to a Jang conspiracy against the Shamshers if a change of regime at Kathmandu suited Calcutta's interests. Under these circumstances, Bir Shamsher considered it essential to strengthen relations with China. Near the end of 1885 a letter was addressed to the Amban at Lhasa justifying the assassination of Ranodip Singh and requesting the Emperor, "as in former cases, to bestow upon [Bir] the title of 'Valiant Prince,' together with an official uniform."[45] The Amban recommended acceptance of the request to Peking, but it was not until August 28, 1889, that a Chinese envoy finally arrived in Kathmandu with the official letter of patent and appropriate robes, for which he was "feted on a scale twice as grand as usual."[46]

Bir Shamsher again wrote to China in 1886, requesting that the periodic mission be allowed to proceed to Peking—some four years late, according to the quinquennial schedule. The mission,

---

43 *Secret E*, No. 6, September 1888: Order signed by the Prime Minister, Commander-in-Chief, Raj Guru and other high officers, June 21, 1888.
44 *Secret E*, No. 136, June 1892: Lt. Col. H. Wylie to GOI, May 21, 1892.
45 *Peking Gazette*, Aug. 17, 1886: Memorial from Wen-Shih to Emperor enclosing text of Bir Shamsher's letter. (GOI, *Secret E*, No. 353, October 1886.)
46 Buddhiman Singh *Vamsavali*, *op. cit.*

headed by Rana Bikram (the son of Tej Bahadur Rana who had led the 1877 mission), left Kathmandu on September 14, 1886. Like its two immediate predecessors, this mission remained in China and Tibet for approximately five years—in contrast to the 18 months which had been normal prior to 1850—and returned to Kathmandu only in June 1891.

What explains the extended stays of these missions in China? Internal disruptions may occasionally have been a factor, but at no time were these so troublesome as to prevent the return of the missions at an earlier date. The commercial character of the missions—e.g., the disposition of opium loads—may have detained them in China for longer than the time needed to present gifts to the Emperor, but certainly not for 5 years. The delay in the return to Kathmandu must have been deliberate, and presumably reflected the Darbar's desire to have some form of diplomatic contact in China that could (1) obtain reliable intelligence on developments there vital to Nepal's interests and (2) establish direct relations with the Peking court, thus circumventing both the Ambans and the Tibetan government.

At first the British authorities attached little importance to the 1886 mission, but gradually they began to evince growing concern regarding the character of Sino-Nepali relations. This can be ascribed, in part, to the delicate negotiations then in progress between the British and the Chinese concerning Burma, Sikkim and Tibet, and the possible effect a Nepali-Chinese alliance would have on the outcome of those talks. The Foreign Department Secretary, H. M. Durand, commented that the mission was "undesirable" and that "sooner or later we shall have trouble with China all along the Himalayas," but concluded that "I am afraid we cannot help it."[47]

The Secretary's brother, Major E. L. Durand, who was then the Resident at Kathmandu, added to Calcutta's apprehensions by his reports of the reception given to the Chinese envoy who brought the patent of title for Bir Shamsher. The Resident commented:

It is perfectly monstrous that the Chinese should be allowed to come all through their country like this as masters, and abuse their women, and be bowed down to, when the British Resident is a prisoner confined to a patch of valley, and the country closed to all Englishmen, whilst they depend upon us for everything.[48]

---

[47] *Secret E*, August 1889, K.W. No. 1 of Consultation No. 27: H. M. Durand note, June 12, 1889.
[48] *Ibid.*, January 1890, K.W. No. 2, Consultations No. 254–63: Major E. L. Durand to Calcutta, Sept. 2, 1889, demiofficial letter.

The Resident charged that Chandra Shamsher, Bir's brother and second in line for succession to the Prime Ministership, "always asserts openly that Nepal is subordinate to China, and is in no way so to the Government of India." He concluded that "the settled policy of the Darbar is to play off China against us, and to make use of a pretended subordination to that power as a safeguard against the spread of any influence over this country."[49] Reports were also prevalent in India, spread assiduously by the Nepali refugees, that Nepal and China had concluded a secret alliance inimical to the interests of the British Government.[50]

Calcutta decided that it was time to consider more fully the nature of Nepal's relationship to both India and China. Major Durand recommended that the British should assert to Nepal:

The fact of the supremacy of the British Government (recognized in a way by Jung Bahadur), the fact of the absolute dependence of Nepal upon the generosity and liberality of Government, and the fact that no outside claims or interference with our undoubted protectorate could be tolerated in regard to any State on this side of the Himalayas.[51]

The Foreign Secretary, who had earlier concluded that Nepal was "in a position of quasi-subordination to us,"[52] argued:

If the Chinese really attempt to establish their influence in Nepal we must object, and revise our relations with that State, not I think a very difficult matter with all Jung Bahadur's descendants under our protection.[53]

The "mission" question arose again in 1893 when, during another of Nepal's periodic disputes with Tibet, Bir Shamsher wrote the Amban requesting permission to send a deputation to Peking. Major Indra Bikram Rana, a grandson of Bam Bahadur, was selected to head the mission, which left Kathmandu in August 1894 and, like its immediate predecessors, remained in China for several years, returning only in March 1901.

The letter to the Emperor that was sent with the mission became the subject of correspondence between Calcutta and Kath-

---

49 *Ibid.*, October 1890, Consultation No. 89: Major Durand to Calcutta, Sept. 4, 1890.
50 See, for instance, the letter of the "Jetha Maharani" (Mother of King Prithvi Bir and a refugee in India) to Governor-General Lansdowne, *ibid.*, November 1889, Consultation No. 84. Oct. 10, 1889.
51 *Ibid.*, January 1890, K.W. No. 2, Consultations No. 254–63: Major Durand to Calcutta, Oct. 22, 1889, demiofficial.
52 *Ibid.*, June 1888, K.W. No. 1, Consultations No. 250–81: Note by H. M. Durand, July 11, 1888.
53 *Ibid.*, August 1888, K.W. No. 1, Consultations No. 152–97: Note by H. M. D(urand), Aug. 5, 1888.

mandu. The first version of the letter that the British saw was a translation of the Chinese text as published in the *Peking Gazette*. Calcutta considered the terminology used in addressing the Emperor as "excessively submissive" and brought the question to the attention of the Nepal Darbar. Bir Shamsher replied that there had been no alteration in the customary form of address to the Emperor in this letter. He provided the Resident with the Nepali version of the letter, which was strikingly different in tone from the text that appeared in the *Peking Gazette*.[54] In the former, the Emperor was addressed respectfully, but essentially as an equal; in the latter, the Nepali king appeared as a humble petitioner before the Emperor.

The explanation is one that should be familiar to all specialists in Chinese history. The Amban, on receiving the Nepali text of the letter, translated it into Chinese, using the extravagant honorific forms considered appropriate by the Peking Court! When this became clear, Calcutta instructed the British Minister at Peking to inform the *Tsungli Yamen* (Foreign Office) that "the submissive expressions in the Nepalese letters are not regarded by Her Majesty's Government as an acknowledgement of vassalage, or indeed as anything more than a purely formal and complimentary style of address."[55] This ended the ambiguity that had on occasion been evident in the British attitude toward Nepali-Chinese relations. The alleged subordination of the Kathmandu court to the Ch'ing Emperor was thenceforth dismissed by Calcutta as a fiction, both *de jure* and *de facto*, and no longer was a consideration in the Indian government's Himalayan frontier policy.

THE CAMPAIGN TO "OPEN" TIBET

Frustrated in its earlier efforts to establish commercial relations with Tibet, Calcutta decided in 1885 to send a mission to Lhasa. China's consent to the deputation was again obtained from the Peking court, but it soon became apparent that Lhasa was still not inclined to recognize the Chinese passport nor, indeed, to concede that China had the right to make decisions affecting Tibet. As a countermeasure, apparently, Lhasa instigated disorders in the Chinese-administered districts in eastern Tibet directed at the Catholic mission at Batang. This immediately embarrassed China's

---

54 For a translation of the Nepali text of this letter, see *Secret E*, No. 123, September 1894; for a translation of the Chinese text, see *ibid.*, No. 119.
55 *Ibid.*, No. 37, January 1896: Secretary of State for Foreign Affairs to British Minister, Peking, Oct. 15, 1895.

relations with both the French and the British, diverting their attention to the Burma-Yunnan border area. Finally, a Sino-British convention was signed in July 1886 delimiting the northeastern frontier of upper Burma (recently annexed by the British), for which "in deference to Chinese susceptibilities the Government of India consented to forego their intention of despatching a Mission to Lhassa."[56]

The next crisis on the frontier arose in Sikkim, where the ruler, Chogyal Thutob Namgyal, was suspected of harboring pro-Tibetan sentiments. At Lhasa's insistence, he agreed to close the route to Tibet through Sikkim. To assist him in this project a Tibetan force crossed the Jelep La in 1886 and occupied the Lingtu area of Sikkim, astride the main route from Kalimpong to the Chumbi valley. Calcutta ordered the Chogyal to come to Darjeeling to explain these developments, but he declined the invitation on the ground that the express permission of the Tibet government was required.[57] The British were then preoccupied with the threatening situation on the northwestern frontier, but finally sent a detachment into Sikkim in March 1888 which forced the Tibetans to withdraw to Tibet. The Tibetans returned reinforced, however, and it was not until September 1888 that they were again expelled. China and Britain commenced negotiations in 1889 and finally signed a convention on March 17, 1890, under which Peking recognized the exclusive supremacy of the British government over Sikkim and allowed the government of India to establish a trade mart at Yatung in Tibet.

One major flaw in this settlement—the failure to obtain the assent of the Tibetan government—soon became painfully apparent to the British. In 1895 a Tibetan official informed the British trade agent at Yatung that the Tibetan government did not recognize the validity of the 1890 convention and the supplementary 1893 agreement concluded with the Chinese.[58] The British complained repeatedly to Peking over Lhasa's failure to abide by the two conventions. The Chinese were in no position, however, to force the Tibetans to observe the terms of these agreements, and perhaps were not inclined to do so.

Nepal's attitude toward these developments was initially influenced by the determination to protect what remained of its position in the trans-Himalayan trade structure. When the Macauley mission was under consideration in 1886, for instance, Bir Sham-

---

[56] H. H. Risley, *The Gazetteer of Sikkim*, Introduction, p. vii.
[57] *Ibid.*, p. viii.
[58] Aitchison, *op. cit.*, vol. XIV, p. 17.

sher tried to dissuade the British from sending the expedition,[59] while at the same time he encouraged Tibet's defiant attitude towards the mission. The contretemps in Sikkim in 1888 came as an unpleasant surprise, however. Kathmandu felt that Tibet had overplayed its hand and urged Lhasa to seek a peaceful settlement of the dispute.[60] Perturbed by this attitude, Lhasa sent an envoy to Kathmandu in the spring of 1888 to demand that Nepal adhere to the terms of the 1856 treaty. Otherwise, he said, Tibet would withhold the annual tribute to Nepal and would pay the British instead.[61] Bir was disturbed by this prospect, but was not prepared to antagonize Calcutta by aiding the Tibetans. He wrote Lhasa, offering again to mediate the dispute. The Tibetans considered this an unfriendly gesture, and rejected the offer. Nor were the British interested in having Nepal as the "arbiter between the British Government and Tibetan authorities," and Bir's efforts to assume a central role in the settlement of this dispute came to naught.

Peking's concessions to the British in the 1890 convention on Sikkim once again demonstrated the basic weakness of the Chinese position in this region. Bir quickly readjusted his foreign policy, which just a year earlier had shown indications of a pro-Chinese bias, and sought again to improve relations with the British. For his cooperation on the recruitment question and for having thwarted the Sikkim Raja's attempt to flee to Tibet through eastern Nepal in 1892, the British Government overcame its previously squeamish attitude towards Bir Shamsher's murder of his uncle, and presented the prime minister with a K.C.S.I. (Knight Commander, Star of India).[62] The British rendered further assistance to Bir at this time by ordering that "sufficient surveillance should be exercized over the (Nepali) refugees to prevent their making British territory a base for active hostilities against the Nepal Darbar."[63] From that time on, the refugees in India ceased to be a serious

---

59 *Secret E*, July 1886, K.W. No. 3, Consultations No. 744–95: F. W. Wilson, Officiating Resident, to Calcutta, Apr. 16, 1886.

60 *Secret E*, No. 325, July 1888: Nepali Vakil at Lhasa to Bir Shamsher, May 26, 1888.

61 *Secret E*, K.W. No. 1, Consultations No. 307–45, July 1888: Major Durand to Calcutta (demiofficial), June 28, 1888.

62 London had indicated that Bir's implication in the assassination of Ranodip Singh should disqualify him for a K.C.S.I. However, Governor-General Lansdowne, closing his eyes to the evidence, wrote London absolving Bir of guilt. (*Ibid.*, June 1892.) Much to the British Resident's indignation, Bir Shamsher failed to show a sense of gratitude for the honor bestowed on him but instead complained that he had not received a G.C.S.I. (Grand Cross, Star of India) as had Jang Bahadur. (*Ibid.*, K.W. No. 2 to Consultations No. 285–90: Colonel Wylie to Calcutta, May 28, 1892.

63 *External A*, May 1892, Consultation No. 180, Under-Secretary, GOI, to Chief Secretary, U. P. Government, May 5, 1892.

threat to Bir's authority, although, of course, Calcutta could always revive the threat of British assistance to the refugees if the Kathmandu Government got too far out of line.

After 1895 there was steady deterioration in British-Tibetan relations, partly because of internal developments in Tibet. The Thirteenth Dalai Lama, Thupten Gyatso, assumed full powers in 1895, the first of his incarnation in the 19th century to survive the attainment of his majority. The new Dalai Lama was a staunch nationalist, determined to protect Tibet from excessive foreign influence, whether Chinese, British, Nepali or Russian. He used the Sino-Japanese war of 1894–95 and an uprising of the Muslim population in western China to reduce even further the limited influence of the Ambans in Tibet. Convinced that Tibet's nominally subordinate relationship to China could no longer serve as an effective buffer to direct British pressure on Tibet, the Thirteenth Dalai Lama looked elsewhere for support. Nepal had proved to be an unreliable ally, more concerned with maintaining good relations with the British and Chinese than in protecting its historical interest in the trans-Himalayan area. The only other major power with a substantial stake in central Asia was Russia, and the introduction of this factor—or rather, the threat of its introduction—dominated Himalayan politics during the next decade.

Several factors had induced the British to revive their efforts to "open" Tibet: trade with Tibet and China, fear of Russian expansion, and the determination to protect British interests in the course of the expected dismemberment of China. But if the impetus for expansion across the Himalaya was compelling, the obstacles were equally complex. China should not be alienated completely, for British interests were far greater in China proper than on the northern frontier of India. Moreover, there was always the danger of forcing China into an alliance with Russia or France if the British pressed too determinedly on the border areas. Nor could Nepal's reactions be ignored, for this small but stubborn Himalayan kingdom was a vital link in the politics of India's northern border as well as in the maintenance of British rule in India itself. There was also the question of England's relative position in the fierce competition for imperial expansion among the Western colonial powers. British activity in the Tibet region had repercussions not only in Asia but also in Europe and Africa, a fact which, in London's view, Calcutta often failed to weigh sufficiently. Finally, topographical factors were of considerable importance, for the expenses involved in trans-Himalayan adventures usually appeared to most British officials to far outweigh the benefits, political

or commercial, derived therefrom. But the 19th century was still
the era of empire builders, and the attraction of a "forward policy" was to prove irresistible to the British Indian officials on the
frontier.

7

Nepal and the
Pax Britannica

LORD Curzon's appointment as Viceroy of India in January 1899 heralded an important change in the government of India's policy in the Himalayan area. Previously, the British, in their relations with Tibet, had usually used the Peking government as intermediary. China's inability, however, to impress upon Lhasa the necessity of observing the various Sino-British agreements in regard to Tibet, and the political revolution in Tibet that followed the Dalai Lama's seizure of power in 1895, convinced Curzon of the necessity of dealing directly with the Tibetan authorities, even at the price of antagonizing Peking, whose sensitivity on this question previous British governments had felt it expedient to placate.

The decision to negotiate directly with Lhasa raised the question of the channel of communication between India and Tibet, since the Lhasa authorities had repeatedly refused to correspond directly with the British. Curzon contemplated using the Nepal government for this purpose. He hinted strongly to Bir Shamsher on one occasion that he would appreciate an invitation to visit Kathmandu so that, as he wrote a friend, he "might endeavour to get the Nepalese Government to allow a party to attack Mount Everest."[1] The significance of a British "mountaineering" expedition to the Nepal-Tibet border was as obvious as the political and international implications of a visit to Kathmandu by Curzon. Bir Shamsher proved "unexpectedly obdurate," however, and went

---

[1] L. J. L. D. Ronaldshay, *Life of Lord Curzon*, vol. II, London, 1928, pp. 166-67.

only so far as to proffer an invitation to visit the Nepal Terai for a "tiger shoot."[2]

The "Boxer Rebellion" in China in mid-1900 further complicated British-Nepali relations because of Calcutta's decision to include a Gurkha Rifles unit in the Indian army detachment sent to China. Bir reacted negatively to this, though he was reluctant to press on Calcutta the obvious fact that this could seriously embarrass Nepal's relations with China. Bir even assured the British Resident, Colonel Loch

with perhaps a suspicious quickness in seizing the point, that his doubt and hesitation do not arise from the consideration of Nepal and Chinese relations, but the suggestion which he himself put forward that the regiment would be put out of caste from crossing the sea, and that recruiting would consequently be hurt.[3]

Curzon replied curtly that Gurkha regiments in the British army had crossed the sea on previous occasions without loss of caste, and in July 1900 the First Battalion of the Fourth Gurkha Rifles was sent to China.[4]

The year 1901 was of great importance in Nepali politics as well as to the Himalayan region as a whole. On January 2, Curzon informed Kathmandu that he would be pleased "to accept the invitation to shoot in the Nepal Terai which has more than once been extended to him since he came to India."[5] Reluctantly, and scarcely even politely, Bir Shamsher extended the requested invitation, noting however that due to his ill health he would not be able to accompany the Viceroy. And indeed on March 4, 1901, before Curzon's visit had begun, Bir Shamsher died under rather mysterious circumstances. His successor, Deb Shamsher, followed Bir's example and refused to go personally to the Terai to meet the Viceroy, but acceded to the request of his younger half-brother, Chandra Shamsher, who asked to be allowed to escort Curzon on the "hunt." What these two brilliant and ambitious men discussed in their meetings in the Terai in April can only be conjectured, but it seems improbable that Nepali internal politics and the situation

---

2 *Ibid.*

3 *Secret E*, August 1900, Consultation No. 200: Note by W. J. Cuningham, June 30, 1900.

4 *Ibid.*, August 1900, Consultation No. 213; Curzon to Loch, July 1, 1900. Curzon expressed some doubts about this decision, and stated that if he had been consulted in advance he would have advised against it. However, inasmuch as the decision had been announced, the Viceroy thought it would be an improper precedent to reverse it merely to mollify Nepali sensitivity on this point. *Ibid.*, August 1900, Consultation No. 211: Note by Curzon, June 30, 1900.

5 *External B*, February 1901, K.W. No. 1, Consultation No. 40: Calcutta to Colonel Loch, Jan. 2, 1901.

in Tibet were ignored. On June 26, 1901, about two months after his return to Kathmandu from the Terai, Chandra staged a successful coup d'état. Deb Shamsher was obliged to resign and eventually was allowed to proceed to India. Recognition of Chandra's seizure of power came almost immediately from Calcutta, arousing even deeper Nepali suspicions concerning the nature of the Terai talks between Curzon and the new prime minister.

It was also in 1901 that Russian-British rivalry over Tibet began to assume serious proportions, partly because of a misunderstanding over a Tibetan delegation that visited Russia in 1900–01. This mission was led by Dorjieff (known as the Tsenye Khenpo or Ngawang Lozang to the Tibetans), a Buriat Mongol subject of the Tsar who had achieved a position of confidence in the Dalai Lama's retinue. Russian interest in Tibet was not a recent development. In the early 1870's a Russian officer, Colonel Prejavalsky, had attempted on two occasions to reach Lhasa, but had been frustrated in both instances by the Tibetan authorities. The Russians then changed their tactics and attempted to utilize their Mongol Buddhist subjects, and particularly the Buriats, in establishing contacts with Lhasa. A number of Buriats were usually to be found studying in the various monasteries in Tibet. Dorjieff, who first went to Tibet as such a student, later served as a confidential adviser to the Thirteenth Dalai Lama.

The mere hint of Russian interest in Tibet was enough to cause worried consultations in Calcutta. There was no particular apprehension over a potential Russian military threat to India by way of Tibet, but the introduction of Russian influence on the northern border would vastly complicate British relations with the Himalayan border states—Bhutan, Sikkim, Nepal, Tibet and Kashmir. With the advantage of hindsight, it is apparent that Russia's interest in Tibet was not so much in mischief-mongering in the Himalayan area and India as in the more immediate problem of Russia's relations with the Mongol communities of central Asia. The great influence wielded by the Dalai Lama over the Mongols made Tibet an important factor in Russian calculations. Tibet under British domination would have been as serious a threat to the Russian position in central Asia as Tibet under Russian influence would have been to British India. Both the British and the Russians preferred an autonomous Tibet under the nominal suzerainty of China or, if this was no longer feasible, an independent Tibet.

A flood of rumors concerning Tibetan-Russian relations reached India in 1901–02 from various sources, including the Nepal Darbar. Most of these centered around the Dorjieff "mission" to St. Petersburg, which allegedly sought and obtained explicit

promises of aid from the Russians.[6] The Peking press also reported
the conclusion of a "secret" Sino-Russian agreement under which
St. Petersburg promised to uphold China's territorial integrity in
exchange for Peking's relinquishment of its claim to sovereignty
over Tibet, presumably in favor of Russia![7] Despite repeated denials
from responsible Chinese and Russian officials, Calcutta strongly
suspected that such an arrangement existed.

It is also apparent that the ambitious and energetic Chandra
Shamsher saw in Russian-British rivalry over Tibet an opportunity
to derive certain advantages for himself and Nepal, and he played
an important part in the events leading up to the 1903 Younghusband expedition. Nepal's policy objectives toward Tibet underwent a major change in the early years of Chandra's rule. Nepal's
once near-monopoly in trade with Tibet was no longer the most
important consideration, for by 1900 Kalimpong had already replaced Kathmandu as the principal entrepôt for trans-Himalayan
trade. Nepali merchant families continued to control the greater
part of this trade, for they still enjoyed a privileged position in
Tibet, but the centers of their operation were now Kalimpong and
Darjeeling rather than Kathmandu. In any case, Nepal no longer
derived any considerable revenue from trade with Tibet. Chandra
assumed that in the broader context of a British-Russian clash—
possibly resulting from a conflict of interests in Tibet—Nepal
would have opportunities to expand its political influence in Tibet, and perhaps could even act as the instrument for the expulsion
of Russian influence from Tibet with British authorization and
assistance.

Chandra became one of the more assiduous abettors of British-
Russian rivalry. A veritable flood of rumors concerning Russian
activity in Tibet, not easily subject to either verification or dis-
proof, had their origin in Kathmandu. The Coronation Darbar at
Delhi in January 1903 provided Chandra with an unprecedented
opportunity to impress upon the Viceroy the necessity for taking
prompt action in Tibet to forestall the Russians. The comments of
Sir Louis Dane, then Foreign Secretary of the Indian government,

---

[6] The Japanese pilgrim-explorer (and agent), Ekai Kawaguchi, was in Tibet at this
time and reported to the British, via Sarat Chandra Das, that he had seen several
hundred camel-loads of Russian arms arrive in Lhasa. (See his *Three Years in Tibet*,
Calcutta, 1909, pp. 505–06, and Shakabpa, *op. cit.*, p. 203). This must have been a
pure fabrication on his part, probably induced by Japan's interest in arousing British-
Russian rivalry in central Asia, as no Russian arms were found in Tibet by the
Younghusband expedition.

[7] For the text of this alleged agreement see Great Britain Foreign Office, *Papers Relating to Tibet*, London, 1904, Enclosure No. 49; Extract from the *China Times*, July
18, 1902, p. 140.

are particularly revealing with respect to the role played by Chandra in the shaping of Curzon's Tibet policy. He later noted:

All this was going on while the Coronation Darbar of 1903 was in progress, and that great man Maharaja Sir Chandra Shumshere came down as a guest of the Government of India. Lord Curzon was taking a great interest in the details of the Darbar himself, and had actually adopted the unusual measure of saying that on this account he had not time for the usual State visits and return visits to the Indian Princes. I met Sir Chandra Shumshere at the station, and I looked after him as Foreign Secretary. I was struck with the marvellous man he was. Much to my surprise, he at once opened up the subject of the serious misgivings he had of the movements of these Russians on the Nepal border, and expressed his desire to see the Viceroy. . . .

I went to Lord Curzon and humbly submitted that I thought he ought to see Sir Chandra. Lord Curzon said, "I cannot possibly do it. I have not seen any of the great Indian chiefs." I then gently reminded him that Nepal was not in India, and that his receiving a distinguished foreign guest would in no way affect his attitude as regards the other visitors. He was very unwilling, but eventually said, "I will see him for ten minutes."

The Maharaja was invited, and, like another great man, he "came, saw and conquered," and the ten minutes expanded into an interview of an hour and a half. During that time all relations with Nepal were put upon a very satisfactory basis. Since the time of the great Maharaja Jung Bahadur, they had been rather frostily polite only, but thereafter they became most cordial and intimate . . .

You saw in the map how the Nepal kingdom dominates all our military and civil routes in Northern India. It would have been quite impossible to have conducted any arrangements in Tibet with an unfriendly Nepal because it absolutely flanks the entry to Tibet. The Maharaja was only too ready to give his assistance, and he gave it with a full heart.[8]

These remarks are of particular significance in the light of the fact that it was only a few days later that Curzon sent his famous letter of January 8, 1903, to London recommending an expedition to Tibet. In this communication Curzan said, in part:

We should contemplate acting in complete unison with the Nepalese Durbar throughout our proceedings, and we would even invite them, if thought advisable, to take part in our mission. We believe that the policy of frank discussion and co-operation with the Nepalese Durbar

---

[8] Louis Dane's comments at the February 7, 1939, meeting of the East India Association in London following the lecture by M. Milward, "Nepal: 'The Land that leads to Paradise' " published in *The Asiatic Review*, April 1939, vol. XXXV, pp. 258–59.

would find them prepared most cordially to assist our plans. Not the slightest anxiety has been evinced at our recent forward operations on the Sikkim frontier; and we think that, with judicious management, useful assistance may confidently be expected from the side of Nepal. Our anticipations on this point may have been confirmed by a recent interview between His Excellency the Viceroy and the Prime Minister of Nepal, Maharaja Chandra Shamsher Jang, at Delhi. The Nepalese Government regards the rumours of intrigue in Tibet with the most lively apprehension, and considers the future of the Nepal State to be directly involved; and, further, the Maharaja is prepared to co-operate with the Government of India in whatever way may be thought most desirable, either within or beyond the frontier, for the frustration of designs which he holds to be utterly inconsistent with the interests of his own country.[9]

There seems little doubt that Curzon's letter was directly inspired by his talks with Chandra, who urged on the Viceroy the feasibility and necessity of punitive action against Tibet. Nor does it seem plausible that Curzon had intended to raise the question of an immediate forward thrust into Tibet prior to his talk with Chandra, as he would then not have been so reluctant to hold the interview.

The London government, in its reply to Curzon's letter of January 8, agreed that

having regard to the geographical position of Tibet on the frontiers of India and its relations with Nepal, it is indispensable that British influence should be recognized at Lhasa in such a manner as to render it impossible for any other Power to exercise a pressure on the Tibetan Government inconsistent with the interests of British India. . . . As regards Nepal, His Majesty's Government have noted with satisfaction the language held by the Minister of Nepal when he met Your Excellency at Delhi, and the terms of his subsequent letter. . . . Nepal has hitherto held its own without difficulty against Tibet; but for this reason Nepal is rightly sensitive as to any alteration in the political positions of Tibet which would be likely to disturb the relations at present existing between the two countries. His Majesty's Government fully recognise that the establishment of a powerful foreign influence in Tibet would disturb those relations, and might even, by exposing Nepal to a pressure which it would be difficult to resist, affect those which at present exist on so cordial a basis between India and Nepal.[10]

However, London was also cognizant of the strong suspicions the Russians had entertained concerning British activity on the Tibet frontier. Discussions with the Russians on central Asia were just begining and a British expedition to Tibet might seriously endanger the course of these negotiations. Further, a "forward policy"

---

[9] Great Britain, Foreign Office, *Papers Relating to Tibet*, London, 1904, p. 156.
[10] *Ibid.*, Secretary of State for India to Curzon, Feb. 27, 1903, pp. 183–85.

toward Tibet would require, inevitably, a public statement regarding China's claim to sovereignty in Tibet, which the British then, as later, wanted to avoid, if possible.

Curzon continued to press London on the issue, particularly after Lhasa once again indicated in mid-1903 its unwillingness to negotiate with the British and announced its intention to resist them with force if necessary. Developments in China, as well as the imminent outbreak of warfare between Russia and Japan (with whom the British had formed an alliance in 1902), apparently influenced the attitude of the London government. On October 1, 1903, the Younghusband mission, which had proceeded earlier to the Sikkim-Tibet border to conduct negotiations with the Tibetans, was authorized to cross the border, to occupy the Chumbi valley, and to advance to Gyantse in Tsang Province if necessary. In December, Younghusband led a strong military detachment (which included the 8th Gurkha Rifles) across the Jelep pass into Tibetan territory. After defeating the poorly armed Tibetan forces in a number of engagements, he advanced first to Gyantse and finally to Lhasa, which was occupied on August 3, 1904.

During these events, Chandra Shamsher fulfilled his promises of support to Curzon. Chandra's offer of troops was declined, but Calcutta did accept the loan of several thousand yaks and porters for transportation purposes.[11] The Nepali Vakil's report from Lhasa were forwarded to Calcutta by Chandra, and these served as the single most important source of information on the attitude of the Tibetan authorities—which may help explain some of the misconceptions entertained by the British on developments within Tibet. After the Younghusband expedition had reached Lhasa, the Nepali Vakil, in conjunction with a representative of the Bhutan government, figured prominently in the negotiation of the convention at Lhasa on September 7, 1904, between the British and the Tibetans.

In his correspondence with the Tibetan authorities, Chandra had urged Lhasa to seek a peaceful settlement with the British, arguing that better terms could be obtained before rather than after a military expedition had been sent to Tibet. When relations between Tibet and Calcutta reached a crucial stage in the latter

---

11 The porters supplied by Chandra were described by one eye-witness as "practically an impressed gang." They proved to be both "discontented and refractory" and were kept under control only with great difficulty. (E. Candler, *The Unveiling of Lhasa*, London, 1905, p. 90.) The yaks were also of questionable value, as most of them died before being put to use. Chandra had offered the loan of ten regiments of the Nepal Army to the British for the expedition, but these had been politely declined after due consideration had been given to the offer. [*Political and Secret Letters from India*, vol. 197, 1903 (IOL): Resident to GOI, Oct. 24, 1903.]

half of 1903, Chandra clarified Kathmandu's view of its treaty obligations in another letter to the Tibetan Kashag:

It is laid down in the treaty concluded . . . between the Governments of Nepal and Tibet that this Government will assist Tibet in case of invasion of its territory by any foreign Rajas. Consequently, when a difference of opinion arises between you and any one else, it is incumbent on me to help you to the best of my power with my advice and guidance in order to prevent any troubles befalling you from such differences, and the manner in which you have managed this business not appearing commendable, the assistance to be rendered to you by me at this crisis of your own creation, consists in giving you such advice as will conduce to the welfare of your country . . . Should you fail to follow my advice and trouble befell you, there would be no way open to me to assist you in any other way in the troublesome situation brought about by you without listening to my advice and following a wayward course of your own.[12]

Thus, Chandra interpreted Nepal's obligations under the 1856 treaty as consisting of the duty to extend advice and counsel rather than armed assistance in case of aggression against Tibet by a foreign power!

This letter was disconcerting, to say the least, to Lhasa, which tried to explore further the attitude of the Nepali government. A Tibetan official, the Dheba of Kuti, accompanied by several Chinese officers, was sent to Kathmandu around the beginning of 1904, ostensibly to present Chandra with the robes and decorations associated with the Chinese title he had received earlier, but also carrying a letter from the Dalai Lama. By that time, the British expeditionary force was already in Tibet, preparing for the march on Lhasa. In his reply, Chandra merely reiterated his view that Tibet was at fault in the dispute and strongly urged Lhasa to seek a settlement with the British as soon as possible.[13] The Dalai Lama vigorously denied Tibet's culpability, and pointed out to Chandra that it was British encroachment on Tibetan territory that had brought on the dispute. He requested Nepali mediation and asked Chandra to send a "well experienced officer" to help settle the dispute or assist in the conclusion of a treaty.[14]

Chandra Shamsher wrote Lhasa that it was "already too late" for Nepal to send anyone to mediate the Tibetan-British dispute but authorized the Nepali Vakil at Lhasa, whom the Tibetans distrusted, to serve in such a capacity if the Dalai Lama so desired. To

---

12 "Papers Relating to Tibet," *op. cit.*: Chandra Shamsher to Tibet Kalons, Aug. 27, 1903.
13 *Ibid.*, Chandra Shamsher to Dalai Lama, n.d., but sent in June 1904.
14 *Ibid.*, Dalai Lama to Chandra Shamsher, July 8, 1904.

the Tibetan request that Nepal's representative "try to fix the boundary at the old line fixed by His Majesty the Chinese Emperor and that not a span of our territory should be taken away," Chandra assured Lhasa that the British "do not covet your country, and therefore have no desire to annex any part of it." Chandra also referred to the report that the Dalai Lama was planning to flee from Lhasa on the approach of the British detachment, and urged him to remain at Lhasa and protect his people, for to flee would be "like a captain deserting a ship in mid-ocean."[15] By the time this letter reached Lhasa, however, the Lama had fled and the British were in control of the city and were in the process of negotiating an agreement with those Tibetan authorities who had remained behind. For his "valuable support" in this enterprise and for the improvements he had inaugurated in the recruitment of Nepalis for the "Gurhkha" regiments in the British Indian army, Chandra was made a G.C.S.I. in January 1905, an honor that did little to enhance his reputation among the Tibetans.

THE "FORWARD POLICY" IN REVERSE

By the end of 1904 it was obvious to London that the Younghusband expedition had created far more problems than it had solved. The strain placed upon relations with both Russia and China by the sudden eruption of a dominant British influence to the north of the Great Himalayan barrier made immediate withdrawal from Tibet imperative—in the opinion of London if not that of Calcutta. The flight of the Dalai Lama to Mongolia, where he established direct contacts with Russian officials, was even more intolerable. At London's insistence, therefore, the expeditionary force withdrew from Tibet in 1905 on terms that were less punitive than those initially imposed on the Tibetan government in the 1904 Lhasa convention.

The British next moved to reassure China and Russia. Peking, which had refused to recognize the Lhasa convention, was placated by the agreement signed between the two powers on April 27, 1906, in which London engaged "not to annex Tibetan territory or to interfere in the administration of Tibet." In exchange, Peking confirmed the 1904 Lhasa convention in its amended form, and guaranteed "not to permit any other foreign state to interfere with the territory or internal administration of Tibet."

---

15 *Ibid.*, Chandra Shamsher to Dalai Lama, Aug. 6, 1904. The curious simile used here, which must have baffled the Tibetans, leads one to suspect that the letter was written for Calcutta's rather than Lhasa's edification.

Russia, weakened by its defeat in the Russo-Japanese war and the tremendous internal upheaval of 1905–06, was also more interested in stabilizing the situation in central Asia than in taking advantage of England's temporary embarrassment or of the Dalai Lama's invitations to intervene in Tibet. A convention was signed at St. Petersburg on August 31, 1907, in which both England and Russia recognized China's suzerain rights in Tibet and agreed (1) to respect the territorial integrity of Tibet and to abstain from interference in its internal administration, and (2) to treat with Tibet only through the Chinese government as intermediary. This constituted a major reversal of British policy toward Tibet even though Russia agreed that the government of India, because of its geographical position, had "a special interest in the maintenance of the *status quo* in Tibet." Russia, however, also made it clear that it would not remain indifferent if the British should disturb that *status quo.*

Although there is ample ground for disputing the wisdom of Curzon's "forward policy" in British imperial terms, it was at least a rational policy from the standpoint of the security of India's northern borders. The drastic policy changes introduced in late 1905 by the new Liberal Party government in England and Curzon's successor in India, Lord Minto, constituted a sacrifice of India's interests for those of the Empire, the long-range consequences of which are still being felt today. If the British had been as straightforward in their support of Tibet as the Russians were to be in regard to Outer Mongolia, Tibet's independence might eventually have been recognized by China. It was London's deliberate ambiguity on this question, as well as its inability to resist the temptation to play both ends against the middle on the "suzerainty" issue, that encouraged China to maintain an irredentist position on Tibet long after it had been effectively excluded from the exercise of any significant influence, much less authority, in that country.

Thus, ironically, the only power involved in the 1903–05 proceedings that emerged with any tangible advantage was China. Peking had watched developments in Tibet with evident concern but a sense of helplessness. The Amban's position at Lhasa was so tenuous, being more dependent upon Tibetan tolerance than on Chinese power, that even his numerous offers to mediate the dispute with the British had been rudely rejected by Lhasa. The Amban's efforts to bolster his position by expanding his bodyguard to 2,000 men had been disapproved by Peking. With what must have been a sense of desperation, he then applied to the Nepal Darbar for the loan of a thousand Nepali troops! Kathmandu, however, feared that this would complicate relations with both Tibet and India, and expressed its inability to meet this request.[16] Even more embarrassing to the Amban was the manner in which the Tibetans ignored Peking's disposition of the Dalai Lama in 1904, treating the imperial rescript as an illegal intrusion into Tibetan affairs.

The near-chaos in the Tibetan administration after the flight of the Dalai Lama and the withdrawal of the British expeditionary force, however, presented the Chinese with an unexpected opportunity to reestablish a presence in Tibet. Under the ruthless but competent leadership of General Chao Erh-feng, a Chinese army launched operations aimed at bringing the eastern-Tibet border area under direct Chinese administration. The Tibetan forces had been badly mauled by the Younghusband expedition, and were in no position to offer effective resistance in Kham. By 1909 most of this area was under relatively effective Chinese control.

The Dalai Lama, meanwhile, had left Mongolia in 1906 but had not returned to Tibet. The 1906 Peking convention and the 1907 St. Petersburg convention made it obvious to the Dalai Lama that he must seek an accommodation with the Manchu court. With this end in view, he came to Peking in September 1908. Hoping to obtain an implicit recognition of his autonomous status, the Dalai Lama requested that he be allowed to address the Emperor directly, as his predecessors had done before 1793. This was refused, however, and instead the Dalai Lama was offered a humiliating Chinese title, "Our Loyal and Submissive Vice-Regent" with the stipulation that on his return to Tibet

he must be careful to obey the laws of the Sovereign State, and must promulgate to all the goodwill of the Court of China. He must exhort the Tibetans to be obedient and follow the path of rectitude. He must follow the established custom of memorializing us, through the Imperial Amban, and respectfully await our will.[17]

In his talks with the Foreign Office, the Chinese insisted that the terms of the 1906 Peking convention be carried out—i.e., that China's suzerainty be recognized by the Tibetans.

These terms were totally unacceptable to the Dalai Lama, who decided to return to Lhasa as quickly as circumstances would permit. An opportunity arose with the deaths of Emperor Kuang-hsu and the all-powerful Dowager Empress in mid-November 1908. The Dalai Lama left Peking three weeks later without having

---

16 *Political and Secret Letter from India*, Secret Dept. No. 44, Oct. 28, 1909 (IOL).
17 Imperial Decree of Nov. 3, 1908, *Peking Gazette*, as quoted in Eric Teichman, *Travels of a Consular Officer in Eastern Tibet*, London, 1922, pp. 19–20.

reached an agreement with the Chinese government. It was, however, eleven months before he finally returned to Lhasa—just ahead of a Chinese army, as it turned out.

One of the first acts of the Dalai Lama on his return was to appeal to England, several European powers and the United States to intercede with Peking and obtain the withdrawal of the Chinese troops. He also requested armed assistance from Nepal under the 1856 treaty. The response from all quarters was discouraging. Both the British and the Nepalis made it clear that they would do nothing to impede the advance of the Chinese troops so long as their respective rights in Tibet were not violated.[18] Unable to mount a successful resistance and unwilling to accept Chinese terms, the Dalai Lama once again fled from Lhasa in February 1910, this time to India. For the second time since 1904, the Chinese deposed the Dalai Lama and asked the Panchen Lama to assume the Regency, an honor he again declined. The Amban, Lien-yu, became the real ruler of the country, in conjunction with the Chinese military commanders. Tibet was brought under firmer Chinese control than at any time in its past history.

The amazing success of the Chinese campaign in Tibet seems to have given rise to unrealistic expectations as to Peking's capacity to adopt its own "forward policy" throughout the Himalayan region. Indeed, as early as February 1907, the junior Amban at Lhasa, Chang Yin-t'ang, had written Peking regarding the urgency of strengthening relations with Nepal. He advocated that China

send a special envoy to this country in order to publicize to its people our prestige and beneficence, to explain the necessity of establishing a close reciprocal reliance between them and us and to conclude a secret offensive and defensive alliance between Nepal and Tibet.[19]

Chang contacted the Nepali Vakil at Lhasa and told him that Tibet and Nepal "being united together like brothers under the auspices of China should work in harmony for the mutual good." He also inquired about the possibility of obtaining Nepali arms or soldiers for the Amban's guard at Lhasa, but was again turned down on both counts by the Nepal Darbar.[20]

---

[18] Peking justified the dispatch of an army to Tibet by citing the Anglo-Chinese 1908 Tibet Trade Regulations, which made China responsible for the protection of telegraph lines from the British trade marts in Tibet to the Indian frontier!

[19] *Ch'ing-chi-Ch'ou* . . . , vol. III, Chuan 2, p. 33: telegram from Chang Yin-t'ang to the Foreign Office, Peking, February 1907. Chang repeated these recommendations in a later communication (*ibid.*, Chuan 5, p. 10, December 1907).

[20] Sir Charles Bell Collection (IOL), Nepal Note Book, Mss. Eur-F-80, Nepal letter of Apr. 20, 1907.

The establishment of Chinese authority in Tibet in 1910, however, greatly increased the potential for the development of closer relations with both Nepal and Bhutan, whose ties with the British Indian Empire were still ambiguous in some respects. British policy at this stage of developments was to allow China "practically complete control" over Tibet, but to resist any Chinese attempt to interfere south of the Himalayan crest. In a note to the Peking government dated February 26, 1910, the British Minister to China declared:

Great Britain, while disclaiming any desire to interfere in the internal administration of Tibet, cannot be indifferent to disturbances of the peace in a country, which is her neighbor and on intimate terms with neighbouring States on her frontier, and especially with Nepal.[21]

In its reply, Peking referred to Nepal as a "feudatory" of China, and maintained that Bhutan and Sikkim were both states in friendly relations with China.[22]

The Chinese government adopted an even stronger position in its note of October 28, 1910, which argued that "Nepal has forwarded tribute to Peking for years past and has long submitted to vassalage to China. Bhutan likewise is a vassal State of China."[23] In its reply, dated January 17, 1911, the British government stated bluntly that it would act, "and advise the Nepalese Government to act, upon the assumption that Nepal is not a vassal but wholly independent of China." Furthermore, any attempt by Peking to exercise influence over Nepal and Bhutan could not "possibly be tolerated."[24] China refused to back down, however, and the British government finally declared "that they will be bound to resist any attempt on the part of the Chinese Government to impose their authority or in any way to intervene in either of these two States."[25] With the outbreak of the 1911 revolution in China and the expulsion of the Chinese from Tibet, the question of Nepal and Bhutan's status vis-à-vis China became purely academic. But at no point during this period did any Chinese government concede the independence of those two states or the British government's paramount authority there.

---

21 Great Britain Foreign Office. *Tibet: Further Papers from September, 1904 to May, 1910*, London: H. M. Stationery Office, 1910, p. 209.
22 Secret Department, May 21, 1910 (IOL), Prince Ch'ing to British Minister, Apr. 18, 1910.
23 *Secret E*, No. 204, January 1911: The Wai-wu-pu (Foreign Office) to the British Minister, Peking, Oct. 28, 1910.
24 *Ibid.*, No. 253, July 1911: British Minister, Peking, to Prince Ch'ing, Jan. 17, 1911.
25 *Ibid.*, No. 279, July 1911: British Minister, Peking, to Prince Ch'ing, May 10, 1911.

NEPAL AND CHINA

Probably no one had been more embarrassed by the vacillating British policy toward the northern border in the 1905–10 period than Chandra Shamsher of Nepal. The Prime Minister had reversed Kathmandu's traditional policy discouraging direct British-Tibetan relations at the time of the Younghusband expedition, but none of the expected advantages—with the very important exception of the improvement in Nepali-British relations—had actually materialized. The Chinese military campaign in eastern Tibet made a renewal of direct diplomatic contacts with the Peking authorities advisable, and Kathmandu therefore sought permission for the periodic mission to proceed to China. Peking, which was also eager to improve relations with Nepal, agreed immediately. The mission, headed by Bharat Bahadur, left Kathmandu in August 1906 and spent nearly four years on its journey. The British were again irritated by the submissive language used in the Chinese version of the letter to the Emperor, and also by Nepal's being classified as a "dependency beyond the border of China" in the Chinese Imperial Gazetteer, but were reassured on both points by Chandra Shamsher.

Kathmandu did not appear to be greatly agitated by China's "forward policy" in Tibet in its early stages, and indeed perceived several possible advantages for itself. In 1907, for instance, Chandra succeeded in obtaining additional modern arms from the British, using the volatile situation in eastern Tibet as his most persuasive argument. There were also potential concessions to be won from the Chinese, who were eager to enlist Nepal's support in their campaign to transform Tibet into a Chinese province. Nepal may even have felt that it had more to gain from a Chinese-dominated Tibet than from an autonomous government at Lhasa under strong British influence. The Tibetans suspected that Nepal wanted a Chinese presence in Tibet as a potential balance to British India. Lonchen Shatra, the Tibetan Minister, later alleged that during the Chinese advance on Lhasa in 1910, the Nepali Vakil repeatedly warned the Tibetans against resisting, and "by this bad advice Chinese troops were enabled to enter Tibet."[26]

Whatever Nepal's initial reactions to the Chinese move into Tibet may have been, the course of developments there eventually aroused apprehensions in Kathmandu. The Chinese were scarcely

---

[26] Bell, *Portrait of the Dalai Lama, op. cit.*, p. 116.

established in Lhasa before Chandra wrote the British, on March 11, 1910, asserting Nepal's "unfettered" right to protect its interests in Tibet and, at the same time asking if there was anything in the Peking or St. Petersburg conventions obligating the British or Russians to intervene in case Nepal should move forcefully in Tibet.[27] The British replied in the negative, but did insist that Kathmandu consult the government of India before taking any action in Tibet likely to lead to hostilities and that it follow any advice offered to it.[28]

The Kathmandu Darbar seems to have been genuinely offended at the presumptuous Chinese claims to suzerainty over Nepal, which Chandra Shamsher characterized as an "unwarranted fiction" and a "damaging reflection on our national honour and independence."[29] The substance of the Chinese position on China's relationship to Nepal was not a surprise to Kathmandu. It was embarrassing and potentially dangerous, however, to have these claims become an issue of public contention between China and Great Britain, and Chandra hastened to repudiate them. When reports reached Kathmandu in late 1910 that Peking was considering sending a mission to Nepal to confer a new title on Chandra Shamsher, he instructed his representative in Lhasa to discourage the Chinese from doing so, ostensibly on the ground that he did not want to incur any new obligations to China.[30]

Perhaps the greatest disappointment to Chandra Shamsher was the fact that the position of the Nepali traders in Tibet had not improved after the Chinese had assumed direct control over the Tibetan administration. Indeed, the Amban wrote the Darbar questioning the exercise of extraterritorial rights by the Vakil under the 1856 treaty now that the Imperial Chinese police were responsible for the maintenance of public order in Tibet. This struck at the heart of Nepali privileges in Tibet and elicited a strenuous objection from Chandra Shamsher.[31] Nevertheless, there was chronic dissension between the Amban and the Nepali Vakil on this point, and it was one factor that helped shape Kathmandu's reaction to the events leading up to the expulsion of the Chinese from Tibet in 1912.

There were some positive aspects to China's presence in Tibet,

27 Secret Department, No. 93, July 21, 1910 (IOL): Memorandum from Chandra Shamsher to British Resident, Mar. 11, 1910.
28 *Ibid.*, British Resident to Chandra Shamsher, June 15, 1910.
29 *Secret E*, No. 164, January 1911: Chandra Shamsher to British Resident, Nov. 19, 1910.
30 *Ibid.*, No. 166, January 1911: British Resident, Nepal, to GOI, Nov. 7, 1910.
31 *Ibid.*, No. 8, January 1912: Amban to Chandra Shamsher, Sept. 1, 1911, and Chandra's reply, Nov. 21, 1911.

of course, particularly with respect to Nepal's relations with the government of India. For instance, Chandra Shamsher used the Chinese claims to Nepal in a series of maneuvers aimed at extracting concessions from the British on issues that had rankled Kathmandu for some time. These concessions included (1) granting him the rank of ambassador during his visits to India or London and (2) deletion of the reference to Nepal as a "Native State" in the 1906 edition of the Imperial Gazetteer of India. Such steps were necessary, Chandra argued, to convince Peking of Nepal's independent status and discourage Chinese assertions of suzerain rights in the state. He also renewed his suggestion, first broached in 1907, for a new treaty that would recognize Nepal's independence in more specific terms, and sought to obtain more arms to meet the alleged Chinese threat to Nepal.[32]

The government of India was prepared to make some minor concessions to Nepal with respect to the importation of arms and machinery and also to reassure Kathmandu regarding its Tibetan interests. The British agreed to use their influence at Peking to guarantee that administrative changes in Tibet should not adversely affect Nepal's existing rights in that state, and also promised to "support and protect Nepal in the event of an unprovoked attack from any quarter." But Chandra's requests for ambassadorial status, a new treaty, and a revision of the Imperial Gazetteer were politely rejected, thus ending his hopes for a more positive recognition of Nepal's independence. The British were prepared to reconfirm Lord Elgin's pledge, made in 1894, that they had "no intention or design of interfering with Nepal's autonomy," but they were not willing to surrender their right to exercise ultimate guidance over Nepal's foreign policy. The Resident was instructed to inform Chandra that Nepal's status lay somewhere between that of independent Afghanistan and the "feudatory States of India."[33]

Whether Nepal would eventually have had greater success in its attempts to play off the Chinese against the British was never really put to the test, for the 1911 revolution in China resulted in the abrupt expulsion of the Chinese from Tibet. With his usual persistence, Chandra sought to extract every conceivable advantage in this volatile situation. He told the British that Nepal preferred "to see Tibet restored to its proper status of practical independence" and was prepared to aid the Tibetans in attaining that objective. At the same time, however, he declared that if the British allowed China "a free hand in Tibet," Nepal would move to "rec-

32 *Ibid.*, No. 693, July 1911, Note by E.W. Clarke, Jan. 4, 1911.
33 *Ibid.*, No. 701, July 1911, British Resident to Chandra Shamsher, May 1, 1911.

tify the boundary" with Tibet "so that the political frontier may coincide in future with the natural boundary"[34] i.e., the Bhairab Langur range in the Kuti-Kerong area.

Kathmandu's role in the struggle between the Chinese and Tibetans in 1912 was of major importance, for the Nepali Vakil in Lhasa functioned as the mediator in the negotiations that led to the withdrawal of the Chinese forces. Territorial gains were not forthcoming, but the prestige of the Vakil was enhanced and the position of the Nepali trading community considerably improved—if only temporarily. There was even the prospect that Nepal would emerge as Tibet's "protector"—a status that had appealed to successive Nepali Governments since at least 1791—in view of the government of India's apparent determination to play a neutral role in the Sino-Tibetan dispute.

The diplomatic finesse employed by the Nepali Vakil in these developments, moreover, allowed Nepal to assist Tibet in ridding itself of the Chinese without at the same time unnecessarily antagonizing the latter. Indeed, General Chung-yen, the Chinese commander, was so convinced of Nepal's good will that he wrote proposing a "union of Nepal with the Five Affiliated Races of China," and suggesting the deputation of a "special delegation to Peking for orders and advice."[35] Chandra Shamsher replied politely to this incredible invitation, but stated "that as Nepal is an ancient Hindu Kingdom, desirous of preserving her independence and her separate existence, she cannot entertain the idea of such a union."[36]

The real question, of course, was not a Nepal-China union but whether the traditional relationship between the two states would be continued. Doubts over the wisdom of allowing Nepali missions to proceed to Peking on a regular basis had been expressed in both Calcutta and Kathmandu even prior to the expulsion of the Chinese from Tibet. When the Amban suggested in mid-1911 that a Nepali mission leave for China the following year, the British Resident informed Chandra Shamsher that this should be done only after consultation with the government of India.[37] The mission was first postponed and then cancelled, when Chandra, on British advice, repudiated the Chinese interpretation of the significance of the mission and terminated the system. This consti-

---

34 Secret Department, No. 20, May 16, 1912 (IOL), British Resident to GOI, Apr. 22, 1912.
35 *Secret E*, No. 240, August 1913: Gen. Chung-yiu to Chandra Shamsher, Feb. 23, 1913.
36 *Ibid.*, No. 248 Chandra Shamsher to Gen. Chung-yiu, Mar. 16, 1913.
37 *Ibid.*, No. 66, February 1912, British Resident to GOI, Dec. 10, 1911.

tuted a formal abrogation of diplomatic relations between Nepal and China, and four decades passed before they were resumed.

THE SIMLA CONVENTION

When the Chinese withdrew in early 1913, Tibet attained a status of *de facto* independence unencumbered by even informal or tacit ties to China. The Dalai Lama moved to make this official when, on February 13, 1913, he issued a proclamation announcing the termination of all ties with China. The previous month the Tibetans had also concluded a treaty with Mongolia in which it was stated that both powers "having freed themselves from the Manchu dynasty and separated themselves from China, have become independent States."[38]

The Chinese Republic refused to recognize Tibet's independence, and there were intermittent hostilities on the Tibet-Szechuan frontier during 1913. The British government therefore proposed a tripartite conference to settle the terms of relationship between Tibet and China as well as to delimit the boundary between Tibet and India. Lhasa agreed almost immediately and Peking after some delay, and representatives of the three governments inaugurated a series of meetings at Simla on October 13, 1913. The major points at issue were those concerning Sino-Tibetan relations. The positions taken by China and Tibet were so far apart that four months of negotiations failed to provide a solution. At that point, the British representative, A. H. McMahon, proposed a compromise under which (1) Tibet would be divided into two zones— Inner and Outer Tibet; (2) Outer Tibet (i.e., Central Tibet) would enjoy complete autonomy, and Inner Tibet (i.e., most of the area to the east of the upper Yangtze) would continue to be administered by China; and (3) Outer Tibet would recognize China's suzerainty. Lhasa was dissatisfied with some aspects of the proposal, but finally accepted the terms. China disliked the terms even more than the Tibetans, and eventually refused to ratify the agreement, on the ground that the boundary between Outer and Inner Tibet proposed by the British was unacceptable.

China's intransigence on this question was not unexpected, and provision had been made to deal with the situation. The clauses solely concerning Tibet and India came into effect with their ratifications of the treaty; the clauses affecting China, includ-

38 Richardson, *op. cit.*, p. 265.

ing British and Tibetan recognition of Chinese suzerainty in Tibet, were "suspended" pending Peking's ratification. The Chinese have claimed that their nonratification invalidated the entire convention, including the clauses concerning Tibet and India. Obviously, that would be the case only if the Tibetan government lacked the capacity to conclude an international agreement on its own authority. This is a complex legal question which need not be discussed at length in this study, but it should be noted that Tibet functioned from 1913 to 1950 with all of the attributes of a sovereign political entity. Although formal diplomatic relations were not established with other states, there were numerous instances during the 1913–50 period in which other governments, including China, accepted the legitimacy of Tibet's international actions and treated with it as an independent state.

The Simla convention inaugurated a period of unprecedented peace and stability along the entire Himalayan frontier under the watchful supervision of the British government of India. In effect, Tibet became part of the buffer system between India and China, and the major area of instability shifted from the Himalayas to the Tibet-China border. Occasional border conflicts erupted on the eastern Tibet-Szechuan frontier, with large-scale hostilities on at least two occasions—in 1917–18 and 1931–32—that required cease-fire agreements. Both China and Tibet continued to assert extensive territorial claims against each other, but in fact a relatively stable border alignment was achieved, based upon the upper Yangtze as the dividing line.

The trend of developments in Tibet since 1912 had tended to deemphasize Nepal's importance in British frontier policy. Kathmandu and Lhasa were placed upon a level of approximate equality by the British, who were primarily concerned with keeping relations between the two states on an even keel. Controversies between Kathmandu and Lhasa, usually involving the status of Nepali subjects in Tibet, were commonplace, but they were mild in comparison with what they had been in the past.

The one exception was a dispute in 1928 in which Chandra Shamsher threatened an invasion of Tibet if Lhasa did not accept the Nepali government's demands. It was probably not strictly accidental that this confrontation coincided with a temporary deterioration in Tibetan-British relations. The dispute concerned the arrest in 1922 of an alleged Nepali subject by the Tibetan authorities in the residence of the Nepali Vakil at Lhasa. The controversy had long since become dormant when Chandra decided to revive it in 1928 as part of a general complaint over the treatment of Nepali subjects in Tibet. Nepal mobilized its forces and allocated Rs.

2,500,000 as a war fund. It is doubtful, however, that the Darbar seriously considered resorting to hostilities or believed that the British would have allowed a war on the frontier. In any case, Chandra Shamsher's death in November 1929 ended the crisis. Shortly thereafter, at the request of a British mission to Lhasa, the Tibetan government proffered an apology for the 1922 incident, which Kathmandu readily accepted.[39]

NEPAL AND BRITISH INDIA, 1914–45

Chandra Shamsher had made the "alliance" with the British the basic theme in his foreign policy, even at the sacrifice of traditional Nepali goals. On several occasions he had been sorely disappointed by the failure of this policy to bring the advantages expected, but no valid alternative policies were available to the Darbar. Nepal became a virtual appendage of the British Indian empire, responsive to the requirements implicit in the alliance with the British.

During World War I, for instance, Kathmandu loaned the Government of India ten battalions of the Nepal state army and facilitated recruitment for the Gurkha battalions in the British Indian army. Approximately 55,000 Nepalis were recruited into those units during the war, and many of them served in the European or the Middle Eastern theater as well as in the 1919 Waziristan campaign in Afghanistan, with great distinction and heavy casualties. Thousands more volunteered for such other units as the Assam and Burma Military Police, the Dacca Police Battalion, the Army Bearer Corps, and the Labour Corps. It was widely felt that the British owed Nepal, and Chandra Shamsher, a generous demonstration of their gratitude for services rendered during the war. The character of the gesture became the subject of delicate and prolonged discussions between the two governments. Chandra was made an Honorary General in the British army and an Honorary Knight Grand Cross of St. Michael and St. George, and was thereafter addressed as "His Highness" by the British. The Prime Minister, however, had in mind something more tangible—preferably real estate. In 1919, he proposed the restoration of those sections of the Terai that had been ceded to the British in 1816 and had not

---

[39] Some British officials suspected that there was a relationship between the Nepali-Tibetan dispute and Lhasa's assent to the reception of a "semi-official" Chinese mission in 1930, the first to come to Tibet since 1912. David MacDonald, for instance, reported that the Tibetan government had appealed to China for assistance against Nepal in case of an invasion. [Bell Collection (IOL), Mss. Eur. F. 80, "Tibet Random Notes," No. 92: MacDonald to Bell, July 8, 1930].

been restored in 1858. The Viceroy replied that "it is clearly impossible that the reward should take the form of territory previously ceded" and instead offered an annual "gift" to Nepal of Rs. 1,000,000. Chandra was disappointed, but accepted the gift—which went into his private treasury—"as a lasting benefit . . . just as much as an accession of territory."[40]

Even more satisfactory, perhaps, to Nepali opinion in general, were the changes in designation of the Resident to British Envoy and the Residency to Legation in June 1920. In announcing the new nomenclature, the government of India declared that "this decision is intended to emphasize the unrestricted independence of the Kingdom of the Gorkhas, which is on an entirely different footing from that of the Protected States of India."[41] The earlier reluctance of the British to make overt gestures recognizing Nepal's "unrestricted independence" rather than "domestic autonomy" had obviously disappeared by 1920.[42] Chandra Shamsher was therefore encouraged to renew his proposal for a new treaty during the visit of the Prince of Wales to Nepal in 1921. The suggestion met with a sympathetic response from the British this time, and negotiations were begun in Kathmandu shortly thereafter. Nevertheless, it took nearly two years of leisurely negotiations to produce a draft agreement for, as the British Envoy noted, "there were . . . certain points both of principle and of detail involved which required very careful consideration, and the weighing of literally every single word."[43]

In the treaty signed December 21, 1923, at Sugauli—where the 1816 treaty had also been concluded—Nepal finally obtained an "unequivocal" recognition of its independence.[44] In the first clause, both governments agreed "mutually to acknowledge and respect each other's independence, both internal and external." The scope of Nepal's independence, however, was limited somewhat by the third clause, which obligated each government "to exert its good offices" to remove causes of "any serious friction or misunderstanding with neighbouring States whose frontiers adjoin theirs." Although defined in terms of mutual obligation, in fact this meant

---

40 *The Pioneer* (Lucknow), Jan. 29, 1920.

41 *The Times* (London), June 4, 1920.

42 Presumably, the change of policy on this question by New Delhi was not solely a reflection of British gratitude toward Nepal for its assistance during World War I. It also coincided with Gandhi's first nationwide "civil disobedience" movement. It is probable that the British wished to encourage Nepalis to think of themselves as beyond the ambit of the Indian nationalist movement and thus more readily available for use in controlling Indian resistance to British rule.

43 W. F. O'Connor, *On the Frontier and Beyond*, London, 1931, p. 309.

44 For the text of the treaty and accompanying notes, see *Accounts and Papers*, vol. 14, State Papers, Session, Jan. 8–Oct. 9, 1924, vol. XXVI (1924), CMD 2112.

that Kathmandu would continue to "consult" the government of India on relations with Tibet, Sikkim, Bhutan and China. In clause 5, Nepal gained the right to import arms and ammunition without previous government of India approval so long as "the intentions of the Nepal Government are friendly and that there is no immediate danger to India from such importations." Here again, however, this right was limited in practice, if not in theory, by Chandra's agreement, in a note that accompanied the treaty, to furnish details concerning such imports to the British Envoy.

Nepal gained further recognition of its independent status in 1934 when the British Government agreed to the establishment of a Nepali Legation at London. Kathmandu had decided to seek direct diplomatic relations with London when the growth of the nationalist movement in India raised doubts about the future of the British Empire in south Asia. The envoy in Kathmandu was thenceforth designated Envoy Extraordinary and Minister Plenipotentiary in recognition of Nepal's more exalted international status. But again the change was more in form than in substance, as the envoy continued to be drawn from the middle level of the Indian Political Service. As late as 1944, Prime Minister Juddha Shamsher could still protest that the envoy was merely a political agent and not a minister "for all Your Excellency's uniform and in spite of your 17 gun salute."[45]

Nepal's contribution to the Allied war effort from 1939 to 1945 far exceeded that made during World War I. Immediately on the outbreak of war, Juddha Shamsher followed his predecessor's example in 1914 by offering the loan of ten battalions of the Nepal state army for use in India. The British also received permission to recruit 22 more Gurkha battalions for the British Indian army, as well as a large number of Nepalis for other Indian army units, the Burma Rifles, Assam Rifles and Kashmir infantry. In all, "well over 200,000" Nepalis served in British units during the war,[46] primarily on the Burmese, Middle Eastern and North African fronts, where they again proved their magnificent fighting qualities at a heavy cost of life.

The period from 1905 to 1914 was of crucial importance in the Himalayan area as a whole new pattern of political relations emerged out of a complex of rivalries and conflicts. The Simla con-

---

[45] Nepal Foreign Office Records (1944): Prime Minister Juddha Shamsher to the British Envoy, Lt. Colonel Betham, Jan. 22, 1944.
[46] Lt. Colonel G. Betham, "Nepal," *Journal of the Royal Central Asian Society,* XXXV (January 1948), p. 20.

ference failed to solve the fundamental problems that had been created by the events surrounding the British and Chinese forward policies in Tibet, but it allowed for the postponement of a solution without causing extreme disequilibrium. Thus, it was possible to discern in 1914 the main characteristics that marked inter-Himalayan relations for the ensuing 30 years. Not until India achieved independence in 1947 and the Chinese Communists emerged victorious in 1949 was the precarious *modus vivendi* achieved so painfully in 1912–14 irretrievably upset.

None of the powers involved was particularly satisfied with the trend of developments after 1914. Tibet attained a *de facto* independence, but one that depended upon British good will and Chinese weakness because of Peking's refusal to ratify the Simla agreement. Lhasa, remembering British policy in the 1910–12 period, could scarcely have considered the government of India a reliable source of support, and must have suspected that New Delhi would desert it again in a similar situation. China was even less willing to accept the 1914 settlement on a long-term basis. Nationalist sentiment as well as geopolitical considerations made it imperative for China to insist upon the sanctity of its traditional frontiers, which it conceived as including Tibet. Thus, it was only to be expected that China would continue its efforts to bring Tibet into its own political framework.

By 1914 the British had achieved their most important political aim north of the Himalayas—an independent Tibet which could serve as a buffer between India and both Russia and China. In the wake of developments after 1900, however, London had become convinced of the inadvisability of an active "forward policy" in the trans-Himalayan area. British interests in Tibet were to be protected exclusively through diplomatic and economic means, and London was determined to avoid all obligations to Tibet that would commit the British to military support of the Lhasa regime. The British position in Tibet thus depended in part upon Chinese weakness, and Lhasa adjusted its policy accordingly. Unlike Nepal and Bhutan, which grudgingly accepted British "guidance" in the international sphere in exchange for internal autonomy, Tibet continued to exercise a considerable degree of independence in formulating its foreign policy. Lhasa was not even averse to seeking a settlement with the Chinese detrimental to British Indian interests or to approaching Russia and Japan for support against both the British and the Chinese. A fortunate combination of circumstances in the three decades subsequent to the Simla conference allowed the Tibetans sufficient latitude to function effectively in this manner. Nevertheless, the impermanent character of the situation was evident throughout the first half of the 20th century, as post-1950 developments so dramatically indicated.

Nepal's interests, both political and economic, had suffered a grievous injury in the 1905–45 period. The trade with Tibet now flowed almost exclusively through the Sikkim-Chumbi route, made secure after 1905 by the establishment of British trade agencies in Tibet. Chandra Shamsher's hopes for the expansion of Nepal's political influence in Tibet had been rudely shattered by the series of events leading to the expulsion of the Chinese from the Himalayan area in 1912, as Lhasa was bitter over Kathmandu's failure to honor its obligations under the 1856 treaty in either 1903–04 or 1910–12. Nepal found itself competing with Tibet for the favor of the government of India rather than serving as an instrument for the protection of British interests in Tibet, as Chandra had once thought possible. Nor could Kathmandu be completely satisfied with the exclusion of Chinese influence from Tibet. Thenceforth Nepal's foreign relations were solely with British India and Tibet, thus depriving Kathmandu of even the limited flexibility it had enjoyed in foreign-policy formulation prior to 1912.

A word on the Rana regime's foreign-policy record during the century of its rule in Nepal would be appropriate. That record has been the subject of bitter and undeviating abuse from most Nepali political and intellectual leaders during the past two decades, but a fairer and less emotional appraisal should now be possible. No doubt the Ranas, from Jang Bahadur to Mohan Shamsher, adjusted their foreign policy to a framework designed in its essentials by the government of India. This has galled contemporary Nepali nationalist sentiment, which derides the Ranas as "lackeys" of the imperialist British.

The question, however, is whether any conceivable alternative policies would have protected Nepal's independence and, indeed, obtained formal British recognition of the Kingdom's sovereign status in the comity of nations—no mean achievement in the prevailing circumstances. The answer is almost certainly in the negative. Jang Bahadur and Chandra Shamsher deserve recognition as two of the great nationalist heroes of Nepal. Whether they were acting in the interest of the nation or the Rana family—or both, as is most likely—is incidental from the broader historical perspective. The fact is that they devised policies suitable to the period in which they lived and implemented those policies with considerable sophistication and skill. In the process they made possible the emergence of Nepal as an independent state after the demise of the British Raj in India.

Part IV
A Place
in the World,
1945-70

8

The Politics
of Revolution,
1945-54

PEACE in 1945 brought neither political stability nor tangible re-
wards to Nepal, but rather a series of momentous events both
within and outside the country that posed a severe challenge to the
Rana regime. The Darbar faced the problem of rehabilitating perhaps 200,000 veterans of the war whom the British demobilized
quickly and with minimal financial assistance. Many of these men,
moreover, had been exposed to the insidious subversive influence
of the Indian nationalist movement in one form or another, and
were harbingers of a whole complex of dangerous thoughts on their
return home to Nepal. Scattered throughout the hill areas of the
country, they provided a potentially explosive component in communities that had always before been the bulwark of the regime
that happened to hold power in Kathmandu.

The challenge posed by the return of the war veterans could
probably have been mastered by the Ranas if it had not coincided
with the withdrawal of the British from India and the transfer of
power to the Indian National Congress. The Ranas had long since
been identified as inveterate opponents of that section of the nationalist movement of India led by the Congress, with its modernist,
democratic, "antifeudal" proclivities. Since the time of Chandra
Shamsher there had been a tacit arrangement between the Nepali
and British authorities under which Indian "subversive elements"
who sought refuge in Nepal were kept under surveillance and occasionally even arrested and extradited in exchange for similar
British-imposed restrictions on the activities of anti-Rana Nepalis
in India. The British had also used the reliable Gurkha units in the

Indian Army to control internal disorders on several occasions, making these "mercenaries" and their Rana "merchandisers" the special object of distaste among a broad segment of the articulate Indian public.

The Ranas had not been so shortsighted, however, as to place complete reliance on the perpetuity of British rule in India. Early in the game, several members of the family sought to establish a discreet working relationship with nationalist elements in the Indian political movement, looking ahead to the day when the British would no longer be a viable source of support. The faction in India with which the Ranas had the greatest affinity was the religiously orthodox, narrowly communal Hindu Mahasabha, which regarded both the British and the Congress party as anathema.[1] Rana ties with this extremist group were so intimate that in 1924 a Hindu Mahasabha leader even proposed the election of Chandra Shamsher as president of the party! The Mahasabha journals also served as a propaganda media for the Rana regime, both before independence and for some time thereafter. As late as 1946 the Nepal government played host to a prominent Mahasabha leader, Dr. B. S. Moonjee, who lauded the Ranas for having consistently upheld Hindu ideals of polity. This source of support proved to be of limited utility to the Ranas once India regained its independence, but it did provide the Ranas with channels of communication to some prominent non-Mahasabha Indian leaders, including several of the more conservative members of the Congress party.

NEW FOREIGN POLICY DIRECTIONS

The prospect of British withdrawal from India was a bitter pill for the Ranas, and it was some time before they were prepared to accept the need to make major policy adjustments to meet the new situation. The events surrounding the Hindu-Muslim riots in northern India in 1946 persuaded some leading Ranas that the process of disintegration then emerging would eventually force the British to abandon plans for the early transfer of power. This comforting thought was dealt a shattering blow in August 1946, however, when an interim government was formed in India under the Congress leader, Jawaharlal Nehru. It was now evident to even

---

[1] Chandra Shamsher also attempted on one occasion to establish contacts with the Gandhi movement in India through the medium of a Nepali Gandhian, Tulsi Mehar, who later established a *khadi* (hand-woven cloth) center in Kathmandu. Juddha Shamsher, however, put a stop to these activities when he was prime minister of Nepal in the 1930's.

the most obdurate Rana that their regime would soon have to be accommodated to an Indian government led by a party that had ample grounds for resenting the interventionist role the Ranas had played in India politics since the time of Jang Bahadur.

The first casualty was the Darbar's traditional isolationist policy and its principal corollary, the restriction of diplomatic relations to states with whom Nepal interacted directly on various levels. The Nepali legation at London and the British legation at Kathmandu were raised to embassy status, thus modifying the system under which the two governments had usually contacted each other through the medium of the government of India. Kathmandu then moved to expand diplomatic contacts beyond the British-Indian-Tibetan relationship in late 1946 when missions were sent to the United States and Nationalist China to test the response of those governments to Nepali overtures on diplomatic relations.[2]

The response in Washington was favorable. A treaty of friendship and commerce between the two countries was signed in Kathmandu in April 1947—four months before the transfer of power in India—and diplomatic relations were established ten months later. To the disappointment of the Ranas, however, it was decided that resident embassies would not be established in their respective capitals; the American ambassador in New Delhi was also accredited to Kathmandu and the Nepali ambassador in London to Washington.

The mission to Nanking met with less success, more because of Chiang Kai-shek's preoccupation with his Communist rivals than a lack of interest. Kathmandu made no further overtures to China at that time, but the advantages of diplomatic relations with Nanking continued to intrigue the Ranas. That hoary old Nepali theme, the use of China as a counterpoise to the ruling power in India, was now revived and indeed expanded to include the two major Western powers with an interest in the area. The Communist victory in China in 1949, however, acted as a damper upon the Rana regime's interest in diplomatic relations with Peking, but the idea was kept in abeyance rather than dropped. Kathmandu also enthusiastically accepted the Indian invitation to the Asian Relations Conference in New Delhi in March 1947, viewing participation as a demonstration

---

[2] Diplomatic contacts between the Nationalist Government in China and Nepal had not ceased entirely after Chandra Shamsher formally terminated the relationship with the Manchu Court in 1912. Chiang Kai-shek sent missions to Kathmandu in 1930, 1932, 1934 and 1946, ostensibly to bestow Chinese titles on newly inaugurated Rana Prime Ministers. Reportedly, these missions also discussed issues of common interest, including the establishment of diplomatic relations, with the Nepal Government. Kathmandu, however, saw no particular advantage in this so long as China was excluded from Tibet, particularly as it might have embarrassed Nepal's far more important relations with both New Delhi and Lhasa.

of its sovereign status to the world as well as an opportunity to interact with other independent Asian governments.

This dramatic reversal of one of the basic operating principles in Nepal's relations with foreign powers was formally adopted as policy by Prime Minister Mohan Shamsher in May 1948 when he declared:

In modern times it is neither possible, nor desirable for any state to keep itself in isolation from the world's affairs. It shall be our policy therefore to enter into diplomatic relations with all such countries that seek our friendship. It is evident that we shall require much help and co-operation from abroad in our nation-building project. We hope we shall obtain such needful assistance and co-operation from our neighbouring and friendly countries.[3]

Nepal was "eager to develop close friendly relations" with the United States, he continued, as well as with China, Tibet, France, the Netherlands, Belgium "and such other countries as well."[4] In conformity with this new policy, Nepal formally applied for admission to the United Nations in February 1949. It was frustrated on that occasion by the Russians (who questioned Nepal's "sovereign status," much to the indignation of the Nepalis), but this act constituted the conclusive step in the "opening" of Nepal to the world.

Relations with India.—It must have come as a pleasant surprise to the Ranas to discover that the attitude of the Congress government in India was not nearly as unfriendly as had been anticipated. The two governments concluded a "standstill agreement" under which India's status as the successor power to the British was recognized and the terms of relationship between Nepal and India as they existed prior to independence were retained. Thus India accepted, at least implicitly, the 1923 treaty in which Nepal's internal and external sovereignty had been recognized. This tended to reduce Kathmandu's fears that it would be treated as another of the Indian "native states" that were coerced into accession to the Indian Union in 1947 and 1948. It now seemed possible to the Darbar that relations with the Congress government in New Delhi could be established on essentially the same basis as those with British India, and to the mutual advantage of both countries. This would involve the retention of such arrangements as the Gurkha recruitment program and Nepali military assistance to India in crisis situations in exchange for an Indian commitment to support the Rana regime against both internal and external enemies.

---

[3] *Nepal Today* (New Delhi, Hindu Outlook, 1950), p. 47.
[4] Ramji Upadhyaya, *Nepal ko Itihas* (History of Nepal), Banaras, pp. 398–99.

It was particularly encouraging to the Ranas that the Congress government was eager to retain the system under which Nepalis were recruited into the Indian army. On August 9, 1947, one week before independence, a tripartite agreement was concluded between the British, Indians and Nepalis under which the existing Gurkha regiments were divided, four being allotted to the British and six to the Indians. Almost immediately thereafter, the Indian Government authorized a seventh regiment, formed mainly from the large number of Nepalis in the British Gurkha regiments who opted for service in the Indian Army. However critical the Congress party may have been about the use of the Gurkhas by the British, their value was quickly recognized. The Ranas sought to counter some of the criticisms levied against the recruitment system in Nepal by specifying that these units should not be used against Nepal, other Gurkhas (i.e., British Gurkha units), Hindus or "unarmed mobs." No restrictions were imposed, however, on their use against armed Muslim mobs in India—e.g., Kashmir—or against any external enemy, including Pakistan and China. Unlike the agreement with the British on recruitment, which was initially made subject to renewal every five years, the agreement with India remains operative as long as neither side formally requests its abrogation.

The Nepal Darbar made several gestures in the 1947–50 period which seemed to be designed to facilitate the process of accommodation with the Government of India. Prime Minister Padma Shamsher announced on May 16, 1947, that basic constitutional reforms aimed at associating the people with the government to a greater extent than in the past would be introduced shortly. This was in response to both small-scale but persistent internal disorders in Nepal and to the expressed views of several prominent Indian political leaders that a liberalization of the Rana regime was long overdue. At Padma Shamsher's request, a three-man team of Indian constitutional experts, led by Sri Prakash Gupta, was brought to Kathmandu in 1947 to advise the Darbar on political reforms. The moderate bent of the advisory team reflected the Indian predilection for what Nehru later termed the "middle way" approach.

The constitution promulgated by Prime Minister Padma Shamsher on January 26, 1948, reportedly adhered closely in most respect to the recommendations in the Sri Prakash report, and was therefore assured a favorable reception in New Delhi. At the Darbar, however, a powerful faction within the Rana family led by the commander-in-chief, Mohan Shamsher, was not prepared to accept even limited political reforms that might in the future diminish the preeminent position of the Rana family. The cautious Padma Shamsher was intimidated into offering his resignation in April 1948, and the new prime minister, Mohan Shamsher, quietly postponed implementation of the constitutional provisions.

In retrospect, this act may have doomed the Rana regime to early extinction, as it deprived the Darbar of much of its flexibility in dealing with both the Indian government and the domestic opposition. New Delhi's response to these events was only mildly critical, to be sure, and the prospect of a decisive Indian intervention in Nepali politics still seemed reasonably remote. Moreover, Mohan Shamsher was confident of his capacity to mollify the Indian government in other ways. During the Hyderabad and Kashmir crises in mid-1948, for instance, he offered New Delhi the loan of ten Nepal Army battalions at a time when the resources of the Indian Army were badly strained. The offer was accepted with thanks, and the Nepali detachments played an important role in the maintenance of public order in northern India during that difficult transitional period. Later, in 1950, Mohan Shamsher publicly promised that Nepal would come to India's aid whenever this was required.

The Rana regime no doubt won several merit badges from New Delhi for these generous gestures, but this did not change the conviction of Nehru and most other Indian Government leaders that at least limited political reforms were essential if an upheaval was to be avoided in Nepal. Describing the Indian approach in this period, Nehru stated:

We have tried for what it is worth to advise Nepal to act in a manner so as to prevent any major upheaval. We have tried to find a way, a middle way, if you like, which will ensure the progress of Nepal and the introduction of some advance in the ways of democracy in Nepal. We have searched for a way which would, at the same time, avoid the total uprooting of the ancient order.[5]

The "middle way" became a consistent theme in Indian policy toward Nepal until and after the 1950–51 revolution, and other considerations, including the strategic importance of the area, had to be fitted into this political framework. The terms of implementation of this policy, of course, changed substantially in the course of time, but this was due primarily to the determined resistance of the obtuse Mohan Shamsher and other leading Ranas to even modest political reforms.

Oppositional Politics in Nepal.—The intransigence displayed by Mohan Shamsher and his brothers not only complicated policy-

---

[5] *Jawaharlal Nehru's Speeches (1949–53)*, Publications Division, GOI, 3rd cl., 1963, pp. 176–77.

formation in New Delhi but also forced the emerging oppositional forces in Nepal and within the Nepali community in India to adopt increasingly extremist tactics and objectives. The anti-Rana movement had first assumed organized form in India in January 1947 when a number of Nepali political workers under the leadership of B. P. Koirala founded the Nepali National Congress (NNC). Taking advantage of the general breakdown of British surveillance of Nepali political activity in India, the new party launched a general strike movement at Biratnagar in March 1947 and a *satyagraha* (nonviolent resistance) campaign in various urban centers in Nepal the following month. Neither movement was a conspicuous success. But the mere fact that popular-based agitations could be organized came as a traumatic shock to the Ranas. This was an important factor in Prime Minister Padma Shamsher's decision in May 1947 to introduce constitutional reforms, which in turn encouraged the NNC to adopt a relatively moderate position with regard to both long-range objectives and immediate tactics.

The triumph of the reactionary Mohan Shamsher faction in mid-1948, however, once again redirected the opposition groups toward a more extreme program. The core strength of the anti-Rana movement was considerably enhanced at this time by the organization of a second opposition party, the Nepali Democratic Congress (NDC). The main figures behind the new party were two wealthy Ranas, Subarna Shamsher and Mahabir Shamsher, whose branch of the family had been virtually excluded from power by an inter-familial struggle in 1934. Both the NNC and the NDC prepared to launch movements aimed at the overthrow of the Rana regime, the former through nonviolent (*satyagraha*) means and the latter by any tactics that had a chance for success. The two groups finally agreed upon a merger in March 1950 with the formation of the Nepali Congress. It was also agreed that the new party would forego the exclusive use of *satyagraha* tactics and would commence preparations for a revolutionary movement in Nepal that did not abjure the use of violence.

The 1950 Treaty.—The 1947 standstill agreement between India and Nepal had been devised as a temporary expedient pending negotiation of a new treaty relationship. It was not until C. P. N. Singh assumed office as ambassador to Kathmandu in mid-1949, however, that discussions on the treaty finally got under way. In the talks, the Indians insisted upon liberalization of the Nepal administration as a *quid pro quo* for its formal acceptance of the Rana regime. Mohan Shamsher was not disposed to make such concessions, however, and he engaged in dilatory tactics in the hope that developments on both sides of the Himalaya would eventually force New Delhi to come to terms with his Government with no conditions attached.

Bijaya Shamsher, the prime minister's son and the Director-General of the Nepal Foreign Office, was finally sent to New Delhi in the last week of November 1949. There were substantial differences between the two sides, but the major obstacle was still India's insistence upon political reforms in Nepal. At the government of India's urgent request, therefore, Mohan Shamsher made a state visit to New Delhi in February 1950. Nehru exercised his persuasive talents on the Nepali prime minister, but was not able to convince him of the necessity for reforms.

Other factors entered into the calculations of both governments at this point and helped pave the way for an agreement. The Nepali opposition parties in India had been distressed with the Indian government's apparent willingness to strike a bargain with the Rana regime. Several of the opposition leaders attempted to use their access to the government and to publication media in India to question the Rana regime's *bona-fides* and long-range objectives. Nepal's application for U.N. membership, for instance, was characterized as anti-Indian in motivation. Rumors about the Darbar's alleged intention to "lease" eastern Nepal to the United States and to conclude a "secret" treaty with Pakistan[6] were also circulated widely by the Nepali dissidents. Although there was no substance to these reports, the Ranas were unable to persuade the Indian public and press of this, and thus found themselves involved in a losing battle with the Nepali Congress in efforts to influence public opinion in India.

Far more crucial, however, was the Chinese Communist threat to "liberate" Tibet, first announced by Radio Peking in November 1949. Mohan Shamsher tried to play upon New Delhi's growing concern over China's intentions by stressing the staunchly anti-communist sentiments of his administration. The opposition leader, Dr. D. R. Regmi, turned this argument on its head when he warned that "if the Government of India adopted a policy of helpful co-operation with the Ranas on the plea of counteracting Communist infiltration from the north," the Nepali people in frustration would "be compelled to seek support from their northern neighbour" in the struggle against the Ranas.[7] B. P. Koirala took a different tact in an apparent effort to outbid the Ranas for India's support. He proposed common Indian-Nepali defense and foreign

---

6 *Amrita Bazar Patrika* (Calcutta), Dec. 29, 1949.
7 *Ibid.*, Nov. 16, 1949.

policies,[8] a position that later exposed him to charges that he had been prepared to "sell" Nepal to New Delhi in exchange for Indian support.

The government of India was still convinced of the efficacy of the "middle way" policy, and was not receptive to the arguments advanced by either the Ranas or the Nepali opposition leaders. In a foreign-policy statement to Parliament on March 17, 1950, Nehru restated the basic principle of his policy:

We have advised in earnestness the Government of Nepal, to the extent a friendly Power can advise an independent nation, that in the inner context of Nepal, it is desirable to pay attention to the forces which are moving in the world, the democratic forces and forces of freedom, and put themselves in line with them.

He rejected out of hand B. P. Koirala's suggestion of a military alliance between the two countries, but declared:

apart from any kind of alliance, the fact remains that we cannot tolerate any foreign invasion from any foreign country in any part of the Indian sub-continent. Any possible invasion of Nepal would inevitably involve the safety of India.[9]

This was the first occasion on which Nehru stated explicitly what later became a consistent theme in India's defense and foreign policy—namely, that so far as security matters are concerned, India's border lies along the Himalayas even in areas where the territory of independent or autonomous states intrude.

Mohan Shamsher had returned from his state visit to India in February 1950 with the text of two treaties as drafted by the Indian Government. Bijaya Shamsher, who returned to Delhi for further talks in April, indicated Darbar's willingness to sign the treaties virtually as proposed if India did not insist that the signing ceremonies be accompanied by political reforms in Kathmandu. As the situation to the north was becoming increasingly threatening, New Delhi apparently decided that it was essential to reach an agreement with the Ranas before the Chinese had established themselves in Tibet. Treaties of "peace and friendship" and of "trade and commerce" were therefore signed by the representatives of Nepal and India in Kathmandu on July 31, 1950, and were subsequently ratified by both governments.

The key clauses in the treaty of peace and friendship are articles 2, 5, 6, and 7.[10] Article 2 obligates both governments "to in-

---

[8] *The Statesman* (Calcutta), Feb. 21, 1950.

[9] *Parliamentary Debates*, pt. II, Mar. 17, 1950, Col. 1697–98.

[10] For the text of the treaty, see Girilal Jain, *India Meets China in Nepal* (New York, Asia Publishing House, 1959), appendix E, pp. 164–65.

form each other of any serious friction or misunderstanding with any neighbouring State likely to cause any breach in the friendly relations subsisting between the two Governments." The "letters of exchange" that accompanied the treaty—which were not made public until 1959—carries the principle of consultation even further by stipulating that—

Neither Government shall tolerate any threat to the security of the other by a foreign aggressor. To deal with any such threat the two Governments shall consult with each other *and devise effective countermeasures.*[11]

This did not constitute a formal military alliance, but it did impose specific obligations on both governments that are unusual in treaties of "peace and friendship."

Article 5, granting the Nepal government the right to import "arms, ammunition or warlike materials and equipment necessary for the security of Nepal" through India, was inserted at the insistence of the Darbar, which had often bristled in the past over the British Indian government's efforts to regulate such traffic. The procedures "for giving effect to this arrangement" were to be worked out through joint consultations. There do not appear to have been any formal or procedural restrictions placed upon Nepal's right to acquire arms, but tacit agreement on the sources from which arms would be obtained later became a part of the working arrangement between the two countries.

Articles 6 and 7 of the treaty obligated each of the states to extend reciprocal rights to citizens of the other with respect to participation in industrial and economic development, trade and commerce, residence, and ownership of property in each other's territory. Although this obligation has been fully applied to Nepalis resident in India, who enjoy virtually equal rights with Indian citizens in these respects, the reverse has not been the case for Indians resident in Nepal. Traditional restrictions on the right of Indians and other foreigners to engage in commerce, purchase land, reside in certain areas, and own industrial establishments have by no means been eliminated, presumably with the tacit consent of the Indian authorities.

The treaty of trade and commerce signed on the same date became the subject of intense controversy in Nepal from the very beginning. Nepal gained the right to import and export goods through India without the payment of Indian excise or import du-

---

[11] Jawaharlal Nehru, *India's Foreign Policy: Selected Speeches, September 1946–April 1961* (New Delhi, Ministry of Information and Broadcasting), 1961, p. 374 (emphasis supplied).

ties, an improvement over the terms of the 1923 treaty. The Nepali business community took strong exception to article 5, however, which stipulated:

The Government of Nepal agrees to levy at rates not lower than those leviable for the time being in India customs duties on imports from and exports to countries outside India. The Government of Nepal also agrees to levy on goods produced or manufactured in Nepal which are exported to India, export duty at rates sufficient to prevent their sale in India at prices more favourable than those of goods produced or manufactured in India which are subject to central excise duty.[12]

In the Nepali view, what India granted in another section of the treaty had been, in effect, taken away by this clause.[13] Furthermore, the cumbersome procedures established for the transit of goods through India under the trade treaty became the object of strong criticism in Nepal. Demands for revision of the treaty were voiced almost immediately after its ratification, and the Ranas were accused of "antinationalism" for having accepted an "unequal" treaty.

THE 1950–51 REVOLUTION

The new treaties with Nepal, implicitly accepting the legitimacy of the Rana regime, had just been ratified when startling developments to the north of the Himalayas forced the government of India to reconsider basic features of its foreign and defense policies. On October 7, 1950, the Chinese Communists launched a sudden attack against the Tibetan garrison at Chamdo in eastern Tibet. No further advances were made at that time toward central Tibet,[14] but on October 25 Peking Radio announced that orders had been issued for the "liberation" of the whole of Tibet. The following day, New Delhi strongly protested against the use of force in Tibet. In a curtly worded reply, Peking asserted that Tibet was an integral part of China and that "no foreign interference" would be tolerated. The presence of Chinese troops along the Himalayan border, a prospect considered relatively remote just a few weeks earlier,

---

12 For the text of the trade treaty, see *Parliamentary Debates*, appendix I, Annexure 25: Second Session: July–August 1950, pp. 198–201.
13 See, for instance, comments by B. P. Shrestha, "*An Introduction to the Nepal Economy* (Kathmandu, 1962), pp. 140–41; and G. D. Pathak, "Nepal's Trade with Her Neighbour—The Trade Pact of 1950," *Nepal Review*, I:6 (Sept. 30, 1963), pp. 6–7.
14 Chinese Communist units in Sinkiang, however, moved into western Tibet during the 1950–51 winter months, violating Indian territory in the Aksai Chin area of Ladakh in the process.

now became an imminent possibility. Nehru's China policy, based upon the continuance of Tibet's role as an autonomous buffer between China and India, was in total disarray.

New Delhi took only a few days to devise a new China policy to meet the situation. The Indian government had already decided some months earlier that military intervention across the Himalaya was unrealistic,[15] as the Indian army was already overburdened with demands for its services in south Asia. The frantic appeals from Lhasa for Indian and Nepali assistance against the Chinese invaders were therefore ignored,[16] and Tibet was advised to make the best deal possible with Peking. Nehru considered it inevitable that China's sovereignty (rather than the more ambivalent suzerainty) in Tibet would have to be recognized. Through "quiet diplomacy," however, he hoped to assist the Dalai Lama's government to retain a broad degree of autonomy as well as to protect at least those aspects of India's privileged position in Tibet that pertained to trade and official representation.

At almost exactly the same time as these dramatic events in Tibet, the situation in Nepal also reached a crisis stage in October–November 1950. The Nepali Congress had decided earlier that year to launch an armed struggle in Nepal as quickly as circumstances would permit. The revolt was scheduled for August, but was twice postponed because of the difficulties encountered in obtaining arms. Meanwhile, several party workers were sent to Kathmandu to organize a massive terrorist campaign aimed at the assassination of some of the leading Ranas. Betrayed almost immediately to the Kathmandu police, they were brought to trial before a Rana court. King Tribhuvan had been in contact with the Nepali Congress and other anti-Rana elements for several years, and his position was tenuous at best. Faced with threats of deposition by the Ranas, the king took refuge in the Indian embassy on November 6 and requested political asylum in India. Under pressure from India, Mohan Shamsher reluctantly allowed the king to leave Nepal in an Indian Air Force plane on November 10. In the early hours of the following morning, Nepali Congress units based in India launched simultaneous attacks upon Birganj and Biratnagar in the Nepal Terai, and the revolution was finally under way.[17]

---

15 See Robert Trumbull's despatch from New Delhi, *New York Times*, Feb. 16, 1950, 12:3.

16 As a matter of course, Kathmandu referred to New Delhi the Tibetan request for aid and was told, according to one informed source, that India had no plans to intervene militarily in Tibet and that Nepal should follow the Indian example.

17 Most of the account that follows is based upon extensive interviews with some of the leading participants on all sides in the 1950–51 revolution. No documentary evidence is presently available to support some of the analysis and conclusions, but

The government of India's role in these and subsequent events has long been a subject of controversy. King Tribhuvan had contacted the Indian ambassador, C. P. N. Singh, prior to seeking refuge at the embassy, but he took this step on his own initiative rather than at the instigation of the Indian authorities. Similarly, it was at Tribhuvan's request that the Indian government applied arm-twisting tactics in obtaining Mohan Shamsher's permission for the king to leave Nepal. Nehru's "middle way" approach had now been redefined to make the survival of the monarchy, with King Tribhuvan on the throne, the central theme.

The relationship between the Indian government and the Nepali Congress-led revolution is considerably more obscure. Many Nepali residents in India had been active in the Indian nationalist movement, occasionally even as members of the Congress party. Their ties with Indian political and governmental leaders were, consequently, very close in some cases. The Nepali Congress secretary-general, Surya Prasad Upadhyaya, for instance, had shared a prison cell with the Indian Congress leader, Rafi Ahmed Kidwai, during World War II. Kidwai, now a Union minister and a confidant of Nehru, served as the principal channel of communication between the Nepali revolutionaries and New Delhi during this crucial period. B. P. Koirala's relationship with the Indian Socialist leader, Jaya Prakash, to whom he had provided asylum in the Nepali Terai during the war, proved of vital importance in gaining the Socialists' indispensable assistance in launching the 1950 movement.

These contacts were used by the Nepali Congress in mid-1950 to test New Delhi's attitude toward the proposed shift from nonviolent to violent tactics. The response was generally unfavorable. The Indian government, eager to pressure the Rana regime into conceding political reforms, encouraged the Nepali Congress to commence a program of active resistance in Nepal, but recommended that only nonviolent tactics be employed. The Nepali leaders protested that the party was in no condition psychologically or physically to launch a massive *satyagraha* campaign, and persisted in its preparations for an armed revolution. New Delhi finally gave its qualified consent to the change in tactics on condition that

1) the scope and objectives of the struggle were well-defined and restricted—i.e., it supported Indians "middle way" policy by pressuring the Ranas into political reforms but did not threaten the regime itself; and

there is a surprisingly wide degree of agreement among these various sources on most of the major events.

2) preparations for the struggle did not "compromise" Delhi, which in clear language meant that the Nepali Congress would have to obtain arms and other forms of material assistance from sources other than the government of India.

This was less than the Nepali Congress had hoped for, but at least it allowed the party some room for maneuver in preparing for the revolution.

In its appraisal of the situation, New Delhi believed that the Nepali Congress could be a thorn in the side of the Ranas but doubted the party's capacity to launch a revolutionary movement without a substantial increase in the quantity of arms in its possession. Overtures from the party for assistance in obtaining arms were rejected by New Delhi, which feared that an armed revolution in Nepal might lead to political disintegration. Apparently the Indian authorities were unaware of the contacts which the Nepali Congress had established with the socialist government of Burma through the intermediation of the Indian Socialists.[18] A private airline company, Himalayan Aviation, the managing director of which was the Nepali Congress leader Mahabir Shamsher, was used to transport arms from Burma to India. A plane-load of arms was landed at an abandoned World War II airfield in northern Bihar on November 3 and was quickly distributed to the *mukti sena* (liberation army) units of the Nepali Congress poised on the India-Nepal border.

The news that King Tribhuvan would be flown out of Kathmandu on November 10 impelled the Nepali Congress to take action before preparations had been fully completed. The order went out to strike immediately, and the attacks on Birganj and Biratnagar were launched early in the morning of November 11. They apparently came as a surprise, and not a particularly pleasant one, to the government of India. According to several Nepali sources, Nehru was furious, as this development threatened to upset his calculations of the variables involved in implementing a "middle way" policy. He criticized the Nepali Congress for not having adhered to nonviolent tactics and rejected the party's urgent plea for the arms and supplies required by the detachment that had seized Birganj. This rejection led to the withdrawal of the detach-

---

18 Bhola Chatterji, the Indian Socialist who went to Rangoon to arrange the arms shipment for the Nepali Congress, has given a detailed account of these events in his invaluable study, *A Study of Recent Nepalese Politics*, Calcutta, World Press, 1968. Kidwai had been kept informed about the Nepali Congress' search for arms but had not been told about the favorable response from the Burmese Socialists nor about the arrangements for transporting arms to India.

ment across the border on November 20. The Indian authorities denied the Nepali Congress access to the Indian railways in transporting men and equipment, and imposed a ban on flights over Nepali territory by Indian airlines, including Himalayan Aviation. On New Delhi's advice, King Tribhuvan refrained from issuing a statement aligning himself with the revolutionary forces, thus depriving the Nepali Congress of this essential element of support at a critical time.

The government of India's response to this series of events, however, was complicated by the unyielding position taken by the Rana regime. On November 7, the day after the King had taken refuge in the Indian embassy, Mohan Shamsher formally deposed Tribhuvan and placed his 4-year old grandson, Jñanendra, on the throne. Kathmandu immediately requested recognition of the new ruler by the nations with which it had diplomatic relations—India, Great Britain and the United States. India's response was first indicated in the reception given to King Tribhuvan on his arrival in India on November 11. Nehru and other cabinet officials were at the airport to greet him, and Tribhuvan was extended the honors due the head of a sovereign state.

Several weeks elapsed before London and Washington reached a decision on the recognition question. According to an authoritative Nepali source, the British government was initially prepared to agree to Kathmandu's request, and informed the Nepali ambassador in London that Jñanendra would be recognized in a few days. The Foreign Office, even under the Labour Party government, was still strongly predisposed in favor of the Ranas. Moreover, the British had just signed a treaty of peace and friendship with Nepal on October 30, 1950, providing for improved recruitment facilities for the British Gurkha regiments. London may have feared that a change of regime in Nepal would endanger this arrangement.[19] Washington was more divided on the question, but would probably have gone along with London. The British postponed recognition, however, when they learned that Kathmandu was sending a mission to New Delhi for discussions with the government of India, for the last thing London wanted was to recognize a new ruler who might be disowned subsequently by both Nepal and India. By this time, New Delhi's strong opposition to recognition of Jñanendra was

---

19 M. P. Koirala's statement at this time that the Nepali Congress opposed the employment of Nepalis "as mercenary soldiers by foreigners for imperialist purposes" did not reassure the British on this question. Indeed, even the Indians were concerned until M. P. Koirala explained that this policy did not apply to India, as "India's defence is our defence." (B. Chatterji, *op. cit.* pp. 115–16.)

clearly evident, and neither the British nor the Americans were prepared to break with India on that question.

Negotiations between the Indian and Nepali governments were begun in New Delhi on November 27 upon the arrival of Bijaya Shamsher and Keshar Shamsher, the foreign and defense ministers. Progress was very slow, however. The Ranas were prepared to accept a limited liberalization of their administration but rejected the Indian demand that King Tribhuvan be restored to the throne.

The adamant attitude of the Ranas, combined with the threatened collapse of the Nepali Congress revolution and with British and American procrastination on the recognition question, caused the Indian Government to adopt a somewhat different tack. While New Delhi had been irritated by the repeated failure of the Nepali Congress to follow its advice, the total collapse of the revolutionary movement had to be prevented if the Ranas were to be pressured into a political compromise. The Indians therefore agreed to look the other way when the Nepali Congress obtained arms, mostly rifles, from Sheikh Abdullah in Kashmir and other sources.

Even more important was the consolidation of India's diplomatic support behind King Tribhuvan, and thus by implication behind the anti-Rana movement in Nepal. On December 6, 1950, Nehru made the strongest statement yet on his government's views when he told Parliament:

From time immemorial, the Himalayas have provided us with magnificent frontiers. . . . We cannot allow that barrier to be penetrated because it is also the principal barrier to India. Therefore, much as we appreciate the independence of Nepal, we cannot allow anything to go wrong in Nepal or permit that barrier to be crossed or weakened, because that would be a risk to our own security.

India would "continue to recognize" King Tribhuvan, he declared, while appealing to the "great Powers . . . to make every effort to solve the present tangle by negotiation or other peaceful means." This was in fact a warning to the United States and Great Britain against the recognition of the new ruler in Nepal. "We are a patient government," he added. "Perhaps we are too patient sometimes. I feel, however, that if this matter drags on, it will not be good for Nepal and it might even make it more difficult to find the middle way we have been advocating."[20]

The Indian position having been so clearly stated, the two Nepali envoys, Bijaya Shamsher and Keshar Shamsher, returned to

---

[20] *Jawaharlal Nehru's Speeches (1949–53), op. cit.*, p. 252.

Kathmandu on December 8 with an Indian memorandum proposing a compromise formula:

1) An elected constituent assembly to draft a new constitution;
2) An interim government with "popular' (i.e., Nepali Congress) representation but a Rana prime minister; and
3) Recognition of King Tribhuvan.

This coincided with a new upsurge in the revolutionary movement, due in part to the influx of arms from Kashmir and elsewhere. Biratnagar and several other towns in the Nepal Terai were captured, and large areas of the eastern and western hills came under rebel control. The Rana family was badly divided upon the proper course of action, with the younger Ranas and the less-favored branches of the family demanding acceptance of the Indian terms. Nehru again warned the Darbar on December 21 "that the longer political reforms and a satisfactory settlement are delayed in Nepal, the greater the danger to Nepal's security and internal tranquility."[21] King Tribhuvan also added his support to the three-point proposal in his first public statement since coming to New Delhi 6 weeks earlier.

The Nepali government finally replied to the Indian memorandum on December 24. Mohan Shamsher agreed to an interim government and the election of a constituent assembly within three years, but he made no mention of King Tribhuvan's status. Bijaya Shamsher returned to New Delhi 2 days later and was told that the government of India would not modify its demand for Tribhuvan's restoration to the throne. Having failed to obtain external support and with the internal situation deteriorating rapidly—the garrison at Palpa, the key to the government's position in the western hills, deserted to the rebels in early January—Mohan Shamsher had no alternative but to capitulate. On January 8, 1951, he issued a public proclamation announcing that as "no friendly country having diplomatic relations with us has recognised the new king," Tribhuvan would be restored to the throne and a cabinet with "popular representation" would be formed.[22]

King Tribhuvan and Nehru both welcomed the announcement, and the latter expressed the hope "that all attempts at violent change will cease." This "advice" to the Nepali Congress was not heeded immediately, however, as the rebels were angered by the sudden termination of the revolutionary movement just when it seemed on the verge of success. B. P. Koirala, Subarna Shamsher and M. P. Koirala hurried to New Delhi on January 14 to argue their

21 *The Hindu*, Dec. 23, 1950, 4:3.
22 *Ibid.*, Jan. 9, 1951, 4:6.

case with the Indians, but to little effect. The Indian authorities agreed that the Rana regime would probably topple if the revolution continued for a few more weeks, but they were not convinced that the Nepali Congress had the capacity to organize a stable government in its place. A transitional period was still considered essential, and this meant continued Rana participation in the administration during the interim period. Moreover, the stated willingness of the Nepali Congress to work with the small Nepal Communist party had not reassured the Indians about the reliability of the revolutionary leadership in the increasingly difficult situation on the Himalayan frontier.

The Nepali Congress was in no position to impose terms on the Indian government and King Tribhuvan. After receiving verbal reassurances on the selection of the "popular" representatives in the interim government, therefore, the party president, M. P. Koirala, issued a cease-fire order to the rebel forces. Some units refused to obey the order and continued the struggle, but this was a futile gesture of annoyance that was doomed to failure. Negotiations between the Nepali Congress and the Ranas began in New Delhi in early February under the supervision of King Tribhuvan. With considerable prodding by the Indians, an agreement was reached on February 7. Under the "Delhi compromise," as it quickly became known, it was agreed that a ten-man cabinet equally divided between Nepali Congressmen and Ranas would be set up under the Prime Ministership of Mohan Shamsher. King Tribhuvan and the Nepali Congress leaders returned to Kathmandu on February 15 and met with a tumultuous reception. Three days later, on February 18, a ten-man cabinet was appointed by King Tribhuvan, the first instance since 1847 that the King of Nepal had employed the sovereign royal powers at his own discretion.

The Rana period had officially ended even though a Rana remained as prime minister. But a full-fledged democratic system was not installed in its place and, in the view of the Nepali Congress, the 1950 revolution was "incomplete." The decisive battles in this struggle, however, had not been fought in the hills of Nepal but in the halls of New Delhi where the Indian insistence upon a "middle way" solution had dominated the proceedings. The social and economic objectives of the revolution had been abandoned, or postponed, under the Delhi compromise. Emphasis was placed primarily upon the achievement of a viable political system involving both the custodians of the *status quo* and the proponents of change, under the attentive supervision of the government of India. A more thankless task and one less likely to succeed under these auspices can scarcely be imagined.

ALIGNMENT WITH INDIA

To speak of a "Nepali foreign policy" in the period immediately following the 1950–51 revolution would probably be incorrect. Indian influence on questions of external relations was so all-pervasive as to make foreign policy formulation by Kathmandu irrelevant or redundant. New Delhi's concept of Nepal's interests was accepted almost automatically in Kathmandu, at least at the official level. Indeed, it is probable that some Nepali leaders tended to be overresponsive in this respect, interpreting even casual suggestions by the Indians as advice to be acted upon. At that stage of developments, the Indian government may have been prepared to allow Nepal greater latitude in defining foreign policy objectives and more initiative in their implementation than the cautious authorities in Kathmandu were prepared to accept. On a number of occasions, the Nepal government not only tamely followed New Delhi's guidance but actually took the initiative in seeking it. That the Indians began to take Kathmandu too much for granted, and tended to act in a rather cavalier and condescending fashion with regard to their own prerogatives, is therefore hardly surprising.

The definition of policy toward the three "border states" of Nepal, Sikkim and Bhutan had been a perplexing problem for independent India. Several high-level Indian officials, including Deputy Prime Minister Sardar Vallabhai Patel, are reported to have urged at one time the accession of the border states to the Indian Union on the same basis as the Indian "native states."[23] The decision on this issue, however, was made by the External Affairs Ministry, whose head was Prime Minister Nehru, rather than by Home Minister Patel.

The policy as it was finally formulated rejected accession to the Indian Union in favor of acceptance of the separate status—differentially defined—of the border states in exchange for recognition of India's "special interests" on the Himalayan frontier. The charac-

---

[23] For some time after 1947, a basic inconsistency existed in the attitude of Indian officials over whether the border states had been independent prior to 1947 or a *de facto* part of the British Indian empire. As late as Dec. 6, 1950, Nehru was still characterizing Nepal's independence as "only formal" during the British period as its "foreign relations were strictly limited to the Government of India." This was incorrect factually as well as questionable under international law.

Curiously enough, there has been an equally persistent inconsistency on this question among Nepali intellectuals, who often stridently criticize the Ranas for their alleged subservience to the British while at the same time insisting with equal vehemence that Nepal has always been independent and never recognized British "parmountcy."

ter and scope of these "special interests" were determined by a complex of factors, including historical precedents, strategic considerations and internal political conditions, and thus varied substantially. Sikkim's autonomy was severely limited, both internally and externally. Bhutan's internal autonomy was recognized, but India retained the right to "advise" that state on foreign relations. Nepal emerged with the fewest legal restrictions on its sovereignty, as it was obligated only to consult with the Indian government on certain foreign policy questions. In fact, however, New Delhi played a much more active role in Nepal than in Bhutan during the first decade after independence.

Undoubtedly the most controversial symbol of Indian intervention in the immediate postrevolution period in Nepal was the Indian ambassador, C. P. N. Singh. He was reputed to be the single most influential person in Kathmandu, and one who quickly became the "bête noire" of every Nepali politician currently out of office. It was C. P. N. Singh, for instance, who was generally credited with having arranged M. P. Koirala's appointment as prime minister in November 1951, whereas it had been generally assumed that his more popular half-brother, B. P. Koirala, would head the first non-Rana government. According to stories widely circulated in Kathmandu, the Indian ambassador often intervened personally in the processes of government, on one occasion even dominating the proceedings of a conference of district-level officials. His politicking became so objectionable in some quarters in Kathmandu that B. P. Koirala was constrained to charge C. P. N. Singh with deliberately setting Nepali leaders against each other. If India and Nepal were to remain friends, the Nepali Congress leader stated, the ambassador would have to be replaced.[24]

A combination of factors allowed C. P. N. Singh such latitude in Kathmandu politics. King Tribhuvan had not established a satisfactory working relationship with most of the Nepali Congress leaders, and therefore tended to look to the Indian ambassador for advice on how to handle both the old Ranas and the new party politicians.[25] The heterogeneous Mohan Shamsher cabinet, with its careful balancing of irreconcilable elements, could function even half-way successfully only under constant Indian supervision and prodding, which C. P. N. Singh was only too willing to provide. Perhaps of equal importance, however, was the lack of effective in-

---

24 *Times of India*, Feb. 22, 1952, 6:8.
25 King Tribhuvan's private secretary, Govinda Narayan, was an Indian civil servant deputed to Nepal for this purpose. Narayan reportedly exercised a substantial influence over the King and, moreover, served as the channel of communication between the Palace and the Nepali political parties and public.

stitutional control over the ambassador by the recently established External Affairs Ministry of the government of India. C. P. N. Singh was thus able to interfere in Nepali politics to an extent that not only violated the spirit of his office but was at times in contradiction to Indian policy.[26]

C. P. N. Singh's successor, B. K. Gokhale, held a more correct view of his function in Nepal, and criticisms directed at the embassy gradually ceased. Other forms of what was considered Indian interference, however, became evident, and the public outcry in Kathmandu increased in intensity by several decibels between 1951 and 1954. The principal objects of attack were the various Indian advisory missions to Nepal, and in particular the Indian military mission that arrived in Kathmandu in February 1952 to assist in the reorganization and training of the Nepali army. An abortive coup d'état by the supporters of Dr. K. I. Singh in January 1952 had raised in critical form the question of the loyalty and competence of the military establishment. The Nepali government, after consultation with an Indian team that visited Kathmandu in late January, requested New Delhi's assistance in this high-priority job.

Probably no other decision of the two governments could have struck more directly at popular sensitivity. The Nepali people had long taken pride in the reputation of the "Gurkhas" as fighters. That *madhesis* (plainsmen) were now being asked to "teach the Gurkhas how to soldier" was an insult to national self-respect, already badly battered. Added to this was the more pragmatic consideration that the reorganization program involved the reduction of the army from 25,000 to 6,000 men. This caused extreme resentment among those dismissed from service, and the tendency was to blame the Indian military mission rather than the Nepali government. The mission, which originally had been scheduled to complete its task in one year, stayed on indefinitely. It became an object of public abuse and dissent, however, and strong objections were raised to the role assigned the Indian military personnel in northern border posts on the access routes between Nepal and Tibet. Radio communications between the northern border and Kathmandu were made the responsibility of Indian technicians assigned to the checkposts, allegedly because the Nepal army lacked both the trained personnel and equipment to carry out that vital function efficiently. Under this arrangement, the Indian and Nepali gov-

---

26 India inherited a full-fledged secretariat structure for internal administration from the British but had to create an External Affairs Ministry after 1947. Some of the early Indian Ambassadors, such as Sardar K. M. Panikkar in China and C. P. N. Singh in Nepal, were allowed considerable latitude in the implementation of foreign policy because of the inadequate institutionalization of their roles.

ernments had equal access to the information radioed back to Kathmandu or elsewhere in Nepal and India, a privilege which New Delhi highly valued but some Nepalis strongly resented.

Less sensational, perhaps, but potentially more critical was the resistance within the Nepal Secretariat to the activities of Indian advisors assigned to that hidebound institution. Two Indian advisors on administrative reorganization arrived in Kathmandu in April 1951, but were withdrawn rather abruptly ten months later, reportedly because of the objections raised by Nepali government servants.[27] A more high-powered advisory team was sent to Nepal in May 1952, again to advise on administrative reorganization and on Indian economic assistance to Nepal. After approximately a month, they produced a long, detailed report on the Nepali administrative system with an equally long list of suggestions for its reorganization. The model followed was the Indian civil service, but with some perceptive modifications to suit Nepal's traditions and experiences. This report provided the framework for the 1953 reorganization of the Secretariat into eleven departments, but most of its recommendations were never fully implemented.

Somewhat different in character, but no less irritating to Nepali government servants, was the practice under which Indian officials were brought directly into top positions in the Nepal Secretariat in administrative rather than advisory roles. The first attorney-general of Nepal, for instance, was an Indian attorney, and the reorganization of the Nepali police was for a time entrusted to an Indian police officer. Only a few Indians actually ever served in such capacities in the Secretariat, and these for relatively short periods, but this practice agitated Nepali government servants who feared that Indians might soon monopolize the key posts in the government.

Furthermore, the propensity of Nepali high officials, including King Tribhuvan and most of the ministers, to visit New Delhi for advice during Nepal's periodic political crises, was another cause for resentment among the Kathmandu public. This practice started in April 1951 when the Rana-Nepali Congress coalition cabinet trooped *en masse* to New Delhi to work out a compromise settlement of their differences in consultation with the Indian govern-

---

27 Nehru told the Indian Parliament that the two advisors had been withdrawn upon completion of their work (*The Hindu*, Mar. 1, 1952, 4:7). This seems unlikely, however, since another two-man mission was sent to accomplish the same task three months later. That mission complained that only a few of the "Reports, Rules and Instructions" prepared by the first team of advisors were still available when they reached Kathmandu three months later! [*The Buch Report on Administrative Reorganisation of the Government of Nepal* (mimeographed copy), p. 1.]

ment. Prime Minister M. P. Koirala made the trip again in January 1952, this time to find out what Nepal's position should be on foreign-policy questions. Nehru's rather condescending comment in February 1952 indicated the extent to which New Delhi accepted these responsibilities. He declared:

We have taken particular care not to interfere. We have given advice on some occasions. On two occasions the Prime Minister was here and the King was also here once or twice. We naturally discussed various matters and gave advice, and in two matters more particularly we are closely associated, in matters of foreign policy and defence, not by any formal agreement but simply because both matters are common to us.[28]

It may have seemed "natural" to Nehru that Nepali officials were so eager to obtain Indian advice, but to the Nepali public this was indicative of a servile disposition. As one Nepali politician remarked, "When Nehru caught a cold, M. P. Koirala sneezed."

The Indian economic aid program also became a subject of controversy in Nepal.[29] Criticism was initially directed at the high priority assigned to improving the communication network in the country—e. g., Gauchar airport near Kathmandu and the highway (Tribhuvan Rajpath) connecting Kathmandu with India. Some Nepalis charged that these projects were intended to facilitate Indian control of Nepal, even though New Delhi had reluctantly approved the road construction program on the urgent insistence of the Nepali government. The manner in which Indian assistance was channelled through the Planning Commission rather than the External Affairs Ministry in New Delhi was also considered a slur on Nepal's national sovereignty, because it seemed to place Nepal on the same standing as an Indian state.

But the greatest uproar came with the conclusion of the Kosi project agreement in April 1954, which provided for the construction of extensive flood-control, power and irrigation facilities on the Kosi River near the Nepal-Bihar border. The entire cost of the project, initially estimated optimistically at Rs. 400,000,000, was to be borne by India. Although this was ostensibly a generous act on the part of New Delhi, the Kathmandu politicians and press soon discovered any number of flies in the ointment: Nepal received only a minute proportion of the total irrigated land; India would benefit more from the power resources developed than Nepal; the water-storage facilities would ruin some of Nepal's richest agricul-

---

28 *Hindustan Times*, Feb. 16, 1952.
29 For a summary account of the Indian aid program in Nepal in the 1951–54 period see E. B. Mihaly, *Foreign Aid and Politics in Nepal: A Case Study* (London, Oxford University Press, 1965), pp. 42–50.

tural lands in the eastern Terai because of the accumulation of silt; and Nepali peasants were discriminated against in the payment of compensation. The greatest volume of invective, however, was directed at the supposed violation of Nepal's sovereign rights in the project areas in Nepal, which, it was claimed, had somehow been ceded to India.[30]

The three occasions in the 1951–53 period in which Indian army or police units were sent into Nepal at the request of the Nepali government to control the activities of "lawless elements" also contributed to the deterioration in relations between the two countries. The capture of Dr. K. I. Singh, the controversial ex-Nepali Congress leader who had refused to accept the Delhi compromise, was the objective on two of these occasions, while the seizure of Bilauri, a market town in the far-western Terai, by a large force under a local rebel leader, Bhim Dutt Pant, led to the third Indian intervention. Dr. Singh and Pant attained the status of minor national heroes in some quarters in Nepal, to the detriment of the reputation of both the Nepali and Indian governments. Kathmandu's inability to control these lawless factions by its own means and the willingness of India to come to the assistance of the Nepali government were both widely criticized.

Anti-Indian sentiment had thus become widespread in Kathmandu by 1953, and was threatening to become a major factor in Nepali politics. In part, such sentiment reflected real grievances that were perhaps the inevitable result of India's efforts to assist and support the "forces of stability" in Nepal, increasingly identified with the monarchy in the minds of the Indian officials. By the time of the collapse of the first Nepali Congress cabinet in August 1952, New Delhi had decided that the throne was the only institution in Nepal capable of achieving some degree of political stability and economic progress. The political party system was considered too volatile to be a dependable agent of modernization. It was one of the anomalies of this period that the trend toward the concentration of power in the throne and the corresponding diminution in the role of the party leaders was initiated with considerable reluctance by King Tribhuvan on New Delhi's advice.

The criticisms of India thus frequently had a political motivation that derived from the direction rather than the fact of Indian intervention. The NNC leader, Dr. D. R. Regmi, stated this explicitly when he declared: "We do not complain of interference

---

[30] This criticism seems to have been based on the fact that the Indian Government was allowed to purchase land in Nepal to facilitate the construction of Kosi Project dams and barrages. The sovereign powers of the Nepal government over such lands, however, were in no way impaired by the terms of the Project agreement.

by the Government of India. Today the main question is not that of interference but in whose interests this interference is working."[31] Dr. Regmi's comment pointed to what was fast becoming a regular feature of Nepali politics. When in office, Nepali political leaders strenuously denied reports of Indian interference; when out of office the same leaders as strenuously decried such interference.

Under the circumstances, it is not surprising that the Indian government consistently underestimated the depth of resentment in Nepal against overt Indian interference, attributing the occasional public outbursts to the antics of disgruntled leaders of insignificant parties or to procommunist elements. The massive anti-Indian demonstration that accompanied the arrival of an Indian parliamentary delegation in Kathmandu in May 1954, therefore, was a severe shock to Delhi. The Nepali government blamed the demonstration on the opposition parties, but this could not disguise the fact that these organizations could use anti-Indian slogans to arouse substantial popular backing. This became even more apparent in September 1954 when a procommunist front successfully organized an "Anti-Indian Interference Day" in Kathmandu without the open support of most of the major political parties. Obviously, India had much fence-mending to do in Nepal, particularly in the context of developments elsewhere in the Himalayan area that would soon challenge New Delhi's paramountcy throughout the entire frontier region.

THE DIVERSIFICATION POLICY

In the last stages of their rule, the Ranas had introduced what was later termed the "diversification policy." Initially this involved the expansion of Nepal's diplomatic relations, first with the United States and then with France. The policy was extended on a limited and experimental basis to external economic relations shortly before the overthrow of the Rana regime, when on January 23, 1951, the United States and Nepali ambassadors in New Delhi concluded an agreement under the Point 4 program providing for American assistance in the surveying of Nepal's mineral resources. Implementation and expansion of this agreement was delayed by the February 1951 political change, but the interest of the Nepali government in diversified sources of economic assistance remained constant. Finally, the U.S. Technical Cooperation Mission established an office in Kathmandu in January 1952, and the American aid program in Nepal then became institutionalized.

---

[31] *Hitavada*, 18 April, 1952, 3:5.

It can safely be presumed that the Indian government had at least tacitly consented to the inauguration of American aid program in Nepal. Similarly, New Delhi did not obstruct the most important form of British economic assistance to Nepal—the recruitment of Nepalis for the British Gurkha units in Malaya—although it did insist upon changing the enlistment procedures. The four British recruitment depots in India were closed in 1952, but New Delhi did not object to the supplementary agreement of July 1953 between Nepal and the United Kingdom under which a British recruitment depot was set up at Dharan in eastern Nepal. Nor were the Gurkha recruits into the British service denied the right of transit across India, so long as they "went in mufti and as individuals,"[32] despite the strong protests of leftist and "anti-imperialist" elements in India.

There were, however, carefully defined limits upon India's acceptance of diversification. Suggestions from nonofficial Nepali sources for the revision of the 1950 trade treaty, for instance, were ignored.[33] While New Delhi supported Nepal's application for membership in the United Nations, it discouraged the immediate expansion of Kathmandu's bilateral relations beyond those states which already had accredited diplomatic representation—India, Great Britain, the United States, France and Tibet. Diplomatic relations with China, the Indians advised, should be delayed until New Delhi had placed its own relations with Peking on a firmer legal basis. Relations with Pakistan and the Soviet Union were also discouraged as untimely, with the implication that it might be quite a while before these would be considered appropriate. As will be seen, however, changes occurred much more rapidly than either the Indians or Nepalis expected.

NEPAL'S CAUTIOUS APPROACH TO CHINA

The steady growth of anti-Indian sentiment in Nepal would not have been so alarming to New Delhi if it had not coincided with a shift in the regional power balance due to the emergence of China as a major participant in the politics of the Himalayan area. To some Nepalis, it was now apparent that there was an alternative,

---

[32] Nehru's statement in Parliament, Aug. 8, 1952 (*Hindustan Times*, Aug. 9, 1952, 1:6).

[33] However, the Government of India did not insist upon the full application of all provisions of the 1950 treaty. The Nepal government did not impose excise duties on Nepali exports to India, for instance, without incurring Indian objections to this violation of the treaty. Furthermore, the Indian excise duty on Indian exports to Nepal was paid to the Nepal Government (Mihaly, *op. cit.*, p. 91).

and an increasingly attractive one, to Indian "paramountcy." By late 1951, a number of prominent Nepali leaders were already beginning to demand that as an integral part of Nepali foreign policy, diplomatic relations with China be established.

While India's cautionary advice against rushing into diplomatic relations with China was probably the chief reason for Kathmandu's studied disinterest in this question in the 1951–54 period, there were several other considerations as well. The methods used by Peking in 1950–51 to impose China's "historical" claim to Tibet inevitably raised apprehensions in Nepal. What are the limits of China's historical claims?—Kathmandu asked. After all, Mao Tse-tung had once listed Nepal as one of the "dependent states" the British had seized from China,[34] and who could be sure that Nepal would not share the same fate as Tibet? In the circumstances, a non-committal approach seemed advisable until China's intentions were clearer, and it is probable that Kathmandu would have evaded the first Chinese overtures on the question of diplomatic relations in mid–1951 even if India had advised otherwise.

The flight of Dr. K. I. Singh and a number of his followers to Tibet after the collapse of the January 1952 abortive coup further complicated Nepal's relations with China. Home Minister Surya Prasad Upadhyaya told newsmen on February 9, 1952, that the Tibetan authorities had been asked to extradite K. I. Singh and that he believed "they will accept our request."[35] Lhasa did not comply, however, and the refugees were given asylum, first at Shigatse, then near Lhasa, and finally in Peking. Reports were current in Kathmandu that the Tibetans had agreed to surrender K. I. Singh but that the Chinese had intruded and prevented his extradition. Fears were expressed in both Nepal and India that the volatile and popular K. I. Singh would be used by the Chinese to mount a communist guerrilla war in Nepal. It was only after his removal to Peking in 1954 that their concern on this question gradually subsided, encouraged in part by reports—later proved accurate—that Chinese "brain-washing" techniques had failed to impress the hard-headed, stubborn K. I. Singh.

There was, finally, the question of China's attitude toward Nepal's rights in Tibet under the 1856 treaty.[36] Kathmandu still valued these rights very highly and was eager to retain as many of

---

34 Mao Tse-tung, *"The Chinese Revolution and the Chinese Communist Party,"* in *Mao Tse-tung hsüanchi* (Selected works of Mao Tse-tung), Peking 1951–60, 4 vols.
35 *The Tribune,* Feb. 11, 1952, 5:6.
36 When the Nepali Vakil at Lhasa came home on leave in the winter of 1961–62, for instance, the Nepal government had to deny persistent rumors in Kathmandu that China had instructed Nepal to withdraw its diplomatic mission from Lhasa (*Hindustan Times,* Dec. 31, 1951).

them as possible. It was with evident satisfaction, therefore, that the Nepali government learned in early 1952 that there was no immediate prospect of substantial modifications in Nepali-Tibetan relations. On March 7 an emissary of the Dalai Lama arrived in Kathmandu bearing the annual Rs. 10,000 payment to Nepal, accompanied as usual by a large party of Tibetans who purchased a wide variety of supplies for the Tibetan government.

A letter from the Dalai Lama, handed over to the Nepali Vakil in Lhasa on March 14, strengthened Kathmandu's optimism, as the head of the Tibetan government wrote: "I have every hope that there will be no hindrance to continuing the age-old relations between my Government and yours. I pray to God that our relations may become stronger than ever."[37] It was reported that the Nepali government was so encouraged by these developments that it even considered raising the status of its representative at Lhasa to that of ambassador,[38] perhaps on the assumption that the Dalai Lama's letter also reflected the views of the Chinese.

There was at this time a rather subtle divergence between the Nepali and Indian positions on China's status in Tibet. New Delhi formally terminated direct relations with the Dalai Lama's government and implicitly recognized China's sovereignty in Tibet when it signed an agreement with Peking on September 15, 1952, converting the Indian mission at Lhasa to a consulate-general. But as late as April 5, 1954, Prime Minister M. P. Koirala was still describing Nepal's relations with Tibet as "independent of Chinese control," by implication, at least, seeming to question China's claim to sovereignty in Tibet.[39] This occurred, moreover, after Peking had informally approached Nepal concerning revision of the 1856 treaty and had taken steps—prematurely, in strictly legal terms—to invalidate the treaty even before talks had begun. China instructed the Dalai Lama to cancel the annual payment to Nepal in 1953, and the Nepali Vakil at Lhasa was informed that his right to hear cases involving Nepali subjects in Tibet would no longer be recognized.

THE 1954 SINO-INDIAN TREATY AND NEPAL

The government of India had been reconciled to the necessity of placing relations with Tibet on a new foundation through an agreement with China since at least 1951, but it was not until the last day of 1953 that discussions on this subject were initiated in

---

[37] *The Statesman*, Mar. 15, 1952, 7:2.
[38] *Hindustan Times*, May 2, 1952, 5:3.
[39] *The Statesman*, Apr. 7, 1954, 3:3.

Peking. After four months of intensive negotiations, an agreement was signed regulating trade and pilgrim traffic between India and Tibet and fixing the number and location of trade agencies each government was to be permitted to establish in the territory of the other. The preamble of the treaty also included the first exposition of what became known as the *panchshila* principles—i. e., the "five principles of peaceful coexistence."

The Sino-Indian treaty had an immediate impact on Nepal's China policy. M. P. Koirala had declared only a few weeks earlier that his government did not intend to surrender Nepal's rights in Tibet under the 1856 treaty. On May 1, 1954, however, just two days after the signature of the pact, King Tribhuvan and Foreign Minister D. R. Regmi flew to New Delhi for discussions with the Indian government. In these talks, which ended on May 6, Nepal was advised to place its own relations with Tibet on a new basis, conforming in general to the terms of the Sino-Indian treaty. D. R. Regmi told newsmen in New Delhi on May 8 that should China "approach us formally, we will do the right thing at the right moment."[40]

That New Delhi had no intention to share Nepal as a "sphere of influence" with China, however, was clearly indicated in the *aide mémoire* handed to D. R. Regmi at the conclusion of the talks. This document, which was first published in a Nepali weekly in 1958, summarized the Indian government's views on the relations between the two states as agreed upon in mutual discussion since 1951: It has been previously agreed between the Governments of India and Nepal that there should be a co-ordination of foreign policies on matters relating to international affairs in so far as they affect each other. In the course of talks held in May in Delhi between the Foreign Minister and some Ministers of the Nepal Government and the Prime Minister and the External Affairs Ministry of India, this was confirmed and it was decided that in order to give effect to this policy of co-ordination:

1) there should be close and continuous contact between the two Governments in regard to their foreign policies and relations, in so far as they affect each other;
2) in any matter under consideration by the Government of India which may relate to Nepal, the Government of India will consult the Government of Nepal;
3) the Government of Nepal will likewise consult the Government of India in regard to any matter relating to foreign policy or relations with foreign powers, with a view to a co-ordinated policy;

---

[40] *Hindustan Times*, May 8, 1954, 1:4.

4) in particular, in matters relating to the relations of Nepal with Tibet and China, consultations will take place with the Government of India;

5) the Government of India agree to arrange that wherever the Government of Nepal wishes, Indian Missions abroad will undertake to represent the Government of Nepal and to look after Nepalese interests;

6) all Foreign Missions of the Government of India will be instructed to give all possible help and assistance to Nepalese nationals;

7) the two governments will from time to time exchange information relating to foreign affairs and relations with foreign powers in so far as they affect each other.[41]

While the *aide mémoire* conformed in general to the spirit of the 1950 Indo-Nepali treaty and "letters of exchange," it imposed additional obligations on both governments with regard to the co-ordination process. This note had been drafted by the Indian Government, but there is no doubt that it reflected the considered opinion of both Kathmandu and New Delhi. In his May 8 press conference, for instance, D. R. Regmi declared that Nepal's foreign policy is "very much allied to that of India," and suggested that joint consultations between the foreign ministers of both countries should become a regular feature.[42] Nehru was even more specific when he told Parliament on May 18 that he had "reiterated" to King Tribhuvan and D. R. Regmi that Nepal should "coordinate its foreign policy with India."[43]

There appears to have been some confusion in both Kathmandu and New Delhi as to whether the Indian advice on China meant that Kathmandu should merely revise its treaty relations with Tibet or should also establish diplomatic relations with China. As late as September 5, 1954, D. R. Regmi was still denying press reports that the M. P. Koirala government was considering "normalizing" relations with the Peking regime.[44] Three weeks later, however, he welcomed Premier Chou En-lai's statement that China was prepared to exchange diplomatic representation with Nepal, and said that "we are willing to give serious thought to the proposal whenever it reaches us."[45]

There was a further delay at this point, however, as Nepali-

41 *Jhyali*, July 8, 1958, p. 2. The original *aide mémoire* was presumably in English. The version given here is a translation from the Nepali text as it appeared in *Jhyali*. Thus, there may be minor terminological changes from the English original but none that alter meaning of the text.
42 *The Statesman*, May 9, 1954, 8:6.
43 *The Hindu*, May 20, 1954, 7:1.
44 *The Statesman*, Sept 8. 1954, 5:3.
45 *Hindustan Times*, Sept. 28, 1954, 9:6.

Chinese relations constituted one of the subjects for discussion between Nehru and Chou En-lai during the Indian Prime Minister's state visit to China in October 1954. M. P. Koirala met Nehru in Calcutta both immediately before and after the latter's tour of China. Apparently the Indian government received—or at least thought it received—the assurances from Chou En-Lai that Nehru had been seeking. In a press conference at New Delhi shortly after his return, Nehru strongly implied that Peking had recognized Nepal as an exclusive Indian sphere of influence and that, moreover, he had been assured that China had no intention to use Dr. K. I. Singh to lead a procommunist guerrilla movement in Nepal. "I do not think that Dr. K. I. Singh will function in the future," he stated. On the question of diplomatic relations between Nepal and China, Nehru said "that is a matter which the Nepalese government no doubt will deal with in its own way,"[46] in effect giving Nepal the green light to undertake serious discussions with Peking on this subject. Negotiations between the Chinese and Nepali ambassadors in New Delhi started the following month.

Thus, by the end of 1954, a number of developments were already under way that were to have a tremendous impact on Nepal's foreign policy. The pace of change proved to be much faster than either New Delhi or Kathmandu had originally contemplated. In the early stages, at least, this was not due to initiatives on the part of China but to changes within Nepal stemming from the death of King Tribhuvan on March 13, 1955, and the succession to the throne of King Mahendra. The new ruler of Nepal proved to be a very different man from his father, both temperamentally and with regard to his views on Nepal's role in the international community.

---

[46] *The Hindu*, Nov. 15, 1954, 8.4.

9

New Directions
in Foreign Policy,
1955-60

THE accession of King Mahendra to the throne on March 13, 1955, did not bring about any immediate changes in the content or direction of Nepali foreign policy. Indeed, the two outstanding events during the first year of the new reign—Nepal's admission to the United Nations and the establishment of diplomatic relations with the Communist Chinese Government—represented the culmination of policies initiated by previous governments.

The talks in late 1954 between the Nepali and Chinese ambassadors in New Delhi regarding diplomatic relations had been inconclusive, to Peking's regret.[1] A six-man delegation headed by the Chinese ambassador in India, General Yuan Chung-hsien, was therefore sent to Kathmandu in late July 1955 for talks with the Nepali government. After five days of intensive and secret negotiations, an agreement was reached on August 1 which called for diplomatic relations between the two states based upon the now-familiar five principles (*panchshila*) of peaceful coexistence. The Chinese ambassador in New Delhi was accredited to Nepal but, in conformity with Indian wishes, a resident embassy was not established in Kathmandu at this time.

Shortly thereafter, and probably as a direct consequence of the Sino-Nepali agreement, King Mahendra pardoned Nepal's most famous political exile, Dr. K. I. Singh, who returned to Kathmandu to receive a hero's welcome. To the astonishment of the Nepali public, however, Dr. Singh became an ardent exponent of closer

---

[1] See the report of the New China News Agency (NCNA), Mar. 4, 1955.

relations with India and warned of dangers involved in contacts with China. This set him apart from virtually every other political party leader in Nepal, who were at least vocal advocates of a balanced relationship between that country and its two neighbors.

But the two events in 1955 that were to have perhaps the greatest impact on Nepal occurred beyond the borders of the state. The first of these was the unpublicized but nonetheless serious boundary dispute between India and China along the western Himalayan border, near the Nepal-Tibet-India trijuncture in that area. Even more important was the outbreak of a massive rebellion against Chinese Communist rule among the turbulent Khampas of eastern Tibet, which for a time endangered Chinese control of that area as well as access to central Tibet from the east.

MAHENDRA'S NEW LOOK IN FOREIGN POLICY, 1956–59

King Mahendra's avoidance of new initiatives in foreign policy during the first ten months of his rule can probably be attributed to the chronic crisis in the domestic political and economic situation, which held top priority. The intimate and necessary relationship between domestic politics and foreign policy quickly impressed itself upon the new ruler, however, and a drastic reorientation of some of the basic principles and processes that had guided Kathmandu's external relations was introduced in early 1956. The first portent of Mahendra's new look in foreign policy was the startling appointment of Tanka Prasad Acharya—a self-proclaimed leftist with poorly disguised anti-Indian proclivities, who headed an insignificant political party, the Praja Parishad—as prime minister on January 27, 1956. In his first press conference, three days later, the new prime minister expressed his government's determination to modify Nepal's "special relations" with India in the direction of "equal friendship" with all countries, thus giving a novel dimension to Kathmandu's diversification policy. He was prepared to accept "aid without strings" from all friendly countries, such as India, China, Britain, and the United States, France and the Soviet Union, Tanka Prasad declared, and would also seek to amend the 1950 Indo-Nepali trade treaty in order to establish direct trade relations with third countries.[2]

The response from the Nepali public and the Chinese government was equally enthusiastic. The Chinese ambassador to India

---

[2] *Gorkhapatra*, Jan. 30, 1956.

and Nepal, General Yuan Chung-hsien, arrived in Kathmandu for a four-day visit on February 3, 1956, to announce that China was prepared to extend economic assistance to Nepal. Prime Minister Acharya expressed his appreciation for this "friendly gesture" and stated that his government would soon take up with Peking the question of Nepali-Tibetan relations and the demarcation of the northern border.[3] Official missions were exchanged between Nepal and China shortly thereafter, Vice Premier Ulanfu representing Peking at King Mahendra's coronation in May 1956 and Balchandra Sharma, a Praja Parishad leader, heading a Nepali delegation to China two months later. While in Kathmandu, Ulanfu expressed China's "sympathy" with Nepal's efforts toward economic development,[4] strongly implying Peking's interest in joining the aid-giving community in Kathmandu.

Ulanfu also prepared the way for Sino-Nepali talks on Tibet, and a second Chinese delegation, headed by the new ambassador to India and Nepal, Pan Tzu-li, arrived in Kathmandu on August 14, 1956. Negotiations with the Nepali Foreign Minister, Chuda Prasad Sharma (a close associate of Tanka Prasad), continued for approximately a month, culminating in the signing of a treaty on September 20, 1956.[5]

The preamble of the treaty reaffirmed that the five principles (*panchshila*) of peaceful coexistence should serve as the basis of relations between the two states. The other main provisions were:

1) all past agreements between Nepal and Tibet were abrogated;
2) Nepal was allowed to establish trade agencies at Lhasa, Shigatse, Kerong and Kuti in Tibet, and China was given the right to establish an equal number of trade agencies in Nepal at locations to be determined later;
3) Nepali merchants were permitted to trade at Lhasa, Shigatse, Gyantse and Yatung,[6] and an equal number of trade markets in Nepal would be specified for the use of China when this became necessary;
4) pilgrimage by Nepalis and Tibetans in each other's territory would continue according to "religious custom;" and
5) traders involved in local trade in the border regions of Nepal and Tibet "may do as they have customarily done heretofore."

In the exchange of notes that accompanied the signing of the treaty, a number of additional provisions were agreed upon:

---

[3] *Asian Recorder*, I:59 (Feb. 11–17, 1956), p. 678.
[4] See report by the NCNA, May 7, 1956.
[5] For text, see *New Developments in Friendly Relations between China and Nepal* (Peking, Foreign Languages Press, 1960, pp. 1–6).
[6] These last two trade markets were for Nepali merchants who used the Sikkim-Chumbi Valley trade route.

1) Nepal could immediately establish a consulate-general at Lhasa and China could, at some mutually agreed later date, establish a consulate-general at Kathmandu;
2) Nepal agreed to withdraw its military escorts at the various Nepal government offices in Tibet within six months;
3) Nepali residents in Tibet lost all the extraterritorial rights and special privileges that they had enjoyed under the 1856 treaty; and
4) direct wireless telegraphic service between Lhasa and Kathmandu would be established at some later date.[7]

In contrast to the treaty, which went into effect only after the exchange of ratified copies by both governments, the provisions of the notes became operative immediately—i.e., on September 20, 1956.

It is obvious that several of the more important provisions had been incorporated into the notes that accompanied the agreement rather than in the treaty itself. A concern for secrecy does not seem to have been the motivation in this instance, as the notes were made public almost immediately. One possible explanation is that the Chinese wanted the stipulations included in the notes to go into effect immediately rather than to await completion of ratification procedures. There were important centers of opposition to the treaty in Kathmandu,[8] and it seemed probable that the ratification process on the Nepali side would be long and involved. And indeed, China returned the ratified copy of the treaty to Kathmandu on November 16, 1956, but it was not until January 17, 1958, that Nepal finaly handed over a ratified copy of the treaty to Peking. There was a touch of mystery about all this, for the Nepali government claimed that the treaty had actually been ratified on March 7, 1957, but failed to explain the ten-month delay in the transmission of the ratified copy to China.[9]

Developments in Sino-Nepali relations came thick and fast in

---

[7] *New Developments in Friendly Relations*, pp. 7–14.

[8] The Nepali Businessmen's Association of Tibet, for instance, had presented a list of guidelines to the Nepal Government requesting that their rights to trade and acquire property in Tibet be left as defined in the 1856 treaty (*The Statesman*, Aug. 21, 1956). Although the Nepali trading community was dissatisfied with some of the terms of the 1956 treaty, they welcomed the limited legitimization of their commercial activity in Tibet. It was fully understood that Chinese goodwill was essential to the liberal implementation of the treaty, and Peking actually gained a valuable and effective lobby in the Nepali business group with trade interests in Tibet. The journal, *Nepal Bhasa Patrika*, for instance, that voices the interests of this group, has consistently followed a pro-Chinese line or at least avoided anything to which the Chinese might object.

[9] Dr. K. I. Singh, during his brief tenure as prime minister, denied that Nepal had ratified the 1956 treaty and charged that the Acharya government had been inattentive to Nepal's interests in its negotiations with the Chinese! (*Samaj*. Sept, 28, 1957.)

the latter part of 1956. On September 25, as a concession to Chinese sensitivity, the Nepali government imposed severe restrictions on mountaineering expeditions into the Himalayan range. The next day, Tanka Prasad Acharya left on a ten-day tour of China, the first Nepali prime minister to visit a country other than India for nearly half a century. The Chinese regime conjured up its usual massive reception for visiting dignitaries, much to the delight of the egocentric Tanka Prasad, whose public statements during the tours were considered excessive even in Nepal, not to mention India.[10]

On the more mundane side, Prime Minister Acharya concluded an economic assistance agreement with the Chinese government on October 7 under which Peking promised Nepal Rs. 20 million (in Indian rupees) in cash and Rs. 40 million in "machinery, equipment, materials and other commodities" during the next three years,[11] to be used for the construction of a cement factory and a paper mill. The Chinese also agreed that "no technical personnel shall be dispatched to Nepal in connection with the aid," thus disclaiming any intention to establish an aid program office in Kathmandu. This aspect of the aid agreement was welcomed by the Nepali public, which contrasted it to the elaborately administered American and Indian aid programs. The outright grant of currency with no restrictions on its utilization was interpreted in Kathmandu as signifying China's recognition of the capacity of the Nepalis to administer their own economic development program without outside supervision.

This was nonsense, of course, as the later closely supervised Chinese aid projects clearly demonstrate. In this instance, however, China's primary motivations were political rather than economic, and presumably Peking had reconciled itself to having the aid squandered even before making the offer. The first installment of the currency aid, Rs. 10 million, was received on February 3, 1957, and was mostly used to meet the Nepali government's existing obligations on projects under the American and Indian aid programs, which may have startled even the inscrutable Chinese. A year later, the second installment was employed in a futile effort to bolster the exchange rate of the Nepali rupee vis-à-vis the Indian rupee.[12] Nothing was left from the currency grant for its stipulated purpose—i.e.,

---

10 *Survey China Mainland Press* (SCMP), No. 1381, Oct. 2, 1956.

11 For the text, see *New Developments in Friendly Relations, op. cit.*, pp. 15–16. Girilal Jain states that China had originally proposed to give Rs. 40 million in currency and Rs. 20 million in material, but that this was "modified in response to India's views. . . . The details of how this amendment was negotiated must still remain secret" (*op. cit.*, p. 48).

12 E. B. Mihaly, *Foreign Aid and Politics in Nepal: A Case Study*, New York, Oxford University Press, 1965, p. 96.

to meet local expenditures on the Chinese-aided paper mill and cement factory. Neither of these projects, however, was inaugurated within the stipulated period nor was any of the Rs. 40 million in material aid actually provided. Nevertheless, the lack of substantive achievements did not seem to diminish the enthusiasm of the Kathmandu public, which still considered the Chinese aid program a model worthy of emulation by other aid-giving countries.

Peking Redefines its Role in Nepal.—During the initial stages of its intensive interaction with Nepal, the Chinese authorities were careful to avoid any blatant and direct challenges to India's preëminent position south of the Himalayan crest. Premier Chou En-lai's visit to Kathmandu from February 25 to 28, 1957, however, marked a significant change in Peking's approach, for thenceforth its concern for Indian sensitivities was considerably muted. The premier's reference to the "blood ties between Nepal and China"[13]—i.e., between the Chinese and those Nepali ethnic groups of Mongoloid origin—was calculated to raise blood pressure in New Delhi, for the Chinese had now begun to compete openly with the Indians in the use of cultural and racial factors in influencing the Nepali public. Since that time, Chinese propaganda in Nepal has subtly encouraged the concept of "Bhotia Raj" (rule by the Bhotias or Mongoloids), particularly when directed at the Newar community in Kathmandu valley or the Limbu and Kirati communities in the eastern hills. That propaganda has taken various forms, including contributions to Newari cultural and philanthropic organizations and an emphasis on the supposed Buddhist ties between the Chinese people and the Nepali Bhotias. The Chinese Buddhist Association, for instance, served as hosts to Nepali Buddhist delegations in 1959 and 1964, and also contributed Rs. 500,000 for a Buddhist hostel in Kathmandu. As it has finally worked out, the Indians have tended to direct their attention toward the "Hinduized" communities, both Indo-Aryan and Mongoloid, in Nepal whereas the Chinese have concentrated on the Buddhist-oriented elements among the Mongoloid groups.

It was also during Chou En-lai's visit to Nepal in February 1957 that a road link between Kathmandu and Tibet was first proposed, although apparently by Prime Minister Acharya on this occasion. The Khampa revolt in eastern Tibet and the delicate stage in relations with India made the proposal unfeasible technically and dangerous politically for China, and Chou En-lai reportedly expressed the inability of his government to assist the project at this time. The ebullient Tanka Prasad, however, was encouraged to

---

13 *Samaj*, Jan. 27, 1957.

proceed on his own. Construction of the section of the road in Kathmandu valley commenced almost immediately, only to be halted indefinitely with the resignation of the Acharya government in mid-1957.

In addition to these new trends in China's policy, a number of other developments in Nepal's external relations in 1956–57 distinguish that period from the Tribhuvan regnum. The 1956 vote in the U.N. General Assembly on the Hungarian question, in which Nepal voted with the West against the Soviet bloc, was welcomed with great enthusiasm by the Nepali public. This had little or nothing to do with anti-Russian sentiment, of course, or with concern over Hungary's sad fate. What satisfied the public was the fact that this was the first major issue in the U.N. in which Nepal had not voted with India,[14] thus establishing Nepal's credentials as a sovereign and independent state in an international forum. Another significant event was the 4th Congress of the World Buddhist Fellowship held in Kathmandu on the occasion of the 2,500th anniversary of the birth of Gautama Buddha in what is now the Nepal Terai. Buddhist monks and scholars from thirty-two countries attended the congress, which was inaugurated by King Mahendra on November 17, 1956. The four-day congress was a resounding success. Nepal took pride in having hosted its first international gathering, and in having established cultural relations with several other countries directly rather than through India as the intermediary.

The Indian Reaction.—New Delhi extended a general approval to the efforts to "normalize" relations between Nepal and China, presumably on the assumption that these would develop under India's general supervision. When, however, these relations began to develop at a quickened pace and in unexpected directions, the Indian government suddenly took alarm, particularly as there was simultaneously an unpublicized deterioration in its own relations with China. No longer could New Delhi take for granted Peking's recognition of Nepal as an Indian "sphere of influence" within which a minimal Chinese role would be defined in consonance with Indian-devised limitations. On the contrary, by late 1956 New Delhi found itself reacting to Chinese initiatives in Nepal. The Indian offer of Rs. 110 million in economic assistance for Nepal's first five-year plan, for instance, was announced shortly

---

[14] According to a reliable Nepali source, the new Nepali delegate to the U.N., Rishikesh Shaha, voted on this issue without having received instructions from Kathmandu. Whether the Acharya government would have concurred with Shaha's decision is doubtful, but there was nothing to be done once the vote had been cast. The Nepali public, and later the government, cheered this example of Nepal's independence from Indian guidance as a triumph for nationalism.

after Tanka Prasad had returned from Peking with a Chinese aid agreement. While it is probable that it was the timing rather than the substance of the Indian aid offer that had been affected by the Chinese assistance, the potential for the encouragement of competition in aid-giving was exposed in sharp relief.

In the latter half of October 1956, President Rajendra Prasad of India made a four-day state visit to Kathmandu, his first trip to a foreign country since assuming office in 1951. He was given a friendly reception, and the usual statements reaffirming the two countries' historical and cultural ties were exchanged between the President and King Mahendra. Nevertheless, the ultrasensitivity of the Nepali public was clearly evident in the political controversy aroused by the President's seemingly innocous remark at a royal banquet that "any threat to the peace and security of Nepal is as much a threat to the peace and security of India. Your friends are our friends and our friends yours."[15] Similar sentiments had been expressed by Indian officials on numerous occasions in the past without anyone's taking offense, but that was before the shift from "special relations with India" to "equal friendship with all." Some Nepali political party leaders affected to perceive ominous nuances in the President's statement, ranging from "India wants Nepal as a satellite" to "India wants to foist her own enemies on Nepal." Although both of these conclusions may or may not have been correct, there was nothing even implicit in Rajendra Prasad's comment to warrant such interpretations. The Indians were learning the hard way that what were once strictly profunctory remarks were now fighting words to the Nepali elite.

New Delhi's dissatisfaction with the trends in Nepal, and in particular with the Acharya government, was reflected in the unusual welcome given to the Nepali prime minister's most vocal critic, Dr. K. I. Singh, upon his visit to New Delhi during the first half of October 1956. The former "red bandit," who had twice been apprehended in Nepal with Indian assistance, now found himself an honored guest in India, and met both Prime Minister Nehru and Home Minister Pandit Pant. In a press conference in New Delhi on October 11, Dr. Singh strongly opposed the establishment of more foreign embassies in Kathmandu, and criticized the economic aid agreement that Tanka Prasad had concluded a few days earlier with China. He also asserted that the Acharya government had erred in surrendering Nepal's traditional privileges in Tibet under the 1856 treaty without simultaneously securing the rectifi-

---

[15] *Speeches of President Rajendra Prasad, 1952–56*, New Delhi, Publication Division, Government of India, pp. 67–68.

cation of the Nepal-Tibet border through the restoration of the territory Nepal had lost in the 1792 treaty.[16] Alarmed by the warm reception given to Dr. Singh by the Indian government and press, Prime Minister Acharya made a state visit of his own to India in December 1956 to explain his China policy to the skeptical Indian government and public, but the manner in which he was received, if formally correct, was decidedly cool.

In evaluating these developments, it should be kept in mind that Tanka Prasad, though enthusiastic about the role he had been selected to play in foreign policy innovations, was more an instrument through which King Mahendra implemented his own program than a framer of policy. It was also the King who finally decided in mid-1957 that Nepal may have gone too far too quickly in expanding relations with China and that a new balance should be struck. On July 14, 1957, the King dismissed the coalition Acharya cabinet and, twelve days later, appointed a new government headed by Dr. K. I. Singh. Internal political considerations influenced the King's astonishing choice of prime ministers, but it seems probable that foreign policy was at least of equal importance.[17]

The Singh ministry constituted an abrupt if transient aberration in the general trend of foreign policy in Nepal. Once again "special relations with India" became the dominant theme, and further "diversification" was postponed if not abandoned. Dr. Singh announced that China and the Soviet Union would not be allowed to establish embassies in Kathmandu, nor would Nepal seek to extend its own diplomatic relations beyond the existing level for the time being. He rejected the suggestion that Nepal should formalize relations with its other major south Asian neighbor, Pakistan, and instead issued the most explicit statement ever made by a Nepali official, either before or since, supporting India's position on the Kashmir question. On the Gandak River project, which Nepali nationalists had made into a symbol of resistance to Indian domination, the prime minister accepted the draft agreement submitted by New Delhi and appointed a special committee to evaluate the proposal as the first step in the direction of an agreement.

The Indian government was not unresponsive to Dr. Singh's welcome gestures. New Delhi promised Rs. 100 million in support of the Singh government's hastily contrived 2-year development plan, as well as immediate assistance in meeting the food crisis that

---

16 *Hindustan Times*, Oct. 12, 1956; and Girilal Jain, *op. cit.*, p. 57.
17 Tanka Prasad blamed his dismissal on India (*Hindustan Times*, Aug. 26, 1957) and dubbed K. I. Singh as "paid agent" of India. He later told an Indian journalist that New Delhi had maneuvered his dismissal (Girilal Jain, *op. cit.*, p. 52).

had reached serious proportions in various parts of Nepal. A break-through was even made on the delicate matter of negotiations for the revision of the 1950 trade treaty. Although little progress was made in these discussions, the foundation for the eventual amendment of the treaty in 1960 was laid.[18]

By late 1957, the Singh ministry had become both a political embarrassment and a potential threat to the Palace, and was suddenly dismissed from office on November 19.[19] The King had used the Acharya ministry to transform Nepal's special relationship with India into a triangle involving China, and had then employed Dr. K. I. Singh as a counterfoil to absorb public discontent in the necessary task of restoring a balance. The policy pursued during these ministries has generally been characterized as "pro-China" for the Acharya cabinet and "pro-India" for the Singh cabinet. King Mahendra, of course, was not motivated by either sentiment but rather by a determination to gain for Nepal a greater degree of flexibility and independence in dealing with both of his dangerous neighbors.

Having accomplished his purpose to a considerable extent, and with nothing to be gained from the further use of front men in either external or internal policy, King Mahendra introduced a period of direct rule. The emphasis in foreign policy was placed on a second theme in the diversification program—the extension of Nepal's international intercourse beyond its immediate neighbors, with the object of involving major outside powers as countervailing forces against both India and China. Perhaps the most significant aspect of the new tactical approach was the relatively little attention paid to gaining even the tacit concurrence of New Delhi—an indication of the steady decline in India's capacity to exert an automatic veto on such questions. The extent of the decline of India's influence should not, however, be overestimated. Pressure tactics of many kinds, both economic and political, could still be employed by New Delhi with telling effect upon Kathmandu, but the Indian authorities seem to have preferred using more subtle methods to influence the Nepal government rather than the application of di-

---

[18] The Indian Government had presented to the Acharya government a draft of the 1950 trade treaty which, according to Tanka Prasad, removed Indian customs restrictions on Nepali imports from and exports to foreign countries but on "the condition that permission from India was required for the import of goods into Nepal." (*Halkhabar*, Feb. 9, 1960.) If correct, these terms were not acceptable to the Nepal government, and the talks never started.

[19] K. I. Singh also attributed his dismissal to "foreign intervention," and on this occasion the U. S. Government was given the credit for having contrived his removal from office (Girilal Jain, *op. cit.*, p. 63).

rect pressure. Their tactics were greatly facilitated by the fact that the Indian ambassador at that time, Bhagwan Sahay, was one of the most effective diplomats ever to have served in Kathmandu and was a confidant of King Mahendra as no Indian has been before or since.

From the Nepali viewpoint, one of the more important developments in the direction of diversification was the agreement reached with the United States in January 1958 under which both governments established resident embassies in their respective capitals. This was the opening wedge for the opening of embassies in Kathmandu by a number of states, including China and the Soviet Union. Although New Delhi had consistently discouraged such diplomatic contacts in the past, it did not raise strong objections on this occasion. The Indians realized that a Chinese embassy, or at least the consulate-general provided in the 1956 treaty, could not long be postponed, and they apparently were content to have the American embassy in Kathmandu as a potential source of support for their own purposes.

King Mahendra also moved to strengthen relations with Great Britain; on April 17, 1958, he renewed the agreement on Gurkha recruitment for ten years rather than the previous five year period. Such recruitment was popular with the "military tribes" in the hills, but sentiment among Kathmandu-based politicians and intellectuals on the matter was decidedly critical. To mollify the latter group, the King formally terminated the Indian military mission in mid-1958, a move which did not seriously effect operational procedures, as the few Indian officers still in Nepal as part of the mission were retained as advisors at staff Headquarters.

King Mahendra also revived and expanded the "diversification" program through the establishment of diplomatic relations with a number of countries. At the time of K. I. Singh's dismissal in November 1957, Nepal had diplomatic relations with five countries; by mid-1960, the number had increased to twenty-four. Probably the most important action of the King in the foreign-policy field during the direct-rule period was his state visit to the Soviet Union in June 1958, during which it was agreed that resident embassies would be established in Moscow and Kathmandu and that Russia would embark on an aid program in Nepal. The advent of this new contender in the "cockpit of international politics," as Nepalis sometimes characterize Kathmandu, aroused strong apprehensions in Washington and even some concern in nonaligned New Delhi. Perhaps it was too much to expect the Americans and Indians to perceive at that time that the Russians would become an unofficial and private ally in the implementation of some aspects of their separate but related anti-China policies!

THE FIRST ELECTED GOVERNMENT

In the settlement that ended the 1950 revolution, general elections had been promised for 1952 or 1953, but for various technical and political reasons eight years went by before they were actually held. It is rather surprising, in view of the incessant harping on foreign "interference" in Nepal, that foreign policy questions played a relatively minor role in the 1959 election campaign. There were the customary exchanges of wild allegations concerning the vast quantities of money that foreign powers—usually unspecified—were pouring into the country to influence the election. None of these charges were ever authenticated, however, and it is doubtful that such funds actually were available in sufficient quantity to affect significantly the outcome of the 1959 elections.

The Nepali Congress, the party most closely identified with the 1950 revolution, won an overwhelming victory in the elections, gaining two-thirds of the seats in the lower house of Parliament, and King Mahendra called upon the president of the party, B. P. Koirala, to form the first elected government. The party's democratic-socialist domestic policy had been reasonably well defined in the various programs issued since 1956, but there was less certainty as to its position on foreign policy. That section of the party's lengthy election manifesto, for instance, merely stated that its foreign policy

will be based on equal friendship with different countries. The Nepali Congress will not join any war bloc and will make use of her U.N. membership for the achievement of peace. The Nepali Congress will maintain full friendship with her great neighbors.[20]

The stock cliches were there, but it remained to be seen how the new prime minister and his closest associates, men with strong views on most subjects, including foreign policy, would interpret and apply these guiding principles.

The formation of the Nepali Congress government coincided very closely with other major developments in the Himalayan area: the outbreak of a full-scale rebellion against Chinese rule in Tibet, the escape of the Dalai Lama to India, and a major dispute between India and China over the border between Kashmir State (Ladakh) and Tibet. The critical problem for the new government was to evolve a balanced foreign policy that would alarm neither of her

---

[20] Nepali Congress, *Chunao Ghoshanapatra* (Election Manifesto), Kathmandu, Kalpana Press, 1958, p. 15.

growling neighbors but would reflect a general political approach that was prodemocratic in content and unsympathetic to communist ideology and communist regimes. That approach was implicit in the statement on Tibet issued by the two Nepali Congress general secretaries, S. P. Upadhyaya and Ganeshman Singh, on April 3, 1959, after the election but before the B. P. Koirala government had taken office. In criticizing Chinese actions in Tibet, the two party officials argued that the communists had violated the 1951 Sino-Tibetan treaty "as well as other treaties signed by China with other nations." They suggested that China should apply "the Leninist principle of self determination to Tibet" and placed the Hungarian revolt of 1956 and the revolt in Tibet on the same footing. "The Tibetan events," they concluded, "have provided a warning to all the nations of Asia."[21]

This frankly critical appraisal of China's policy toward Tibet immediately raised questions concerning the foreign policy of the Nepali Congress government that was then preparing to take office. B. P. Koirala clarified the party's position on April 17 when he stated that it is "absurd to suggest that recent Tibetan developments will affect our traditional relations with our great neighbour China." He denied that the recent statement by the party's general secretaries portended "any shift in our foreign policy because of the happenings however unhappy in Tibet," but he also reiterated the view that recent events in Tibet have

affected the people of Nepal deeply, and it has exercised the emotion of nationalist elements in our political life. You all know how sensitive we Nepalese are on the question of nationalism and the preservation of our national way of life.[22]

Two weeks later, on May 2, 1959, the Nepali Congress adopted a resolution on Tibet which went even further in characterizing Chinese action in Tibet as within the "19th century imperialist tradition" and asserted that "it would be a reactionary step if China tries to establish its sovereignty over Tibet on the basis of old standards. . . . It is a breach of the Chinese promise of autonomy that has caused the Tibetans to rise in a national revolt and as such it is the duty of China to satisfy them by giving them what they want."[23] B. P. Koirala told the party's M. P.'s two days later that his government's foreign policy would continue to be based on neutrality and nonalignment, but repeated that "China must unequiv-

---

21 *Kalpana*, Apr. 3, 1959.
22 *Commoner*, Apr. 18, 1959.
23 *Kalpana*, May 2, 1959 (emphasis supplied).

ocally allow Tibet to exercise full autonomy within the 1951 Sino-Tibetan agreement."[24]

The Nepali Congress leadership appeared to be badly shaken by the developments in Tibet and were uncertain when they took office on May 27, 1959, just how these would eventually affect Nepal's foreign policy. Their immediate response, as might be expected, was directed at achieving a broad degree of harmony with the government of India on the policy to be pursued to meet this new and potentially dangerous situation on the Himalayan frontier. Private talks had been held between Nehru and King Mahendra in late May, which set the stage for the Indian prime minister's visit to Kathmandu the following month.

The Nepalis obtained an insight into Nehru's views at a public meeting in Kathmandu on June 13 when he rather abruptly dismissed the *panchsila* approach to foreign policy with the cryptic comment: "Panchshila? Kahan hai Panchshila? Kaun manta hai Panchshila?" (Panchshila? Where is Panchshila? Who observes Panchshila?) He met separately with both King Mahendra and B. P. Koirala to discuss (1) strengthening Nepal's northern border posts, if necessary, with the assistance of Indian personnel; (2) revision of the 1950 trade treaty; (3) Indian economic assistance; and (4) the Tibetan situation.

The joint communiqué issued by the two prime ministers on June 14 noted that "there was an identity of views, the policies of the two countries, both in the international and domestic spheres, being animated by similar ideals and objectives." In what was widely interpreted as a reference to Tibet, the communiqué asserted that "the Prime Ministers are further convinced that in the interests of peace as well as national and human progress no country should be dominated by another and colonial control in whatever form should end." The statement concluded with the comment that "there is no conflict of interest between the two countries, and they face similar problems and have common approaches."[25] This constituted the closest approximation to the terms and spirit of the 1950 "letters of exchange" and the 1954 "aide mémoire" that any Nepali government had publicly agreed to since King Mahendra's accession to the throne.[26] On the basis of these talks, and of Indian promises of financial and material support, the Nepali government

---

24 *Motherland*, May 5, 1959.
25 *Asian Recorder*, V:27 (July 4–10, 1959), pp. 2748–49.
26 Although King Mahendra did not sign the joint communiqué, he had held private talks with both Nehru and B. P. Koirala and, presumably, had not objected to the language used by the two prime ministers.

announced a 100 percent increase in defense expenditures for 1959–60, primarily aimed at strengthening northern border defenses.

Nehru had been given an exceptionally friendly welcome on his arrival in Kathmandu, but it was not long before the opposition parties and pro-China elements began to raise alarms. The Indian prime minister's caustic remarks on *panchshila*, for instance, while obviously aimed at China's failure to abide by these principles in its relations with India, was interpreted to mean that New Delhi felt no obligation to follow the *panchshila* principle of noninterference in its relations with Nepal. Even stronger objections were raised in regard to the joint communiqué, which, in the views of many Nepalis, constituted an abandonment of the policies of "equal friendship to all" and "nonalignment in the Sino-Indian dispute." B. P. Koirala insisted on a number of occasions thereafter that this was not the case and that absolute neutrality, nonalignment and equal friendship were still the basis of his government's foreign policy. But neither his opposition critics nor, perhaps, the Chinese government were convinced.

There is no question that Peking was disturbed by the attitude of the Nepali Congress government on foreign policy, and particularly on Tibet, but the Chinese employed a soft approach at this stage. The Chinese ambassador to India and Nepal, Pan Tsu-li, came to Kathmandu twice in 1959, in late May and again in October, for talks with the Nepali authorities, ostensibly concerning economic assistance but actually in regard to Tibet. Chinese policy in the aftermath of the Lhasa rebellion had raised major problems for Nepali subjects resident in Tibet. A number of them had been arrested by the Chinese in connection with the uprising, and had been denied the right to meet the Nepali consul-general. Trade between Nepal and Tibet had declined drastically because of the restrictions placed on the movements of Nepali traders. The sudden announcement that Chinese currency would be the only legal currency in Tibet threatened to ruin the Nepali traders there, as most of their capital holdings were in Tibetan currency.

Given the tense situation in Tibet in the first half of 1959, the Chinese behaved as reasonably as could be expected. By September, they were in a position to ameliorate some of the more specific situations complained of by the Nepal Government. Several Nepali subjects under detention in Tibet were released. Most of the travel restrictions on Nepali traders were lifted, and Peking suggested joint Sino-Nepali talks on a new trade treaty. The Chinese also announced that the now illegal Tibetan currency could be exchanged at face value for Chinese currency.

Kathmandu had also moved cautiously on several fronts since midsummer to improve relations with China. B. P. Koirala stated in July that his government would continue to support the Peking regime's right to the seat reserved for China in the U. N., and endorsed India's policy of separating that question from the Tibet issue. A six-man Nepali Buddhist delegation, headed by Bhikshu Amritananda, was allowed to visit China at the invitation of the Chinese Buddhist Association.[27] Moreover, when a resolution condemning China's behavior in Tibet was brought to a vote in the U. N., Nepal abstained.[28] Nevertheless, the Chinese reassurances had only partly convinced Kathmandu, as was clearly indicated by the extensive tours of the northern border area by both King Mahendra and B. P. Koirala in the winter of 1959–60.

In an effort to ascertain more clearly the objectives and policies of the Chinese government in the Himalayan area, B. P. Koirala sent one of his closest associates, Dr. Tulsi Giri, to Peking as the head of the official delegation to China's October celebrations.[29] Dr. Giri's consultations with the Chinese authorities were private, and there was no announcement of the subjects discussed. In public statements after his return, however, Dr. Giri repeatedly stressed China's interest in a peaceful settlement of the dispute with India as well as its willingness to be "reasonable" in its relations with Nepal. In his eagerness to press his views on both India and Nepal, Dr. Giri made a serious *faux pas* in an interview with Indian journalists in Calcutta when he offered the "good offices" of the Nepali government in the mediation of the Sino-Indian dispute. This ran directly counter to Kathmandu's basic policy of avoiding involvement at all costs in its neighbors' quarrels. Dr. Giri claimed that he

---

[27] The glowing account of the condition of Buddhism in Communist China given by Bhikshu Amritananda after his return never mentioned what was happening to Buddhist institutions in Tibet under Chinese rule. Cynics in Kathmandu related this incredible omission to the Rs. 500,000 the Chinese donated to the Bhikshu's Buddhist organization, whose headquarters were at the Swayambhu Nath shrine near Kathmandu.

[28] In his statement in the U.N. concerning the Tibet resolution, the Nepali delegate, S. P. Upadhyaya, emphasized that Nepal had recognized "the special kind of relationship that exists between China and Tibet today," and decried attempts to preserve "traditional ways of life" such as those in Tibet when they stand in the way of progress. (*General Assembly Official Records*, 831st plenary meeting, Oct. 20, 1959, paras. 55–62.) Contrast this with his strongly critical appraisal of Chinese policy in his statement of Apr. 3, 1959.

[29] The official Nepali delegation had been "insulted" by the Chinese Government, according to one Nepali paper, when it was allotted a lower position of precedence (No. 66) than that given to the Nepali Communist Party delegation (No. 44) that also attended the October celebrations. This was one of the few instances in which the Chinese authorities failed to demonstrate a good sense of tact in handling Nepali visitors.

had been misunderstood, and that he had merely offered the Nepali government's cooperation, not mediation.[30] Nevertheless, his off-hand remark was so embarrassing to his colleagues that Deputy Prime Minister Subarna Shamsher hastened to New Delhi to explain to Nehru that China had not proposed Nepal as a mediator and that Kathmandu was not volunteering its services in this capacity.

During Nehru's visit to Kathmandu, B. P. Koirala had accepted an invitation to visit India at some mutually agreeable date. Two events in December 1959 added to the urgency for renewed discussions between the two government leaders. On December 4, the Gandak River project agreement, amended substantially to meet the major Nepali objections, was signed in Kathmandu. Three weeks later, during a debate on foreign policy in the Indian Parliament, Nehru reiterated his government's position that "any aggression against Bhutan and Nepal would be regarded as aggression against India."[31]

Opposition and anti-Indian elements in Nepal moved quickly to exploit both these issues. Public meetings were organized in Kathmandu to protest the Gandak agreement, while the critical comment on Nehru's parliamentary statement was so vehement that B. P. Koirala finally was constrained to explain that the Indian prime minister had merely meant "that in case of aggression against Nepal, India would send help if such help is ever sought. It could never be taken as suggesting that India could take unilateral action."[32] Nehru affirmed that B. P. Koirala's elaboration was "perfectly correct" but also revealed for the first time the terms of the "letters of exchange" that had accompanied the 1950 treaty. This outraged Nepali sentiment even further, and added substantially to the outcry against India's alleged interference in Nepal.

B. P. Koirala arrived in New Delhi in late January 1960 for talks with Nehru and other Indian leaders. The joint communiqué issued by the two prime ministers on January 29 differed substantially in tone and content from the one signed seven months earlier. Reference was made to "a similarity of approach to international problems by the two Governments" but nothing was said about any presumed "identity of interests" or "common approaches." India promised an additional Rs. 180 million in economic assistance and also agreed that revisions of the 1950 trade treaty should "provide for the separation of Nepal's foreign exchange account and the reg-

---

[30] *Kalpana*, Oct. 22, 1959.
[31] *Statesman*, Nov. 28, 1959.
[32] *Asian Recorder*, V: 51 (Dec. 19–25, 1959), pp. 3060–61.

ulation by the Government of Nepal of their foreign trade."[33] In a press conference at Chandigarh two days later, B. P. Koirala said he did not envisage a joint defense arrangement between Nepal and India, as military alliances were "worse than useless." In response to a question concerning the "similarity of approach" mentioned in the joint communiqué, the Nepali prime minister stated that this referred to his government's adherence to the "policy of neutrality enunciated by Mr. Nehru. In the context of the Sino-Indian dispute, we are friendly to both the countries. We want an amicable settlement between the two."[34] The "equal friendship" principle, thus, had now been fully reinstated as an integral part of the Koirala ministry's foreign policy.

B. P. Koirala had set the stage for his projected visit to China and had assured himself of a reasonably friendly reception there. The Nepali prime minister, however, quickly demonstrated to the Chinese that they were not dealing with another Tanka Prasad Acharya. In one of his first public statements in Peking, for instance, Koirala implicitly criticized Chinese policy toward India when he stated: "Notwithstanding its size or might if any power attempts to occupy or control even an inch of territory of another Asian country, such attempts will definitely disrupt peace in the world." He also warned against efforts to suppress freedom-loving people by means of force, which in the context was an obvious reference to Tibet.[35]

The Chinese Communists, however, were not visibly provoked by B. P. Koirala's thinly disguised criticisms, but instead set about to relieve his evident concern over the border situation. This was accomplished substantially through a number of major Chinese concessions in the agreements reached with Koirala on the demarcation of the Nepal-Tibet border, additional Chinese economic assistance to Nepal,[36] and the decision to set up resident embassies in Kathmandu and Peking. A Chinese proposal for a treaty of "peace and friendship" was postponed for further consideration at Koirala's request; but his general satisfaction with the results of his visit to China was indicated in his incredulous remark at Hong Kong that "the Chinese have so much to do in their own country that they have not had time to glance across their borders."[37]

The boundary agreement, signed March 21, 1961, noted that

---

33 *Foreign Policy of India, Text of Documents*, Lok Sabha Secretariat, New Delhi, 1966, pp. 343–4.
34 *Asian Recorder*, VI: 7 (Feb. 6–12, 1960), p. 3158.
35 *Gorkhapatra*, Mar. 16, 1960.
36 For texts of agreements and joint communiques, see *New Developments in Friendly Relations, op. cit.*, pp. 17–28.
37 *Gorkhapatra*, Mar. 28, 1960.

both countries have "always respected the existing traditional customary boundary line," and agreed that "the formal settlement of some existing discrepancies in the boundary line . . . and the scientific delineation and formal demarcation of the whole boundary line" would consolidate the friendly relations existing between the two states. It also called for the appointment of a joint demarcation committee to investigate the situation on the ground so as to determine the places where the boundary was in dispute and to ascertain the state of "actual jurisdiction in these sections." It was also agreed that a twenty-kilometer demilitarized zone would be created on each side of the border, from which "armed personnel" would be excluded and in which only unarmed administrative personnel and civil police would be allowed to operate.

In the economic aid agreement, Peking promised Rs. 100 million in aid in addition to the Rs. 40 million of unspent aid in the 1956 agreement. The new treaty differed from its predecessor, however, in that it provided for technical assistance to Nepal, thus leading to the establishment of a Chinese aid mission in Kathmandu. Peking tried to mitigate the political impact in Nepal of this change in policy by specifying that the Chinese technicians, in contrast to their Indian, American and Russian counterparts, should have a standard of living "not exceeding that of personnel of the same level in the Kingdom of Nepal." Nevertheless, China was now an integral part of the aid-giving community in Kathmandu, with all the advantages and disadvantages, achievements and frustrations, that went with that status.

THE MT. EVEREST QUESTION

Nepali-Chinese relations appeared to have attained an even keel during B. P. Koirala's visit to China, and no one in Kathmandu—and probably Peking—expected a sudden deterioration. In a press conference in Kathmandu on April 4, 1960, however, Koirala casually—indeed, almost incidentally—referred to China's claim to Mt. Everest ("Sagarmatha" to the Nepalis and "Jhomolunga" to the Chinese) as a "very ordinary thing."[38] The intensity of the popular response in Nepal to this comment was unprecedented, and the first anti-Chinese demonstration in the history of the country was organized in Kathmandu on April 21 to support Nepal's claim to the world's highest mountain.

---

[38] *Kalpana*, Apr. 4, 1960.

The Chinese government, which appeared to be genuinely surprised by the onset of a dispute with Nepal on this issue, hastened to repair the damages as best it could. Fortunately for Peking, Chou En-lai had already scheduled a visit to Kathmandu to follow his talks with Nehru in New Delhi on the Sino-Indian border dispute. He arrived in the Nepali capital on April 26 and moved immediately and effectively to relieve Nepali anxieties on the Mt. Everest question. He told newsmen on April 28 that China did not plan to press a claim for Mt. Everest but was prepared to accept the demarcation of a boundary line along the peak.[39] In an address to the Association of Nepali Traders, he endorsed the proposal for a Kathmandu-Tibet highway, and held out prospects for a rapid and mutually profitable expansion of trade relations between the two states. He also obtained the Nepali government's agreement to a "treaty of peace and friendship" which in essence repeated the terms of the 1956 treaty establishing the five principles of peaceful coexistence as the basis of their relationship. After an exceptionally busy and successful four days in Kathmandu, the Chinese Premier returned to India, with Nepali-Chinese relations again on a firm basis—or so it seemed.

The euphoria in Kathmandu did not last long, however. In early May, rumors that a Chinese mountaineering team was poised for an assault on Mt. Everest swept through Kathmandu. Peking denied the story initially even though, according to later Chinese accounts, the team began the climb on May 17 and finally conquered the peak on May 25 under truly astonishing conditions.[40] The Nepali government was disturbed by the failure of the Chinese authorities to request Kathmandu's consent to the climb or, indeed, even to notify it about the expedition. By this act, China had in effect made a claim to share control of Everest, in the process infringing upon one of the proudest symbols of Nepali nationhood. Although the legality of the Chinese position was readily conceded,[41] many Nepalis were distressed that Peking had ignored their sensitivities on the matter.

---

[39] *Halkhabar*, Apr. 28, 1960.

[40] Detailed descriptions of this astonishing climb can be found in *Peking Review* (23), June 7, 1960, pp. 21–22, and (22), May 31, 1960, p. 4. Some western mountaineering sources, aware of the adverse weather conditions in the Everest area in late May, are frankly skeptical about the Chinese claim to have "conquered" Everest, particularly under the primitive conditions described in the Chinese account.

[41] B. P. Koirala told newsmen on May 28 that China was under no obligation to inform Nepal about the expedition but maintained that this did not affect his government's claim that Everest belonged to Nepal and to Nepal alone. (*Asian Recorder*, VI: 26 (June 25–July 1, 1960), p. 3398.

THE MUSTANG INCIDENT

Nepali feelings were dealt an even harsher blow shortly thereafter. On June 28, 1960, Chinese troops fired on an unarmed Nepali police party in the demilitarized zone in the vicinity of the Kore pass in the Mustang section of the Nepal-Tibet border, killing one of the party and capturing seventeen others. According to the Chinese foreign ministry, the Chinese force had mistaken the Nepali party for Tibetan rebels[42] who were then operating on both sides of the border with relative impunity. The two governments disagreed on the actual location of the incident, Peking claiming that it occurred in Chinese territory about one kilometer to the north of the pass while Kathmandu insisted that the site was in Nepali territory approximately 300 meters to the south of the pass. Agreement was never reached on this question, but it is interesting to note that the actual demarcation of the border in that area by a joint team the following year placed *both* sites in Nepali territory.

The Nepali government also protested that the intrusion of an armed Chinese party into this area was in direct violation of the border agreement signed between the two governments the previous March. Peking attempted to explain away this "shortcoming" by noting that the Nepali government had been informed on June 26 that Chinese troops would be operating in the demilitarized zone. Kathmandu admitted that it had received the unilateral notification (although only on the day of the incident), but argued that it had not consented to the Chinese operation, which, therefore, still violated the agreement. The Chinese government admitted that "certain low-ranking personnel" of the Chinese army had been "careless" and agreed to pay Rs. 50,000 in compensation. Chou En-lai wrote B. P. Koirala on July 12 that "it would be meaningless and unprofitable for the two sides to continue to argue over the place of the incident," and suggested that it would be advisable for both governments to establish embassies in each other's capital as well as direct telecommunication contact to help avoid such incidents in the future. In his reply of July 24, the Nepali prime minister agreed that "it would not serve any gainful purpose to continue arguing over the incident," but gave an equivocal reply to Chou's proposal for an early exchange of resident embassies.[43]

42 *China Today*, 5:32 (July 7, 1960), pp. 4–5.
43 The texts of both Chou En-lai's and B. P. Koirala's letters were published in *The Commoner*, July 27, 1960, pp. 2, 6–7.

The behavior of both the Nepali and Chinese governments in the Mt. Everest and Mustang incidents is curious indeed, and it is difficult to avoid the impression that much more lay behind these events than was apparent on the surface. Is it really possible that the Chinese expedition to Everest and the assault on an unarmed Nepali police party were unintentional infringements of Nepal's rights and sensitivities? It seems most unlikely. It is far more reasonable to presume that these were deliberate provocations carried out in such a way as to constitute a subdued but pointed reprimand to the B. P. Koirala government, and a reminder of the ease with which China could create difficulties all along the border.

Peking's motivations are, at best, a matter of speculation. It is not unlikely that the Chinese had been irritated with B. P. Koirala while he was in Peking, in particular by his unresponsiveness to their suggestions with regard to a Kathmandu-Tibet road (which was assuming greater importance because of the virtual breakdown of the vital supply route to Tibet via India and Sikkim) and a Chinese embassy in Kathmandu. Peking must also have been distressed by the way in which B. P. Koirala, or more precisely other leading members of his government and the Nepali Congress, built up what was probably a *pro forma* Chinese claim to Mt. Everest into a major issue in domestic Nepali politics, inevitably giving it an anti-Chinese twist in the process.[44]

The B. P. Koirala government had been virtually unique in the annals of modern Nepali politics during its first year in office because of its restraint in using foreign-policy issues to bolster its domestic political position. This had been a deliberate decision on the part of the Nepali Congress leaders, who had carefully avoided actions or statements calculated to elicit popular applause in Nepal at the cost of exasperating a foreign power. Their attitude was most evident perhaps in relations with New Delhi in which an attempt was made to discuss issues—e. g., Gandak and the trade treaty revisions—on their merits rather than as expressions of popular dissatisfaction. By the spring of 1960, however, the political opposition in Nepal was beginning to achieve some results through its intemperate and emotional criticisms of the Koirala government's foreign policy, and in particular its allegations of a pro-Indian orientation that threatened Nepal's national integrity. The Nepali Congress leadership considered it essential to answer these charges in kind,

---

44 This dispute occurred at an embarrassing time for Peking, which was then involved in a major diplomatic campaign aimed at contrasting Peking's "reasonableness" in its border disputes with neighboring states, and in particular Burma and Nepal, with New Delhi's intransigence in the Sino-Indian border dispute.

and B. P. Koirala, perhaps reluctantly, went along with their decision.[45]

In any case, the Nepali Congress used the Mt. Everest issue and the Mustang incident skillfully in bolstering their political position. The non-Communist parties were maneuvered into temporarily abandoning their anti-Indian tirades in favor of demands that the government stand up to China, while the Nepali communists became half-hearted apologists for the Peking regime. The communists attempted to employ their usual tactic in such situations by diverting the public attention with anti-Indian counterdemonstrations. The massive anti-China rally of April 21 in Kathmandu on the Everest issue, for instance, was followed two days later by a communist-organized demonstration on the Gandak issue.

In using these disputes with China to good effect internally, the B. P. Koirala government had no intention of embittering relations with China on a long-term basis.[46] It was, therefore, quite prepared to make several concessions of its own when Peking adopted a moderate position on the issues in dispute. A Chinese embassy was allowed to open in August 1960, and the joint boundary commission met the following month to inaugurate discussions on the demarcation of the Nepal-Tibet border. In the process, however, the Nepali Congress had deprived the opposition parties of their most effective line of criticism against the Koirala ministry. Moreover, the carefully dramatized exposure of the potentiality of a Chinese threat to Nepal had contributed to a better-balanced perspective as to the country's relations with both its neighbors in the public mind, which, until then, had been almost solely concerned with the "Indian threat."

The conclusion of a new trade treaty with India on September 11, 1960, was another important success for the Koirala government, as it signified the achievement of a goal that had evaded that government's predecessors for a decade. Virtually all of the major Nepali complaints against the existing trade system were satisfied in the new agreement:

---

45 Two organizations affiliated with the Nepali Congress, the *Nepal Tarun Dal* (Nepal Youth Organization) and the *Nepal Chhatra Sangh* (Nepal Student Association), were chiefly instrumental in the organization of anti-Chinese demonstrations in Kathmandu (*Swatantra Samachar*, Apr. 21, 1960).

46 The minor role played by B. P. Koirala and other members of his government in the exploitation of the Mt. Everest and Mustang issues by the Nepali Congress for domestic political advantages was probably carefully calculated to avoid directly involving the government in the campaign. This made it much easier for the prime minister to settle these disputes with China.

1) Nepal was no longer obligated to "clear" the terms of trade relations with third countries with the Indian government.
2) The joint exchange account for foreign currency administered by India was terminated and Nepal was granted a separate exchange account.
3) Transit facilities within India for Nepali imports and exports were to be defined in conformity with the usual international conventions.
4) Nepali trade traffic in transit through India was exempted from Indian customs or transit duties.
5) Trade between India and Nepal was exempted from customs duties and quotas except as specified by the two governments.

In the letters of exchange that accompanied the treaty, Kathmandu agreed that goods imported by Nepal from third countries would not be reexported to India, and New Delhi allowed the Nepal government to continue to impose duties on goods imported from or exported to India at its own discretion. The response to the new agreement in the Nepali trading community and general public was enthusiastic, and the reputation of the Koirala government had never been higher—at least on foreign-policy matters.

THE FALL OF THE KOIRALA GOVERNMENT

It would be interesting to know how much these developments in Nepal's relations with India and China motivated King Mahendra in his dramatic dismissal and arrest of the Koirala ministry on December 15, 1960, and the abrogation of the parliamentary system of government a few days later. The King had obviously lost all confidence in the capacity of the opposition parties to challenge the dominance of the Nepali Congress within the parliamentary system, particularly now that the opposition had been effectively deprived of the potentially explosive foreign policy issue. The King must have concluded that the opposition parties were at best doubtful allies in the expected confrontation between the monarchy and the Nepali Congress.

Taken at their face value, the King's public statements following his coup strongly implied that foreign policy considerations had played an important part in his decision. "Anti-national elements," he proclaimed, had "received encouragement to a large degree" from the Koirala government. "As it is our ultimate responsibility to safeguard nationalism and sovereignty . . . We hereby dissolve the Cabinet as well as both houses of Parliament."[47] No specific al-

---

47 Royal Proclamation of Dec. 15, 1960, *Dainik Nepal*, Dec. 15, 1960.

legations, however, were ever made against B. P. Koirala or his colleagues in this respect,[48] nor were any significant changes made in foreign policy until late 1961, when a whole new series of factors intruded. In making these vague charges against the Nepali Congress, King Mahendra may have hoped to discredit the Koirala government in the eyes of the Nepali public without directly affecting his own relations with foreign powers. But B. P. Koirala's credentials as a bona fide nationalist, primarily concerned with protecting Nepal's national interests, had been firmly established during his eighteen months in office. There was no more substance to the allegations that he was an Indian agent or even "biased toward India" than there was later to the charge that King Mahendra was pro-Chinese.

---

[48] An Indian journalist reported in March 1961 that King Mahendra, in an interview, had accused B. P. Koirala of planning to merge Nepal into India (*Indian Nation,* Mar. 22, 1961). Such an accusation seems highly unlikely, however, and the report probably reflected either a misunderstanding or misinterpretation of the King's remarks by the correspondent.

10

Crisis in Relations
with New Delhi,
1961-62

BECAUSE of the suddenness and thoroughness with which King Mahendra planned and implemented the December 15, 1960, royal coup, it encountered little more than token resistance. Hundreds of Nepali Congress leaders were arrested. Hundreds more fled to India where, under the leadership of Deputy Prime Minister Subarna Shamsher (who was in India at the time of the coup), the party was reorganized into an opposition in exile. A party conference was held at Raxaul, just across the border in Bihar, in mid-January 1961. The resolutions adopted were moderate in tone, merely petitioning the King to release political prisoners and reconvene Parliament. The conference, however, also secretly decided to "build a resistance movement" to the "King's autocratic regime,"[1] which would necessarily be directed from India, inasmuch as the Congress organization had disintegrated in Nepal.

In the Indian press and among Indian political leaders, almost unanimous denunciation greeted the news of the dismissal and arrest of the Koirala ministry. The Indian Government's public reaction was more restrained, but it nevertheless evinced a deep distress over the Nepal events. Nehru's first comment was merely an expression of regret at this "setback" to democracy,[2] but he was more explicit a few days later when he described the King's allega-

---

[1] P. N. Chowdhury, "From Non-Violence to Violence," *Nepal Today*, I:11 (May 1, 1962), 109.
[2] *Lok Sabha Debates*, XLIX (25), Dec. 16, 1960, Col. 5973–77.

tions against the Nepali Congress as "vague charges" and characterized the coup as "a complete reversal of democratic process."[3]

Although New Delhi usually emphasized the "setback to
democracy" theme, it was in fact the potential for political instability which the Indians perceived in the King's "rash" action that
caused them far greater concern. New Delhi underestimated Mahendra's capacity to stabilize his regime and control the emergence
of oppositional forces. Under the Koirala government, Nehru commented, "for the first time Nepal had some order of Government
which was trying its best to improve things."[4] He doubted that the
royal regime shared this capacity and determination, and feared
that the consequence might well be a political upheaval in the central Himalayas which, in the context of the Sino-Indian dispute,
could easily get out of control.

The Indian government's position at this time, therefore, cannot properly be categorized as hard-line anti-royal regime. Indeed,
New Delhi took several steps in the first half of 1961 that had the
effect of bolstering the King, presumably with that result in mind.
In April, for instance, the two governments signed four agreements
under which India promised aid totaling Indian Rs. 13.2 million
for development purposes. The following month, in New Delhi,
there were talks on the 1960 trade treaty, during which the Indian
Government agreed to alleviate some of the difficulties that Nepalis
still faced in the transit of imports and baggage through India. Discussion also got under way on the Gandak project, and these led
to an agreement to establish a joint coordination committee that
would meet periodically to consider problems arising in the implementation of the program. These concessions to the royal regime,
minor though they may have been, had a considerable political
impact in Kathmandu, where all political factions were carefully
evaluating New Delhi's policy toward the King.

The tactics employed by the Nepal government at this critical
period were classic Mahendra, with various so-called spokesmen
for the regime taking widely varying and even contradictory positions on major issues. It was *de rigeur* at this stage, for instance,
for the foreign affairs minister, Dr. Tulsi Giri, to take a conciliatory
position toward India while the home minister, Bishwabandhu
Thapa, was outspokenly critical of New Delhi, the King usually
being somewhere in between in his public statements. Later, the
roles of the supporting actors changed, Dr. Giri taking the anti-
Indian, pro-Chinese position and Rishikesh Shaha, the finance

---

[3] *Rajya Sabha Debates*, XXXI (17), Dec. 20, 1960, Col. 2707–10.
[4] *Loc. cit.*

minister, counselling "quiet diplomacy" in Nepal's contentious relations with India. The positions assumed publicly by various ministers were, of course, not necessarily indicative of their true sentiments, but were determined by the role-fulfillment functions assigned to them by the King, who in his way gained greater flexibility in his own handling of troublesome neighbors.[5]

The King was also able to exploit the nationalist sentiments of the hypersensitive Nepali elites by stigmatizing the opposition forces as puppets of a foreign power. Indeed, it would appear that on occasion Mahendra deliberately gave an anti-Indian orientation to his foreign policy in order to solidify popular support behind the royal regime. It was to his political advantage to pose the alternatives as an Indian-influenced democratic government or his own autocratic but independent rule.

PEKING'S REACTIONS TO THE COUP

In contrast to India, the People's Government of China maintained a discreet silence on the royal coup, merely reporting the event without editorial comment. This may have reflected a sense of satisfaction stemming from the realization that the changeover brought opportunities that were ripe for exploitation. Peking had usually been scrupulously correct in its official relations with the Koirala ministry, but its preference for the authoritarian royal regime may have been reflected in the series of agreements concluded between the two governments in the months following the coup. Although the preliminary negotiations on some of these questions had started while the Nepali Congress was still in office, King Mahendra consistently won more favorable terms from the Chinese than B. P. Koirala could have reasonably expected.

The Nepal-China Joint Boundary Commission, for instance, was in session at the time of the coup, and combined teams were touring the border areas and preparing reports based on their investigations. The dismissal of the Koirala ministry did not interfere with these proceedings, which concluded on schedule in mid-January 1961. The second session reconvened in Peking a few days later to scrutinize the survey reports. One month later, an agreement was reached in which a series of points on the border were mutually affirmed, and joint survey teams were again sent to the border to demarcate the boundary between these points.

---

[5] We cannot be certain whether this was an example of deliberate statecraft or whether the ministers themselves perceived personal advantages in such role fulfillment. It is apparent, however, that the King not only allowed but encouraged this practice.

The third session of the commission was inaugurated in Kathmandu on July 31, 1961, to finalize the terms of agreement. Of the eleven areas originally in dispute, China had conceded four to Nepal during B. P. Koirala's visit to Peking and two others thereafter. In the final negotiations, the survey reports supported the Nepali claims to four more disputed areas. It was only in the Kimthanka section of the border, in the Mt. Yayamba area well below the southern slope of Mt. Everest, that the Chinese claim was upheld, and even here two small villages were allotted to Nepal.

On August 28, 1961, it was announced that agreement on a draft boundary treaty had been reached and that an *ad hoc* map had been prepared delineating the border in all but three places— Mt. Everest and the trijunctures on the eastern and western sections where the boundaries of Nepal, Tibet, India and Sikkim met. The extent of China's territorial claims in the Everest area were never made public, but they reportedly included not only the peak but the southern slope of the mountain as well.[6] Earlier, Mao Tse-tung had suggested to B. P. Koirala that the peak be placed under joint sovereignty and the crest made the boundary line, but the Nepali Prime Minister had rejected this offer. At the third session of the Joint Boundary Commission, China for the first time stated its claim to Everest in writing, and then again proposed Mao's "joint sovereignty" formula. The offer was again rejected, and King Mahendra publicly reiterated Nepal's claim to the peak on August 29, 1961. Consequently, when the fourth session of the Commission met in Peking a week later, the only issue on the agenda was the framing of a compromise formula on the Everest question that would be acceptable to both governments.

Consulations on the improvement of Sino-Nepali economic relations had also been initiated in the spring of 1961. Peking sent an economic delegation to Kathmandu in May to discuss Chinese aid projects. In September a protocol to the 1960 aid agreement was concluded, under which Peking agreed to give Nepal hard currency (sterling or dollars)[7] to the value of Indian Rs. 10 million and commodities valued at Rs. 25 million as a gift to be used to provide the

---

6 On a Chinese map published in 1955, the boundary was shown as including Mt. Everest and the area approximately five miles to the south as Chinese territory. This map first came to public notice in Nepal in October 1959 when a Russian map based on the Chinese map was circulated in Kathmandu. (*Swatantra Samachar*, Oct. 21, 1959). Presumably, it was this map about which B. P. Koirala queried the Chinese during his visit to Peking in March 1960, this in turn leading to the dispute over Mt. Everest. For details, see Padma Bahadur Khatri, "Nepal-Chin Sima Sandhi" (Nepal-China Border Treaty) *Gorkhapatra*, Mar. 7, 1962.

7 *Gorkhapatra*, Sept. 6, 1961.

local currency required for Chinese-aided projects—a paper mill, a cement factory and a shoe factory.

PAKISTAN ENTERS THE PICTURE

An important aspect of Nepal's diversification program has been the strengthening of contacts with the Afro-Asian bloc of states. Kathmandu eagerly sought participation in various formal and informal regional arrangements such as the conference of the heads of nonaligned states at Belgrade in September 1961, to which King Mahendra himself led the delegation. In the drafting of the conference agenda, the Nepali representative emphasized "non-intervention and non-interference in the internal affairs of nations."[8] Ostensibly directed at the colonial powers, the Nepali contribution in reality was aimed at India, another participant in the conference.

After profusely lauding nonalignment at Belgrade, King Mahendra proceeded to Pakistan, a member of two military pacts, on a six-day state visit. The Koirala ministry had formally established diplomatic relations with Pakistan in 1960, but no further steps had been taken at that time, and this was the first instance in which a top-level Nepali leader had visited Pakistan in his official capacity. The King, aware of New Delhi's interest in these proceedings, ignored the efforts made by President Ayub Khan to raise political questions in public and merely expressed the hope that "relations between our two countries can be strengthened by better commercial and cultural exchanges."[9] Pakistan, which sought common ground with Nepal in their respective difficulties with India, accepted the overture at its face value. A trade delegation was sent to Kathmandu in April 1962 to discuss trade relations between the two states and an air-link between East Pakistan and Kathmandu. A Nepali delegation returned the visit a few months later, and a trade treaty, providing for mutual most-favored-nation treatment, was signed October 19, 1962. A series of talks at Karachi in January 1963 culminated in a trade and transit treaty providing for the free movement of goods between the two countries without customs or transit duties. This was viewed in Kathmandu as a major contribution to the economic diversification program.

---

8 Yadu Nath Khanal, "What Nepal Expects from the 'Neutral Summit,'" (text of the statement by the Nepali Foreign Secretary at the bureau meeting of the Belgrade Conference), *Gorkhapatra*, Aug. 8, 1961.
9 *Sagarmatha Sambad*, Sept. 12, 1961.

CLOSER TIES WITH CHINA

The traveling season for King Mahendra had only begun with his return from Belgrade and Pakistan. On September 25, 1961, the Nepali monarch set off on a 17-day state visit to China and Outer Mongolia which proved to be one of the most critical events of his rule. On his arrival in Peking, King Mahendra was greeted by Liu Shao-chi as an "esteemed friend of the Chinese people." The Chinese made several subtle attempts to maneuver the King into public anti-Indian declarations, but with no success. Indeed, several of his more pointed remarks appear to have been directed at China, perhaps as a discreet warning that he did not take Chinese professions at their face value. On one occasion, for instance, the King quoted Liu as having stated in a private conversation that China "might have a tendency to ignore just and rightful claims, and the rights and susceptibilities of her small neighbors."[10] A few days later he commented:

History notes that China defeated other races and was also vanquished. But I believe the Communist Government of . . . China will take lessons from history and not adopt the path of encroachment upon and interference in the political sovereignty and territorial integrity of her neighbors. China should make all possible efforts not to repeat past mistakes.[11]

Nepal was eager to have China's friendship, the King implied, but on terms compatible with the country's independence.

The stated purpose behind the King's visit to Peking had been the signing of a boundary agreement, which occurred on October 5. The terms were essentially those prescribed by the boundary commission.[12] With regard to Mt. Everest, an ambivalent formula was devised which merely stipulated that the boundary passed through the peak. Presumably there is joint sovereignty, but this was not explicitly stated, and both Nepal and China have continued to claim exclusive sovereignty. In his first public statement after his return, for instance, the King told his countrymen that Everest continued to belong to Nepal "as usual," but there is nothing in the treaty terms to warrant this conclusion and China has not conceded the Nepali claim.

Another significant point in the boundary treaty concerned

---

[10] The text of the King's address was broadcast by Nepal Radio on Oct. 7 and summarized in *The Hindu*, Oct. 11, 1961.
[11] *Gorkhapatra*, Oct. 7, 1961.
[12] *Peking Review*, IV (42), Oct. 20, 1961, pp. 5–8.

the trijunctures at the eastern and western ends of the border. New Delhi had made known its views on this question to the third session of the boundary commission in August 1961, but it had no voice in the final agreement between Nepal and China. Nevertheless, the treaty drew the alignment at the trijunctures in conformity with the watershed principles as suggested by India. Peking also agreed that the Nepal-Tibet border had been delimited by tradition and did not require redefinition except in places where the two governments' concepts of the "traditional customary boundary line" differed. This was a position that India had argued in vain in its own border dispute with China. For these reasons, and because the Indians hoped that the treaty might contribute to stability in a difficult section of the Himalayan frontier, New Delhi officially welcomed the boundary agreement and suggested that the application of the same principles to the Sino-Indian dispute would facilitate a solution

The Kathmandu-Tibet Road Agreement.—A surprise ingredient of the package settlement concluded by King Mahendra was the totally unexpected signature on October 15, the last day of his visit to Peking, of an agreement on the construction of a road between Kathmandu and Tibet. Dr. Tulsi Giri, who had accompanied the King, signed the agreement for Nepal, possibly because Mahendra preferred to keep his own name off of what was certain to be a highly controversial document to which New Delhi would raise strenuous objections. He may also have wanted to demonstrate quietly his dissatisfaction with the pressure tactics which, according to some sources, the Chinese had employed in obtaining his assent to the road agreement. And indeed, that agreement had several curious aspects. In all of the King's previous meetings with the Chinese in Peking, the subject of a road agreement had not been raised by either side. Suddenly, on the day before his departure, the Chinese presented a draft road agreement to Mahendra, and in such terms as to imply that implementation of the boundary treaty depended upon a favorable response on the road question. Having been badly outmaneuvered for once, the King was in no position to resist the pressure.[13]

---

13 The official Nepali position regarding the road agreement is that King Mahendra took the initiative and that the Chinese, "after a cursory glance at His Majesty's proposal, gave their assent." [Rishiram, "Kathmandu-Lhasa Sadak" (Kathmandu-Lhasa Road), *Swatantra Samachar*, June 11, 1962, 18. See also the report on King Mahendra's interview with the Hindustan Samachar news agency in *Dainik Nepal*, Feb. 7, 1962.] This does not conform with the accounts of the negotiations by several sources, which make it clear that the proposal came from the Chinese. Nor is it reasonable to assume that King Mahendra would have waited until the last minute to bring up the subject with the Chinese, or that Peking would have given its assent

Under the terms of the road agreement,[14] China promised monetary aid to Nepal amounting to £3.5 million for construction work in Nepali territory, and also agreed to supply the necessary experts, technicians and equipment. One clause in the treaty, reportedly inserted at King Mahendra's insistence, specified that Chinese assistance should be provided only "at the request of His Majesty's Government," thus theoretically giving Kathmandu the final voice in the implementation of the project. The significance of this clause, however, was obscured by another provision which stipulated that the Chinese aid must be given by June 30, 1966. Presumably, this was only an obligation on China to provide the aid by the latter date, if requested, rather than an obligation on Nepal to undertake the road project by that date, but the terminology employed was not clear.

The potential importance of the road to Peking can be deduced from the extreme urgency with which the Chinese approached the project, despite a severe domestic economic crisis that placed a heavy strain on China's limited foreign exchange reserves. Obviously this was more than good-neighborliness or even the desire to expand Chinese influence in a susceptible area. Perhaps China's approach in this instance can be better understood in terms of the chronic difficulties Peking then faced in supplying its large military establishment in Tibet. The roads into Tibet from the east (Szechuan) and northeast (Tsinghai) traverse extremely difficult terrain, are expensive to maintain, particularly during the rigorous winter season, and were subject to sabotage and blockage by Khampa rebels. The road from the northwest (Sinkiang) was easier and safer, but it crossed the Aksai Chin plateau which was then in bitter dispute between India and China.

The logistical problems of the Chinese were further complicated by New Delhi's 1960 ban on trade in strategic goods with Tibet, thus eliminating what had been China's primary source of supply for many commodities. The potential value to Peking of the Kathmandu-Tibet road was greatly increased by this development, as India's trade blockade was not extended to Nepal as it had been to Sikkim and Bhutan. Rice from the surplus-production areas in the Nepal Terai and manufactured goods and other essential supplies (e.g., petrol) could still be imported into Tibet from Nepal more easily, quickly and cheaply than directly from China. The road therefore was an attractive proposition economically,

---

after "a cursory glance." The restructing of these events by Nepali publicists can probably be attributed to the need to project the royal image in terms of successful initiatives in all dealings with foreign powers that involve Nepal's national interests.
14 *SCMP* (2611), Nov. 21, 1961, pp. 32–33.

politically and strategically, and a few minor territorial concessions on the Nepal-Tibet border were a low price to pay as a *quid pro quo*.

Despite the circumstances under which the road agreement had been concluded, the Nepali government perceived several potential political and economic advantages for itself that made the agreement attractive. Relations with India were deteriorating, and King Mahendra was increasingly apprehensive that New Delhi would attempt a repetition of 1950–51. The road agreement provided the King with a badly needed bargaining weapon in negotiations with India. The strategic significance of the road, the first to breach the Himalayan barrier, was readily apparent, and the King was not being unrealistic in assuming that India would be prepared to pay a high price to avert this threat to its hard-pressed defense and security system on the northern frontier.

Publicly, however, the Nepali authorities belittled the political and strategic significance of the road and instead stressed its economic importance to Nepal. Harking back to Kathmandu's traditional status as the principal entrepôt for trans-Himalayan trade—lost when the route through Sikkim was opened after 1905—Nepalis envisioned the road as a means by which past glories and profits could be recaptured. The road would also provide Nepal with an alternative source of manufactured and other goods, thus lessening its dependence upon India.

The reaction in the Indian press to the road agreement was unanimously unfavorable, indeed almost frenetic, but the government of India maintained a discreet silence. The official position was that Nepal had not violated the letter of the 1950 treaty by its failure to consult with New Delhi on the matter prior to the formal conclusion of the treaty. Nehru told Parliament on November 27, 1961, that he was "not satisfied" that India's interests were unaffected by the road,[15] but that was as far as he was prepared to go in public. Nepali government sources dismissed the alarmist accounts of the road in the Indian press and Parliament as unwarranted intrusions into Nepal's domestic affairs that, moreover, were prompted by basic misunderstanding of the significance of the agreement. Communism would not enter Nepal "in a taxi cab," King Mahendra argued.[16] The Indian Government, however, was far more concerned with the possibility that Chinese troops might use the road to enter Nepal in tanks.

Even more important, perhaps, was the gap the road made in the Indian economic blockade of the Chinese forces in Tibet. Kath-

---

[15] *The Hindu Weekly Review*, Dec. 4, 1961, 15:2.
[16] *Gorkhapatra*, Nov. 14, 1961.

mandu recognized the validity of New Delhi's position on this point, and itself imposed a limited ban on the exportation of strategic goods—including iron products, cement, petrol, kerosene and coal—to Tibet on December 6, 1961. Five months later, Nepal agreed to extend the ban to include Indian-produced goods imported into Nepal. This left a wide divergence in the two governments' trade policies, however, as goods imported into Nepal from third countries could still be transhipped to Tibet if they were not on the banned list.

The Nepali authorities, of course, understood the strategic implications of the road, and did what was possible within the context of the agreement and Chinese insistence upon immediate implementation to direct the construction program along the least dangerous lines. The Chinese survey teams, which undertook their tasks in early 1962 as soon as weather conditions permitted, proposed two alternative routes—one through the Rasua Garhi pass in the Kerong area and the other via Kodari on the route to Kuti.[17] The former, which was shorter by nearly 20 kilometers and traversed easier terrain, was preferred by the Chinese. The Nepal Government, however, insisted on the Kodari route. Kathmandu has never explained its choice, but it is possible that the Nepali authorities hoped to prolong the construction period as much as possible. Peking, anxious to get the project under way immediately, agreed to the Kodari route. Within a remarkably short time, work on the road was in progress and Nepal could only go along with the Chinese construction timetable.

THE NEPALI CONGRESS RESISTANCE AND THE INDIAN ROLE

Although there had been sporadic acts of resistance to the royal regime in the early fall of 1961, the coordinated, wide-scale terrorist campaign organized by the Nepali Congress leaders in In-

---

[17] The passes at Rasua and Kodari, cut deeply by rivers having their origin in the north of the Himalayan crest, are only 13,000 to 14,000 feet above sea level, and therefore are two of the lowest all-weather passes in the entire Himalayan range. Both the routes also follow river valleys most of the way to Kathmandu valley, thus easing construction problems considerably even though bridges would have to cross the rivers at a number of points. For nearly four-fifths of its route, the Kodari road follows the Indravati, Sunkosi and Bhote Kosi rivers, averaging 2,000 to 4,000 feet in altitude. While there are numerous small bridges and culverts, only five large bridges are required, the longest about 580 ft. in length. Nepal usually prefers to refer to the road as the Kathmandu-Kodari highway (or as it is now called, the Arniko Rajpath) thus deemphasizing the connecting link with Tibet. The road does not stop at Kodari, the last point on the Nepal border, however, but continues to Kuti, where it

dia broke out only late in the year, after King Mahendra had gone to China. The sequence, we can safely assume, was not coincidental, nor is there reason to doubt that the Indian authorities had given the Nepali rebels the green light. What cannot be ascertained from existing sources is whether New Delhi's decision followed the Kodari road agreement or whether King Mahendra was constrained to seek closer relations with China because he knew that the Indians were about to unleash the Nepali Congress and was uncertain about the extent of support promised to the rebels.

These widespread but scattered disorders and terrorist acts never constituted a serious threat to the royal regime, but they did contribute to a dangerous deterioration in Nepali-Indian relations. Kathmandu repeatedly demanded pledges of noninterference from New Delhi as well as guarantees that the rebels would not be granted sanctuary on Indian soil. The Indian authorities reassured Kathmandu that "no trouble will come to Nepal from India," but they insisted that it was not possible for them to take legal action against Nepali political refugees who had not violated Indian law or who were not the subject of extradition procedures initiated by the Nepali government.

The public dialogue between New Delhi and Kathmandu throughout 1962 focused on these two issues. However, this was in part a façade behind which the two governments carried on a debate on more fundamental aspects of their interrelationship. The course of events in this period exacerbated all facets of Nepali-Indian relations, for their general foreign policy lines seemed to be moving in divergent directions on a number of levels and a confrontation of some sort was perhaps inevitable. The Nepali rebels in India contributed to the situation, but they were more a symptom than a cause of the worsening of relations. This general framework should be kept in mind in analyzing the trend of developments in 1962 that otherwise might appear to be senseless and even suicidal.

The earliest diplomatic exchanges in late 1961 were clothed in the usual polite verbiage, but the language gradually became blunter as the rebel raids increased in intensity. King Mahendra appealed in early January 1962 for support, stirring nationalist feeling with the charge that the exiles "are trying to undermine the cause of the country from foreign soil."[18] Later that month,

---

connects with the Chinese road to Shigatse and Lhasa, as well as with the 600-mile network of roads the Chinese have constructed paralleling the Nepal-Tibet border for its entire distance.

[18] Official English version of the speech by King Mahendra at Kathmandu on Jan. 5, 1962.

tempers rose even more when the King was allegedly the target of an assassination plot while touring the Janakpur area in the central Terai. Dr. Giri charged that the unsuccessful "assassins" had come from India and that "no local person had a hand in the attempt." He placed the blame for the incident on "Indian in-action" and charged New Delhi with "irresponsibility" for having failed to check these raids "from Indian bases."[19] An anti-Indian demonstration took place in front of the Indian embassy in Kath-mandu on January 26, and its official inspiration was only indif-ferently disguised.

Meanwhile, Kathmandu had issued warrants for Subarna Shamsher and other rebel leaders in connection with the Janakpur incident, and India's "cooperation" in the apprehension of the al-leged instigators of the assassination attempt was requested. Just how India was expected to cooperate, however, was not clear, as extradition of the rebel leaders was not demanded under the rel-evant treaty with India. King Mahendra stated on February 6 that India had been asked "to surrender these people," but New Delhi replied that this would be illegal so long as they had not violated Indian laws. India was prepared to initiate extradition procedures if requested, but the spokesman for the Government noted that the treaty barred extradition for political offenses and that criminal charges had to be supported by *prima facie* evidence. Kathmandu was not prepared for this, and instead ordered seventy-six of the most prominent Nepali exiles to return home by March 23, 1962, on pain of forfeiting all their property in Nepal.

In a curious tactical by-play on January 31, a spokesman of the Nepali Foreign Ministry announced that "unidentified aircraft" were dropping arms to Tibetan rebels in the Mustang area. The Nepali army was incapable of handling the well-armed Khampas on its own, he blandly declared, and if the Chinese should feel threatened by the rebels and should demand the right to send troops into Nepal to bring the Tibetans under control, there was little Kathmandu could do but comply with the request. He drew a parallel with the incident in 1951 when Indian troops entered Nepal to apprehend bandit gangs operating on both sides of the border—ignoring the fact that this had been at the invitation of the Nepali government. But the most intriguing aspect of the state-ment was that, according to Dr. Giri, Peking had never raised this question with Kathmandu.[20] New Delhi, ostensibly appraising the statement at its face value, reiterated its promise to come to Nepal's

19 *Nepal Samachar*, Jan. 24, 1962, and *Naya Samaj*, Jan. 30, 1962.
20 *The Overseas Hindustan Times*, Feb. 9, 1962, 7.

assistance in meeting external aggression. Kathmandu thereupon dropped the matter, but only after denying the accuracy of the original statement by their own official.

The Nehru-Mahendra Meeting.—The steady deterioration in Indo-Nepali relations was alarming to officials in both governments, who agreed that a meeting between the Indian prime minister and the King of Nepal was the best hope for improving the situation. Nearly three months were spent in the preliminary maneuvers for the meeting, however, as neither side wished to appear to be taking the initiative. The King, who finally arrived in New Delhi on April 18, 1962, assumed a hard-line position from the very beginning, emphasizing the necessity for states to abide by the *panchshila* principles "not only by words but also by deeds."[21] According to press reports, the meetings between Nehru and Mahendra were marked by frank and sharp exchanges. Mahendra insisted that Nepal's internal troubles were solely the handiwork of rebels based in India, and Nehru, arguing his old line that fundamental economic and political factors were at the root of the disturbances, proposed another "middle way" solution based upon a compromise settlement between the royal regime and the Nepali Congress. This was totally unacceptable to the King, and the only concrete result of their discussions was the agreement to establish joint commissions when necessary to ascertain the facts about the terrorist incidents.

Nehru also attempted to convince the King that India was not hostile either to him personally or to his regime. The monarchy and the Nepali Congress were India's two best friends in Nepal, Nehru argued, and with the Nepali Congress in difficulty it would be foolish indeed for New Delhi to alienate the King. Although this was an accurate assessment of the official Indian policy, Mahendra's skeptical response was certainly not unrealistic in view of the Indian record in the 1950–51 period and in recent months. Nehru had even less success in his efforts to discuss Nepal's relations with China, including the question of the Kathmandu-Tibet road. The King reiterated his public position that the road had only economic significance and was of little immediate strategic importance because it was a long-term project that would be under construction for years. In any case, he concluded, it was too late for Nepal to back out of the agreement.

By April 22, the substantive part of the talks had ended and it soon became apparent that neither side had made any significant concessions. Mahendra told Nepali journalists in New Delhi that

---

[21] *Rashtriya Sambad Samiti*, Apr. 19, 1962.

Nehru had given a "convincing assurance that the Government of India would not permit Indian soil to be used as a base for anti-Nepal activities," and that he, Mahendra, was "now convinced more than before that he will fulfill his promises."[22] The joint communiqué—reportedly drafted by Nehru—issued the following day, however, indicated that the Indian prime minister had not accepted Mahendra's contentions on the source of disorder within Nepal.[23] Nehru was even more explicit on that point two weeks later when he told newsmen that Indian soil could not be used to mount raids on Nepal, but that "peaceful agitation" by Nepali exiles "can be carried on here."[24] Mahendra had failed to achieve the main objective of his visit, which was to persuade the Indian authorities to impose restrictions on the activities of the Nepali rebel leaders in India.

The Mahendra-Nehru talks did nothing to arrest a further deterioration in the relations between the two states, and in fact they probably hastened the process. The raids continued, and the Nepali government became even more vehement in its allegations that the raiders were using Indian soil as their base. Joint commissions met to investigate two of these incidents, but disagreed on the interpretation of the data presented. The language employed by the Nepali government, both in its notes to New Delhi and in publicity releases, became increasingly undiplomatic and even abusive.[25] In another sudden shift of tactics in early July, however, King Mahendra reorganized the Council of Ministers, replacing Dr. Giri as foreign minister with the less controversial but equally volatile Rishikesh Shaha. Dr. Giri had increasingly become identified as an advocate of closer ties with Peking as a counterfoil to the threat of Indian intervention, whereas Shaha had usually expressed a preference for "quiet diplomacy" in relations with India, arguing that there were limits to New Delhi's patience with the bombastic tone of statements and notes emanating from the Nepali foreign ministry.

The new foreign minister was given an opportunity to demonstrate whether "quiet diplomacy" would be more productive than Dr. Giri's aggressive tactics. Shaha flew to New Delhi on September 4 for a series of talks with Nehru and other leading members of the Government. He returned to Kathmandu eleven days later bearing a noncommittal letter from Nehru to Mahendra which made it

---

22 *Ibid.*, Apr. 23, 1962.
23 *India News*, I:2 (May 4, 1962), 8.
24 *The Statesman Overseas Weekly*, June 23, 1962, 11.
25 See, for instance, S. P. Gyawali (Attorney-General of Nepal), *Friendship on Trial*, Kathmandu, Dept. of Publicity, 24 pp:, and Prakash Bahadur K. C., *Hostile Expeditions and International Law*, Kathmandu, Dept. of Publicity, 1962, 62 pp.

evident that he had not accomplished his objective. Indeed, Nehru advised the King to open "friendly negotiations" with the Nepali Congress. In the wake of a series of stormy cabinet meetings, Shaha was dropped from the ministry, along with the quiet diplomacy approach, and the King himself now charged that "anti-national elements have been receiving all sorts of help, facilities and cooperation in the friendly country, India."[26]

The hard line toward India was revived, and relations between the two countries worsened to such an extent in the ensuing three weeks that even a rupture of relations appeared possible. That would have been a disaster for Nepal, however, and the royal regime could not have allowed matters to go so far. Until this point, New Delhi's support of the Nepali rebels had been largely nominal, in both material and diplomatic terms. The Indian authorities had allowed the Nepali Congress and affiliated political groups in India to organize and direct terrorist and other disruptive incidents in Nepal, but had not provided them with any sizeable quantity of material assistance. New Delhi tried to exploit the rebels in its own campaign to pressure King Mahendra into major concessions, both to his internal opposition and to India with regard to relations with China. The objective, however, was not the overthrow of the royal regime but changes in its foreign and domestic policies—in essence, a restatement of the middle-way policy enunciated by Nehru a decade earlier.

The failure of Shaha's mission to New Delhi and his abrupt dismissal from the cabinet clearly indicated to the Indian government that the King was still not disposed to make the basic concessions demanded of him. New Delhi, therefore, reconsidered its own tactics and decided in late September to escalate its support of the Nepali rebels one notch by imposing an unofficial and undeclared economic blockade of Nepal. A number of minor incidents on the border were used to rationalize a total interruption of trade relations between the two countries. For several days, the flow of essential commodities into Nepal was halted, although no formal ban was placed on their exportation. Kathmandu's vehement, almost hysterical response, to this new tactic was a reflection of its vulnerability to such pressure. King Mahendra was placed in a situation in which he would have had to make major concessions to the Indians and the Nepali Congress, for alternative sources of supplies were not available. To his incredible good fortune, however, dramatic developments intervened elsewhere on the Himalayan frontier which he was able to exploit to immense advantage.

---

[26] *Asian Recorder*, VIII: 42 (Oct. 15–21, 1962), 4841–42.

THE SINO-INDIAN BORDER WAR AND NEPAL

On October 5, 1962, simultaneously with the crisis in Indo-Nepali relations, the Chinese foreign minister, Ch'en-yi, told the audience at a banquet in Peking to celebrate the first anniversary of the Nepali-Chinese boundary treaty that "in case any foreign army makes a foolhardy attempt to attack Nepal . . . China will side with the Nepalese people."[27] This gratuitous and vague offer of support must have been received in Kathmandu with mixed feelings. After all, it was not the Indian army but rather Indian economic pressure with which Nepal had to contend, and Chinese support in this respect was at best of limited value. Nehru's comment that Peking was "showing off" was to the point. Although the royal regime welcomed support from any source in those trying days, there was good reason to expect that the principal consequence of Ch'en-yi's remark would be to increase New Delhi's determination to force a settlement on Nepal that would make such dramatic gestures meaningless in the future.

In any case, it is probable that Ch'en-yi's statement was directed more at developments elsewhere on the Himalayan frontier than at Nepal.[28] In the latter half of October 1962, a limited but nonetheless large-scale border war flared up when Chinese military forces moved across the Indian border at the extreme eastern (NEFA) and extreme western (Ladakh) ends of the frontier. The Indian forces in NEFA were badly mauled, and the Chinese seized virtually the entire area on the Ladakh-Tibet border that was in dispute. Having attained their major objectives, the Chinese imposed a unilateral cease-fire which the battered Indian forces also respected, and by mid-December a tenuous peace had been restored.

The immediate response of the royal regime to these hostilities must have been one of relief, for New Delhi hastened to make fundamental changes in its Nepal policy. The unofficial economic blockade was lifted, and trade began to flow across the border again. The Nepali Congress leaders, on the advice of the government of India, first suspended their agitation in November and then formally terminated it the following month. King Mahendra had survived both Indian economic pressure and a concentrated

---

27 *NCNA*, Oct. 6, 1962.
28 Peking's implied offer of military support to Nepal has never been repeated subsequently, and presumably the timing of Ch'en-yi's statement was determined by events on the Sino-Indian border rather than in Nepal.

and determined assault by his major domestic opposition, without having made substantial public concessions to either. He emerged from the crisis in relations with India, which at one point he had seemed to push beyond the limits imposed by geopolitical and economic factors, with his prestige greatly enhanced and the opposition forces discredited. For this, the King owed Peking a profound word of thanks.

11

The Politics of
Balance, 1963-70

APPARENTLY even King Mahendra had been convinced by the traumatic events of the fall and winter of 1962 that some adjustments in foreign policy were in order. Relations with India could not be allowed to continue in a state of semi-crisis without adversely affecting the security and integrity of both countries. New Delhi's offer of a rapprochement based on acceptance and support of the royal regime, therefore, was welcomed by the King, who, for his part, did what he could to hasten the restoration of friendly relations. This could not, however, be accomplished by sacrificing Nepal's relations with China, in view of the frightening imbalance of military power along the Himalayan frontier after the 1962 war and, even more important, the basic operating principles of Nepali foreign policy.

The long and difficult process of redefining the terms of relations between Nepal and India had actually started at least as far back as 1955, when King Mahendra ascended the throne. Considerable progress had been made, particularly during the period in which the Nepali Congress government was in office, when the foundation for a new interrelationship appeared to have been firmly established. This collapsed in the aftermath of the December 1960 royal coup. By late 1961, some aspects of the pre-1951 relationship between the two governments had reappeared, with both New Delhi and Kathmandu sometimes reciprocally miscalculating motivations and objectives.

After "unofficial" visits to Kathmandu were made in 1963 by Lal Bahadur Shastri, Bhagwan Sahay and Dr. Karan Singh, the process of redefining the terms of relationship was resumed and within two years had been largely completed. The remodeling of

250

the relationship of the two countries has been based for the most part on tacit understandings, rarely discussed in public even by implication, rather than on explicit agreements. The outside observer can deduce their existence from the behavior of the responsible authorities, but has to infer their content. It seems, however, that the essential ingredient has been New Delhi's acceptance of the need to use the utmost restraint both in word and action in exploiting the tremendous potential for effective interference in Nepal that India still possesses. The concept of an Indian sphere of influence along the entire southern Himalaya is now muted, at least for public consumption, and Indian officials carefully refrain from statements that might have such an implication. For its part, Nepal exercises its sovereign power with more consideration for India's preoccupation with security and defense questions than was evident in the 1961–62 period. Consultations between the two governments now take place periodically at various levels. The exchange of formal visits by the highest officials of the two countries has been regularized in order to guarantee that the momentary irritations which still trouble their relationship do not get out of hand before being thoroughly discussed at a responsible level.

The price that India has paid for its virtually unconditional support of the royal regime has been the progressive alienation of noncommunist, antiregime forces and leaders in Nepal.[1] The long-range significance of this factor is disturbing to New Delhi, which understands that the present political system, dependent as it is upon an active and vigorous monarch, may not prove very durable. The other plausible alternatives, however, probably appear even less attractive. Material assistance to the "democratic forces" at this stage might well have political and economic consequences that are more threatening than the existing situation and would, furthermore, present China with an excuse to intervene in similar fashion. Furthermore, Indian officials have learned from experience that any government set up in Nepal with New Delhi's assistance would soon feel compelled to adopt a noisily anti-Indian posture in order to prove its nationalist credentials to the Nepali public. New Delhi, therefore, prefers to maintain informal friendly contacts with a broad spectrum of Nepali political leaders, but on terms that patently do not threaten King Mahendra. The assumption is that

---

1 Nepali political refugees in India occasionally threatened to go to China for support if India did not provide the necessary backing, particularly after the 1962 border war. This did not make much of an impression on Indian officials, who strongly doubted that China was interested at that time in giving any Nepali opposition group, including the pro-China faction of the Nepal communist party, the magnitude of support in both materials and men that would have been required to overthrow the royal regime.

in the event of the collapse of the present regime, should Mahendra suddenly disappear from the scene, the Indian Government would be in position to assist the noncommunist forces in gaining an ascendancy in the country. Otherwise, of course, it might have to intervene directly itself, something New Delhi would prefer to avoid at almost any cost except the establishment of an overtly pro-Chinese regime in Nepal.

ECONOMIC ISSUES

With both sides studiously playing down potential political controversies, discussions between the two governments since mid-1963 have usually focused on problems in their economic relations. Nepal is still resentful of its status as an adjunct to the dominant Indian economy, badly exposed as that economy is to all the setbacks and catastrophies that have plagued Indian agriculture and industry in recent years. If there is a food shortage in India and New Delhi imposes strict controls on the movement of food grains, farmers in the food-surplus areas of the Nepali Terai are vitally affected. Inflation in India inevitably means inflation in Nepal, and there is little the authorities in Kathmandu can do to control price rises.

Even the success of Nepal's trade diversification program is dependent upon India's cooperation. In the quarterly talks inaugurated in 1963 concerning the terms of transit through India for Nepali imports and exports and related questions,[2] and in appropriate international gatherings, Nepal has become a highly vocal spokesman for the rights of landlocked countries. It led the fight at the 1964 International Trade and Development Conference (UNCTAD-I) at Geneva, which recommended a 23-clause convention on this subject for approval of member-states. At UNCTAD-II, held in New Delhi in early 1968, Nepal presented a nine-point program that would have further expanded the obligations of coastal countries to landlocked states if it had been accepted.[3]

Nepali officials occasionally refer regretfully to India's non-ratification of the 1964 Geneva convention, inferring that New Delhi is reluctant to accept these obligations. Although India may

---

[2] K. N. Shrestha, "Byapar Tatha Parivahan Sambadhi Simhavalokan Varta" (Trade and Transit Review Talks), *Gorkhapatra*, Dec. 5, 1964.

[3] For an authoritative Nepali statement on this question, see Devendra Raj Sharma, "Some Reflections on the Treaty of Trade and Transit between Nepal and India," *Rising Nepal*, July 27, 28, 29, 30 and 31, 1969.

object to some provisions of the draft convention, it has made a number of major concessions with regard to the handling of Nepali goods in transit through India. The bond system, which Nepali trading firms had found so irksome, was abolished in 1963. The following year India agreed to provide unrestricted transit facilities for goods being shipped from one part of Nepal to another via India. In December 1966, New Delhi exempted Nepali goods in transit through India from Indian laws and also agreed to provide a "separate and self-contained space" for Nepali cargo at Calcutta port. The issuance of export and import licenses by the Nepali government, at India's insistence, for all Nepali goods in transit through India was terminated two years later. A number of problems still persist, mostly involving Nepali complaints against the alleged inadequacy of transportation and storage facilities in India and the allegedly excessive service charges imposed on Nepali goods, but they are either of minor significance or, as in the case of transportation facilities, probably incapable of solution for technical reasons at this time.

The periodic trade talks held since 1963 have also contributed substantially to improving Nepal's terms of trade with India. The main issues in contention were (1) the procedures under which excise duties levied by India on Indian goods exported to Nepal are refunded to the Nepali government; (2) discrepancies in the Nepali tariff schedule which are disadvantageous to Indian imports; and (3) New Delhi's policy with regard to Nepali manufactured goods exported to India. In 1963, India agreed to revise the procedures for the refund of excise duties to Nepal to expedite repayments. This did not end the problem, however, as Nepal next claimed that additional duties of various kinds levied by the Indian government on Indian factory products should also be refunded. New Delhi rejected this demand, but in 1968 did agree to a lump-sum payment, in place of such duties, to be used for industrial development in Nepal.

A controversy over Nepali manufactured goods utilizing indigenous raw materials, primarily finished jute products, is of more recent origin. New Delhi decided at one point to impose a surcharge —paid by the Indian importer—on such products equal to the excise duty levied on similar Indian goods. Kathmandu protested that this was a violation of the 1960 trade agreement. A compromise was finally reached in November 1968 under which Nepal agreed to impose excise duties at eighty percent of the Indian government's rate, on Nepali manufactured goods in which indigenous raw materials had been used. These products would then have free entry into India, in theory giving them a substantial price advantage over

Indian products on the Indian market. In practice, however, production costs in Nepal have tended to run substantially higher than those in India, and the twenty percent preference on excise duties has not been sufficient to make these products competitive.

A more serious disagreement arose in 1968 over the importation into India of Nepali manufactured goods which utilize raw or semiprocessed material imported from third countries—mostly synthetic textiles and stainless steel utensils. The rationale behind India's objections to this trade has never been made explicit by New Delhi, whose precious foreign exchange reserves are not utilized in the acquisition of the raw materials or in the import of the finished product. Presumably, New Delhi is apprehensive over the likelihood that Indian business and industrial interests would be tempted to invest heavily in such industries in Nepal, where government controls and restrictions are much less onerous and where needed foreign exchange is more readily available. They may also suspect that Indian businessmen use foreign currency obtained illegally to finance the importation of the required materials into Nepal, and that this practice does have an indirect effect upon India's foreign exchange position.

This question was raised at the November 1968 trade talks between the two governments. Nepal agreed, reportedly with considerable reluctance, to restrict the number of industries dependent upon imports from third countries to the 1967–68 level, and New Delhi agreed to allow the free import of these manufactures into India under existing regulations. Obviously, this can only be a temporary expedient, while the two governments seek more permanent solutions to this and several other interrelated questions. Nepal cannot be expected to accept such a limitation on its industrial development on a long-term basis. What is required, of course, is a better understanding between the two governments over the terms on which Indian business interests are permitted to invest in Nepal, but this would be possible only if both New Delhi and Kathmandu were to modify their basic policies on this question.

Probably the most serious problem remaining in trade relations between the two countries, however, concerns the extensive smuggling across their long, open border.[4] Traditionally, this involved the unregulated and uncontrolled transport and sale of surplus agricultural products from the Nepali Terai to the chronically

---

[4] The extent of this smuggling is impossible to determine, but in a 10-month period in 1968, goods valued at Rs. 1,736,000 were seized by Central Excise and Customs authorities in Bihar alone. (*Hindustan Times*, Dec. 30, 1968). It this was one-tenth of the value of the goods that actually crossed the border illegally, the Indian border police were being unusually efficient.

deficit areas of northern India. Neither government was particularly disturbed by this unofficial trade, as it held advantages for both sides. India obtained ready access to badly needed food grains, and Kathmandu gained huge quantities of Indian rupees, part of which could then be used to purchase food grains at Indian markets more convenient to the lines of communication into the deficit food areas in the hill areas of Nepal, including Kathmandu valley.

The Indian attitude toward this widely prevalent smuggling changed, however, when the system was extended to include goods imported from third countries—mostly China, the USSR and other communist-bloc countries—which enter Nepal under special arrangements that exempt them from the usual custom duties. New Delhi had been unhappy about the practice, since it gave these goods a considerable advantage over similar Indian products, and on basically uneconomic terms. The Indian government could not raise legitimate objections to this trade, but it did object repeatedly to the smuggling of these products into India and demanded that the Kathmandu authorities establish an effective system of controls. Kathmandu pointed out that it was Indian commercial interests that were the most active participants in this illicit trade. Nepal could not move effectively against them on that issue, the Nepalis argued, without violating the spirit of the 1960 trade agreement, inasmuch as Indian businessmen could not be prevented from purchasing these products on the Nepali market. Nor would it be possible to prevent the reexport of such goods into India without major revisions in the open border system, something both governments would prefer to avoid. Finally, Nepal's economic development is so dependent upon its capacity to attract substantial Indian investment that no government in Kathmandu can be reasonably expected to impose restrictions that would be counterproductive of this goal. The Indian government has somewhat more latitude in the matter, but the imposition of stricter regulations on this comparatively minor infringement of the legal trade structure might well have serious and unfavorable repercussions on the total trade structure as well as on India's general position in Nepal.

Nepal also has its share of complaints against Indian policy on trade between the two states. Kathmandu has recently protested to New Delhi about the restrictions imposed on the entry of food products into India by the Indian government's "food zone" policy, under which the transport of food grains across state lines in India is strictly regulated. Under this program, Nepal can export food grains only to states immediately adjacent—Bihar, West Bengal, and Uttar Pradesh—and therefore cannot take full advantage of the higher prices prevailing in other states, particularly in south

India. Nepal has requested free access to the entire Indian market, but New Delhi has not so far been disposed to make a concession that would violate its basic food policy. Presumably, however, the food-zone system will be abandoned or at least modified in India when (and if) the food situation improves, in which case this particular subject of controversy between Nepal and India would be eliminated.

Another chronic problem that has absorbed the attention of the Nepal government concerns the relationship between the Indian and the Nepali rupee, both of which until recently were legal tender and freely interchangeable in Nepal. The Indian rupee was the chief medium of exchange in the Terai and much of the hill area, whereas the Nepali rupee was restricted for the most part to Kathmandu valley and surrounding areas. In 1961, the Nepali government launched a long-range campaign aimed at making Nepali currency the only legal tender in the country.[5]

The program proceeded relatively smoothly if not spectacularly until mid-1966, when New Delhi suddenly devalued the Indian rupee after having given Nepal only very short notice. In what was widely acclaimed as a declaration of economic independence, the Nepali government refused to follow India's example. The Nepali rupee was revalued vis-à-vis the Indian rupee—from 160 N.C.–100 I.C. to 101.60 N.C.–100 I.C.—while the exchange rate between Nepali currency and other foreign currencies was maintained at its previous level. It soon became apparent, however, that this brave but foolish act had been motivated more by political than economic considerations. In one stroke, for instance, the value of Indian and U.S. foreign aid[6] was reduced by approximately forty-five percent. The trade structure between India and Nepal was also thrown into disarray, with the result that the prices of most imported commodities rose rapidly. Even the program for the "nationalization" of the Nepali rupee suffered a setback as the public's confidence in the currency was shaken by the unrealistic exchange rate with the Indian rupee.

By the end of the year the Nepali government had recognized its mistake, but it was uncertain about how to rectify the situation without suffering a tremendous loss of prestige. The British devaluation of the pound in 1967 provided Kathmandu with the loop-

---

[5] The Nepali finance minister estimated in 1963 that Indian currency in circulation in Nepal amounted to approximately Rs. 200 million, which indicates the magnitude of the task the Nepal government faced in implementing its currency program. *Asian Recorder*, IX:30 (July 23–29, 1963), p. 5326.

[6] Most U. S. economic assistance to Nepal is given in the form of Indian rupees drawn from the large holdings the U. S. Government has accumulated in this currency under the P.L. 480 (wheat loan) program in India.

hole it needed, and the Nepali rupee was also devalued at this time, thus avoiding acute political embarrassment for the government. Nevertheless, the experience has been a useful lesson on the limitations of Nepal's economic viability and autonomy. The program for widening the use of the Nepali rupee has been continued and has met with some success. The Indian rupee, although no longer legal tender, is still freely exchangeable, and it will probably be some years before it has been completely replaced.

POLITICAL DISPUTES

While overtly political controversies have usually been soft-pedaled by both India and Nepal since the two powers achieved a *modus vivendi* in 1963, a number have come to public attention. The most widely publicized is the minor border dispute over approximately 3,200 acres of land in the Narasahi-Susta area on the Nepal-Bihar border, usually refered to as the "Susta dispute." The dispute has led to headlines in the Kathmandu press and to occasional anti-Indian demonstrations by Nepali nationalist and pro-Chinese elements (although it should be noted that these usually occur in congruence with other crises in Nepali-Indian relations). The dispute, which first arose in the 19th century and then several times thereafter, is the result of the periodic shifting of the course of the Gandak River, which forms the boundary in this area. The two governments have not yet agreed upon the principles that should be used in deciding disputes of this kind. Nepal insists upon the boundary delimited in the 1817 treaty between Nepal and British India, while India proposes that the more generally accepted principle under which the boundary follows the river course should be applied in this and similar cases.

Another, and potentially more serious, source of disagreement between the two countries is the system under which Nepali citizens are recruited into the Indian army. The number of "Gurkhas" actually serving in Indian army units of various kinds far exceeds the nominal limitations imposed by the tripartite 1947 agreement on recruitment between Nepal, India and the United Kingdom, particularly since New Delhi authorized six new "mountain" divisions after the 1962 border war with China. Probably a majority of the "Gurkha" recruits in these new units are Nepalis who are now residents of India, Sikkim or Bhutan, but a large number are still drawn from the hill area of Nepal. As the latter go down to the plains voluntarily and are recruited on Indian soil, however, they do not violate Nepali national law nor Nepali-Indian treaty relations, and the Nepali government therefore has so far made no effort to interfere with the movements of these recruits.

Some Kathmandu intellectuals and political activists have long objected to the recruitment system, which it considers detrimental to Nepal's national integrity and, moreover, liable to involve the country in disputes with the third powers against whom the Gurkha units are employed. The Nepali government has been reluctant to propose modifications in the recruitment system, both because of possible complications in relations with New Delhi and London and the disastrous economic consequences in the hill areas of Nepal which provide most of the volunteers. The communities in those areas are dependent upon the recruitment system for what little economic viability they now enjoy. It is the principal alternative source of employment to farming in an area that already suffers badly from overpopulation and land shortage, while the pay and pensions of the servicemen are often the major source of capital for their home areas.[7] Much of the development in educational and commercial services, meager as these appear to be, can be attributed to the investment of savings, pensions and related earnings by ex-servicemen.

The hill communities and the Ex-Servicemen's Association, potentially one of the most powerful political forces in the country, have generally opposed the abolition of the recruitment system. In 1969, Prime Minister Kirtinidhi Bisht made what seemed to be a concession to the Kathmandu-based critics of the system when he stated that the recruitment of Nepalis into the British army might be terminated. In actual fact, however, he apparently was merely making as much political capital as possible out of London's decision to reduce, and probably eventually eliminate, the Gurkha units from the British forces serving in Southeast Asia when they are withdrawn in the 1970's. The initiative in this instance did not come from Nepal, and there are as yet no indications that Kathmandu intends to modify in any way the far more important—in political and economic terms—recruitment into the Indian armed forces.

The Nationality Question.—The large number of Nepalis and Indians residing, respectively, in India and Nepal has given rise to many problems. The Nepali community in India numbers well over one million, many of whom are second- or third-generation residents of India and thus qualified to claim Indian citizenship.

---

[7] See John Hitchcock, "A Nepalese Hill Village and Indian Employment," *Asian Survey*, I:9 (November 1961), 15–20.

But confusion on the nationality question is rampant in this community, and it is not uncommon for Nepali Indians to opt for the citizenship that is most convenient in any given situation, even on such matters as the acquisition of passports. Neither Nepali nor Indian laws permit dual citizenship, and the legal restrictions on its *de facto* practice have been defined more precisely in recent years.[8] Nevertheless, there is still considerable room for maneuver in this complex intermingling of populations, and most of the descendants of migrants in both Nepal and India can easily claim citizenship in their country of origin if they should be so disposed.

To date, the most serious political controversy between the two governments on the migrant-community question was caused by the flight of several hundred Nepali political leaders and workers to India after the 1960 royal coup against the Nepali Congress government. The termination in December 1962, however, of the resistance campaign directed by the Nepali Congress mitigated that dispute considerably. New Delhi's restrictions on the activities of the political refugees became increasingly tighter, until finally in 1967 the Indian authorities warned the Nepali editors of two papers published in India against indulging "in any political activity which would prejudice our friendly relations with Nepal or for making personal attacks on His Majesty the King."[9] The release of B. P. Koirala and the simultaneous pardon of Subarna Shamsher and many of his associates in October 1968 settled that particular problem for the time being. Nepali officials will doubtless continue to resent the procedure under which opponents of the existing regime in Kathmandu seek and obtain refuge in India, where they are susceptible to exploitation by the Indian government for its own purposes.[10] But it would be a rash Nepali leader who would suggest that India should revise its liberal policy on the admission of political refugees, in view of the uncertainties and volatility of politics in Nepal.

Perhaps the most potentially explosive issue with regard to

---

[8] Frederick Gaige's doctoral dissertation at the University of Pennsylvania analyzes in detail the nationality question in Nepal.

[9] *Gorkhapatra*, Aug. 12, 1967. The Indian government has rejected Nepali suggestions that similar restrictions should be imposed on the Indian press on the grounds that such an action would constitute an unjustifiable violation of the constitutional provision guaranteeing freedom of the press in India.

[10] B. P. Koirala, for instance, has made his residence in Banaras, India, since his release from prison in 1968. While there is no indication that he intends to revive the campaign of resistance to the royal regime, the possibility of this is a source of concern to the Nepal Government. It may be one factor in the deterioration in relations between New Delhi and Kathmandu in mid-1969, discussed later in this chapter.

these migrant communities, however, is the Nepali government's long-term policy of *de facto* discrimination against the large *Terai wala* (Terai inhabitant) community of Indian origin.[11] Many of these families have resided in Nepal for several generations, but still maintain close social and economic ties across the nearby border with India. There is the same confusion with respect to their nationality and allegiance as there is for many of the Nepalis resident in India. The provisions of the Nepal Citizenship Act are so ambiguous in some respect that it is difficult to determine in strictly legal terms which of the *Terai walas* are qualified to claim Nepali nationality.

Presumably this complicated issue would have been settled automatically within a generation if Kathmandu had not introduced legislation that, as interpreted by both officials and the court, discriminates against Nepali residents of a non-hill-community origin. The 1961 Industrial Enterprises Act, for instance, restricted small-scale cottage and village industries to Nepali "nationals," and the 1963 *Muluki Ain* (legal code) barred "foreigners" from inheriting or acquiring an escheat on immovable property. The most controversial measures, however, were the 1964 Land Reform Act, under which land cannot be sold to foreigners, and the 1964 Ukhada Land Tenure Act, which stipulated that land can be registered only in the name of Nepali nationals. Given the uncertainty as to the nationality of many Terai landowners and tenants, these laws could play havoc with the landholding and land-use system in the Terai. It is not surprising, therefore, that many Nepalis of Indian origin suspect that the primary objective of the land reform program, at least as perceived by the hill-dominated Central Secretariat, is the eviction of landowners belonging to Nepali families of Indian origin in order to open this fertile area, now being cleared of the malarial scourge, for settlement by land-hungry hill peoples.

Such discriminatory legislation, if directed against Indian nationals, violates the 1950 Indo-Nepali treaty which guarantees citizens of each country equal treatment in the other. At the time of the conclusion of that treaty, however, it had been agreed that Nepal's "special circumstances" might require Kathmandu to protect its nationals against "outside competition." India had insisted that such protection be mutually agreed upon. Kathmandu's failure to consult with New Delhi before enacting legislation discriminating against Indian nationals may, therefore, constitute a violation of the 1950 treaty. The Indian government presented Nepal

[11] The present size of the Terai community of Indian origin cannot be precisely determined from available census data, but it numbered between 2 and 2.5 million in the 1961 census, or approximately 20–25 percent of Nepal's total population.

with an aide memoire on the subject in June 1966,[12] and Mrs. Gandhi also discussed it with King Mahendra during her visit to Kathmandu in October of that year. The Indian government's policy has been to wait and see how thoroughly Kathmandu implements the discriminatory legislation. The West Bengal, Bihar and Uttar Pradesh state governments were instructed to keep an accounting of the number of Indian nationals evicted from their lands in the Terai. Only a few families having been affected so far, and New Delhi has not raised any public objection to the procedure.[13] If mass evictions should occur, however, India might decide to react more vigorously, perhaps even by threatening retaliatory measures against Nepali residents in India who now enjoy equal rights with Indian citizens.

Himalayan Federation.—The concept of federation of Himalayan states has been broached on a number of occasions since 1947, and usually has received wide publicity in both the Indian and Western press. The general theme has been that this is a gigantic Chinese plot concocted with the enthusiastic cooperation of some expansion-minded Nepali political leaders to the detriment of India's defense and political interests.

There appears to be little if any substance to this allegation, however. The idea of a federation was first broached by the Chogyal of Sikkim shortly before the British withdrew from India, and his proposal was that it should consist of the three political units in which lamaistic Buddhist culture was dominant—Tibet, Sikkim and Bhutan. The concept was revived in Nepal by Tanka Prasad Acharya during his tenure as prime minister, when it was redefined to include that country as well as Sikkim, Bhutan and some of the hill areas of India. Its reception in both New Delhi and the royal palace in Kathmandu was reported as distinctly hostile, and Tanka Prasad quickly dropped the subject. Occasionally since that time, the federation project has been resurrected by Nepali politicians or publicists, but never with any notable persistence or enthusiasm in view of the studied disinterest of the Nepali government. Regardless of what interest China may have in the project, Kathmandu realizes that a federation is totally impractical under existing con-

---

12 See the statement by Dinesh Singh in the Indian Parliament on Dec. 2, 1966 (Press Information Bureau, Government of India).

13 The official figures on the land-reform program (December 1968) showed that nearly 240,000 acres of excess lands had been found, almost entirely in the Terai area. However, only about 82,000 acres had actually been acquired by the government. No information is available as to the number of cases in which excess holdings over the maximum permitted were involved; there was one report, however, of the eviction of a family from its entire landholding because it could not prove Nepali citizenship (*Jana Awaz*, December 1968).

ditions in South Asia, and that overt support of the scheme on its part would only needlessly complicate relations with India, to no useful purpose.

Nepal does not have direct diplomatic or economic relations with its two Himalayan area neighbors, Sikkim and Bhutan, whose foreign relations are "guided" by New Delhi. Kathmandu's primary concern has been with the large Nepali communities in these two small principalities. Indeed, the federation proposal has sometimes been defended in Nepal as a means of reuniting these migrant communities with their motherland, an important factor behind the generally negative response of the Buddhist monarchies of Sikkim and Bhutan to any form of association with Hindu Nepal.

If all goes as planned, Bhutan will be admitted to the United Nations in 1971 or shortly thereafter, and this probably will be followed by the establishment of diplomatic relations with a number of countries, including Nepal. We may yet witness a revival of the informal alliance that existed between Nepal and Bhutan at critical points in their past histories. At the least, we can expect a similarity in views on international questions, for Bhutan regards Nepali foreign policy as sound and worthy of emulation. A *de facto* alliance, however, would not provide the basis for federation, except perhaps under conditions of political and national disintegration in India.

KATHMANDU AND PEKING

With the exception of one brief period in 1967, there have been no serious strains in the relations between Nepal and China, at least publicly, since the royal coup of December 1960. Diplomatic exchanges between the two governments have usually been polite and friendly, if somewhat superficial. Peking has been accommodating, on the whole, even on some occasions when there was ample reason for the Chinese to express displeasure over the trend of developments in Nepal. When Kathmandu first applied to the United States and Great Britain for military assistance in 1963, for instance, the Chinese reportedly made angry verbal objections in private but never publicly denounced the Nepali government in the vehement language they often use in describing other recipients of Western military aid. Nepal's rejection of a Chinese proposal for the construction of a road connecting the food-surplus areas of the Terai with the Kathmandu-Tibet road was another setback for Peking, but the Chinese exercised restraint in their handling of Kathmandu in this instance as well. Nor did the last-minute cancellation in 1964 of a Chinese-aided road project in the Terai, at Indian and American insistence, provoke the Chinese to an angry response, even though that project was handed over to the Indian aid program for completion in what can only be described as a disdainful lack of concern for Chinese sensitivity.

The extreme care the Chinese have taken in coddling the royal regime has also been reflected in their failure to offer substantial support, both material and moral, to procommunist, antigovernment forces in Nepal. If reports are correct, the Chinese Embassy in Kathmandu provides the pro-China factions of the Nepal Communist party only with sufficient funds to maintain a precarious existence in exile in India, but not enough to make it a real threat to the royal regime. Presumably, China is prepared to coexist with King Mahendra, at least at this stage of developments, rather than support his domestic enemies, who in any case are too weak and divided to pose much of a challenge. The effusively laudatory references to the King emanating on the proper occasions from high sources in Peking are scarcely what would be expected from the advocates of people's liberation, but they do fit in well with general Chinese tactics in Nepal and elsewhere throughout the Himalayan area.

Although Sino-Nepali relations are correct, it would probably be an exaggeration to characterize them as intimate. King Mahendra has not visited China since the 1962 Sino-Indian border war, even though he has travelled abroad extensively during that period. A number of Nepali high officials, including Crown Prince Birendra, have made the journey to Peking, but they of course are not in a position to make basic policy decisions tht would commit their government. Kathmandu now places emphasis almost exclusively on the improvement and expansion of economic relations with China, and these preferably on terms that do not expose Nepal to intensive Chinese political pressure.

The caution displayed by Kathmandu in promoting political relations with China can probably be attributed to the chronic behind-the-scenes, low-keyed tension in their relationship that finally came to public attention in 1967. There has been a series of developments since 1963 that the Nepali authorities have found disquieting, and even potentially threatening. Chinese construction teams on the Kodari road and other aid projects have made a practice of showing Chinese propaganda movies to surrounding villages and distributing communist literature and Mao buttons. The Nepali government eventually became so disturbed over the wearing of Mao buttons by Nepali students and peasants that it decided to concoct a Mahendra button as a symbol of nationalistic sentiments. The publication of a photo depicting Nepalis saluting a portrait of Mao and a poem by an unnamed Nepali journalist lauding Mao as "the leader of all exploited people"[14] in the *Peking Review* of March 10, 1967, also caused an uproar in Kathmandu. On this occasion, the "guided" Kathmandu press was allowed to criticize the Chinese publication, a sure sign of official displeasure as well.

The Nepali government was also embarrassed several times by vehement Chinese denunciations of India, the United States and the Soviet Union at public functions in Nepal. This violated the Government's "rule" that overt propaganda against one power by another in Nepal is contrary to the country's neutrality policy. The propensity demonstrated by Chinese technicians working on aid projects in Nepal to act as if they were a power unto themselves has also irritated Nepali public opinion. In 1968, for instance, Chinese personnel seized and maltreated an Indian and a Nepali journalist and a Western photographer at the Chinese-aided Sunkoshi hydroelectric project. As the Nepal press pointed out, this was not an isolated incident, but was a common occurrence at Chinese project sites.

There have also been a number of reports that Chinese workers on various projects have indulged in intelligence-gathering and subversive operations in addition to their regular duties. The discovery of an arms cache in 1964, reportedly brought into the country from Tibet along with road construction equipment, was confirmed by the authorities but with no public assignment of responsibility. An embarrassment to both Peking and Kathmandu, perhaps, was the statement by a Chinese defector who had worked on the Kodari road but had somehow made his way to Taiwan—with, if rumors are correct, Indian and American assistance. He charged that the bridges on the Kodari road were being constructed to carry vehicles (tanks?) weighing up to 60 tons rather than the 15–17 ton limit stipulated in the building stipulations. Nepali government officials have never verified this allegation, but it is generally accepted as correct by both the Nepali public and the various foreign missions in Kathmandu whose officers have travelled on the road.

These events provided the background for what was to become the only public dispute between Nepal and China in recent years. On June 17, 1967, approximately 200 Chinese Embassy officials and project technicians, led by the ambassador, gathered at the Kath-

---

14 The June 2, 1967, issue of *Peking Review* reported that the Nepalis who attended the inauguration of the Kathmandu-Kodari road by King Mahendra on May 26 had shouted: "The great leader Chairman Mao is the red sun which shines most brightly in the hearts of the people of the whole world." According to one Nepali journal, however, "Nobody else heard the Nepalis present on the occasion praising Mao as 'the red sun.'" (*Nepal Times*, June 16, 1967.)

mandu airport to welcome two of "Mao's warriors" who had just been expelled from India. The crowd, disappointed when the two men were not on the flight from New Delhi, became unruly, shouting anti-Indian and pro-cultural revolution slogans. The Indian Government lodged a strong protest against this demonstration with Kathmandu, and reportedly was assured that such incidents would not be repeated. Officials of the foreign ministry met with the Chinese embassy staff to express their dissatisfaction with these events.

Until this point, both sides had been reasonably polite even in private, but this was not the case in the next episode of the "perils of Maoism." In late June 1967, a "fun-fair" was organized at Kathmandu to celebrate King Mahendra's 48th birthday. On July 1, the Chinese stall at the fête was attacked by a crowd of Nepali students who reportedly objected to the display of a large portrait of Mao with no accompanying picture of King Mahendra. After being dispersed by the police, the demonstrators moved toward the center of the city, where they stoned a Chinese Embassy jeep and partially sacked the Nepal-China Friendship Association library. The "fun fair" was closed immediately, two days earlier than scheduled.

A strongly worded New China News Agency (NCNA) report dated July 9, 1967,[15] accused U.S. "imperialists," Soviet "revisionists" and Indian "reactionaries" of having instigated the Nepali "hooligans" who had perpetrated "this vile anti-China outrage." It also directly accused the Nepali authorities of having "approved and supported this anti-China outrage" and of having banned Nepalis from wearing Mao buttons and carrying the Mao "quotations" handbook.

Before the anti-China outrage by the hooligans, the Nepalese Government was aware of it. At the time of the outrage, the Chinese side had time and again demanded that the Nepalese Government stop the outrage. However, the Nepalese Government did nothing about it.

The NCNA report also disclosed that a protest note, submitted to the foreign ministry on July 5 had warned that the "imperialists, revisionists and reactionaries" who encouraged such activities "will break their own skulls" and those who follow them "will suffer from the consequences of their own actions."

The following day, the Nepali foreign secretary protested to China about the "false and baseless reports" in the NCNA statement. The Chinese reply of July 21 rejected the protest and repeated the charges. This was the last that was heard of the incident in public, however, and later exchanges between the two govern-

---

[15] *News from China* (published by the Chinese Embassy in Kathmandu), July 9, 1967.

ments were again restrained in tone. What had induced Peking to take a position directly critical of the Nepali government? It is possible, of course, that there was some substance to China's angry allegations, as the "fun fair" events were indeed curious. But this episode also coincided with an assertively aggressive stage in China's cultural revolution, when angry notes were being exchanged with Burma and Cambodia—like Nepal, unusual recipients of such messages. Peking's primary motivation may have derived from internal developments only remotely connected with foreign policy. There is also the possibility that the Chinese government felt that a stage had been reached in Nepal where the Kathmandu authorities required an indirect but pointed reprimand, such as that given to B. P. Koirala in 1960, to restore Nepali-Chinese relations to a more acceptable level. The tensions that developed between the two governments concerning the Mao button and similar questions may seem minor in retrospect, but in the context of the cultural revolution they could have loomed large in Peking's calculations.

PROGRESS ON DIVERSIFICATION

The motivation behind many of Nepal's foreign and domestic policies continues to be the maximum diversification of its political and economic relations with the outside world, but its government now seems more cognizant of the limitations placed on that objective by the country's geopolitical and economic situation. Nepal has entered into diplomatic relations with an increasing number of states, but has considered it expedient for financial reasons to limit its diplomatic representation abroad. Kathmandu has also carefully restricted active participation in regional and international organizations to those in which its interests are directly involved and where its nonalignment policy is not likely to be put to the test. One important exception to this general rule, however, was Nepal's acceptance of a seat on the Security Council of the United Nations in late 1968, which may well force the government to take positions on specific international disputes such as the Middle East or Kashmir— a dilemma that it would prefer to avoid. The prestige of service on the Security Council, symbolizing Nepal's full acceptance as an equal in the international community, was enough, however, to overcome any reluctance that may have been felt about the political complications that may ensue.

Remodeling the Trade Structure.—Most of the activity in the diversification program has centered on Kathmandu's intensive efforts since 1961 to diversify trade relations. China continues to occupy first place in Nepal's calculations, and indeed it is Peking that is primarily responsible for whatever degree of diversification has been achieved. New trade agreements were concluded between the two governments in 1964, 1966 and 1968, but these served more to change the directions and terms of trade than to increase its volume. One of the primary objectives of China in the negotiation of these agreements has been to eliminate the role of the private Nepali trader in Tibet and to replace the traditional trade structure between Nepal and Tibet with direct state-to-state trading. This was accomplished for the most part in the agreement signed in Peking on May 2, 1966.[16] In anticipation of this development, Kathmandu had already closed its trade agencies at Kerong, Kuti and Shigatse in the winter of 1965–66, and had announced that the Lhasa agency would also be closed shortly because it was no longer required.[17] The number of Nepalis in Tibet declined from about 5,000 in the early 1960's to a few hundred by 1968.[18] According to a Tibetan source, the Chinese imposed further restrictions on the movement and residence of "all foreigners" (now only Nepalis) in Tibet in August 1968, making it difficult for them to continue even the limited legal trade still allowed them.[19]

The Chinese also moved at the same time to eliminate both the local trade carried on by the inhabitants of the Nepal-Tibet border area and the traditional transborder pasturage usage system under which pastures on both sides of the boundary were used at different times of the year by Nepali and Tibetan herdsmen. The 1956 Sino-Nepali trade treaty, which had specifically allowed the continuation of both these customary practices, was extended for another five year period in August 1962. The Nepalis raised this question in the May–June 1968 trade talks in Peking, but the Chinese were unwilling to agree to a further extension.[20] As a result, the economy of the border area in which these traditional privileges had long played an important role has been adversely affected.

The trade policies of the Chinese and Nepali governments—

---

16 In contrast to previous practices, the text of the 1966 trade agreement was not made public. Was this to save the Nepali government the embarrassment of having to admit that it had agreed to the elimination of private trade with Tibet? The text of the agreement is given in Avtar Singh Bhasin (ed.), *Documents on Nepal's Relations with India and China*, Bombay, 1969.

17 China may have paid a high price to obtain Nepal's consent to the elimination of private trading in May 1966. That same month, it offered economic assistance for the construction of five new factories, and in July it agreed to help Nepal through its crisis arising from the revaluation of the Nepali rupee and also promised an additional Rs. 150 million in economic aid.

18 See Kuladharma Ratna, "Sino-Nepalese Trade," *Rising Nepal*, July 26, 1968.

19 "Chinese Tighten Control," *Tibetan Review*, 1:9 (September 1968), p. 7.

20 See the statement by Foreign Minister Kirtinidhi Bisht in the Rashtriya Panchayat (*Gorkhapatra*, Aug. 13, 1968).

the latter under considerable pressure from India—have had the cumulative effect of bringing the legal trade between Nepal and Tibet to a virtual standstill. China does not allow the import into Tibet of most of the traditional items of trade, chiefly luxury goods. By agreement with New Delhi, Kathmandu has banned the reexport of all goods brought into Nepal from India as well as most goods imported from third countries via India. Food grains, even if produced in Nepal, have also been placed on the restricted list. Thus, the majority of the commodities the Chinese would be anxious to obtain from or through Nepal cannot be exported to Tibet. The only general exception to this complicated trade ban are the special agreements that have been concluded each year since 1964 in connection with the Hindu festival of Dushera, under which Nepali rice is bartered for Tibetan goats that are used in the sacrificial ceremonies marking this important religious festival in Nepal.

A substantial illegal trade between Nepal and Tibet still exists, of course, mostly in items such as petrol, lubricants and food grains that are on Kathmandu's banned list but fetch fantastic prices from the Chinese in Tibet. Indeed, it is probable that the Nepali traders still in Tibet have been allowed to remain there because they are essential to the operation of the smuggling system. Neither the Chinese nor the Nepali authorities exert much effort to control this illegal trade so long as it stays within certain limits both in quantity and in content. New Delhi frowns on this trade officially, and occasionally registers a quiet protest to Kathmandu when it appears to be exceeding established limitations. However, the Indians apparently would rather see the smuggling continue at its present level than press the question too vigorously with Nepal, thereby possibly endangering the tacit agreements with Kathmandu limiting the legal trade with Tibet.

All in all, trade with Tibet has declined drastically in recent years, even when smuggling is taken into consideration, but on the other hand Nepal's commerce with China proper has increased substantially in the same period. This rise is due primarily to the system under which the local-currency costs of Chinese-aided projects in Nepal are met by the sale of Chinese consumer goods given gratis to the National Trading Limited (N. T. L.) established by the Nepal government to handle state-to-state trading. Nepali exports to China, mostly jute products, have also increased to some extent. Virtually all of this trade is conducted via Calcutta, as it is still incomparably less costly to use the Indian transit system than the extensive road network linking China with Tibet and Nepal. The Kodari road, which Nepalis once lauded as vital to their country's economic development, is now seldom used for trading purposes and only an occasional jeep or truck is to be seen on this expensive roadway.

Nepal's efforts to use East Pakistan for a further diversification of its economic relations has also been a failure. The trade agreement between Nepal and Pakistan signed October 19, 1962, called for a total annual trade of Rs. 20 million under most-favored-nation provisions. The development of that trade depended upon Indian cooperation in making transport and travel facilities available, and this has been the subject for discussion between New Delhi and Kathmandu on several occasions since 1963. An agreement "in principle" was reached on October 23, 1963, but further negotiations were necessary to settle the terms of transit between East Pakistan and Nepal. Indeed, the trade talks actually broke down on one occasion over India's insistence upon the imposition of service charges that were estimated to amount to only Rs. 15,000 per year, but a compromise settlement was accepted three months later.

At Kathmandu's urgent request, communication and storage facilities have been provided for Nepal's transit trade at Radhikpur (West Bengal), a railhead on the India-East Pakistan border. The 1965 Indo-Pakistani war, however, brought the little trade that had developed between Nepal and East Pakistan to a complete halt, and communications between India and Pakistan had not yet been reestablished by the end of 1969. Nepali goods can be brought to Radhikpur, but it was only in the spring of 1970 that they were allowed to be transported a short distance across the border to the railhead in East Pakistan. Thus, the main channel of communication between Nepal and Pakistan has been the airline service between Kathmandu and Dacca. That service is of considerable political importance to Kathmandu, as it was the first with a country other than India,[21] but obviously its economic importance is very limited.

Besides establishing trade relations with Japan and several Western countries, Nepal has also entered into a number of trade agreements with the Soviet Union and eastern European states. These latter agreements are usually based on barter arrangements and, because of the limited quantity of Nepali goods available for export, cannot play a very prominent part in Nepal's total trade picture. At one time the Soviet Union did provide consumer goods for sale by the N. T. L. to meet local currency costs on Russian-aided projects,[22] but recently the Russians appear to have dropped this approach for more traditional trading procedures.

---

[21] In 1968, direct air connections between Bangkok and Kathmandu, via Calcutta, were also inaugurated.

[22] The Russians introduced this practice, which was later copied by the Chinese.

These intensive efforts to diversify Nepal's trade structure—in the course of which Kathmandu several times endangered its vital economic and political relations with India—have had minimal results at best. Imports from Pakistan during the first three years of the trade agreement amounted to Rs. 575,000 rather than the projected Rs. 20 million per annum, and they have since declined even further. On the other hand, the trade with China has made some impact on both the internal and external commerce of Nepal. Because of the noneconomic terms of that trade, however, doubt exists as to its long-term significance. The Chinese consumer goods brought into Nepal by the N. T. L. are priced competitively, and in some instances have even pushed similar Indian commodities off the Kathmandu market. The N. T. L. obtains these goods free, however, and the prices set in Nepal bear no relation to production costs. Nepali visitors to China have reported that the same goods are often more expensive on the Chinese market than they are in Kathmandu. How long Peking will find it advantageous, either for political or financial reasons, to continue to provide goods on such terms is uncertain, but most of these commodities probably could not compete on purely economic terms on the Nepal market.

By 1968, the Nepali authorities had gained a reasonably accurate assessment of both the potentialities and the limitations of the trade diversification policy. Despite its best efforts in the past decade, India still accounts for at least 90 percent of Nepal's total trade, legal and illegal. Further diversification is being sought, but Nepal is now more concerned with improving the trade system with India, and particularly with gaining access to markets in India for Nepali products.[23] Trade with India has been increasing rapidly since 1960, indeed in absolute terms far more than with the rest of the world. Nepal is thus still a part of the broader Indian economic and commercial system, although now on terms that are somewhat more acceptable to Kathmandu.

Diversification of Aid Sources.—Nepal considers the maximum diversification of sources of foreign aid an essential corollary of its nonalignment policy, aimed at avoiding overdependence upon any one power. Moreover, Kathmandu has succeeded in creating an atmosphere of competition among the aid-giving states, which has had the effect of increasing the quantity of aid available. In view of these developments, Nepal usually has strongly opposed proposals to coordinate the programs of the aid-giving states, either on specific projects or as a totality.

The government's insistence on diversification and minimal

---

23 *Gorkhapatra*, Nov. 24, 1968.

coordination has not been implemented without some adverse effects on Nepal's total economic development program. The entire planning process within the Nepali government, for instance, has often been an exercise in futility in which wasteful duplication of efforts by the various foreign aid programs has had to be permitted and indeed even encouraged.[24] The inauguration of vitally needed programs has also been seriously delayed on occasion by the propensity of the Nepali government to bargain with the various foreign aid suppliers. The Karnali River project is a case in point. Kathmandu decided at an early stage in the planning of this project that Nepal's third major river system should not be turned over to India for development as had been the Kosi and Gandak Rivers. Nepal tried for several years to find an alternative source of support —the U.S., the U.S.S.R., Japan, the U.N., the World Bank, and the Asian Development Bank. None of these were interested, however, and Kathmandu finally had to conclude that India was the only feasible source of support after all. Further delays were caused by Kathmandu's insistence that this should be a Nepali-administered project utilizing Indian financial and technical assistance, in contrast to the Koshi and Gandak projects which were Indian-administered as well. An agreement in principle was reached with India, but the terms are still being negotiated. This stage could have been reached at least 5 years earlier if the Nepali government had then been prepared to accept some of the inevitable limitations on its diversification program.

To compensate for the lack of coordination in its development program due to the diversity of sources of aid, the government has sought to define a set of priorities into which foreign-aid programs should be fitted. The list varies from time to time, but they have generally followed this order: (1) communications, (2) power, (3) agriculture, (4) administrative and political infrastructure, (5) industry, and (6) education and social services. In actual fact, however, these priorities have been determined to a great extent by the policies of the aid-giving states in deciding which programs to support. Nepal's development budget, which until 1969 had been kept separate from the regular administrative budget, has been almost totally dependent upon foreign aid. The government makes a nominal contribution to the development budget, varying from twenty

---

24 On several occasions, Nepal has deliberately acted to create situations in which the aid-giving states would be encouraged to compete against each other. Usually this had involved competing for specific projects, but at times Nepal has also maneuvered the establishment of competing projects in the same field. An interesting example of this was the assignment of exactly the same projects to the communist ideological rivals, China and Yugoslavia.

to forty percent, but only rarely is much of that allocation expended.

Even under these conditions, the basically different approaches of the aid-giving states would assure Nepal broad flexibility in the formulation of the development budget if full diversification were a reality. This is not yet the case, however, and perhaps never will be. The Chinese, Russian and assorted other smaller aid programs are very useful to Nepal, but are not vital. The Indian and American aid programs, on the other hand, together constitute between sixty and seventy percent of the total aid given Nepal,[25] and moreover are concentrated in the fields having the highest priorities. On purely economic grounds then, it might be argued that Nepal would develop faster and more efficiently if Kathmandu was less concerned with diversification and more prepared to accept coordination of foreign aid programs. Because of the inevitable political consequences of such a change in policy, however, it is unacceptable to Nepal, which would then be exposed more than ever to big-power domination. This attitude is one which Nepal holds in common with most other Afro-Asian states in which nation-building political considerations have a priority over economic development.

Diversification in Defense.—The outbreak of the Sino-Indian border dispute in 1959 placed heavy new burdens of responsibility on the Indian army, which inaugurated an intensive expansion and reequipment program. The capacity of India to provide Nepal with its arms requirements—as specified in the letters of exchange to the 1950 treaty and the annex to the 1947 agreement on Gurkha recruitment—was severely inhibited after 1960 by India's own needs. The 1962 Sino-Indian border war demonstrated to Kathmandu that reliance could not be placed on the capacity of the Indian army to meet aggression, either direct or indirect, from the north, and that the fighting strength of the Nepali army would have to be increased immediately. Discussions on this and related questions were held with General J. N. Chaudhri, chief of the Indian army staff, during his visit to Kathmandu in June 1963. India was sympathetic, but was in no position to offer tangible assistance.

At this point, the Nepali government decided upon a limited application of the diversification policy to the defense field. The Americans and the British were approached in the fall of 1963 with a request for military aid, and this was also a subject of discussion during Dr. Tulsi Giri's visits to Washington and London in September–October of that year. The British and American govern-

---

[25] It is difficult to calculate the quantity of foreign aid actually given to Nepal, because at times quite substantial amounts offered with considerable publicity are never actually expended.

ments moved slowly on this issue, primarily because of their concern over New Delhi's reaction. Protracted negotiations were carried on with the Indian government in late 1963. The Indians first suggested that the aid be channeled through their own military assistance program, but this was unacceptable to Kathmandu, which was interested in soliciting a direct, if limited, American and British involvement in Nepal's defense. New Delhi finally accepted the Nepali position, and a tacit agreement on their respective roles was reached between India, the United States and the United Kingdom.[26]

Washington and London thereupon informed Kathmandu in February 1964 that they were prepared to provide a small quantity of military assistance on a short-term basis. The Nepali government presented a "shopping list" to the United States and Britain which, though modest, included heavy, sophisticated weaponry. Under the program as finally approved, however, only light arms and support equipment (medical, signal, jeeps and trucks) were included. The arms were provided by the British, as the Nepali army was already largely equipped with British weapons, while the support equipment came from the U.S. The military assistance, valued at $4 million equally divided between the United States and the United Kingdom, began to reach Nepal in October 1964. Several small units were also sent on a short-term basis to train the Nepalis in the use of the equipment, but no military assistance program office as such was set up in Nepal.

In the summer of 1964, India and Nepal renewed their discussions on the Indian military assistance program. An agreement was reached between the two governments in January 1965 under which New Delhi agreed to underwrite as far as possible the entire requirements of the Nepali army. American and British assistance would be sought only when India was not in a position to supply the necessary equipment. Nepal was also to continue using the Indian army's staff colleges for the training of its own officer corps. In mid–1965, Nepal submitted to the United States and the United Kingdom a second shopping list amounting to approximately $3 million. As neither of these governments wanted to supersede New Delhi's responsibilities in this respect, they advised Nepal to seek its requirements from India first. In 1967, the commander-in-chief of the Nepali army and the Nepali defense minister made seperate visits to India, during which Nepal reportedly obtained most of the desired military equipment from that source.

---

[26] An agreement between the U.S., the U.K. and India would probably have been consummated if Nepal had not objected to this tripartite coordination of programs as contrary to its diversification objective.

Notwithstanding the Nepali government's periodic reaffirmation of its devotion to nonalignment, noninvolvement and equal friendship with India and China, it is apparent that Kathmandu continued to play a limited but significant role in the Indian security system in the Himalayan border area, as indeed it had for several decades before 1950. Changes introduced by King Mahendra in the *modus operandi* of Nepal's foreign policy since coming to the throne in 1956 modified the forms of affiliation with India but left the terms virtually unchanged. The 1950 treaty and letters of exchange, which imposed certain obligations on both governments, was never formally repudiated by either side. Indian army technical personnel were stationed at checkposts and other strategic locations along the Nepal-Tibet border until 1970, and an Indian Military Liaison Group continued to function at Nepali army headquarters in Kathmandu a decade after the formal withdrawal of the Indian Advisory Military Group. India is still the main source of supply for the Nepali army and provides most of the training for Nepali officers and technicians. Furthermore, the large number of "Gurkhas" in the Indian army constitutes a bond between the two countries of incalculable significance,[27] and one that is constantly being renewed and expanded. And finally, there is the unilateral Indian pledge to defend Nepal against aggression (China being the only potential threat), which New Delhi has never withdrawn even though, at Nepal's request, it is now more circumspect in the public references to that pledge.

This tacit alignment on security questions was for the first time seriously challenged by responsible Nepali officials in 1969. In May of that year, the Nepali Foreign Minister visited New Delhi for talks with the External Affairs Ministry and requested the withdrawal of the Indian technical personnel on the northern border and a change in the status of the Indian Military Liaison group. Discussions on these questions were renewed during the visit of the Indian Foreign Minister, Dinesh Singh, to Kathmandu in mid-June.

Until that point, both sides had pursued their negotiations quietly and with no apparent intention to escalate them into a full-blown public controversy. Dinesh Singh's inept handling of the negotiations, combined with the disclosure in the Indian press of the terms of the "secret" January 1965 arms agreement, may have caused the Nepali government to change its tactics. In a re-

---

27 The author was in Pokhara valley in western Nepal in 1964 at the time it was visited by President Radhakrishnan of India. Hundreds of ex-servicemen thronged the airport at Pokhara to welcome the President, many of them wearing their Indian army uniforms and medals.

markable and untypical interview with the *Rising Nepal*,[28] Prime Minister Kirtinidhi Bisht questioned some aspects of the basic relationship between India and Nepal on security matters. He charged India with having failed to inform Nepal, as required by the 1950 treaty, about important developments in its relations with the U.S.S.R., the U.S., Pakistan and China that affected the general security situation in the Himalayan area. "This shows," he added, "that India itself had assumed and has led Nepal to assume that exchange of information in such cases is not necessary," implying that the 1950 treaty provisions were no longer operative and that Nepal was not obligated to consult with New Delhi on its own relations with third powers. He also called for the withdrawal of the Indian army technical personnel and the Indian Military Liaison Group, inasmuch as their functions had now been completed. Referring to the 1965 Arms Assistance Agreement, the publication of which had been embarrassing to the royal regime, he asserted that the Indian government had "verbally advised" Nepal to cancel it rather than to amend it as Kathmandu had suggested. In accordance with this advice, he stated, his government had written to India "and as far as Nepal is concerned, the agreement no longer exists."

This interview caused a furor of activity on both sides, and numerous discussions and exchanges of communications between the two governments. By the end of 1969, India had agreed to the withdrawal of the military mission immediately and of the technical personnel by the end of 1970, and it appeared that additional substance might be added to Kathmandu's "nonalignment" policy. It was impossible to determine whether this would actually be the case, however, as it was still difficult to distinguish rhetoric from reality. For instance, although it is too early to be certain about this, it is probable that the Nepali government was using the "withdrawal" demand as a ploy in its more important campaign to wring concessions from New Delhi on trade and aid (the Karnali project) questions. Kathmandu might never have raised the controversy to the public level if it had not been for Dinesh Singh's heavy-handed response to Nepal's demands and the suspicion that the "secret" information published by the Indian press had been deliberately leaked to journalistic sources by responsible Indian officials. Nepal was not seeking yet another confrontation with India, but obviously it has to play the few cards it holds when circumstances demand.

How far Kathmandu will actually go in redefining its relationship with India on the security question is still uncertain. The 1950

---

28 *Rising Nepal*, June 25, 1969.

treaty has not been formally repudiated. If the 1958 precedent is any guide, it is probable that the Indian military mission will be replaced by a similar body under another name and that New Delhi will continue to receive the intelligence data that it had obtained until now from its technical personnel on the northern border in one form or another. Even the 1965 arms assistance agreement still appears to be operative on a *de facto* basis. No changes in the system under which Nepalis are recruited into the Indian army have been suggested by any responsible source, and Nepal will continue to provide a substantial proportion of the military force with which India confronts both China and Pakistan. It is also safe to conclude that Nepal continues to base its own defense and security policy on the assumption of automatic assistance from the south in the event of aggression, direct or indirect, from the north, and will be careful not to endanger this relationship with India.

Diversification in trade, aid and defense may, therefore, be an attractive political slogan in Nepal, but it is a policy that has very rigidly defined practical limitations which are sometimes underestimated by everyone involved. Nepalis are prone to proclaim every move in the direction of diversification as a nationalist achievement. Alarmed Indian journalists (and an occasional Western member of the profession), assuming that this means a weakening of ties with India and a corresponding greater sense of dependence upon China, take up the cry. But is this the case? It is obvious that relations between India and Nepal in 1969 differ substantially from what they were in the 1951–55 period, but it is open to question whether they are now any less intimate and crucial to both sides in real terms. Similarly, China has a far greater role in Nepal in 1969 that it had in 1950, but this was perhaps an inevitable consequence of the Chinese conquest of Tibet. To the extent that it is able to determine the course of events, Nepal has succeeded in establishing a balanced relationship with India and China which to date has been satisfactory to Peking without altering the essential aspects of the ties between New Delhi and Kathmandu. Nevertheless, the basic decisions determining Nepal's future continue to be made on the international level, and caution, induced by uncertainty, must continue to be a characteristic of the Nepali response to new developments.

12

A Perspective on Nepal's Foreign Policy

THROUGHOUT this study, one of the themes emphasized has been the existence of several factors in Nepal's international relations that have operated more or less continuously for at least the past two centuries.[1] The specific policies pursued by the various governments in the Himalayan area may have varied from time to time in accordance with changing circumstances, but certain basic considerations have delimited both the style and the content of their responses to external influences and challenge. These are as important in the 20th century as they were in the 18th, technological developments and ideological innovations notwithstanding.

It is obvious, for instance, that topographical and geographical factors have had a tremendous influence in establishing the parameters of policy formulation, both for the countries of the Himalayas and others bordering thereon. A sense of physical isolation combined with a basically ethnocentric world view seems natural in a region characterized by rugged mountain chains and primitive communication systems. The governments of the area usually have perceived their political independence as primarily a consequence of their jealously guarded isolation. For in all the border states—Nepal, Tibet, Bhutan and Sikkim—the general policy followed was to discourage and obstruct efforts to improve and facilitate access

---

[1] Some of the themes analyzed in this chapter are drawn from my article (co-authored with Roger Dial), "Can a Mini-State Find True Happiness in a World Dominated by Protagonist Powers—The Nepal Case," *The Annals of the Academy of Political and Social Science*, Vol. 386, (November 1969), pp. 89 101.

into and through this difficult region. Indeed, only in the middle decades of the 20th century, when the capacity of the Himalayan border states to control regional developments had been severely impaired, has any real effort been made to improve communications.

Their policy of deliberate isolation was maintained by the border states even though it often deterred their economic development and prosperity. In the 19th century, this attitude bewildered the East India Company officials, whose own decision-making was strongly motivated by economic factors. But British arguments in favor of the expansion of commercial ties between India and the border states—to their mutual advantage—were rarely persuasive to the ruling groups in this area. Even now, when all three of the border states have formally abandoned the isolation policy, some remnants of that tendency can still be detected, as the officials of any of the foreign aid programs in Nepal can readily testify.

The border states, particularly Nepal and Tibet, adopted approaches to foreign policy that were similar in fundamentals though differing at times in nuance and emphasis. Their location between two of the more dynamic and culturally expansive Asian civilizations has strongly colored their world view. As might be expected, the border states have generally been inclined to look more benignly on the neighboring power that is more distant and, therefore, less likely to pose a serious threat. The rulers of Nepal usually have perceived India as the more dangerous of its neighbors, whereas China has been considered as too distant—both in physical and cultural terms—to threaten the country's independence but close enough to serve as a potential source of support. The opposite view was held by Tibet, to whom China was the principal enemy and India a possible ally. The situation was made even more difficult for Lhasa by the fact that on many occasions the interests of Nepal and China in Tibet and elsewhere in the region have seemed to coincide. (This may help explain why Nepalis evidenced such little concern over the Chinese conquest of Tibet in 1951 and were unsympathetic with the valiant but futile Tibetan struggle for freedom in 1959–60.) It was for this reason presumably, that the Tibetans usually discouraged direct Nepali-Tibetan relations or, when this was not practicable, sought to insert themselves as intermediaries between their two troublesome neighbors. The obstacles repeatedly placed by Lhasa in the path of Nepali missions to Peking in the 1789–1912 period may be attributed to this factor, as can the Tibetan government's unsuccessful efforts to retain relations with Nepal in its own hands after 1951.

NEPAL'S NATIONAL IDENTITY PROBLEM

Nepal's sudden and unplanned debut into international society in 1951, although virtually unnoticed by the rest of the world at the time, caused an immediate and severe crisis in its national self-identification. That crisis was perhaps an inevitable consequence of both Nepal's immediate past, which had been characterized by a semisatellite relationship with British India, and the circumstances under which the revolutionary movement finally emerged triumphant. No one could fail to grasp the obvious, namely that Indian support and direction had been essential and that without it victory would have been long delayed. Furthermore, the terms of settlement, the so-called "Delhi Compromise," reflected the objectives of the Indian authorities to a much greater extent than those of the revolutionary leadership. Although the revolution itself was not an Indian product, the results were, and this fact set the tone for the relationship between the two states thereafter.

New Delhi defined the postrevolutionary situation as a "special relationship," a phrase which soon became anathema to the hypersensitive political elites in Kathmandu because of its presumed denigration of Nepal's claims to national sovereignty. The situation became even more unpalatable to the Nepalis because of the obvious lack of confidence among their own leaders, who sometimes took the initiative in soliciting Indian advice and arbitration on even purely domestic matters in the 1951–55 period. Indians interpreted New Delhi's willingness to function in such a manner as indicative of its concern for the democratic process in Nepal and its interest in assisting the country's rapid economic progress. This type of relationship, however, with its patronizing and potentially chauvinistic ramifications, was viewed quite differently by the Nepali public, some sections of which considered India more of a threat than a protector of Nepal's independence.

For the Nepalis, independent, democratic India constituted a far greater challenge, both politically and psychologically, than had the alien, autocratic British Indian polity. The latter had presented what was essentially a straightforward political problem to Nepal—a problem that had appeared threatening only on rare occasions and which had been handled with relative ease by basically simple political responses. The Indian republic, on the other hand, poses a different kind of problem in both ideological and cultural terms, particularly in view of the large proportion of the Nepali population (20 to 25 percent) which is of recent Indian origin. India cannot be treated as an alien power in the same way that the British—or the Chinese—can, as Indian influences at all levels, political, economic, cultural and religious, are too persuasive and integral to Nepali society to be ignored or even easily sublimated. Nepalis must continuously assert, and indeed exaggerate, their differences with Indians in order to justify *in their own minds* their country's national existence. It was inevitable, therefore, that Nepalis should become increasingly agitated by the Indian government's seeming lack of respect for Nepal's political integrity on numerous occasions, and should resent the paternalistic (or perhaps maternalistic is the more accurate term) overtones in the Indian leadership's description of their policy toward Nepal.

King Mahendra, in his carefully calculated campaign aimed at modifying the terms of relationship with India, has elicited an enthusiastic response from most of the articulate Nepali public, including those groups that oppose the King's domestic policies and political system. The magic formulas ("tantra mantra") used to define his foreign policy, as it gradually evolved, were "nonalignment with equal friendship for all" and "diversification." The tactics devised to achieve these objectives were, first, a careful balancing of relevant external forces in order (1) to minimize their capacity to restrict Nepal's freedom of maneuver, (2) to maximize the benefit (e.g., foreign aid) derived therefrom, and (3) to contribute to Nepal's security, and, secondly, a cautious tacking back and forth between Nepal's two great neighbors as circumstances seemed to dictate.

NONALIGNMENT

Although the philosophy of "nonalignment" and its usual corollary, "peaceful coexistence," was adopted only recently by Nepali elites, the policy that it reflects is not. In the 18th century, King Prithvi Narayan Shah may not have used the cliches that have now become so common, but he certainly understood their tactical implications. Nonalignment, however, was plausible only so long as the actuality of China's "presence" in Tibet could be utilized to discourage British India from pursuing a more vigorous "forward policy" on its northern frontier. By the mid-19th century, China was at best a dim shadow on a distant Himalayan horizon, and the only strategy open to Kathmandu was a *de facto* alignment with British power in India. For nearly a century thereafter, Nepal's primary concern in foreign policy was to perceive and define the limits of its association with British India, always seeking the maximum autonomy then attainable within the context of its informal status as an ally of the British.

Somewhat paradoxically, Nepal's nominal readoption of non-alignment as a basic principle of foreign policy in 1951 did not constitute in any way a diminution of its subordinate position within the Indian security system in the Himalayan area. Indeed, at that stage Nepal's nonalignment was both fictitious (because it was borrowed wholesale from India and did not modify, much less terminate, the "special relationship" between those two states) and irrelevant (since it concerned a far-removed and essentially disinterested pair of protagonists, the United States and the Soviet Union). Both Washington and Moscow tacitly regarded Nepal as falling within the Indian sphere of influence—the Russians, in fact, rationalized their vote against Nepal's admission to the United Nations on this ground—rather than as a potential arena of confrontation between their respective blocs. Kathmandu's nonalignment was correctly perceived as a by-product of India's foreign policy, and neither of the super-powers was concerned with changing the situation—all things else being equal.

Nepal's long-time status as a second-rank buffer between south and east Asia gained added importance, if not necessarily viability, with the Chinese conquest of Tibet in 1951, but on conditions not unlike those prevailing throughout the latter half of the 19th century, when the terms were defined by the Indian government. In these circumstances, it was difficult for Nepalis to identify "bufferism" with "nonalignment," for in reality Nepal functioned as an "Indian buffer." In 1955, however, the focus of Nepal's nonalignment policy moved somewhat closer to the Himalayas through the establishment of diplomatic relations with the communist government of China. Yet even this decision was not initially designed to emphasize Nepal's nonalignment, but rather, on the contrary, its alignment with India. Kathmandu's recognition of the Peking regime was directed by New Delhi, and occurred only after Nehru thought that he had obtained China's express recognition that "Nepal was in India's sphere of influence."

Upon King Mahendra's accession to the throne, diplomatic relations with China quickly gained a new significance. But as Nepal's two great neighbors were not yet openly antagonistic, Kathmandu's concept of its role as a buffer gravitated towards that of a "link" between two ideologically distinct but friendly powers. It was in that period that Nepal's historical role as a channel of communication between the civilizations of south and east Asia began to be emphasized by both Nepali officials and intellectuals, often in extravagantly exaggerated terms.

The "link" notion had to be quietly dropped after 1960 in view of intense Sino-Indian hostility in the Himalayan area, but a newly defined buffer concept was introduced by Kathmandu. The slogan of nonalignment which had been adopted in 1956, "equal friendship for all," was gradually reinterpreted to mean equal friendship with India and China. This led eventually to a declaration of nonalignment in the Sino-Indian dispute—that is, the formal "neutralization" of Nepal.

Bufferism then became the product of a balance that Nepal had helped to create and not, as it previously had been, a mere convenience for India. The buffer concept, based as it now is upon nonalignment, both symbolizes Nepal's sovereignty and helps to assure its integrity against external aggrandizement. As defined by King Mahendra, Nepal's national identity is dependent upon the calculated maximization of the unique attributes that distinguish the country from both of its great neighbors. King Mahendra sees in "Nepalism" (that is, a political system that differs in theory and practice from both the Chinese and Indian) internally, and non-alignment and diversification externally, the solution to Nepal's identity crisis.

Questions have been raised from time to time as to whether Nepal is nonaligned in fact as well as in form—and with considerable justification, as has been indicated. King Mahendra has been both tireless and imaginative in his efforts to provide some degree of substance to his post-1960 version of nonalignment, in policy terms as well as psychologically. In the first few years after the 1960 royal coup, for instance, the King usually included both an ostensible pro-Indian and a pro-Chinese minister in his government, he himself carefully taking a position somewhere between theirs. The public position of these ministers may have had little relation to their true sentiments on foreign-policy issues,[2] (indeed, one minister served on both sides at different times during his tenure on the Council of Ministers), but their function as spokesmen for differing policy orientations was vital to the King's adroit manipulation of circumstances in accordance with his interpretation of nonalignment and his determination to give the nonalignment policy as much substance as was consistent with the intimate ties still existing between Nepal and India.

---

[2] It was not strictly coincidental that one of the "pro-Indian" ministers, Rishikesh Shaha, accepted an invitation to visit China shortly after his dismissal from office in 1962, nor that the "pro-Chinese" Dr. Tulsi Giri hastened to India following his resignation in 1964. Both men had played their assigned roles with considerable skill and enthusiasm while in office, but once out of power considered it essential to present themselves to the Nepali public and to New Delhi and Peking as nonaligned.

The U.S. and the U.S.S.R.—Washington and Moscow have been assigned increasingly important roles in Nepal's nonalignment policy since relations between India and China deteriorated to a condition of chronic hostility. The two super-powers are now subsidiary but nonetheless vital elements in Nepal's intricate balancing act, partly as offsets to each other but primarily as counterbalances to both New Delhi and Peking—a new twist to an old tactic.

For their part, Washington and Moscow have been prepared to accept somewhat greater responsibility in Nepal since 1960, and presumably for the same reason—that is, their interest in bolstering India's hardpressed security system in the Himalayan area against both overt Chinese aggression and covert Chinese subversion. New Delhi had previously sought, as a rule, to discourage any substantial increase of third power activity in Nepal, but the glaring exposure of Indian vulnerability and weakness in the 1962 border war with China led to a modification—probably temporary—in that attitude and a reluctant and begrudging acceptance of American and Russian support.

Both Washington and Moscow have found it preferable, indeed absolutely necessary, to offer separate but occasionally complementary support to the Indian position on the northern frontier. The Kathmandu authorities, of course, view this interrelationship from a quite different perspective. Alignments, even when informal and limited in scope, such as those between the United States and the Soviet Union, seriously undermine the efficiency of Nepal's complicated politics-of-balance game. Furthermore, they are contrary to the objectives for which Nepal abandoned its partial isolation policy in 1956 and opened itself to big-power politics—the diminution of New Delhi's capacity to exert at preponderant influence in Nepal. Unfortunately for Kathmandu, it cannot dictate the terms of participation to the players, but can only attempt to channel their activities along more acceptable lines. The Nepalis have considerable room for maneuver, however, because of the widely different approaches of the United States, the Soviet Union and India, as well as their strong aversion to any public manifestation of their common interest in containing China's influence and presence in Nepal.

DIVERSIFICATION: SOMETHING FROM EVERYBODY, SOMETHING FOR EVERYBODY

The program aimed at the maximum diversification of Nepal's political, economic and cultural relations with countries other than India has taken its place alongside nonalignment in King Mahendra's foreign policy. That policy actually had its origin in the last years of the Rana regime when, as later, it was aimed at reducing the potentiality of Indian intervention. During the Tribhuvan period, diversification was not totally abandoned, but it was severely handicapped by Nepal's explicit alignment with India. King Mahendra not only has revived the diversification program but has vastly expanded its scope and significance within the total context of Nepali foreign policy. Sleepy little Kathmandu, in which foreigners had once been a rarity, has now become a "cockpit of international politics," and its substantial diplomatic and aid community is a testimony to the efficacy of the diversification policy.

Political diversification, through the establishment of diplomatic relations with a large number of countries and an active role in the United Nations, was accomplished in a relatively short time and with a minimum of fuss and bother. It did little, however, to alleviate the most critical aspect of Nepal's dependence on India—that is, the country's status as a virtual adjunct of the Indian economy. Some progress in that direction has been achieved since 1960, primarily through the trade- and aid-diversification programs, but these have not yet served to alter Nepal's dependent economic status in any fundamental respect.

More recently, Nepal has experimented with a limited application of the diversification policy on defense and security questions, both through seeking arms assistance from the United States and the United Kingdom and by revising some aspects of its working arrangement with India on defense questions. There were indications in 1969 that the royal regime was again moving in the direction of a more literal interpretation of nonalignment, one that may have important policy consequences. Prime Minister Kirtinidhi Bisht made the most explicit statement yet on this subject by a Nepali government official when in June 1969 he declared, "it is not possible for Nepal to compromise its sovereignty or accept what may be called limited sovereignty for India's so-called security." For the first time some of the basic ties between Nepal and India on security and defense questions seemed to be in real jeopardy. It was still uncertain by the end of 1970 just how far King Mahendra was prepared to go in this respect, or indeed what his real objectives are, but there is no doubt that these policy changes are a logical derivative of his concept of nonalignment.

Another form of diversification—and one that is seldom discussed publicly in Nepal—that may prove of some importance in strengthening Kathmandu's capacity to resist external (i.e., Indian) pressure concerns private investments abroad by Nepali political leaders. From their earliest contacts with Nepal, the British Indian authorities had sought to expand their influence in the Kathmandu Darbar by "rewarding" compliant Nepali officials with gifts or with grants of land in India. Moreover, Nepali political refugees could usually depend upon the British for at least a bare subsistence allowance while in exile in India. Their presence in India was a constant threat to the ruling power in Kathmandu, and was skillfully exploited by the British Indian government to extract concessions from Nepal on several occasions.

The Ranas, aware of the fragility of their political system, further increased this form of economic dependence through extensive investments in land, commerce and industry in India. These were generally profitable, and large fortunes were made by several leading Ranas. But the practice also exposed the regime to Indian pressure at critical moments in its existence and indeed was one factor in the overthrow of the Rana system in 1951. The present political leadership, facing the same dilemma as the Ranas but intent on avoiding exposure to Indian pressure, has diversified its private investments abroad to the extent that the availability of foreign exchange permits. Although "hard data" (in contrast to authoritative gossip) on this subject are not available, it has been suggested that Hong Kong, Geneva and London are now as important to some Nepali leaders' financial viability as Calcutta and Bombay.

TACKING AS A TACTIC

As a sailboat's course must constantly be adjusted in accordance with the wind, it is also necessary for a country in Nepal's exposed geopolitical situation to place greater emphasis on its relationship with one or the other of its neighbors as circumstances seem to demand. "Tacking with the winds" has been a major feature of King Mahendra's foreign policy virtually since the day of his succession to the throne, and one that has been used to good effect on several occasions. His first tentative step toward the reversal of the alignment-with-India policy was the appointment of Tanka Prasad Acharyas as prime minister in January 1956. In moving toward real nonalignment, the new prime minister sought and obtained trade and aid agreements with the communist government of China, for the first time inviting this recent addition to Himalayan area politics to serve as a potential counterbalance to India.

Having reversed the general direction of Nepali foreign policy in sensational fashion, King Mahendra considered it necessary to tack southward a bit in order to give a worried New Delhi time to adjust to the new situation. Tanka Prasad was dismissed in mid-1967, and the vocally pro-Indian (at that time) Dr. K. I. Singh was appointed in his place. The new prime minister announced his intention to reestablish the "special relationship" with India and to keep Nepal's contacts with other powers to a minimum. Having served his purpose, Dr. Singh was summarily dismissed after only three months in office. The King, who ruled directly during the ensuing year, attempted no new initiatives on either the China or the India front, but he did widen the scope of his balancing act through an aid agreement with the Soviet Union and by arranging for the establishment of American and Russian embassies in Kathmandu and Nepali embassies in Washington and Moscow.

Another period of dextrous backpedaling in the general trend of Nepal's foreign policy came with the appointment of the first elected government headed by B. P. Koirala in the spring of 1959. This was not due to any basic disagreement between the ruling party, the Nepali Congress, and the King on foreign policy issues, as has been suggested, but rather to the fact that the new government's assumption of office coincided with an anti-Chinese rebellion in Tibet and with the public admission by New Delhi that it was involved in a serious border dispute with China. Uncertainty as to the limits of Peking's objectives in the Himalayan area induced the Kathmandu authorities to reemphasize and strengthen ties with India. The joint communiqué issued by B. P. Koirala and Nehru during the latter's visit to Nepal in June 1959, for instance, harkened back to the days of the Tribhuvan era in its reference to an "identity of interests" between the two states.

As the crisis eased in Tibet and it became apparent that China was limiting its territorial claims in the region to areas in dispute with India, the Koirala government reverted to a modified version of King Mahendra's balance politics. A new aid agreement was signed with China, and the two governments agreed to hold border talks. Furthermore, during his return visit to India in early 1960, B. P. Koirala was careful to avoid any reference to a presumed "identity of interests." There was still some ambivalence in his attitude toward China, however, which was reinforced by a series of incidents in mid-1960, including a border patrol clash on the Nepal-Tibet frontier and a dispute over Mt. Everest, that led to a temporary deterioration in Sino-Nepali relations and quiet consultations with New Delhi on the new situation. Peking's obvious determination to avoid a major confrontation with Nepal, however, gradually lessened Kathmandu's apprehensions, and by the end of 1960 Nepal's relations with both India and China were back on an even keel.

Undoubtedly the most strenuous tacking exercise by King Mahendra occurred in the period following his dismissal of the B. P. Koirala government in December 1960. The presence of a large number of Nepali Congress refugees in India, together with New Delhi's evident dissatisfaction over the trend of developments in Nepal, left the King with no viable alternative except an approach to China for support. He had to pay a high price—the Kathmandu-Tibet road—but he did manage to gain some concessions from Peking in the form of a border settlement and new trade and aid agreements as well as an ambiguous promise of assistance in the event of "foreign" interference in Nepal. Even more important, although of course not a direct consequence of King Mahendra's frantic maneuvers, was the Chinese attack on India's frontier regions in the fall of 1962. New Delhi was forced to revise its policies radically throughout the Himalayan area, to Kathmandu's great advantage.

The 1962 border war was therefore a godsend to King Mahendra, but certainly not an unmixed blessing. He was seriously distressed over the acute imbalance in Indian and Chinese military strength in the Himalayan area, as this threatened to undermine an essential feature of his delicate balance policy. Any further weakening of the Indian position was not to his advantage, hence King Mahendra welcomed the overtures from New Delhi for a rapprochement, symbolized by a tacit arrangement which curtailed the activities of antiregime elements in India and by the conclusion of several agreements on trade and security questions.

Except for a temporary aberration in relations with Peking in 1967, due perhaps as much to internal developments in China's "cultural revolution" as to Chinese dissatisfaction with certain of Kathmandu's foreign-policy decisions, Nepal's relations with both of its neighbors proceeded relatively undisturbed until 1969, when trade, aid and security questions again led to a minor crisis in Indo-Nepali relations. Both India and China have usually—but not always—confined their efforts to influence developments in Nepal to ways acceptable to the royal regime rather than through overt support of dissident forces of various political persuasions. Thus, King Mahendra's intricate balance-cum-tacking act has not only produced a greater degree of discretion for his government in international affairs but also a measure of security against potentially subversive internal forces in Nepal.

Nevertheless, tacking northward or southward as the occasion demands is a tactic rather than a policy, and one moreover with severe limitations on its utility. Whenever King Mahendra has felt compelled to seek closer ties with China, pundits in India and the

West have taken up the cry that Nepal is "moving into the Chinese camp." This is a basic misconception, however, of both the King's motivations and of the pendulum character of the tacking tactic. Nepal's economic dependence upon India may be resented in Kathmandu, but it is rarely forgotten in foreign policy decision-making.

Similarly, on security questions, it is probably still true that to the Nepali authorities defense means defense against China. This is not to imply that defense against India is a less serious problem for Kathmandu, for there have been several occasions in the past—and these may be repeated—when the greatest threat to the existing regime in Nepal has been from the south. However, strategic conceptualization about defense against Indian intervention has always been handicapped by the lack of alternatives, as Kathmandu learned in the early 19th century. Nepal is not capable of offering resistance unaided to a determined Indian program of intervention, but only in alignment with another major power. In the Himalayas, this could only be China. In view of Nepal's historical experience, however, as well as the Nepali perception of China's role in the Himalayas, alignment with China is neither feasible nor attractive.

China's policy in the Himalayan area has usually had twofold objectives, both before 1951 and to some extent thereafter. These aims were (1) the isolation of Tibet from neighboring areas in all directions with which Lhasa had traditional political, economic and cultural ties, and (2) the gradual Sinicizing of the border areas—and ultimately Tibet proper—through Chinese colonization and acculturation. On the other hand, China has usually demonstrated a limited interest in the areas to the south of the Himalayas except when developments there appeared to threaten Chinese interests to the north of the crest or when the border states could be used to advantage against independence-minded Tibetans or other current enemies of China.

Nepal's foreign policy, therefore, is based ultimately on the assumption that China will not militarily challenge New Delhi's dominant position to the south of the Himalayan crest on anything but a short-term basis, such as the 1962 border war, at least so long as India is functioning politically and is capable of concerted and effective responses to aggression. When Nepali officials assert, rather sanctimoniously at times, that they do not fear Chinese aggression, there is an unspoken but vital addendum: "so long as India is capable of coming to our assistance."

There is, of course, no similar confidence with regard to Peking's probable response in the event of overt Indian aggression against Nepal or of indirect Indian intervention through support of dissident Nepali political factions. The pragmatic Nepalis doubt that China would even consider risking a general war with India unless its own vital interests were somehow involved. America's refusal to challenge the Soviet Union on Hungary or Czechoslovakia, Russia's backdown in the Cuban crisis, and Peking's own noisy but timid response to the U.S. bombing of North Vietnam are all considered to be pertinent lessons. Although Nepal is vital to India's strategic and defense planning, and New Delhi could not safely allow the area to come under a dominant Chinese influence, it must be of secondary importance, at most, in Peking's strategic calculations on China's long and troubled frontier.

The assumption by the Nepali authorities that they can play cozy games with the Chinese in comparative safety, is therefore probably sound, at least under present conditions. It has been a commonplace for both Indian and Western commentators to grossly exaggerate China's military capabilities in the Himalayan area, basing their estimates for the most part on the 1962 border war, in which the Indian army performed very poorly. Such assessments of the situation do not take into account the changes that have occurred since that event in the relative military and logistical position of the two powers, such as the substantial enlargement of the Indian army and the emphasis given thereafter (and only thereafter) to training in mountain fighting. Nor is sufficient attention paid to the basic lesson to be learned from the 1962 war—namely, that China can sustain a major military effort across the Himalayas for only a limited time in the face of determined and unyielding resistance, and then only during the times of the year when the high Himalayan passes are free of snow.[3]

It is reasonable to assume, therefore, that overt, undisguised Chinese aggression aimed at the conquest of Nepal and its absorption into the Chinese Communist empire is a remote possibility. The essential precondition for such a drastic change in Chinese policy would be political chaos in India severe enough to lead to the dismemberment of the Indian republic into several hostile nation-

---

3 Some Western journalists and specialists in Asian studies have argued that China's unilateral withdrawal from the North-East Frontier Agency of India by December 15, 1962, was "voluntary" and indicative of China's limited and nonaggressive intentions in the border war. This analysis disregards completely the topographical and climatic factors that must have been the basic determinant in Chinese decision-making with regard to the terrain and timing selected for the attack and its ultimate objective, and treats the frontier in this area as if it were flat land with easy access in both directions. The fact is, however, that the Chinese had to withdraw by the date chosen or else face the awesome task of supplying a large force, scattered over perhaps 20,000 square miles, by porterage over snowbound passes. Whether the Chinese would have withdrawn voluntarily if the circumstances had been different can only, of course, be guessed.

states. This is not impossible, but it seems improbable. Somewhat higher on the scale of probability is the danger that Nepal could become involved in another limited Sino-Indian conflict, or that the Chinese might make it the target of indirect aggression through support and sponsorship of a Nepali "liberation movement." King Mahendra is confident, however, that his present foreign policy provides the best possible guarantee against either of these contingencies. To attempt to exclude the Chinese from any role in Nepal or to align the royal regime openly with India's anti-China security system would invite Chinese retaliation. Such retaliation would be likely to take far more ominous forms than the circulation of Mao buttons and propaganda films or the financing of noisy but insignificant student and social groups.

Kathmandu can also argue with some logic that India's best interests are served by a policy that preserves Nepal's noninvolvement in any Himalayan confrontation, as this limits the Indian army's immediate responsibilities in a highly strategic but vulnerable section of the frontier. Indeed, given China's present policy, Nepal is probably less of a burden for India as a nonaligned buffer than as a compliant ally. Understandably, it is difficult for Indians, especially some journalists and politicians, to accept this conclusion, and they continue to insist, as they have since 1951, that Nepalis must behave like good, patriotic Indians in meeting the Chinese challenge. It sometimes seems as if many Indians have become so accustomed to thinking of their country as poor and weak that they are unable to adjust to a situation where they are dealing from a position of strength, both in military and economic terms, as they are with Nepal. This kind of thinking further complicates New Delhi's political relations with Kathmandu and discourages the Indians from acting towards Nepal with the spirit of magnanimity that the situation both demands and permits.

The responsible officials in the external affairs and defense ministries have usually taken a more practical position, and have not begrudged Kathmandu its occasional ostentatious show of independence. But they too must be concerned with Nepal's role in any ultimate test of arms with China, unlikely as this may be, and thus have felt constrained to seek tacit reassurances from Kathmandu in this respect. Furthermore, any change in Chinese policy toward Nepal that involved some form of intervention would, of course, necessitate changes in Indian policy in the same direction. Under such circumstances, principles of territorial integrity are rarely decisive in strategic conceptualization. It is naive to assume that India is prepared to defend such remote and comparatively less strategic sections of the frontier as Ladakh and the N.E.F.A. against Chinese aggression and yet docilely to permit Nepal, a dagger aimed at the heartland of northern India, to come under Chinese domination.[4]

The Nepali government must therefore tread a careful path in the conduct of its balance policy in order to forestall an Indian overreaction to a perceived—or misperceived—threat of a Chinese Communist takeover. This problem may become even more threatening for Kathmandu with political instability now a distinct possibility in India. A new leadership may emerge that is less sophisticated than the present one on foreign policy issues and thus more susceptible to mistaking images for reality. This was apparent even in the room for maneuver available to the Indira Gandhi cabinet following the split in the Congress Party in 1969, and was one factor in New Delhi's comparatively tough attitude toward further concessions to Nepal on economic and political questions. Some future Indian government may well conclude that the simplest solution to New Delhi's chronic problems with Nepal would be to replace the existing regime in Kathmandu with one considered more reliable by the Indian authorities. While this would probably prove counterproductive in the long run, it could be accomplished with relative ease in several ways: direct intervention by Indian troops; slightly disguised intervention through the use of the Gurkha units in the Indian army or ex-servicemen resident in India; indirect intervention through support of a Nepali revolutionary movement; or an all-out economic blockade. Any of these tactics would almost certainly prove successful, and there is no third state, including China, that would be likely to give the royal regime the support required to counter Indian intervention.

One of the King's ministers, in a conversation with the author in 1962, predicted the Nepal's fate is likely to be eventual absorption by either India or China, and that furthermore the decisions and actions of the Nepali government would not be crucial in determining the results. Although this sort of pessimism has not disappeared entirely in the intervening years, there is now much greater confidence that Nepal can continue to exploit its geopolitical situation to its own advantage without endangering the country's national existence. It is also apparent, however, that greater independence on foreign policy issues has brought greater responsibility in determining not only Nepal's future but that of the Himalayan area in general.

---

4 It has been suggested that Nepal's likely future is a division of the state under which the plains area (Terai) would be absorbed by India and the hills by China. However, no Indian government would accept such a result unless it was incapable of offering resistance, as New Delhi's basic defense policy is to keep China's military power to the north of the Himalayan barrier.

Selected Bibliography

WESTERN LANGUAGES

Aitchison, C. U. *A Collection of Treaties, Engagements and Sanads Relating to India and Neighbouring Countries.* Vol. XIV. New Delhi: Central Publishing Branch, 1929.

American University, Washington, D.C. Foreign Area Studies Division. *Area Handbook for Nepal (with Sikkim and Bhutan).* Washington, D.C., 1964. 448 pp. (U.S. Dept. of the Army. Pamphlet no. 550–35).

Bacot, Jacques, et al. *Documents de Touen-Houang Relatifs à l'Histoire du Tibet.* Paris: P. Geuthner, 1940. 204 pp.

————. *Le Tibet Révolté: Vers Népêmako, la Terre Promise des Tibétains.* Paris: Librairie Hachette, 1912. 364 pp.

Bahadur, Poorna. *Nepal Behind the Screen.* Kathmandu: Nepal Youth League, 1957. 55 pp.

Bahadur K. C., Prakash. *Hostile Expeditions and International Law.* Kathmandu: Department of Publicity, 1962. 62 pp.

Bell, Charles. *Portrait of the Dalai Lama.* London: Collins, 1946. 414 pp.

————. *Tibet Past and Present.* London: Oxford University Press, 1927, 329 pp.

Bhasin, Avtar Singh. *Documents of Nepal's Relations with India and China, 1949–66.* Bombay: Academic Books, 1970. 295 pp.

Buchanan (Hamilton), Dr. Francis. *An Account of the Kingdom of Nepal and of the Territories Annexed to the Dominion by the House of Gorkha.* Edinburgh: Constable, 1819, 364 pp.

Burrard, Col. S. G., and H. H. Hayden. *A Sketch of the Geography and Geology of the Himalaya Mountains and Tibet.* Calcutta: Government of India, 1907–8. 308 pp.

Cammann, Schuyler. *Trade Through the Himalayas: The Early British Attempts to Open Tibet.* Princeton University Press, 1951. 186 pp.

Chakravarti, P. C. *India's China Policy.* Bloomington: Indiana University Press, 1962. 180 pp.

Chatterji, Bhola. *A Study of Recent Nepalese Politics.* Calcutta: World Press, 1967. 190 pp.

Chatterji, Dr. Nandalal. "The First English Expedition to Nepal," *Proceedings of the Indian History Congress,* 2nd session. Allahabad (1938), 545–53.

Chatterji, Sunita Kumar. *Kirata-Jana-Krti the Indo-Mongoloids: Their Contribution to the History and Culture of India.* Calcutta: Royal Asiatic Society of Bengal, 1951, 94 pp.

Chaudhuri, K. C. *Anglo-Nepalese Relations, From the Earliest Times of the British Rule in India till the Gurkha War.* Calcutta: Modern Book Agency, 1960. 181 pp.

Choudhary, Radhakrishna. "Nepal and the Karnatas of Mithila (1097–1500 A.D.)," *Journal of Indian History*, XXXVI, Pt. 1 (April 1958), 123–30.

Das, Sarat Chandra. *Journey to Lhasa and Central Tibet.* London: Murray, 1902, 285 pp.

David-Neel, Alexandra. *Le Vieux Tibet Face à la Chine Nouvelle.* Paris: Librairie Plon, 1953. 241 pp.

———. "Tibetan Border Intrigues," *Asia* (May, 1941), 219-22.

Desgodins, C. H. *La Mission du Thibet.* Verdun: 1872. 419 pp.

Dial, Roger. *Flexibility in Chinese Foreign Relations: Nepal a Case Study.* (M. A. thesis). Berkeley: University of California, 1967. 249 pp.

Digby, William. *1857—A Friend in Need: 1887—Friendship Forgotten.* London: Indian Political Agency, 1890. 148 pp.

Diskalkar, D. B. "Tibeto-Nepalese War, 1788–1793," *Journal of the Bihar and Orissa Research Society*, XIX (1933), 355–98.

East India Company. *Papers Respecting the Nepaul War.* London: J. L. Cox, 1824. 998 pp.

Eden, Ashley. *Political Missions to Bootan.* Calcutta: Bengal Secretariat Press, 1865. 206 pp.

Filippi, Filippo de (ed.). *An Account of Tibet: The Travels of Ippolito Desideri of Pistoia, S.J., 1712–1727.* London: G. Routledge and Sons, 1932. 475 pp.

Fisher, Margaret W. and Joan V. Bondurant. *Indian Views of Sino-Indian Relations*, Indian Press Digests Project Monograph No. 1. Berkeley: University of California Press, 1956, 163 pp.

Fisher, M. W., L. E. Rose and R. A. Huttenback, *Himalayan Battleground: Sino-Indian Rivalry in Ladakh.* New York, Praeger, 1963. 205 pp.

Fürer-Haimendorf, Christoph von. *The Sherpas of Nepal: Buddhist Highlanders.* Berkeley: University of California Press, 1964. 298 pp.

———. *Caste and Kin in Nepal, India and Ceylon: Anthropological Studies in Hindu-Buddhist Contact Zones.* New York: Asia Publishing House, 1966. 364 pp.

The Gazetteer of Sikhim (with an Introduction by H. H. Risley). Calcutta: Bengal Secretariat Press, 1894. 392 pp.

Giri, Tulsi. *Some Speeches of Dr. Tulsi Giri.* Kathmandu: Department of Publicity, 1964. 39 pp.

Great Britain Foreign Office. *Tibet Handbook.* London: H. M. Stationery Office, 1920. 74 pp.

———. *Tibet Blue Book, 1904–5.* London: H. M. Stationery Office. 620 pp.

———. *Tibet: Further Papers from September, 1904 to May, 1910.* London: H. M. Stationery Office, 1910. 615 pp.

Gupta, Anirudha. *Politics in Nepal; A Study of Post-Rana Political Developments and Party Politics.* Bombay: Allied Publishers, 1964. 332 pp.

Gyawali, S. P. *Friendship on Trial.* Kathmandu: Department of Publicity and Broadcasting (n.d.). 23 pp.

Hagen, Toni. *Nepal: The Kingdom in the Himalayas.* Berne, Switzerland: Kummerly and Frey, 1961. Tr. by B. M. Charleston.

"Historicus" (Rishikesh Shaha). "Nepal-China Relations," *The Nepal Guardian,* No. 2 (June, 1954), 37–47.

Hodgson, Brian Houghton. *Essays on the Languages, Literature and Religion of Nepal and Tibet Together with Further Papers on the Geography, Ethnology, and Commerce of Those Countries.* London: Trubner, 1874. 104 pp.

Huang Sheng-chang. "China and Nepal," *People's China* (1 May, 1956), 8–10.

Hunter, William Wilson. *Life of Brian Houghton Hodgson, British Resident at the Court of Nepal.* London: Murray 1896. 390 pp.

Imbault-Huart, C. C., "Histoire de la conquête du Népal par les Chinois sous le règne de Tc'ie Long," *Journal Asiatique,* 7th series, XII (1878), 348–77.

———. "Un Épisode des Rélations Diplomatiques de la Chine avec le Népal en 1842," *Revue de l'Extrème-Orient,* III (1887), 1–23.

Jain, Girilal. *India Meets China in Nepal.* Bombay: Asia Publishing House, 1959. 177 pp.

Joshi, Bhuwan Lal and Leo E. Rose. *Democratic Innovations in Nepal; A Case Study of Political Acculturation.* Berkeley, University of California Press, 1966. 551 pp.

Kavic, Lorne J. *India's Quest for Security: Defense Policies, 1947–1965.* Berkeley: University of California Press, 1967. 263 pp.

Kawaguchi, Ekai. *Three Years in Tibet.* Banaras and London: Theosophist Office, 1909. 719 pp.

Khanal, Yadunath. *Background of Nepal's Foreign Policy.* Kathmandu: Department of Publicity and Broadcasting (n.d.). 7 pp.

———. *On Nepal-India Relations.* Kathmandu: Department of Publicity and Broadcasting, 1963. 22 pp.

———. *Reflections on Nepal-India Relations.* Delhi: Rakesh Press, 1964. 98 pp.

Khatry, Padma Bahadur. *Non-Aligned Foreign Policy: Its Nature and Necessity.* Kathmandu: Department of Publicity and Broadcasting, 1963. 12 pp.

Kiernan, V. G. "India, China and Sikkim: 1886–1890," *Indian Historical Quarterly,* 31 (March 1955), 32–51.

Kirkpatrick, Captain William. *An Account of the Kingdom of Nepaul, Being the Substance of Observations Made During a Mission to that Country in the Year 1793.* London: W. Miller, 1811. 386 pp.

Kumar, Satish. "Nepal and China," *Indian Journal of Political Science,* XXIV (Jan.–March, 1963), 79–93.

———. *Rana Polity in Nepal: Origin and Growth.* Bombay: Asia Publishing House, 1967. 195 pp.

Lai Tze-sheng. *Le Problème Thibétain.* Paris: A. Pedone, 1941. 186 pp.

Lamb, Alistair. "Tibet in Anglo-Chinese Relations: 1767–1842," part I in *Journal of the Royal Asiatic Society*, Pts. 3 and 4 (1957), 161–76; part 2 in *ibid.*, Pts. 1 and 2 (1958), 26–43.

Landon, Perceval. *Lhasa: An Account of the Country and People of Central Tibet and of the Progress of the Mission Sent There by the English Government in the Year 1903–4.* London: Hurst and Blackett, 1905. 2 vols., paged separately.

———. *Nepal.* London: Constable, 1928. 2 vols., paged separately.

Lévi, Sylvain. *Le Népal. Etude Historique d'un Royaume Hindou.* Annales du Musée Guimet. Paris: Bibliothèque d'Etudes, tomes XVII, XVIII et XIX, 1905–08.

Li Tieh-Tseng. *Historical Status of Tibet.* New York: Columbia University Press, 1956. 312 pp.

Mahendra, His Majesty King. *Nepal-India Friendship: Speeches by H. M. King Mahendra in the Course of the Royal Visit to India (April 18–22, 1962).* Kathmandu: Department of Publicity, 1962. 44 pp.

Mahendra, His Majesty King. *Statement of Principles: Major Foreign Policy Speeches by His Majesty King Mahendra.* Kathmandu: Department of Publicity and Broadcasting, 1962. 39 pp.

Mahendra, His Majesty King. *Statement of Principles: Major Foreign Policy Speeches by His Majesty King Mahendra.* Kathmandu: Department of Publicity, 1964. 44 pp.

Manab, P. B. *King Mahendra's Active Non-Alignment.* Kathmandu: Nepal Printing Press, 1963. 11 pp.

Markham, Clements R. *Narratives of the Mission of George Bogle to Tibet and of the Journey of Thomas Manning to Lhasa.* London: Trubner, 1879. 362 pp.

Mihaly, Eugene B. *Foreign Aid and Politics in Nepal; A Case Study.* New York: Oxford University Press, 1965. 202 pp.

Mukherji, A. C. (ed.) *Life of Maharaja Sir Jung Bahadur of Nepal.* Allahabad: Pioneer Press, 1909. 314 pp.

Mukherji, Baba Purna Chandra. *A Report on a Tour of Exploration of the Antiquities in the Tarai, Nepal, the Region of Kapilavastu; During February and March, 1899.* Calcutta: Archaeological Survey of India, No. XXVI, Pt. 1, 1901. 60 pp. and 32 plates.

Narayan, Shriman. *India and Nepal: An Exercise in Open Diplomacy.* Bombay: Popular Prakashan, 1970. 172 pp.

Nepal. Department of Publicity and Broadcasting. *Nepal-China Boundary Protocol.* Kathmandu, 1963. 14 pp.

New Developments in Friendly Relations between China and Nepal. Peking: Foreign Languages Press, 1960.

Pant, Yadav Prasad. *Nepal's Economic Development on International Basis; An Analysis of Foreign Aid Utilization.* Kathmandu: Educational Enterprise, 1962. 87 pp.

Parker, E. H. "China, Nepaul, Bhutan, and Sikkim; Their Mutual Relations as set forth in Chinese Official Documents," *Journal of the Manchester Oriental Society* (1911), 129–52.

———. "How the Tibetans Grew," *Asiatic Quarterly Review*, XVIII (3rd series) (July–October 1904), 238–56.

Pathak, G. D. "Nepal's Trade With Her Neighbour—The Trade Pact of 1950," *Nepal Review*, 6 (Sept. 23, 1963), 11–12; cont. in 7 (Sept. 30, 1963), 6–7, 13.

Petech, Luciano. *China and Tibet in the Early Eighteenth Century: History of the Establishment of the Chinese Protectorate in Tibet.* Leiden: E. J. Brill, 1950. 286 pp.

————. *Mediaeval History of Nepal.* Roma: Istituto Italiano per il Medio ed Estreme Oriente, 1958. 238 pp.

————. *I Missionari Italiani nel Tibet e nel Nepal.* Roma: La Libreria dello Stato, 1952. 4 parts, paged separately.

————. "The Missions of Bogle and Turner According to the Tibetan Texts," *T'oung Pao*, XXXIX (1949), 330–46.

————. *A Study on the Chronicles of Ladakh.* Calcutta: Calcutta Oriental Press, 1939 (2 vols., issued as a supplement to the *Indian Historical Quarterly*).

Poudel, Bishnu Prasad. *Nepal's Relations with Tibet, 1792–1856.* (Ph.D. dissertation). New Delhi: Indian School of International Studies, 1963. 264 pp.

Pradhan, Bishwa. *Foreign Policy and Diplomacy.* Delhi: Rakesh Press, 1964. 96 pp.

Prinsep. Henry T. *History of the Political and Military Transactions in India During the Administration of the Marques of Hastings, 1813–1823.* London: Kinsbury, Parbury and Allen, 1825. 2 vols.

Ramakant. *Indo-Nepalese Relations: 1816 to 1877.* Delhi: S. Chand & Co., 1968. 390 pp.

Rao, Gondker Narayana. *The India-China Border, A Reappraisal.* Bombay: Asia Publishing House, 1968. 106 pp.

Ratna, Kuladharma. *Buddhism and Nepal.* Kathmandu: Dharmadaya Samaj, Serial No. 38, 1956. 24 pp.

Records of the Ludhiana Agency. Lahore: Punjab Government Press, 1911. 465 pp.

Regmi, Dilli Raman. *Ancient and Medieval Nepal.* Kathmandu, 1952. 178 pp.

————. *A Century of Family Autocracy in Nepal.* Banaras: Nepali National Congress, 1950. 326 pp.

————. "First Anglo-Nepalese Trade Pact," *New Review* (August 1942), 130–41.

————. *Modern Nepal.* Calcutta: Firma K. L. Mukhopadhyay, 1961. 333 pp.

————. "Nepal's Foreign Policy in Relation to India and China" in S. P. Varma and K. P. Misra (eds.), *Foreign Policies in South Asia.* Bombay: Orient-Longmans, 1969, pp. 258–65.

Regmi, Mahesh Chandra. *Land Tenure and Taxation in Nepal.* Berkeley: Institute of International Studies, University of California, 1963–68. 4 vols.

Richardson, H. E. *A Short History of Tibet.* New York: E. P. Dutton & Co., 1962. 308 pp.

Risley, Herbert Hope. "History of Sikkim," *Journal of the Buddhist Text Society of India*, IV, Pt. I (1896), appendix II, 6–16.

Rockhill, W. W. "The Dalai Lamas of Lhasa and Their Relations with the Manchu Emperors of China, 1644–1908," *T'oung Pao*, II, Ser. 2 (1910), 1–92.

————. *Tibet, a Geographical, Ethnographical, and Historical Sketch, Derived from Chinese Sources* (Extract from the *Journal of the Royal Asiatic Society of Great Britain and Ireland*, 1891). Peking, 1939. 291 pp.

Rose, Leo E. "Communism under High Atmospheric Conditions: The Party in Nepal," in Scalapino, Robert A. (ed.), *The Communist Revolution in Asia* (2d ed.). New York: Prentice-Hall, 1969, pp. 363–90.

————. "Sino-Indian Rivalry and the Himalayan Border States," *Orbis*, V, No. 2 (July 1961), 198–215.

————. "Regional Developments in South Asia: Nepal's Role and Attitude," in S. P. Varma and K. P. Misra (eds.). *Foreign Policies in South Asia*. Bombay: Orient-Longmans, 1969, pp. 356–64.

————, and Margaret W. Fisher. *The Politics of Nepal: Persistence and Change in an Asian Monarchy*. Ithaca: Cornell University Press, 1970.

————, and Roger Dial. "Can a Mini-State Find True Happiness in a World Dominated by Protagonist Powers: The Nepal Case," *The Annals* of the Academy of Political and Social Science, vol. 386 (November 1969), pp. 89–101.

Sanwal, Bhairava Dat. *Nepal and the East India Company*. Bombay: Asia Publishing House, 1965. 345 pp.

Schuleman, Gunther. *Geschichte der Dalai-Lamas*. Leipsiz: Veb Otto Harrassowitz, 1958. 519 pp.

Shaha, Rishikesh. *Heroes and Builders of Nepal*. London: Oxford University Press, 1965. 95 pp.

————. *Nepal and the World*. 2d ed. Kathmandu: Nepali Congress, 1955. 54 pp.

Shakabpa, Tsepon W. D. *Tibet, a Political History*. New Haven: Yale University Press, 1967. 369 pp.

Sharma, Jagadish Prasad. *Nepal's Foreign Policy, 1947–1962* (Ph.D. dissertation). Philadelphia: University of Pennsylvania, 1968. 318 pp.

Sharma, Jitendra Raj. *Nepal-India Relations*. Kathmandu: Department of Publicity and Broadcasting, 1963. 40 pp.

Shastri, G. C. *Freedom Loving Nepal*. (n.d.) 10 pp.

Sherring, Charles A. *Western Tibet and the British Borderland*. London: E. Arnold, 1906. 376 pp.

Snellgrove, David. *Buddhist Himalaya*. New York: Philosophical Library, 1958. 324 pp.

————, and Hugh Richardson. *A Cultural History of Tibet*. New York: Praeger, 1968. 291 pp.

Shreshtha, Badri Prasad. *Monetary Policy in an Emerging Economy; A Case Study of Nepal*. Kathmandu: Ratna Pustak Bhandar, 1965. 117 pp.

Teichman, Eric. *Travels of a Consular Officer in Eastern Tibet, To-*

gether with a History of the Relations between China, Tibet and India. Cambridge University Press, 1922. 248 pp.

Tucci, Giuseppi. *Tibetan Painted Scrolls.* Roma: Libreria dello Stato, 1949. 798 pp.

————. *Nepal: The Discovery of the Malla.* Translation from the Italian by Lovett Edwards. New York: Dutton, 1962. 96 pp.

Tuladhar, Tirtha R. *Nepal-China, A Story of Friendship.* Kathmandu: Department of Publicity and Broadcasting (n.d.). 47 pp.

Turner, Samuel. *An Account of an Embassy to the Court of the Teshoo Lama in Tibet.* London: W. Bulmer and Co., 1800. 473 pp.

Ware, Edgar J. *Report on a Visit to Sikkim and the Tibetan Frontier.* Calcutta: Bengal Secretariat Press, 1874.

Waddell, L. Austine. "Tibetan Invasion of India in 647 A.D. and its Results," *Asiatic Quarterly Review,* 3rd series, XXXI (January–April 1911), 37–65.

White, John Claude. *Sikkim and Bhutan.* London: E. Arnold, 1909. 331 pp.

Wright, Daniel. *History of Nepal.* Cambridge University Press, 1879. 324 pp.

Younghusband, Sir Francis. *India and Tibet, a History of the Relations which have Subsisted Between the Two Countries from the Time of Warren Hastings to 1910; With a Particular Account of the Mission to Lhasa of 1904.* London: Murray, 1910. 455 pp.

SOUTH ASIAN LANGUAGES
        (Nepali, unless otherwise specified):

Acharya, Baburam. "Rana Sahi ra Shadyantra" (Rana Rule and Conspiracy), *Sharada,* XXI:5, V.E. 2013 (1957 A.D.), 1–8.

————. "Aitihasik Patra" (Historical Letter), *Purushartha,* I:1, Pous 2006 V.E. (December 1949–January 1950 A.D.), 11–13.

————. "Bhimsen Thapa ko Patan" (The Downfall of Bhimsen Thapa), *Pragati,* II:4 (1957), 115–123.

————. *China ra Tibet Sita Nepal ko Sambandha* (Nepal's Relations with China and Tibet). Kathmandu: Jorganesh Press, 1958. 35 pp.

————. "Sri Sri Jaya Prakash Malla," *Pragati,* 3, No. 1 (1958), 35–85.

————. "Bhimsen Thapa ko Utthan" (The Rise of Bhimsen Thapa), *Rup-Rekha,* V.E. 2017 (January–February, 1961). 5 pp.

————. "Janaral Bhim Sen Thapa ko Parakram ra Unle Samarjang Kampani lai Diyego Danda" (Gen. Bhimsen Thapa's Prowess and the Punishment Meted Out by Him to the Samar Jung Company), *Arti,* Baisakh, (V.E.) 2024 (April 1967), 3–11.

Acharya Dixit, Keshar Mani. "Girban Yuddha Bir Bikram Lai Bharat Bata Nepali Vakil ko Patra" (Letter from the Nepali Vakil in India to Girban Yuddha Bir Bikram), *Sanskrit Sandesh,* I:9, 38–43.

Agrawal, Basudev Sharan. "Himalaya, Ganga ra Nepal" (Himalayas, the Ganges and Nepal), *Sanskritik Parishad Patrika,* I:1 (1952), 17–20.

Bajracharya, Dhanabarjra et al. (eds.). *Aitihasik Patra Sangraha* (A Collection of Historical Letters), part I. Kathmandu: Nepal Samskritik Parishad, 1957. 110 pp.

———. "Girban Juddha Bir Bikram Shah Lai Amar Singh Thapa ko Patra" (Amar Singh Thapa's Letter to Girban Juddha Bir Bikram Shah) *Sanskrit Sandesh*, I:7, pp. 22–26, I:8, 35–38: and I:9, 31–34.

———. *Triratna Saundarya Gatha* (An Account of the Beauty of the Three Jewels). Kathmandu: Nepal Cultural Council, 1963. 317 pp.

Bhandari, Dhundiraj. *Nepal to Aitihasik Vivechana* (Historical Analysis of Nepal). Banaras: Krishna Kumari, 1958. 368 pp.

Bisht, Som Dhwaj. *Shahi Sainik Itihas* (History of the Royal Army). Kathmandu: C. N. J. Shah and N. M. S. Basnyat, V.E. 2020 (1963 A.D.).

Dixit, Kamal (ed.). *Jang Bahadur ko Bilayet Yatra* (Jang Bahadur's Trip to England). Kathmandu: Madan Library, V.E. 2014 (1957 A.D.). 57 pp.

Giri, Tulsi. "Bharat-Birodhi Kaun, Nepal-Prem Kya" (Who is Anti-India, What does Love for Nepal Mean?), *Nepal Sandesh*. (Hindi.) Poush 17, 2023 (January 1, 1967).

Gorkha Vamsavali (The Chronicles of the Gorkha Kings). Banaras: Yoga Pracharini, V.E. 2009 (1952 A.D.). 144 pp.

Itihas Prakas (Lights on History). Kathmandu: Nepal Press, 1955–56. 4 vols., paged separately.

Itihas–Samsodhan (History Corrections). A valuable series of pamphlets published by various Nepali historians and Sanskrit scholars. Contributors included Dhana Bajra Bajracharya, Gautam Bajra Bajracharya, Akrur Kuwinkel, Babu Ram Nepal, Jñan Mani Nepal, Mahesh Raj Pant, Bhola Nath Poudel, Naya Nath Poudel, Mohan Nath Pandey, Shyam Raj Pokhrel, Laxman Satyal, Aishwarya Dhar Sharma, Kumar Dhar Sharma, Ghana Syam Subedi and Maheswar Raj Subedi. 1955–58.

Jñawali, Surya Bikram. *Amar Singh Thapa*. (Hindi.) Darjeeling: Ratnakar Press, 1951. 230 pp.

———. *Nepali Birharu* (Nepali Heroes). Darjeeling: Nepali Sahitya Sammelan, 1951. 87 pp.

———. *Rama Shah ko Jivan Charitra* (A Biography of Rama Shah). Darjeeling, 1933. 25 pp.

———. *Nepal Upatyakako Madhya Kalin Itihas* (Medieval History of the Nepal Valley). Kathmandu: Royal Nepal Academy, V.E. 2019 (1962 A.D.). 338 pp.

———. *Nepal Vijeta Shri Panch Prithvi Narayan Shah ko Jivani* (Life of King Prithvi Narayan Shah, the Conqueror of Nepal). Darjeeling, 1935.

Joshi, Satya Mohan. "Chini Nepali Samskritik Sambandha" (Sino-Nepalese Cultural Relations), *Gorkhapatra*, Sept. 23, 1960.

Lal, Manik. "Rana Haruko Nijamati Prashasan Pranali" (The Civil Administration System of the Ranas). Unpublished Ms. 23 pp.

Lal, Shyam Bihari. "Nepal to Baideshik Byapar ma Ek Adhyayan" (A Study in Nepal's Foreign Trade), *Byapar Patrika*, vol. 2, no. 7, Kartik, V.E. 2021 (October–November 1964).

Naraharinath, Yogi. *Gorkhaliharu ko Sainik Itihas* (Military History of the Gorkhas). Kathmandu: Annapurna Press, 1954. 24 pp.

―――. *Itihas Prakash ma Sandhi Patra Sangraha* (A Collection of Treaties in the Illumination of History), Kathmandu, V.E. 2022 (1966). Published on the occasion of the Spiritual Conference convened at Dang. 786 pp.

―――, and Baburam Acharya, *Sri Panch Bada Maharaja Prithvi Narayan Shah ko Divya Upadesh* (Divine Counsel of King Prithvi Narayan Shah the Great). Kathmandu: Shri Bagiswar Press, 1953. 38 pp.

Nepal-China Friendship Association. *Miteri Gantho* (Ties of Friendship). [A Collection of Articles on Nepal-China Friendship]. Kathmandu, 1963. 41 pp.

Nepali, Chitta Ranjan. "Chautariya Bahadur Saha ko Nayabi Kal" (The Period of the Nayabship of Chautaria Bahadur Shah), *Sharada*, XXII:1, V.E. 2014 (1957 A.D.). 21–29.

―――. *Janaral Bhimsen Thapa ra Tatkalin Nepal* (General Bhim Sen Thapa and the Nepal of His Day). Kathmandu: Jorganesh Press, 1957. 334 pp.

―――. "Yartaman Nepal ko Nirmanma Sri Panch Prithvi Narayan Shah" (King Prithvi Narayan Shah's Role in the Building of Modern Nepal), *Pragati*, Year 3, Issue 2 (n.d.), 78–110.

―――. "Nepal-Chin Yuddha," (Nepal-China War), *Sharada*, XXI:1, V.E. 2013 (1956 A.D.), 202–16.

―――. "Nepal ra British Gorkha Rifles" (Nepal and the British Gorkha Rifles), *Rup-Rekha*, V:4, Bhadra, V.E. 2021 (August–September 1964), 9–16.

―――. "Nepal ra British Samrajya" (Nepal and the British Empire), *Sharada*, XXI:3, V.E. 2013 (1956 A.D.), 11–12.

―――. "Nepal ra Tibet ko Sambandha" (Nepal-Tibet Relations), *Pragati*, Year II, IV:10 (n.d.), 103–15.

―――. *Shri Panch Rana Bahadur Shah.* Kathmandu: Shrimati Mary Rajbhandari, 1964. 154 pp.

―――. "Trayi Shashan" (Triumvirate), *Sharada*, Year 24, Issue 3, Poush, V.E. 2016 (December 1959–January 1960), 1–14.

Pande, Totra Raj and Naya Raj Pant. *Nepal ko Sankshipta Itihas* (An Abridged History of Nepal). Banaras: V.E. 2004 (1947 A.D.). 220 pp.

Pant, Maheshraj. "Nepal-Angrej Yuddha ko Tayari" (Preparations for Anglo-Nepali War), *Purnima*, I:2, Shravan Sankranti, V.E. 2021 (July 16, 1964).

―――. "The Second Stage of Anglo-Nepal War," *Purnima*, 8, Magh 1, V.E. 2022 (January 14, 1966), 41–49.

Pant, Naya Raj, "Damodar Pande Lai Ran Bahadur ko Patra" (Letter from Ran Bahadur to Damodar Pande), *Sanskrit Sandesh*, I:5, 36–43.

Poudyal, Bholanath and Dhanbajra Bajracharya (eds.). *Galli ma Fyak-iyeko Kasingar—Pandit Bhawani Datta Pande le Gare ko Muddrarak-shasa Haru ka Nepali Anubad* (Letters Thrown in the Street . . . Renderings in Nepali of the Mudrarakshasa Drama and Other Sanskrit Works . . .). Kathmandu: Jagdamba Prakashan, 1961. 269 pp.

Sharma, Balchandra. *Nepalko Aitihasik Rup Rekha* (An Outline of the History of Nepal). Banaras: Madhav Prasad Sharma, 1951. 440 pp.

Shrestha, Baburam. "Hamro Byapar Sthiti" (Our Commercial Situation), *Gorkhapatra*, Kartik 16, V.E. 2021 (November 1, 1964).

Shrestha, K. N. "Hamro Vyapar Bastusthiti ra Vikash Path" (Facts About Our Trade and Ways of Its Development), *Gorkhapatra*, Poush 11, V.E. 2021 (December 25, 1964).

Singh, Iman. *Kirat Itihas* (Kirat History). Gangtok, Sikkim, 1952. 72 pp.

Tiwari, Ramji et al. (eds.). *Abhilekh Sangraha* (A Collection of Inscriptions). Kathmandu: Samshodhan Mandal, 1961–63. Volumes 1–9, 11, paged separately.

————, et al. (eds.). *Aitihasik Patra Sangraha (Dosro Bhog)* (Collection of Historical Documents, Part II). Kathmandu: Nepal Samskritik Parishad, V.E. 2021 (A.D. 1964). 126 pp.

————. "Vikram Sambat 1843 ma Bhayeko Kehi Mukhya Ghatana" (Some Important Events of 1786), *Purnima*, 1:2, Shravan Sankranti, V.E. 2021 (July 16, 1964).

Upadhyaya, Ramji. *Nepal ko Itihas* (History of Nepal). Banaras: Subha Hom Nath Kedar Nath, 1950.

————. *Nepal Digdarshan* (A Survey of Nepali History). Banaras: Gopal Press, 1950. 486 pp.

"Vyas." "Nepal-Bharat Vyapar Sambandha, Duwai Rashtra ko Arthik Hit ko Paripati" (Nepal-India Trade Relations, A Means for the Economic Benefit of Both Nations), *Gorkhapatra*, Jestha 30, V.E. 2024 (June 13, 1967), 4–5.

EAST ASIAN LANGUAGES
       (Chinese, unless otherwise specified):

Chang Ming. *Hsi-Tsang Chih-Ta-Shia-Chi Ch'i-Hsien-Chuan* (General Condition and Present State of Tibet). Shanghai, 1933. 22 pp.

Chao Hsien-chung. *T'ang-Kuo Hsiu-Ho Chi-Lueh* [Summary Narrative of the Peace Settlement of the Nepal-Tibet Dispute (1883)] Preface dated May 12, 1888, published privately by author.

Chao I. *P'ing-Ting K'uo-Er-K'a Shu-Lueh* (Summary Narrative of the Subjection of the Gorkhas). From Chuan IV of "Huang-Chao-Wu-Kung Chi-Shang." Yangchow, 1792.

Chi-Chia-Fang-Chi (Description of the Lands of Sakyamuni). Compiled by the Monk Tao-hsuan, completed in 650 A.D. (Japanese edition, *Ta-Tsang-Chin*, vol. 51).

Chin-Ting K'ou-er-k'a Chi-Lueh (Official Summary Account of the Pacification of the Gorkhas). Peking, 1796. 54 plus 4 chuan in 8 vols.

Ch'ing-Chi-Ch'ou-Tsang-Tsou-Tu (Memorials and Correspondence Concerning the Arrangement of Affairs during the latter part of the Ch'ing Dynasty), Peiping, National Academy, 1938, 3 volumes.

Ch'iu-T'ang-Shu (Old History of the T'ang Dynasty). Compiled by Liu Hsu and others in the period from 936 to 946 A.D. Vol. 40, chuan 198, concerns Nepal.

Ch'ou-Pan-I-Wu Shih-Mo (Documents Concerning the Management of Foreign Affairs). Peiping: Palace Museum, 1930.

Fa-Yuan-Chu-Lin (Forest of the Pearls of the Garden of Buddhist Law). Compiled by Tao-shih and completed in 668 A.D. (Japanese edition, *Ta-Tsang-Chin*, vol. 53.)

Hsin-T'ang-Shu (New History of the T'ang). Compiled by Ou-Yang Hsiu, completed in 1060 A.D. Vol. 39, chuan 221, concerns Nepal.

Huang P'ei-ch'ao. *Hsi-Tsang-T'u-Kao* (Maps and Descriptions of Tibet). 1886.

I-tsing. *Ta-T'ang-Hsi-Yu-Chiu-Fa-Kao-Seng-Ch'uan* (Life of the Eminent Monks who travelled to the Western World for Research in Buddhist Law in the Great T'ang Period). Completed about 692 A.D. (Japanese edition, *Ta-Tsang-Chin*, vol. 51.).

Kawaguchi, Ekai. *Chibetto Ryokoki* (Tibetan Travels). Tokyo, 1904. (Japanese.)

Meng-Pao. *Si-Tsang Tsou-Shu* (West Tibet Memorial Reports). No publishing date or place. 10 chuan in 5 vols.

Ming Hui-Yao (Classified Records of the Ming Dynasty). Compiled by Long Wen-pin, no date. Chuan 78 concerns Nepal.

Ming-Shih (History of the Ming). Compiled by Chang Ting-yu and others, 1739. Chuan 331 concerns Nepal.

Ming-Shih-Kao (Draft History of the Ming). Compiled by Wang Hung-hsu, 1714. Chuan 309 concerns Nepal.

Ming-Shih-Lu (Veritable Records of the Ming Dynasty). Nanking, 1940.

Nakamasa Suzuki. *China, Tibet and India—Their Early International Relations.* Tokyo: Hitotsubashi Shobo, 1962 (Japanese).

Ta-T'ang-Hsi-Yu-Chu (Records of the Western Countries in the Great T'ang Period). Compiled by Hsuan-chuang and edited by Pien-chi; completed in 648 A.D. (Japanese edition, *Ta-Tsang-Chin*, vol. 51.)

Tu Yu. *T'ung-Tien* (Encyclopedia of Source Material on Political and Social History). Completed around the end of the 8th century. Volume 46, chuan 190, and volume 47, chuan 193, concern Nepal.

Wei-Tsang T'ung Chi (Topography of Wei and Tsang Provinces). Shanghai: Commercial Press, 1936.

Wei Yuan. *Ch'ien-Lung Cheng K'uo-er-k'a Chi* (Narrative of the Conquest of the Gorkhas under Ch'ien-lung), from "Sheng-Wu-Chi" (Military Exploits of the Ch'ing Imperial Period).

Wu, Chung-hsin. *Hsi-Tsang Chi-Yao* (Summary Narrative on Tibet). Taipei, 1953.

OFFICIAL RECORDS, MANUSCRIPTS, ETC.:

"An Account of the Anglo-Nepal War" (anonymous manuscript compiled in 1855).

Records of the Jaisi Kotha Office (Nepal-Tibet-China Office) of the Ministry of Foreign Affairs, Government of Nepal, 1790–1900.

Records of the British Government of India, 1765–1937, in the India Office Library in London, the National Archives of India in New Delhi and various State Record Offices in Allahabad, Patna and Calcutta.

Private Papers in the India Office Library and the British Museum in London. Particularly important were the papers of Brian H. Hodgson, Henry Lawrence and Sir Charles Bell.

Private Papers of Sylvain Lévi in the Institut des Civilisations Indiennes of the Sorbonne, Paris.

Buddhiman Singh Vamsavali. Nepali chronological manuscript.

Calendar of Persian Correspondence. Calcutta: Superintendent of Government Printing, 1914. 4 vols., paged separately.

NEPALI NEWSPAPERS AND JOURNALS:

The Commoner (English daily), Kathmandu.
Dainik Nepal (Nepali daily), Kathmandu.
Diyalo (Nepali daily), Kathmandu.
Filingo (Nepali daily), Kathmandu.
Gorkhaptra (Nepali daily), Kathmandu.
Halkhabar (Nepali daily), Kathmandu.
Himachuli (Nepali monthly), Kathmandu.
Jhyali (Nepali weekly), Kathmandu.
Kalpana (Nepali daily), Kathmandu.
Karmavir (Nepali weekly), Kathmandu.
Mashal (Nepali weekly), Kathmandu (Communist party organ).
Matribhumi (Nepali weekly), Kathmandu.
Motherland (English daily), Kathmandu.
Navayuga (Nepali weekly), Kathmandu (Communist party organ).
Naya Samaj (Nepali daily), Kathmandu.
Naya Samaj (Hindi weekly), Kathmandu.
Naya Sandesh (Nepali weekly), Kathmandu.
Nepal Pukar (Nepali weekly), Kathmandu (Nepali Congress journal).
Nepal Times (Hindi daily), Kathmandu.
Karmavir (Nepali weekly), Kathmandu.
Nepal Bhasa Patrika (Newari daily), Kathmandu.

Nepal Samachar (Nepali daily), Kathmandu.
Nepal Sambad Samiti (Nepal News Agency), Kathmandu.
News From Nepal (English weekly), Kathmandu. (Published by His Majesty's Government, Department of Publicity and Broadcasting.)
Nepal Gazette (Nepali biweekly, frequent Extraordinary Issues), Kathmandu. (Official periodical issued by His Majesty's Government, Department of Publicity and Broadcasting.)
Pragati (Nepali bimonthly), Kathmandu.
Rashtravani (Nepali weekly), Kathmandu (Gorkha Parishad organ).
Rashtriya Sambad Samiti (National News Agency), Kathmandu.
Rising Nepal (English daily), Kathmandu.
Sagarmatha Sambad Samiti (Everest News Agency), Kathmandu.
Samaj (Nepali daily), Kathmandu.
Samaya (Nepali weekly), Kathmandu.
Samiksha (Nepali weekly), Kathmandu.
Samyukta Prayas (Nepali weekly), Kathmandu (National Democratic party organ).
Samskritik Parishad Patrika (Nepali periodical), Kathmandu.
Sanskrit Sandesh (Nepali periodical), Kathmandu.
Saptahik Samachar (Nepali weekly), Kathmandu.
Sharada (Nepali monthly), Kathmandu.
Swatantra Samachar (Nepali daily), Kathmandu.

INDIAN NEWSPAPERS AND JOURNALS:

Asian Recorder (English weekly), New Delhi.
Amrita Bazar Patrika (English daily), Calcutta.
Himalayan Observer (English weekly), Kalimpong.
Himalayan Sentinel (English weekly), Patna.
The Hindu (English daily), Madras.
Hindustan Times (English daily), New Delhi.
Nepal Sandesh (Hindi weekly), Patna.
Nepal Today (English biweekly), Calcutta (Published by the Nepali Congress-in-Exile).
The Statesman (English daily), Calcutta.
Times of India (English daily), Bombay.
The Tribune (English daily), Ambala, Punjab.

Index